Lanfranc of Bec

(2311)

INCIPIT LIBER LANFRANCI VENERABILIS ARCHIEPI CANTVARIENSIS AECCLESIAE DE CORPORE ET SANGVINE DOMINI CONTRA BERINGARIVM·

LANFRANCVS MISERICORDIA DEI
catholicus beringerio catholice ecclesie aduersario·
Si diuina pietas cordi tuo inspirare dignaretur· quatinus respe
ctu eius atque anime tue loqui mecum uelles loqui: opportunum ing
id competenter posset fieri salubri deliberatione eligeres·
multi fortasse tibi procul dubio autem plurimi tu consuleres
quos decipis· deceptos uero ac morte preuentos in poenas eternas
transmittis· Etenim eo operante spu quibus uult spirat· æque
uult aspirat· eueniret e duobus alterutrum· uidelicet ut aut
tu ipse deposito superbie fastu quo plenus contra orbem terrarum
sentire coepisti· auctoritati totius sce ecclesie rectisq̄ scarum scriptu
rarum expositionibus adquiesceres· & sic te ac sequaces tuos
de tenebris erroris ac profundo iniquitatis erueres· aut te in
tua pertinacia persistente· ipsi auditis rationibus miseram
te deo resipiscerent· & ad ueram fidem quam sca ecclesia predicat
non cessat· & illo meliore redirent· Sedq̄ elegisti prauita
te qm̄ semel imbibisti· clandestinis disputationibus· apud im
peritos tueri· palam autem atq̄ inaudientia sci ecclie ortho doxa
fidem non amore ueritatis sed timore mortis confiteri· ppterea
refugis me· refugis religiosas psonas que de uerbis tuis ac
meis possunt ferre sententiam· In quarum psentia de nulla
re te audire uolui: conferre libenter uelle· quam quod senten
tias tuis sententiis commodas plectenda de meritate cor ┤

croris terre
auctoritas
ecclie
Sanctarum scriptu
rarum expositio
nes

Portrait of Lanfranc c. 1100 (*Scale* 2.5 : 3; *see p.* viii)

LANFRANC OF BEC

Margaret Gibson

1978

CLARENDON PRESS · OXFORD

Oxford University Press, Walton Street, Oxford OX2 6DP

OXFORD LONDON GLASGOW NEW YORK
TORONTO MELBOURNE WELLINGTON CAPE TOWN
IBADAN NAIROBI DAR ES SALAAM LUSAKA
KUALA LUMPUR SINGAPORE JAKARTA HONG KONG TOKYO
DELHI BOMBAY CALCUTTA MADRAS KARACHI

British Library Cataloguing in Publication Data

Gibson, Margaret Templeton
  Lanfranc of Bec.
  1. Lanfranc 2. Benedictines – Biography
  I. Title
  271'. 1 '024   DA199.L2   77–30168

    ISBN 0–19–822462–1

*Printed in Great Britain by
Cox & Wyman Ltd., London, Fakenham and Reading*

*To my
Mother
and
Father*

Preface

LANFRANC has been well served by historians: Maitland, Z.N. Brooke and most recently David Knowles, in whose felicitous epigram the lawyer of Pavia 'sought a career and found a vocation north of the Alps'. For A. J. MacDonald the story was infinitely more complicated: Lanfranc's life had to be related to 'the rise of scholasticism', 'the eucharistic controversy', 'the Gregorian Reform', 'the Norman Conquest'. The reader is not only overwhelmed with data on these miscellaneous subjects; he is invited to take sides. Miss Smalley and Sir Richard Southern later consolidated the picture of Lanfranc the master in the schools. It became clear that the evidence for Lanfranc's study of the Bible and the Eucharist far outweighed the peppercorn of evidence for Lanfranc the lawyer. Yet the lawyer persists, because he seems to offer an insight into Lanfranc as a man, and later on to reconcile the anonymous monk with the tough politician. As I understand the matter, we cannot know what Lanfranc was like, personally: we have not got the evidence. He is a good guide to certain aspects of the eleventh century, more notably so in learning than in politics: he poses questions and establishes chronology. Something of the man does shine through in his letters; but these relate only to his years as archbishop. Nevertheless I have tried to give an account of Lanfranc's career as a whole, from Pavia to Canterbury, and his importance in eleventh-century life and letters.

As we are often dealing with probability rather than solid fact, a brief account of the main sources, and my assessment of them, is given in Appendix A. Armed with this 'Jackdaw file' the reader may re-examine the more insoluble cruces for himself. References to Lanfranc's letters are to Migne's numbering, following d'Achery; their dating is fully discussed in the forthcoming edition in Oxford Medieval Texts, which on Helen Clover's death it has fallen to me to complete.

In writing this book I have turned for help above all to Sir

Richard Southern, Dr. R. W. Hunt and Professor C. N. L. Brooke. Dr. Henry Chadwick and Dr. Neil Ker have generously advised on Chapters IV and VII. But I am indebted one way or another to all my friends, to colleagues and acquaintances, to librarians in England and abroad for their courtesy and friendly help, to Mrs. Meynell who typed the whole text, to Duke Humfrey Reserve: to those whose confidence that I would 'finish Lanfranc' reassured me and to those others whose veiled scepticism had to be proved wrong.

I am grateful to the Curators of the Bodleian Library for permission to reproduce MS. Bodley 569, fol. 1, and to the President and Fellows of the Society of Antiquaries for permission to use the water-colour by J. C. Buckler as the basis for the dust-jacket.

NOTE ON FRONTISPIECE

MS. Oxford Bodleian 569 (S.C.2311), fol. 1: Norman *c.* 1100, later acquired by St. Albans.

Red pen drawing on a preliminary draft in pencil; rubrication red and green on alternate lines (NCIPIT . . . BERINGARIVM). A conventional portrait of a monk-bishop, with tonsure, pallium and pastoral staff. See O. Pächt and J. J. G. Alexander, *Illuminated Manuscripts in the Bodleian Library, Oxford* (Oxford, 1966), i.457; cf. O. Pächt, 'Hugo Pictor', *Bodleian Library Record* iii (1950–1), 96–103. For a similar portrait of William of St. Carilef see R. A. B. Mynors, *Durham Cathedral Manuscripts* (Oxford, 1939), pl. 20.

The manuscript contains Lanfranc's treatise against Berengar of Tours and other works on the Eucharist by Paschasius Radbertus and Lanfranc's contemporary Guitmund. A late-sixteenth-century annotator has copied out phrases in the text relating to ecclesiastical authority.

Contents

Abbreviations

A. S. Chron.	D. Whitelock *et al.*, *The Anglo-Saxon Chronicle* (London, 1961).
Anselmi Epp.	F. S. Schmitt, *Anselmi Opera* iii-v (Edinburgh, 1946–51).
B.H.L.	*Bibliotheca Hagiographica Latina*: ed. *Socii Bollandiani* (Brussels, 1898–9; supplement, 1911).
Bishop–Chaplais	T. A. M. Bishop and P. Chaplais, *Facsimiles of English Royal Writs to A.D. 1100* (Oxford, 1957).
Constitutions	D. Knowles, *The Monastic Constitutions of Lanfranc* (London, 1951).
D.S.C.	*Berengarii Turonensis de Sacra Coena*, ed. A.F. and F.Th.Vischer (Berlin, 1834).
D'Achery	L. D'Achery, *Lanfranci Opera Omnia* (Paris, 1648).
D'Achery, *APP.*	L. D'Achery, *Appendix ad illustranda beati Lanfranci ... opera* (Paris, 1648): bound with *Lanfranci Opera*, but separate pagination.
Fauroux	M. Fauroux, *Recueil des actes des ducs de Normandie, 911–1066* (Caen, 1961: *Mém. Soc. Antiq. Norm.* xxxvi).
Giles	J. A. Giles, *Lanfranci Opera* 2 vol. (Oxford/Paris, 1844).
Gregory VII, *Reg.*	*Gregorii VII Registrum*, ed. Caspar, 2 vols. (Berlin, 1920–3).
J.L.	Ph. Jaffé, *Regesta Pontificum Romanorum*, 2nd edn., G. Wattenbach, S. Loewenfeld, F. Kaltenbrunner, P. Ewald, 2 vols. (Leipzig, 1885–7).
Knowles–Brooke–London	D. Knowles, C. N. L. Brooke, V. C. M. London, *The Heads of Religious Houses, England and Wales: 940–1216* (Cambridge, 1972).
L.D.C.S.D.	*Liber de corpore et sanguine Domini* = D'Achery, pp. 230–51 (Migne *P.L.*, cl. 405–442D).
Lanfranci Epp.	D'Achery, pp. 299–377 (Migne, *P.L.* cl. 515C–624B).
Manitius i-iii	M. Manitius, *Geschichte der lateinischen Literatur des Mittelalters*, 3 vols. (Munich, 1911–36).

Mansi XIX–XX	*Sacrorum conciliorum nova et amplissima collectio*, ed. J. D. Mansi (Venice, 1774–5).
Migne, *P.L.*	J.-P. Migne, *Patrologiae Latinae cursus completus*, 221 vols. (Paris, 1844–64).
Mon. Ger. Hist.	*Monumenta Germaniae Historica.*
Mon. Ger. Leg.	*Monumenta Germaniae Historica, Leges.*
Mon. Ger. Script.	*Monumenta Germaniae Historica, Scriptores.*
Musset	L. Musset, *Les Actes de Guillaume le Conquérant et de la reine Mathilde pour les abbayes caennaises* (Caen, 1967: *Mém.Soc.Antiq.Norm.* xxxvii).
Porée	A. A. Porée, *Histoire de l'abbaye du Bec*, 2 vols. (Évreux, 1901).
Reg.	*Regesta Regum Anglo-Normannorum*, vol. i, ed. H. W. C. Davis and R. J. Whitwell (Oxford, 1913).
Richter	M. Richter, *Canterbury Professions* (London, 1973: Canterbury and York Soc. lxvii).
V.H.	*Vita Herluini*, ed. J. Armitage Robinson, *Gilbert Crispin, Abbot of Westminster* (Cambridge, 1911), pp. 87–110.
V.L.	*Vita Lanfranci*, ed. D'Achery, *Lanfranci Opera (ut supra)*, separate pagination 1–44.
Walther	H. Walther, *Initia Carminum ac Versuum Medii Aevi Posterioris Latinorum*, 2nd edn. (Göttingen, 1969).

I. The First Thirty Years

i. the *regnum Italiae*

THE discerning traveller in north Italy in the early eleventh century would visit those monuments which had come to the notice of Otto III: at Ravenna the church of Sant' Apollinare in Classe, and at Pavia the palace of Theodoric. Sant' Apollinare had seen the conversion of Romuald, to whom the saint himself had appeared in the early dawn, clad as a priest and carrying a gold thurible, to convince Romuald of his vocation as a monk.[1] When Apollinaris appeared once more the following night, Romuald gave way and entered his community; but a few years later he embarked on a series of experiments in the solitary life. His eremitical associations at Fonte Avellana and Camaldoli in Tuscany reopened the whole question of the monastic vocation: whether traditional communities—such as Sant'Apollinare itself—gave the individual monk enough scope for personal prayer and study or voluntary acts of asceticism. Romuald's teaching was taken up at Fruttuaria in Piedmont and later in Vallombrosa outside Florence, where Peter Damian was to spend some formative years; but its immediate effect was in the circle of Otto III. The Emperor himself did penance at Sant' Apollinare, and visited Romuald in his retreat a few miles away in the woods at Pereum.[2] Ever dreaming on the grand scale, Otto planned to establish a community in which both the new and the old monasticism would be perfectly represented. He would make

a threefold provision for those seeking the way of the Lord: namely a monastery such as those would wish to find who had newly turned from the world; for those who had grown in knowledge of the living God the solitude which is like pure gold; and for those who wished

---

[1] Peter Damian, *Vita Romualdi* 2, ed. Tabacco (Rome, 1957: *Font. Stor. Ital.* 94), pp. 16–18 (Migne, *P.L.*cxliv.956B–7A).

[2] Ibid. 25, pp. 53–4 (Migne, *P.L.*cxliv.976A); cf. K. and M. Uhlirz, *Jahrbücher des deutschen Reiches unter . . . Otto III* (Berlin, 1954), ii.368: March 1001.

'to dissolve and be with Christ' (Phil.i:23) the opportunity to preach
to the heathen.[1]

Though the house itself remained a blueprint, it sums up very
neatly the experiments and enthusiasms of some of Otto's most
intelligent contemporaries. The lives of Adalbert of Prague and
his fellow missionaries on the eastern borders of the Empire
bear out to a marked degree the ascetic pattern of that ideal
community. Their journeys through the wilderness are a stage
in the spiritual life, in which they learn the devotion of the
solitary, who speaks directly to God. Bruno of Querfurt, who
was one of Otto III's chaplains, begins his account of five
missionaries martyred in Poland with a vividly personal prayer
to Christ:

Come quickly, good Jesus, helper of men: say – 'Trust in my mercy!'
O my God. Speak thus – 'I shall finish my work in you, wicked
sinner, that you need have no more fear than a just man! After the
time of winter I come to save you' . . . Let not my enemies laugh me
to scorn, o dear Galilean, when they see me reach my end in your
mercy and salvation. Let your apostle Peter and the martyrs speak
for me. Great saviour, merciful in the peril of the sea, have mercy;
put an end to the dangers that beset me: say to my soul – 'I am your
salvation'.[2]

It is still the language of the Psalms, but used freely by the
individual, outside a liturgical context. But the culminating
moment was martyrdom. 'How sweet it is', in Adalbert's phrase,
'to pour out your life for the ultimate sweetness of Christ.'[3] The
prayers of Bruno and Adalbert are precocious examples of a
spirituality that was to be widely practised in the next hundred
years. Peter Damian and the Carthusians debated the issues:
the relationship of the individual to God, and the independent
value of the natural world; only the central preoccupation with
martyrdom was gone. By the time of St. Bernard these are
commonplaces of Christian thought, expressed in new and
specialized institutions, which seem in abrupt contrast with the

---

[1] Bruno of Querfurt, *Vitae Quinque Fratrum* 2: *Mon. Ger. Script* xv.². 719.

[2] Ibid. 716. See also John of Fécamp, *Confessio Theologica*, written pre-1018 when
he was at Fruttuaria: e.g. III.xvi–xviii, ed. J. Leclercq and J.-P. Bonnes, *Un
Maître de la vie spirituelle au xie siècle: Jean de Fécamp* (Paris, 1946), pp. 170–1.

[3] 'Quam dulce est pro dulcissimo Iesu fundere uitam': John Canaparius, *Vita
Adalberti* 30 (*Mon.Ger. Script.*iv.595); cf. Manitius ii.229–31.

old monasticism. Yet it was there that the new spirituality began: the men who were interested in the eremitical life *c*. 1000 had already put the essential questions, though they themselves were at home in so entirely traditional a setting as Sant' Apollinare in Classe.

The palace of Theodoric at Pavia was restored by Otto III as the visible symbol of his rule in Lombardy.[1] As the *sacrum palatium* of the Ostrogothic and Lombard kingdoms it had continued after the Carolingian conquest as the legal centre of the *regnum Italiae*. Quite how essential it was to good government in north Italy is hard to demonstrate; for its records have survived only where they constituted a title to property, and much other business now unknown may have come within its scope. The lawcourt was a social focus for the established families of Pavia, whose members appear from one generation to the next as *iudices sacri palatii*; and it gave the city as a whole status and a sense of independence. For Otto III himself its function was at least as much ceremonial as practical. The emperor or his representative presided there not as an alien but as the legitimate successor of the old kings of Italy. But whereas in his ideal monastery Otto had grasped something of the way in which the religious life would develop in the future, in his refurbished *sacrum palatium* he was trying to restore a traditional structure that was soon to collapse. By the later eleventh century the chances of his political judgement being vindicated were virtually nil.

Lanfranc belonged to the generation for which neither the political nor the religious changes of the eleventh century could be seen at all clearly. Even his immediate successors had a more straightforward choice between the old and the new. Manegold of Lautenbach for example was imprisoned for his support of the new papal position in Germany;[2] Anselm of Canterbury was ready to explore to the limit the fundamental doctrines of Christianity. Lanfranc by contrast had to set against his appreciation of 'modern' scholarship and the new forms of religious life a very solid grounding in the traditional education

---

[1] The best account of early medieval Pavia, in terms of both written and archaeological evidence, is D. A. Bullough, 'Urban change in medieval Italy: the example of Pavia', *Papers of the British School at Rome* xxxiv (1966), 82–130.

[2] Manitius iii.180; cf. Ch. III below.

and outlook of north Italy. Hence he can appear an unadventurous academic and a political trimmer. But it is in just his hesitation between the old and the new, as he swings from one to the other and back again, that the interest of Lanfranc's life and writings may be found.

ii. the law

There is no precise chronology for Lanfranc's early life. Given that he entered Bec as a mature scholar in 1042 and survived until 1089 as an active archbishop, he was probably born *c.* 1010, or a little later. What is known of his younger relatives falls in with this dating: one nephew, Lanfranc, was a monk of Bec in the 1080s, and another, Paul, became abbot of St. Albans in 1077.[1] But these men were the exceptions, who like Lanfranc had come to the north, where their lives were chronicled. Of the family as a whole we know only that it belonged to Pavia, and that Lanfranc's father was—in the words of a Norman monk—'said to be of the order of those who declared the rights and laws of the city'.[2] A Canterbury tradition has preserved the names of both parents, Aribald and Roza,[3] but neither can now be identified in the Pavian records. Yet even without such corroborative evidence we may reasonably see Aribald as in some capacity attached to the lawcourt, probably as a *iudex*, and his family as belonging to the social milieu of the *sacrum palatium*.

The duties of a *iudex sacri palatii* may be seen in a case that came before Alberic, envoy of the emperor Henry II, in October 1018.[4] Alberic held a court in the upper hall of his house in Pavia, having with him Armann, Gisulf, Peter, Adalbert, Bonfilio, Teuzo, Everard, Amizo, Otbert and Lanfranc, all *iudices sacri palatii*, and many others. Bishop Warin of Modena came before them, with Nordilo his advocate, and presented a charter:

---

[1] For the younger Lanfranc (Lanfranc's brother's son) see *Lanfranci Epp.* 43, 45, 47, *Anselmi Epp.* 39, 137–8. He became abbot of St. Wandrille in 1089–90, against the wishes of his superiors.

[2] 'Nam, ut fertur, pater eius de ordine illorum qui iura et leges ciuitatis asseruabant fuit': *V.L.*, cap. 1.

[3] Gervase of Canterbury, *Actus Pontificum*, p. 364.

[4] C. Maneresi, *I placiti del 'Regnum Italiae'* (Rome, 1958: *Font Stor.Ital.* 96**), II.ii.599–605, much abridged.

On 28 August 1018, in the presence of the count of Pavia, Rainard and Roza his wife gave to the church of Modena certain property within the gate *de Viridario* of the city of Pavia: two houses, each with an upper hall, a third with a walled courtyard, and a tower with a chapel of St. Nicholas on the ground floor. The transaction was recorded by Restald, notary of the palace, and witnessed by count Otto, by two of Roza's relatives, and by two imperial envoys, Alberic and Adalbert.

Then bishop Warin and Nordilo his advocate were asked why they presented this charter.

'We do so,' they said, 'lest anyone remain in ignorance that the property in Pavia here enumerated, the two houses with their upper halls, the third with the walled courtyard, and the tower with the chapel of St. Nicholas on the ground floor, belong inalienably to the church of Modena. If anyone disputes this, we are ready to meet him; and moreover we call upon Rainard and Roza the donors, who are here with their notary, to say whether they or their family retain any interest in the said property.'

Rainard and Roza and their notary replied,

That charter which the bishop and his notary present is a true statement of our gift, and all the property therein designated now belongs to the church of Modena. Should we or our family ever seek to recover it, we are liable to a fine.

Then the *iudices sacri palatii* were satisfied, and they declared the case at an end. They ordered Restald the notary to draw up this document for the greater security of the bishop of Modena, and they added their own signatures: Alberic the imperial envoy, and ten *iudices*—Armann, Gisulf and the rest as enumerated. Now the function of the *iudices* here is to recognize that a transaction has taken place, and that it is valid. They are neither judges in the modern sense, nor even advocates arguing a case: they are simply local men of good repute who are versed in the traditional forms of the law. Such men are a familiar constituent of the early lawcourt, whether as Carolingian *scabini* or the *iudices* of twelfth-century England,[1] and their work at Pavia was in this respect no more sophisticated than elsewhere.

---

[1] For the problem in general see H. M. Cam, 'Suitors and *scabini*', *Speculum* x (1935), 190–1 and G. Mor, *L'età feudale* (Milan, 1952: *Stor.Pol. Ital.* I), ii.58. Its bearing on Lanfranc is discussed by R. W. Southern, 'Lanfranc of Bec and Berengar of Tours', in *Studies in Medieval History presented to F. M. Powicke,* ed. R. W. Hunt *et al.* (Oxford, 1948), p. 29.

What distinguished the *iudices* of eleventh-century Pavia was their interest in the law as an intellectual discipline. Although their predecessors had already assembled a primitive apparatus for the Lombard lawcode, these first commentators rarely offer more than a cross-reference or the explanation of a difficult word. The *moderni* by contrast—as they self-consciously called themselves from *c.* 1020 onwards—extend the apparatus to include what may loosely be called case law: the records of memorable disputes as to how in a given situation the law should be interpreted.[1] At the same time Roman civil law was beginning to exert a strong influence on both the content and form of the vernacular codes. Where for example the law of the Lombards conflicted with that of the Salian Franks, Roman law might solve the difficulty, for it was generally applicable to all men: 'lex romana omnium generalis est'.[2] Roman law was regarded as an absolute, founded on universal principles of justice, theoretically coherent and a model of system. By about 1070 (the date is only approximate) the whole Lombard Code had been rearranged according to the subjects treated;[3] and the way was open for its systematic study on a par with the law of Justinian. The work of the whole period *c.* 1020–70 is summed up in the apparatus to the Lombard Code known as the *Expositiones*. Here the arguments of the *moderni* are presented as an academic commentary on the lawcode, following its new systematic arrangement, and prefaced with the typically scholastic exhortation:

The student should distinguish the author's purpose, the use of the work, and the division of learning to which it belongs: whether ethics, logic or physics. This work pertains to ethics, for it treats of the customs of men.[4]

Judging by this introduction, the collection may in its present form be as late as the early twelfth century.[5] Certainly it is a

---

[1] A. Boretius, *Liber Legis Langobardorum Papiensis dictus: Mon.Ger. Leg.* IV.xlvi-xcviii; 290–585. Early glosses are found e.g. in MSS. Milan Amb.O.53+55 and London B.L.Add.5411 (Boretius cod. 3 and 10). See further F. Calasso, *Medio evo del diritto* (Milan, 1954), i.305–15, with references.

[2] Boretius, op. cit., p. 291: 'iuxtaRomanam legem quae omnium est generalis'.

[3] *Mon.Ger.Leg.* IV. 607–40 (the *Lombarda*).

[4] Ibid. 290, line 29–291, line 1.

[5] The *Exporitiones* survive only in MS. Naples B Naz.Brancacciana I.B.12 (*olim* II.B.28) an early twelfth-century book written in the 'Beneventan' script of

text for the schoolroom rather than a handbook for the practising lawyer. The *Expositiones* cannot offer a complete account of the legal developments of the eleventh century; but taken as a whole the arguments of the *moderni* show the intellectual bias of the society in which Lanfranc grew up: there was a lively interest in the law and some energetic argument as to its interpretation.

At the same time it is very difficult indeed to relate the *Expositiones*, which are known only in this one collection, to the other main body of evidence: the notarial records such as the *placitum* of 1018 already quoted. The *Expositiones* often deal with a type of problem for which no notarial records have survived (e.g. criminal law); and even where the subject-matter is similar, the record gives only the final decision, not the preceding discussion. The witnesses to the documents no doubt include many of the *moderni*: but within the *Expositiones* the *moderni* themselves are seldom named. The editor of the *Expositiones* was interested in the debates rather than the protagonists; and even those few whom he does name cannot be reliably correlated with specific *iudices*.

The great exception would appear to be Lanfranc himself. The *Expositiones* contain one crucial discussion of the law of inheritance:

Archbishop Lanfranc put this question to Bonfilio the *iudex*:
> If a man presents a charter in court, and it is challenged; and if both the notary who wrote it and the witnesses are dead, how can he defend the validity of his charter?

Bonfilio replied,
> By custom, he may call twelve oath-helpers, and show two other charters written by the same notary.

Lanfranc:
> Does custom allow no other way?

Bonfilio:
> No.

Lanfranc:
> Then custom is in conflict with the law; for Otto I declared this custom to be 'detestable, dishonest and inadmissible'.

---

southern Italy: see E.A. Loew, *The Beneventan Script* (Oxford, 1914), p. 354. Their arrangement is systematic, like the *Lombarda*; but they have been printed chronologically, in conjunction with the Lombard Code (*Mon.Ger.Leg.* IV.290–581).

At this Bonfilio retired; but William took up his cause and answered Lanfranc thus:

It was not the custom itself that Otto I thought detestable, but its abuse; for men were drawing up false charters deliberately, and then perjuring themselves in their defence. So Otto gave to the *challenger* the option of trial by battle.[1]

Lanfranc's reply is not recorded. It would indeed be difficult to devise one; for William's interpretation is plainly correct. In two other passages 'Lanfranc', not described as 'the archbishop', appears with the same disputants.[2] Now the name 'Lanfranc' alone is too common in eleventh-century Italy to identify Lanfranc of Bec unsupported. The *iudex* of 1018, for example, unless he is witnessing as a minor, must be a different man. But the only possible *Lanfrancus archiepiscopus* is the archbishop of Canterbury (1070–89).[3] So the editor of the *Expositiones* (or, at worst, the scribe of the unique manuscript) must have believed that his defeated disputant was the archbishop of Canterbury at an earlier stage in his career. A similar tradition was current in twelfth-century Normandy, where Orderic Vitalis described Lanfranc's youthful distinction in the lawcourt:

Even as a young orator he frequently got the better of his experienced adversaries in lawsuits, and by his floods of eloquence and apt choice of words defeated his seniors ... He showed so much wisdom in giving legal opinions that lawyers, *iudices* and civil officials all gladly followed his advice.

If, as is probable, Orderic is quoting a lost passage from William of Poitiers, the story was in circulation by *c.* 1070.[4] But how it originated is another question. In the fragment of William's work that has survived Lanfranc appears as the prophetic monk giving counsel to the new Theodosius: this is as much a flower of rhetoric as a historical judgement.[5] The story of the young advocate confuting his elders (whether or not it is William's) has a trace of the same artificiality: it falls in too neatly with the

---

[1] *Expositio* to Guy vi.23: ed.cit., pp. 566–7.

[2] *Expositiones* to Grimoald and Liutprand iii.3: ed.cit., pp. 402–3; 404.

[3] For the multiplicity of 'Lanfrancs' in eleventh-century Pavia see J. Ficker, *Forschungen zur Reichs– und Rechtsgeschichte Italiens* (Innsbruck, 1872), iii.45. There is no known archbishop of the name in eleventh-century Italy.

[4] *Hist.Eccles.* iv (Chibnall II. 248–9).

[5] *Gesta Guillelmi Ducis* i.52.

picture of Christ among the doctors.[1] In the late twelfth century yet another tradition appears in Normandy, when Robert of Torigny couples Lanfranc with Irnerius of Bologna as one of the first great teachers of law. Though the link with Irnerius is chronologically misleading, Robert may have found at Mont-St.-Michel some recollection of Lanfranc's legal studies that had escaped the chroniclers of Bec and St. Évroult.[2] Insecure though these Norman traditions may be, they do lend a certain support to the editor of the *Expositiones* in his identification of 'archbishop Lanfranc'.

But the real corroboration should come from Lanfranc's own writings; and here the evidence again fails us. Allowing that many of his works may be lost, in those that survive the quotations from civil law (Lombard or Roman) are nearly all commonplaces from the *Etymologies* of Isidore and similar books.[3] There is however one striking definition of a phrase in the *Pauline Epistles*:

If a widow has children or grandchildren, then they should learn as their duty to show loyalty to the family and to repay what they owe to their parents and grandparents. (I Tim.5:4, *N.E.B.*)

Lanfranc explains that *parentes* here covers both the direct and the collateral relationship—

'for the whole of that generation is called the *parentela*, as we find in secular law:
   The heir shall inherit according to his place in the family.'[4]

He is quoting Rothari 153 in the Lombard Code, which lists a man's heirs and the order in which they shall be reckoned, to the seventh degree of kinship.[5] Within so wide a collateral relationship an heir is almost certain to be found. Unfortunately this is the one text that need not imply a further knowledge of Lombard law, for it was quoted in the eleventh century in the

---

[1] Luke 2: 46–7.   [2] *Chronicle*, s.a.1030.
[3] Lanfranc's use of the *Etymologies* and cognate works is discussed in Ch. III. Many of his legal turns of phrase have been collected by N. Tamassia, 'Lanfranco arcivescovo di Canterbury e la scuola pavese', in *Mélanges Fitting*, ed. E. Meynial (Montpellier, 1908), ii. 189–201.
[4] 'Parentes uocat quos superius filios et nepotes. Tota enim progenies parentela dicitur, unde et in mundana lege *parens parenti per gradum et parentelam succedere iubetur*': *Comm.Epp. Pauli* (D'Achery, p. 190: Migne, *P.L.* cl. 355B, corrected from MS.Vat.lat. 143, fol. 142v).
[5] *Mon.Ger.Leg.* IV. 35.

quite different context of the prohibited degrees of marriage. Here the text that is generous in determining the scope of inheritance extends intolerably the number of distant relations whom one may not marry. By contrast the Roman reckoning of kinship, which favoured the direct descendant against the collateral, bore less severely on the law of marriage. To some it was unduly lax. Peter Damian for example condemned the reckoning of the prohibited degrees by the Roman rather than the Lombard usage.[1] As the question affected duke William's marriage in the 1050s, we cannot assume that Lanfranc's quotation here (which was written about the same time) comes directly from the Lombard Code.

Perhaps it is anachronistic to expect formal proof of Lanfranc's competence in the law, whether Lombard or Roman. Whatever the reputation of the Pavian lawyers of his childhood, their studies were wholly practical: they were concerned with the interpretation of texts within the lawcourts. There was as yet no question of a 'school' of law, either as an academic tradition or as an institution, which might challenge the established education of northern Italy.[2] It is only in the *Expositiones*, which in their present form are at least half a century later, that law is systematically taught as a text in school. The root of the problem however is not the relation between the practical and the academic study of law, but the relation of law as such to contemporary education. Even in the *Expositiones* it is not an autonomous discipline. The methods employed—tricks and turns of argument and the organization of material—are still essentially those of rhetoric and the allied

[1] Peter Damian, *De parentelae gradibus* (Migne *P.L.*cxlv.191A–204C). The degrees of kinship according to Roman and barbarian reckoning are conveniently expounded by M. Deanesly and P. Grosjean, 'The Canterbury edition of the answers of pope Gregory I to St. Augustine', *Journ.Eccles.Hist.* x (1959), 5–7. cf. R. W. Southern, *The Making of the Middle Ages* (London, 1953), pp. 77–9, with references.

[2] Modern scholars have been loath to relinquish such a school. Among legal historians F. W. Maitland has a vivid account based on the *Expositiones* (which he assumes refers to the early eleventh century): F. Pollock and F. W. Maitland, *The History of English Law*, 2nd edn. (Cambridge, 1898), i.22. Historians of Pavia have argued that the city of Cassiodorus and Boethius and the compilers of Rothari's *Edict must* have had a continuous tradition of legal scholarship: see most recently U. Gualazzini, 'La scuola pavese, con particolare riguardo all' insegnamento del diritto' (with bibliography) and B. Pagnin, 'Scuola e cultura a Pavia nell'alto medio evo', in *Atti IV Congr.Int.Stud.Alto Medioevo: Pavia, Scaldasole, etc.* (Spoleto, 1969), pp. 35–73 and 75–106.

linguistic *artes* of logic and grammar. The *artes* were the substance of education; and as they developed throughout the century the study of law was affected in turn. But law was the beneficiary, not the origin of such changes: it was the material on which the student might use tools which he had acquired elsewhere.[1] Here Lanfranc can be no exception. In the last analysis the degree of his legal expertise is less important than the character of his basic education, however that was applied.

Here the main issue is not in doubt. Lanfranc is a product of the north Italian schools *c.* 1020–30: Pavia certainly, perhaps Vercelli or even distant Ravenna.[2] It was a milieu with a clear academic bias, from which Lanfranc himself in his later career never departed.

iii. the schools of northern Italy

The purpose of education *c.* 1000 was summed up by Gerbert of Aurillac. A man should fit himself, he wrote, both to live well and to speak well.[3] Gerbert had made his own career at the Ottonian court in exactly this way: as a man with the right phrase for the moment. His dispute at Ravenna in 982 with Ohtricus the Saxon shows his formal skill in debate; it is here, rather than in his grasp of the subject-matter, that Gerbert has the edge on his opponent.[4] Again his own teaching at Rheims was directed above all towards proficiency in rhetoric.[5] It was as an orator that the student would succeed in life, whether in the imperial chancery or in Lombard city politics; so he must learn to handle a wide range of subjects aptly and persuasively: to acquire a technique rather than a body of information.

While these considerations apply to Latin Europe as a whole, they are especially relevant to Italy, where there was a greater sophistication in government than outside the Empire, and a certain tradition of public life. The school curriculum reflected

---

[1] Vinogradoff puts the matter in a nutshell: *Roman Law in Western Europe*, 2nd edn. (Oxford, 1929), p. 56.

[2] 'Relicta ciuitate amore discendi ad studia litterarum perrexit. Vbi plurimo tempore demoratus, omni scientia seculari perfecte imbutus, rediit': *V.L.*, cap. 1.

[3] 'Cum studio bene vivendi semper coniunxi studium bene dicendi': *Ep.*44, ed. F. Weigle (Weimar, 1966: *Mon.Ger.Hist.*), p. 73.

[4] Richer, *Historiae* iii.57–65, ed. G. Waitz (Hanover, 1877: *Mon.Ger.Hist.*), pp. 105–9.

[5] Ibid. iii.46–8, ed.cit., pp. 101–2.

the practical needs of that society. It was concerned almost exclusively with the linguistic arts of the *trivium*: grammar, logic and rhetoric. In Pavia itself the grammarian Papias was active in the 1050s. His *Vocabularium*, a great list of difficult or ambiguous words, and his abridgement of the *Institutiones* of Priscian provide dogma for the uncertain—like Fowler's *English Usage*; and judging by their success the need for such guidance was widespread.[1] What has not so far been discovered is new work in grammar as such: it was the indispensable auxiliary rather than a subject in its own right. Nor was there much original work in logic. The basic problems had been recognized since the time of Alcuin: 'substance' and 'accident', genus and species and the permutations of the syllogism.[2] But by the late tenth century a wider range of texts was coming into circulation; the traditional questions were being handled with a new assurance, and they were reaching a larger public. What only Gerbert and a few chosen spirits could comprehend *c.* 980 was within the grasp of Adalbert of Laon a generation later. The educated man was coming to have some knowledge of the elements of logic, even if his main interests lay elsewhere. The dramatic advance however was in the field of rhetoric. The Carolingian schoolmaster had found enough for his needs in Cicero's *Topics* and the *Rhetoric* of Alcuin. While individual writers might borrow devices or tricks of style from the *De inventione* of Cicero or the *Rhetorica ad Herennium*, these primary texts of medieval rhetoric were not discussed in the schools. The early eleventh century saw the first serious attempt to master both the *De inventione* and the *Ad Herennium*, initially with the aid of ancient commentaries and then by revising and abridging these commentaries to make new ones. A south German commentary of *c.* 1020 on the *De inventione* adapts the standard commentary of Victorinus, adding notes from Grillius (who was much rarer) and other passages still which seem to be original.[3]

[1] See Manitius ii.717–24.

[2] The best account of the composition and currency of the *logica vetus* is still A. van de Vyver, 'Les étapes du développement philosophique du haut-moyen-âge', *Rev.Belge.Phil.Hist.* vii (1929), 425–52. See further L. Minio-Paluello, *Aristoteles Latinus* I. i-v (Bruges/Paris 1961), pp. ix-xcvi.

[3] MS. Oxford Bodleian Laud lat. 49, fol. 137v–46: see M. Dickey, 'Some commentaries on the *De Inventione* and the *Ad Herennium* of the eleventh and early twelfth centuries', *Med.Renaiss.Stud.* vi (1968), 1–41. I have laid more emphasis than Mrs. Dickey on the author's use of Victorinus and Grillius.

For the *Ad Herennium* the evidence is appreciably later: it was a school text in the area Parma–Reggio–Milan by about 1040; the first 'modern' commentary belongs probably to the 1050s. This is a crucial development in pure scholarship, which matches (and was no doubt stimulated by) the need for rhetoric in practical life.

The first author to exploit the new rhetorical texts on any scale was the imperial scribe and notary Anselm of Besate. Anselm's career began in the aristocratic circles of Milan cathedral; he was educated *c.* 1040–5 in Reggio and Parma; by 1045 he had joined the imperial chancery and in 1048 he entered the chapel of Henry III: thereafter nothing certain is known of him.[1] Very possibly he died young. Certainly his work lacks the sobriety and equilibrium of middle age. Anselm's *Rhetorimachia*—the rhetorician's battle, on the analogy of the *Psychomachia* of Prudentius—was written in 1046–8 as a kind of fellowship dissertation for the imperial chapel. At first sight it is inspired by *The Golden Ass* (which Anselm could not have known) moderated by the *De Nuptiis* of Martianus Capella. The work is a sustained invective against Anselm's cousin, to whom Anselm explains politely at the beginning that he knows that his charges are untrue—let not the mud stick: it is pure rhetorical convention, authorized by Cicero. At one moment he is describing magical rites in a cemetery at Parma; then he inserts a *novella* of an inept seducer: next comes a vision of the virtues and the arts contending in heaven for Anselm's affections—a smug contrast with the taste of his opponent. These tales now dominate the book. But it was at least Anselm's intention that they should be no more than illustrations to his main theme: the complete exposition by means of concrete examples of the teaching of the *De inventione* and the *Ad Herennium*. In the criminous cousin stealing out of the city to St. John's field by night the reader may see in action some of the 'criteria for building up suspicion' that are listed in *Ad*

---

[1] There is an excellent account of Anselm's life in Karl Manitius' edition of the *Rhetorimachia* (Weimar, 1958: *Mon.Ger.Hist.*), pp. 61–86 (reviewed by D. A. Bullough, *Eng.Hist.Rev.* lxxv (1960), 487–91) and a good survey in English by H. E. J. Cowdrey, 'Anselm of Besate and some north-Italian scholars of the eleventh century', *Journ. Eccles. Hist.* xxiii (1972), 115–24. See further Bullough, 'Le scuole cattedrali e la cultura dell' Italia settentrionale prima dei Comuni', in *Italia Sacra*, ed. Maccarrone *et al.* (Padua, 1964), v. 140–2.

Herennium ii. 3–7.[1] And so throughout the book. If Anselm can be carried away by the excitement of telling a story, the basic idea of his work is still original and attractive: to construct a working model of contemporary rhetoric. The emphasis is always on the specific example, as it might function in a real situation.

The pressure to produce men who could argue, whether as Pavian *iudices* or in the incipient communes of northern Italy, goes far to explain the fundamental scholastic development of the eleventh century: the evolution of a technical vocabulary. The twists and turns of a discussion are marked by *sed contra, e converso, tu autem oppones*—devices which were to be common-place in scholastic discussion. Other phrases are more obviously technical: *secundum proprietatem uerbi* and *ablatio contrarii*. Individually they all derive from well-known texts of the trivium; but taken as a whole they are new. Though a word or phrase may be found verbatim in Boethius, its meaning in eleventh-century parlance is often different or less precise. What was to become the language of Abelard appears in a misleading and miscellaneous guise, now clear cut and now stubbornly ambiguous. But its character is unmistakable. These formulae of distinguishing, objecting, and subsuming are the rough beginning of the scholastic language that was to be agreed throughout Europe. In so far as this lan-guage was hammered out in viva voce discussion, among the earliest centres of its evolution were the cities of northern Italy.

In the mathematical and scientific arts of the quadrivium Italian education was relatively weak: there are few signs of the exploration that had already begun in northern Europe, in the schools of Liège[2] and Rheims. In the great imperial monastery of Pomposa, near Ravenna, Guy of Arezzo made an outstanding contribution to musical notation;[3] but otherwise science and mathematics as school subjects do not come into their own until later in the eleventh century. Even then it is in the south that

---

[1] *Rhetorimachia* ii. 3 (ed.cit., p. 143).

[2] Manitius ii. 225–8; 743–8; cf. T. Gregory, *Platonismo medievale* (Rome, 1958), pp. 1–15.

[3] Manitius ii. 748–56; see further G. Reese, *Music in the Middle Ages* (London, 1941), Chs. 6 and 9.

they flourish, in Monte Cassino and Salerno.[1] In northern Italy the student was grounded in Latin literature and in correct and effective verbal expression. Anything beyond that he studied on his own initiative.

iv. the road to Bec: c. 1030–1042

Lanfranc left Italy about 1030. Crossing the Alps into Burgundy he travelled for some time there and in the Loire valley before finally establishing himself c. 1039 as a teacher in Avranches.[2] Within a few years he had experienced a conversion to the religious life and entered the monastery of Bec. Thereafter his life is reasonably well known, at least externally. It is the 1030s that are so obscure: and yet it is here that the fundamental problems lie. When did Lanfranc leave Italy, and in what circumstances? How long was he itinerant in France? What did he learn in the French schools?

If Lanfranc was still in Pavia in 1024, as is very likely, he witnessed the revolt that swept Lombardy on the death of Henry II. Many years later pope Leo IX described how as a young man he had led the contingent of the bishop of Toul to join the emperor Conrad in Italy, and how he himself travelled back from Milan to Burgundy through a countryside that was hostile nearly the whole way.[3] For a moment German control of North Italy was virtually lost; and although in military terms it was quickly regained, still the rising of 1024 marked a turning-point. In Pavia the palace of Theodoric was destroyed and the system of government for which it stood was in abeyance. For many families it was the moment of choice between outright support of the emperor or of the city;[4] in particular the *iudices sacri palatii* had to decide whether or not they wished to see the old order restored. Where Lanfranc's own sympathies lay we can scarcely even speculate. He seems never to have visited

---

[1] The outstanding figures are Desiderius, abbot of Monte Cassino, (as a patron) and Alphanus, archbishop of Salerno, who was a scholar in his own right: Manitius iii. 75–9; ii. 618–37.

[2] 'Et pertransiens Franciam, *quamplures* magni *nominis scholares secum habens, in Normanniam* peru*enit*; et in Abrincatensi ciuitate demoratus, per aliquid tempus docuit': *V.L.*, cap. 1; cf. *V.H.*, p. 95.

[3] *Vita Leonis*, cap. 7; 10: Migne, *P.L.* cxliii. 472C–3A; 477A–8C.

[4] D. A. Bullough, 'Urban change in early medieval Italy: the example of Pavia', *Papers of the British School at Rome* xxxiv (1966), 116.

Germany, nor even Lorraine: the two great centres of patronage when he was a young man. But he had pupils from Germany, and his works appear in the catalogues of German libraries. All that can be said is that he left Pavia at a time of acute tension between the emperor and the Italian cities. The reasons for his departure may lie here; but there is no certainty that they do.

The scholars whom Lanfranc encountered in France may be called the diaspora of the school of Chartres. Bishop Fulbert, long the doyen of French scholarship, had died in 1028; but his pupils were to be found throughout the Loire valley and the Île de France, and even in the German-speaking world at Speyer and Regensburg.[1] Academically the school reflected Gerbert's teaching at Rheims in the late tenth century. There the whole span of learning had been attempted: on the linguistic side Gerbert had built up his curriculum towards rhetoric; on the scientific he had essayed the mysteries of mathematics. He wrote a treatise on geometry and probably another on the astrolabe; and his *De rationali et ratione uti* is the first independent contribution to logic for over a century.[2] Among his pupils only Abbo of Fleury was so wide-ranging: his scientific work was on a par with Gerbert's, though his only surviving logical writing scarcely rates as original. Abbo was killed in 1004 while still a young man, leaving as his memorial the library at Fleury.[3] None of Gerbert's other pupils was of the same calibre. Adalbert of Laon wrote quite a popular little work on the syllogism, illustrating its various forms by the story of the man who bought a lame mule:

ADALBERT: You have sent me a trashy little mule; its ears are cropped; it is blind and lame: it is useless and worthless in all respects.

FULK: My dear brother, it is your argument that can scarcely

[1] The classic account of the school of Chartres is A. Clerval, *Les Écoles de Chartres au moyen âge* (Paris, 1895); cf. J. Havet, 'Poème rhythmique d'Adelman de Liège', in *Notices et documents . . . Soc.Hist.France . . . cinquantième anniversaire* (Paris, 1884), pp. 71–92. For the link with Regensburg see p. 18, n. 3.

[2] Richer, *Historiae* iii. 46–54, ed. Waitz (Hanover, 1877), pp. 101–4; cf. Manitius ii. 729–42, and further N. Bubnov, *Gerberti Opera Mathematica* (Berlin, 1899).

[3] A. van de Vyver, 'Les oeuvres inédites d'Abbon de Fleury', *Rev.Bén.* xlvii (1935), 125–69, and (posthumously) an edition of Abbo's *Syllogismorum categoricorum et hypotheticorum enodatio* (Bruges, 1966). For the library see further E. Pellegrin, 'Membra disiecta floriacensia', *Bibl.Éc.Chartes* cxvii (1959), 5–56.

stand up. You have not condemned this mule in universal terms, but only declared it unfit for specific duties.
It may be no use for pulling the bishop's carriage; but
have you tried it at ploughing? If it can be used for
anything at all, then it cannot be 'in all respects' useless.

ADALBERT: My condemnation is neither universal nor particular:
for the phrase 'in all respects' cannot be classified in this
way . . . etc.[1]

The use here of the 'joke' example is like Anselm's in the
Rhetorimachia; but Adalbert is working on a less ambitious scale
and with much better known material. He was an informed
patron of letters and a minor satirical poet—in all a very
reputable product of Gerbert's school—but he is scarcely himself an independent scholar.

Fulbert was the contemporary of both Abbo and Adalbert in
Gerbert's school. His surviving work consists principally of the
hymns and liturgical sequences that he wrote for his cathedral,
some moral and mnemonic verses, his prayers and sermons and
a collection of over a hundred letters. The qualities that emerge
are sound judgement, clarity of thought and a good Latin style.
His letters expound and conclude the legal and political
problems which he encounters as bishop, while in his prayers
and hymns he can touch genuine poetry, in his antiphon for
example for the Nativity of the Virgin:

Solem iustitiae regem paritura supremum,
Stella Maria maris hodie processit ad ortum —
Cernere divinum lumen gaudete fideles.[2]

In an age when simple flexible latinity was still rare Fulbert had
a gift of language that was easily as valuable as academic
originality. He made no independent contribution to learning.
His understanding of the trivium is dimly reflected in two
sets of mnemonic verses *On the difference between dialectic and
rhetoric*:

---

[1] G. A. Hückel, 'Les Poèmes satiriques d'Adalbéron', in *Mél.hist.moyen âge*, ed.
Luchaire: *Univ. Paris Bibl.Fac.Lettres* xiii (1901), pp. 180–1 (freely translated and
abridged). Cf. C. Prantl, *Geschichte der Logik im Abendlande*, 2nd edn. (Leipzig,
1885), ii. 58–9.

[2] Migne, *P.L.* cxli. 345A: see Y. Delaporte, 'Fulbert de Chartres et l'école
chartraine de chant liturgique au xie siècle', *Études Grégoriennes* ii (1957), 64.

For they differ in their subject, in their purpose and their use:
Dialectic has a thesis, but hypothesis belongs
To the rhetorician's province—give to each his proper due.
When a question is a *thesis* it is set in abstract terms;
The *hypothesis* is furnished with specific circumstance . . .[1]

This is the ancient metre of *Ecce Caesar nunc triumphat* put to a
new use in the cathedral school. Other verses summarize a list
of weights and measures and the positions of the stars.[2] It is
important to see that these jingles (for they are little more) are
the whole sum of Fulbert's surviving work in the *artes*. Perhaps
he should rather be seen as a librarian. Though the main body
of the cathedral manuscripts was destroyed in 1944, their
contents are roughly known, and several books have fortunately
survived outside Chartres. One of these outliers is the collection
of literary, scientific and medical texts, some with commentaries,
which the monk Hartwic gave to St. Emmeram, Regensburg,
on his return from studying at Chartres. Hartwic's collection
reinforces the impression left by several of the lost manuscripts,
that the fundamental texts of Gerbert's curriculum were available in Fulbert's school.[3] Lanfranc could find in Chartres the
material of scholarship, as Fulbert had grasped these at Rheims.
Had he been of a scientific turn of mind, this would have been
a great gain: but in the trivium we may well doubt whether
there was much in Fulbert's library that was not already available in Italy.

Another fragment of the Chartres library which has escaped
destruction is the collection made soon after Fulbert's death of
his letters, verses and *memorabilia*. It begins with the titles to a
series of miniatures commemorating different sides of Fulbert's
life:

The young man taught his pupils here
The seven arts with zealous care;

The elder shepherd of the Lord
For twenty years proclaimed the word;

[1] C. Pfister, *De Fulberti Carnotensis Episcopi Vita et Operibus* (Nancy, 1885), p. 6.
In MS. Oxford Bodleian d'Orville 158 this poem is preceded (fol. 122) by another
of the same type, now only partly legible.

[2] Pfister, op. cit., pp. 35–7; Migne, *P.L.* cxli. 347B–8B.

[3] Hartwic's book is now Munich Clm. 14272: see B. Bischoff, *Mittelalterliche
Studien* (Stuttgart, 1967), ii. 80–1.

As quick in charitable deed
To find and succour those in need.[1]

Fulbert was a teacher and a collector of books, but he was much more: he was pastor and ruler of his diocese; and it is clear from the letters that he was often called upon to be a politician, either in defence of his own lands or in advising his metropolitan or the king of France. The same qualities are found in his pupils. At St. Florent, Saumur, for example abbot Sigo was remembered as 'learned in humane letters, but more learned in the school of Christ'. His scholarly attainments are less important than his edifying life and his sheer competence in running St. Florent. Abbot Albert of Marmoutiers, Everard of Breteuil, Hildegar of Poitiers all had similar gifts: they were enlightened and conscientious administrators, with sufficient learning for their needs.[2] Fulbert was their well-remembered teacher; but pre-eminently he was a man who understood the art of government, in which their own careers were made. His school was a centre of administrative expertise rather than original thought, and it was the gateway to promotion: these are more convincing reasons for its fame in the world than a breakthrough in pure scholarship.

It is likely that Lanfranc visited Chartres; but he found neither academic guidance nor preferment there.[3] The only French master with whom he may have studied is Berengar, a pupil of Fulbert's in the late 1020s, who was teaching at Tours *c.* 1035.[4] Berengar's discussion of the Eucharist, and the

[1] Pfister, op. cit., p. 3, and L. C. MacKinney, *Bishop Fulbert and education at the school of Chartres* (Notre Dame, Indiana, 1957), p. 57, both from MS. Paris B. N. lat. 14167. This manuscript is discussed in detail by Professor F. Behrends in his edition of Fulbert's letters (Oxford Medieval Texts 1976). The miniatures, of which two survive, were intercalated in the cathedral martyrology at the date of Fulbert's death (10 April): see R. Merlet and A. Clerval, *Un Manuscrit chartrain du XIe siècle* (Chartres, 1893).

[2] See A. Clerval, *Les Écoles de Chartres au moyen âge* (Paris, 1895), pp. 54–5 (Sigo), 67–8 (Albert), 47–9 (Everard) and 49–53 (Hildegar). Sigo's *obit* describes him as 'plurime in studiis liberalibus, sed ulterioris in Christi scola eruditionis': MS. London B. L. Harley 3023, fol. 63.

[3] The only formal evidence of Lanfranc's contact with Chartres is a letter from Berengar (1049) quoting Lanfranc's alleged eucharistic opinions according to Ingelran, *magister scholae* at Chartres cathedral: Migne, *P.L.* cl. 63CD.

[4] See Ch. IV. Tradition had it that Berengar was present at Fulbert's deathbed: William of Malmesbury, *Gesta Regum* iii. 285 (ed. Stubbs, ii. 341).

controversy this aroused, have obscured all trace of his early exposition of the *artes*; and Lanfranc himself was reluctant to admit that he had actually learnt anything from Berengar. He drew for his own pupils at Bec a sharp little vignette of Berengar's lecturing style: the theatrical gestures, the conviction of his own brilliance, and the exaggerated reaction to Lanfranc's criticism. When he was crossed, we are told, on a trivial point of logic, he abandoned the whole subject and took up the theological inquiries that were to lead to so much trouble.[1] Distorted though this anecdote may be, it does indicate that Lanfranc first encountered Berengar as a teacher of the trivium; his methods of argument and verbal analysis may have been in part adopted by Lanfranc—to be used in the end against Berengar himself.

That Lanfranc taught at Avranches, though reasonably well attested, is at first scarcely credible. Western Normandy had suffered so badly from the Viking invasions that there is no record even of a titular bishop of Avranches from the mid-ninth century to the late tenth. The bishops that follow are scarcely more than names: Norgot, Mauger and Hugh; it is only with John of Bayeux (1060–7) that the history of the see can be resumed.[2] In such conditions it is beside the point to conjecture that Lanfranc was *scholasticus* in the cathedral.[3] He could have found in the city neither books nor scribes, to say nothing of pupils ready to hear him. A more reasonable proposal is that he had some association with Mont-St.-Michel, which is only a few kilometres away. Among the Norman houses Mont-St.-Michel had shown an exceptional zeal for collecting and copying manuscripts.[4] No expense had been spared: one scribe travelled to Fleury to copy books, another to Corbie; the collection as a

---

[1] Guitmund of Aversa, *De corporis et sanguinis Christi veritate in eucharistia* i (Migne, *P.L.*cxlix.1428AC); see also Appendix A4b.

[2] *Gallia Christiana* xi. 474A–6B; cf. D. C. Douglas, 'The Norman episcopate before the Norman Conquest', *Camb.Hist.Journ.* xiii (1957), 101–2, and for a similar state of affairs in Coutances J. Le Patourel, 'Geoffrey of Montbray, bishop of Coutances, 1049–93', *Eng.Hist.Rev.*lix(1944), 134ff.

[3] Anselm's visit to Avranches in the late 1050s (*Vita Anselmi* I.v, ed. Southern, p. 8 app.) has tempted some historians to posit a continuous scholastic tradition from Lanfranc onwards: see for example C. Lebreton, 'Les écoles d'Avranches sous Lanfranc et saint Anselme', *Mém.Soc.Archéol.d'Avranches* vi (1873), 493–511.

[4] J. J. G. Alexander, *Norman Illumination at Mont-St.-Michel 966–1100* (Oxford, 1970), Chs.ii–iv: see in particular pp. 35–7; 212–13.

whole was probably the best in Normandy at this date. While its great strength was in *patristica*, there are some historical works, a few Latin poets and one notable collection of logic,[1] including two of the Boethian monographs and the *De Decem Categoriis* with the most up-to-date version of its Carolingian gloss. It was a library in which serious scholarship was possible. On a more practical level, Lanfranc cannot have ventured into these remote parts without a patron. As Suppo of Fruttuaria was then abbot of Mont-St.-Michel, it was perhaps to him that Lanfranc was recommended as a fellow-Italian: certainly he is unlikely to have settled in the area without Suppo's prior knowledge and consent. Both as a scholastic centre and as a source of patronage Mont-St.-Michel looks like one of the missing pieces in the Lanfrancian jigsaw. He could find there (it is argued) protection and encouragement, without in any formal way belonging to the community.

If this is so, Lanfranc may be compared with two other scholars who visited the abbey slightly later on: Robert of Tombelaine and Anastasius the Greek. Robert wrote one of the first 'modern' commentaries on the Song of Songs and Anastasius made a slight, but again fairly early, contribution to the eucharistic controversy.[2] But at the same time, while they were alive to the new developments in scholarship, they were both primarily looking for a more perfect life outside the security of an established monastery—not necessarily in total isolation nor at variance with the older houses, but experimenting with new forms of organization and devotion. They came to Mont-St.-Michel as one of the great shrines of the north, but they soon passed on: Robert to be a hermit on the island of Tombelaine, Anastasius to the Pyrenees. Such a combination of scholar and ascetic was becoming very common by the mid-eleventh century, when the institutional framework for neither was yet clear: the instinct to explore led them equally into modern scholarship and the experimental forms of religious life. In Lanfranc's case the scholar and the monk are in absolute opposition: his conversion is unpremeditated, and irreconcilable

---

[1] MS. Avranches B.Mun. 229: see G. Lacombe, *Aristoteles Latinus* (Rome, 1939), no. 406.

[2] Alexander, op. cit., pp. 12–14, with references. Robert's *Commentary* is printed in Migne, *P.L.* cl.1361–70, and Anastasius' treatise ibid., cxlix. 433B–6A.

with his academic past. But in the long run the scholarly interests return, and the pattern of his life is not dissimilar to that of the learned ascetics of the next generation, though they were to venture further than Lanfranc in both scholarship and the religious life.

II. Prior of Bec *c.* 1045-1063

i. the community

For he realized, learned as he was, that the praise of men is vanity, that indeed all things tend towards their destruction, except him who is eternal and those who seek him ... So he seized on those words of Scripture ... which enjoin that a man should renounce everything, even his own will, to follow him who said—'If any man will come after me, let him deny himself, and take up his cross, and follow me.' (Matt. 16: 24)

THE story of Lanfranc's conversion is told by Gilbert Crispin in his life of abbot Herluin, who had founded Bec in 1034, eight years before Lanfranc's arrival.[1] Though the *Vita Herluini* was not written until 1109–12, Gilbert himself had been given as a child to the monastery *c.* 1055, early enough to have known the community in its first generation. After Herluin's rejection of the world, Lanfranc's decision comes as another example on a smaller scale. Just as the knight had exchanged the service of an earthly lord for a heavenly and the transient for the immutable, now the scholar saw the ancient contrast between the visible world and its creator:

Thou Lord in the beginning hast laid the foundations of the earth; and the heavens are the work of thine hands.
They shall perish, but thou remainest; and they all shall become old as doth a garment;
And as a vesture shalt thou fold them up and they shall be changed; but thou art the same, and thy years shall not fail. (Heb. 1 :10–12)

In becoming a monk Lanfranc had invested in what was real and permanent.

By his strategic allusion to the *Rule*—'even his own will'— Gilbert indicates that Herluin's community was essentially

---

[1] *V.H.*, pp. 95–6; cf. Robert of Torigny, *Chronicle*, s.a.1042. Lanfranc was the thirty-fifth monk to be professed at Bec (Appendix A5b).

Benedictine.[1] But it is at the same time contrasted with every other monastic foundation that existed in Normandy in the 1030s. Mont-St.-Michel, Fécamp, Jumièges, St. Wandrille, St. Ouen, to name only the principal houses, are all implicitly condemned as lax and disedifying beside the earnest little settlement at Bec. Herluin and his monks had no secure income; they existed on black bread and vegetables; the water was scarcely fit to drink: when Lanfranc entered the community it was 'the poorest and most wretched house in Normandy'. In the austerity of its regime Herluin's foundation was more like a group of hermits than a traditional Benedictine monastery. It is a theme that runs through the *Vita Herluini*—not obtrusively, but worked in with considerable art: the renewal of the austerity and simplicity preached by Cassian and exemplified in the *Vitae Patrum*. Herluin himself leads his monks out of the choir to their daily work in the fields, ruling them 'as the early Fathers had done'. Again in the tradition of the Desert monks Herluin, who had no scholastic expertise, could as the Spirit led him expound the Scriptures to the edification of all.[2] Now it is clear that in respect of the poverty of Bec Gilbert Crispin has an axe to grind. By the early twelfth century Bec was rich and established: not on the scale of Mont-St.-Michel and Fécamp, but on the same level of solid respectability as half a dozen other Norman foundations of the mid-eleventh century. The contrast now was between these houses, including Bec, with their lands and wealth and position in society, and the dramatic poverty of the early Cistercians or the model of asceticism offered by La Grande Chartreuse. It was already being said that in the new houses, where renunciation was complete, the principles of Benedict himself (as well as Cassian) were better realized than in the monasteries that enjoyed a steady income and an established place in society. Gilbert is concerned at once to demonstrate that such admired asceticism was already to be found in the early community at Bec and to justify Bec's recent prosperity as the harvest of its original self-denial. His account of the

---

[1] *V.H.*, p. 96; cf. *Rule of St. Benedict*, prologue: 'abrenuntians propriis uoluntatibus'.

[2] *V.H.*, pp. 91 (Herluin's exposition of Scripture), 93 (diet of the monks, their work in the fields, Herluin's rule *more patrum priorum*), 96 (the poverty of Bec).

spartan conditions in which the community began, and the spectacular returns on that austerity, reflect Gilbert's characteristic grasp of contemporary opinion as much as the actual circumstances of 1034.

The only first-hand opinion of the early years of Bec is, exceptionally, Lanfranc's own. Soon after he had entered the community he realized that he had made an irretrievable mistake; for it was not nearly strict enough. He decided to escape and become a hermit, adjusting himself to this harsher way of life by a diet of herbs secretly obtained from the monastic gardener. But his plan was miraculously revealed to Herluin, and he stayed on in the community. As the incident was a proof of Herluin's sanctity, Lanfranc told one other monk, who finally made it known at Bec in the early twelfth century.[1] Lanfranc's reaction to Bec *c*. 1042 is curiously similar to his early cry to be relieved of the see of Canterbury: deliver me from these barbarians, for I can neither help them nor save my own soul if I stay here.[2] In Bec as at Canterbury he settled down to make the best of things; and we do not have to accept his first, perhaps emotional, judgement. Both Lanfranc's disappointment with Bec and Gilbert Crispin's ideal picture reflect the preoccupation of the eleventh-century community with a stricter form of life than it did in fact maintain. St. Anselm said that, had Lanfranc required it, he would have become a solitary in the forest of Brionne.[3] The eremitical life, though it was not practised, was seen as a real option.

By the time the formal *Life* of Lanfranc was written in the mid-twelfth century, the zeal for primitive monasticism had faded. The author of the *Vita Lanfranci* was a contemporary of Theobald of Canterbury and Stephen of Rouen: sophisticated rhetoricians and literary men, whose interests are reflected in the impressive library of mid-twelfth-century Bec. At the same time the community was a centre of serious historical writing, culminating in the *Chronicle* of Robert of Torigny; and it is to this context that the *Vita Lanfranci* belongs. The author has assembled both the written evidence of the *Vita Herluini*, Lanfranc's letters, his conciliar legislation and so forth (all,

[1] William of Cormeilles, *Letter to Abbot William of Bec.*
[2] *Lanfranci Epp.* 1, to Alexander II.
[3] *Vita Anselmi* I.vi.

where they can be verified, accurately rendered) and the oral tradition that was still current as the edifying anecdote. Very little has escaped him: the *Vita Lanfranci* is essentially the final word on Lanfranc from Bec. As the author's outlook and circumstances differ widely from those of Gilbert Crispin, so at one significant point his interpretation of Lanfranc departs from the *Vita Herluini*. He explains that Lanfranc became a monk in fulfilment of a vow. As he was riding through the forest of Brionne, he was set upon by bandits, who robbed him and left him helpless. In his extremity he vowed that if he escaped with his life he would become a monk: what God gave him he would return to God. A contemporary variant of the story has the same crux, that Lanfranc entered Bec not out of a sense of vocation but in payment of a debt.[1] We might feel obliged to accept this explanation, with whatever misgivings, were it not that the conversion of Herluin had already been described in virtually the same terms. Orderic Vitalis, who is a good barometer of ordinary monastic opinion, describes how Herluin was fleeing from an ill-considered skirmish with the count of Ponthieu:

He vowed to God that if he escaped alive from such dire peril he would never fight again, save for God alone. By God's will he came unscathed through all perils; and, mindful of his vow, he abandoned the world and built a cell to the honour of the blessed Mary, mother of God, on his family estate in a place called Bec.

This is a straightforward pact with the Lord, that leaves no room for the growing conviction, the delays and obstacles described by Gilbert Crispin.[2] Stories of this type reflect not how this man or that saw his own vocation, but the fundamental belief that the monk was paying back the life that he owed to God. It is the kind of popular monastic assumption from which St. Anselm constructed his theory of the atonement. The author of the *Vita Lanfranci*, who had no personal knowledge of his subject, is underlining the significance of what Lanfranc did rather than explaining how as an individual he reached his decision.

Within about three years of his arrival at Bec Lanfranc

[1] *V.L.* cap.1; *Miracula S. Nicholai* cap. 8.
[2] *Hist.Eccles.*iii (Chibnall II. 12–13); contrast *V.H.*, pp. 88–91.

became prior, Herluin's first effective assistant in ruling the community. Gilbert Crispin contrasts the multifarious activities of the abbot, overseeing his monastic property and defending it at law, with Lanfranc's retired life within the confines of Bec.[1] In a small house the distinction might not be absolute; but in principle Gilbert can scarcely be wrong. In the formative years of the community, when its liturgical and domestic routine was established at home and its property built up abroad, Lanfranc's duties lay at home. The best guide to the life of a monastery is its customary, the timetable of the house throughout the year, which places it within a specific monastic tradition. The extant customaries of Bec are late: but they can be shown to derive from material of the first half of the twelfth century; and from that in turn the practice of Anselm's priorate has been inferred, and even Lanfranc's. Certainly Lanfranc enforced customs of some kind; and he was later to compile a customary for Christ Church which is still extant: it could well be that his work survives in the customs of Bec. But this is tricky ground. All that we know of the Bec customs associates them with the usage of Fruttuaria: the tradition of William of Volpiano, John of Fécamp and Suppo of Mont-St.-Michel. The book that Lanfranc provided for Canterbury on the other hand is essentially Cluniac: that is, it is sufficiently unlike the hypothetical usage of eleventh century Bec to suggest that Lanfranc was not responsible for both.[2] Furthermore the extant Bec customary reflects the full-scale Benedictine house into which Herluin's community eventually grew; it is no guide to the preceding period of change within which Lanfranc's priorate falls—and, one would think, Anselm's also.

An alternative line of inquiry is to compare the form of worship in Bec with that in other Norman houses. While Lanfranc was prior the community was still using the little church that Herluin and his companions had built in 1041. This was manifestly too small, as were the conventual buildings; and *c.* 1060 Lanfranc began to renew the whole complex. When

---

[1] *V.H.*, pp. 96–7.

[2] *Consuetudines Beccenses*, ed. M.-P. Dickson (Siegburg, 1967), pp. xxix-xli: *Corpus Consuetudinum Monasticarum*, ed.Hallinger, vol.iv. Lanfranc's customs for Christ Church (1079–89) depend on those of Bernard of Cluny (1067); Lanfranc himself left Bec in 1063.

he left for Caen in 1063, the new church was half finished and in 1073 it was complete.[1] This church in turn was extended in the mid-twelfth century, rebuilt in the thirteenth and demolished to about 3 feet above the ground as a result of the Revolution: the present church is the immense and very beautiful eighteenth-century refectory. Though the dimensions of Lanfranc's church could easily be determined by excavation, the visible remains belong to the enlarged church of the twelfth century.[2] Lanfranc's church was on a more modest scale, even for its own day; it was strikingly different from the showpiece that he was soon to build at Caen. It is likely that the liturgy performed within this church was equally simple. At a time when there was great enthusiasm in Normandy for new and elaborate church music, no liturgical composition originated in Bec nor is even known to have been used there: Herluin's community seems to have stood apart from a significant development in contemporary monasticism. It is difficult to maintain, in the light of the endowments, that Bec could not afford music; possibly Lanfranc's own convictions or idiosyncrasies have a bearing on the problem. The great occasions for liturgical composition were the festivals of local saints: the exhortations to the crowds, the processions, the splendid ceremonial in church, the attendant miracles. Now Lanfranc rather distrusted miracles. He was too cautious, and indeed orthodox, to deny that they took place: but he preferred the explanation that did not require them, the divine intervention that was not too crude.[3] When St. Anselm saw a boatload of pilgrims capsize as they came to the shrine of St. Honorine at Conflans, he picked up the saint's skull and waved it in the air as he prayed for their safety.[4] Lanfranc might not have let the pilgrims drown; but it is unlikely that he would have touched St. Honorine's skull. Bec in his time was not renowned for any one cult, such as that of St. Taurin at Fécamp or Nicholas at St.

---

[1] *V.H.*, p. 99. The new church came into use in 1073; but it was not dedicated until 1077 (Robert of Torigny, *Chronicle*, s.a.1073, 1077).

[2] M. de Boüard and J. Merlet, in *Mon.Hist.France* v (1959), 149–56 and 157–72 respectively; cf.R.Liess, *Der frühromanische Kirchenbau des elften Jahrhunderts in der Normandie* (Munich, 1967), p. 269.

[3] *L.D.C.S.D.*, cap.19; cf.*Comm.Epp.Pauli:* 'cum res exigit, miracula fiunt' (Rom. 1:16).

[4] *Miracula S. Honorinae*, ed. Mabillon, *Acta Sanct.O.S.B.* (Paris, 1680), saec.IV.ii. 527; cf. Appendix A4b.

Catherine's, Rouen:[1] the prime occasion of musical invention was absent.

At the same time Bec may have been an early centre of devotion to the Virgin. When William Crispin, abbot Gilbert's father, was beset by his enemies, he called on the Virgin and she appeared (as Venus to Aeneas) to hide him in her cloak. William's grandson, finding himself hard-pressed in battle, called on 'St. Mary of Bec', and was rescued.[2] The first anecdote is so close in date to Anselm's early prayers that it may be seen as the lay side of the same devotion.[3] But the two cults for which we have substantial evidence are later: at Bec itself the cult of St. Nicholas and at the priory of Conflans the cult of the Merovingian St. Honorine. For each there is a considerable series of miracles, running from the late eleventh century to the mid-twelfth. The earliest that can be dated is Anselm's appeal to St. Honorine in 1082; the collections in their present form are both *c.* 1140.[4] By then the community had also amassed a comprehensive collection of relics, recently augmented by the empress Matilda, who made some spectacular gifts of German heirlooms in 1134.[5] Both here and in the cult of the saints Bec could now easily stand comparison with Fécamp and Jumièges.

These are marked changes from the austerity of Lanfranc's day; and they reflect primarily the demands of the outside world. The patrons of Bec—whether small local men like the Crispins or potentates like Matilda—expected two services in return: continuous intercession for themselves and their families, and in times of stress and disaster direct intervention by the saints whom the monastery honoured. The Crispins at least were not disappointed. At the same time there were other, practical

[1] See Y. Delaporte, 'L'office fécampois de saint Taurin', in *L'Abbaye bénédictine de Fécamp* (Fécamp, 1960), ii.171–89; and for the liturgical aspects of the cult of St. Nicholas C. Hohler, 'The proper office of St. Nicholas . . .', *Medium Aevum* xxxvi (1967), 40–8.

[2] *De nobili genere Crispinorum:* D'Achery, *APP.*, pp. 54–6 (=Migne, *P.L.* cl. 739B–42C); cf.*Aeneid* xii.52–3.

[3] Prayers 5–7: *Anselmi Opera*, ed. Schmitt, iii (Edinburgh, 1946), 13–25; trans.B. Ward, *The Prayers and Meditations of St. Anselm* (London, 1973), pp. 106–26. See further H. Barré, *Prières anciennes de l'occident à la Mère du Sauveur* (Paris, 1963), pp. 287–307.

[4] See Appendix A4b.

[5] Porée i.650–5; cf.Robert of Torigny, *Interpolations in William of Jumièges, 'Gesta Normannorum Ducum'* pp. 303–4.

considerations that might attract a patron in the first instance. Duke William himself, Baldwin of Meulles and his brother Richard, who founded the English house of Clare, Hugh of Grantmesnil, William of Vernon, and others familiar in the annals of the Conquest all took an interest in Bec in the mid-eleventh century. Some made only minor donations and soon lost touch; but as a group it was they who ensured the establishment and survival of the community. They determined the conditions under which Lanfranc lived and worked; and in a few cases they even reappear later as patrons of Caen and Canterbury.

ii. the patrons

Bec was founded on Herluin's family lands in the Risle valley, near the castle of Brionne. Its initial support came from Herluin himself and his brothers and from Gilbert, count of Brionne, their overlord: their gifts are confirmed in a charter of 1034 by archbishop Robert of Rouen and Robert the Magnificent, duke of Normandy.[1] Within the year duke Robert had died on a pilgrimage to Jerusalem, leaving as his heir the future William the Conqueror, who was still a child. In 1040 count Gilbert became the boy's 'tutor' or guardian, only to be assassinated a few months later:[2] the castle of Brionne then passed to William's cousin, Guy of Burgundy. In February 1041, when a second charter was drawn up for Bec at the consecration of the new church, Guy ratified the gifts of his predecessor, count Gilbert, and duke William confirmed the original charter and the subsequent acquisitions, adding certain fiscal rights in Brionne.[3] The legal position of Bec had been re-established with very little delay.

How the property of Bec was distributed in 1041 can be seen (nos. a–k) in the map at the end of this book. Two points stand out: that whoever holds Brionne holds Bec; and that Brionne itself lies on the fringe of the area that the dukes of Normandy effectively controlled. South of the line Lisieux—Vernon even

---

[1] Fauroux, no. 98, p. 251. The charter of 1041, here printed, quotes the document of 1034.

[2] Orderic Vitalis, *Interpolations in William of Jumièges*, '*Gesta Normannorum Ducum*', ed.Marx, pp. 155–7; cf. D. C. Douglas, *William the Conqueror* (London, 1964), p. 40.

[3] Fauroux, no. 98, pp. 251–3.

Richard II never had much power. Now most of the early endowments of Bec, slight though they are in quantity, lie either at the border fortresses of Brionne (a, c–e) and Vernon (b) or at Rouen itself (gh). It was all land in which the duke was bound to be interested. In 1047 the strategic importance of Bec itself became embarrassingly clear. Guy of Burgundy joined an alliance against duke William based on lower Normandy, beyond the Risle. Although the revolt was defeated almost immediately at Val-ès-Dunes, Guy held out in Brionne until 1050. William of Poitiers describes the duke's efforts to dislodge him: the siege-towers built by the river below the castle, the campaigns in the surrounding countryside.[1] When William eventually recovered Brionne, he kept it for a while in his own hands before consigning it to the sons of Count Gilbert, Baldwin of Meulles and Richard, subsequently of Clare. Bec had changed allegiance twice in a decade: in 1041 and again during the struggle with Guy of Burgundy in 1047–50.

In the former Lanfranc had no part: he arrived in 1042 at a house whose immediate secular loyalty was to Guy of Burgundy. After Val-ès-Dunes however his position was less secure. It was probably then that duke William ravaged some of the lands of Bec and demanded that Lanfranc himself leave Normandy. But as Lanfranc rode into exile, so the story runs, he met the duke and his entourage: 'Can't you get away quicker than that?' said the duke. 'I could, if I had a decent horse.' William laughed, and sent Lanfranc back to his monastery.[2] During the 1050s Lanfranc came to be trusted by the duke, who regarded him as in some sense an adviser on ecclesiastical affairs; in 1056 Lanfranc assisted archbishop Maurilius in his visitation of St. Évroult.[3] Otherwise however no details survive of Lanfranc's activity at court until 1063, when he became abbot of St. Étienne, Caen.

Over this period the endowments of Bec were notably

---

[1] *Gesta Guillelmi* i.9; cf. Orderic Vitalis, *Hist.Eccles.*vii–viii (Chibnall IV. 82–5, 208–11), with references.

[2] *V.L.*, cap. 3; cf. *V.H.*, p.99. Suppo of Fruttuaria, abbot of Mont-St.-Michel (see above, p. 21), may also have supported Guy of Burgundy. Suppo was exiled in 1048, on grounds which could well have been political: J. J. G. Alexander, *Norman Illumination at Mont-St.-Michel 966–1100* (Oxford, 1970), p.12, with references.

[3] Orderic Vitalis, *Hist.Eccles.* iii (Chibnall II. 66–7).

increased. By 1050 the ancient church of St. Peter in the forest of Ouche was in the hands of Lanfranc and a few others, perhaps to form the basis of a priory. But the donors had second thoughts, and Bec received another church in exchange; St. Peter's itself became the monastery of St. Évroult.[1] Further property was acquired in the region of Brionne and the Risle valley, on the Seine and in Calvados. Duke William granted rights in Bec itself and in the Pays d'Auge, near Lisieux; subsequently in 1063 (the year of Lanfranc's departure) he gave the church near Rouen which became the priory of Bonne-Nouvelle. After the Conquest Bec continued to attract patronage: priories were established at Canchy in Ponthieu (1076), at Conflans-St.-Honorine (1081) and Pontoise (1082), both just west of Paris.[2] By then the endowment in England had begun, and within a few years priories were founded there also.[3] The rapid expansion was matched by a sudden and sustained increase in the number of monks: an increase that may temporarily have strained the economy.[4] By the end of the century however Bec was financially stable and to a considerable degree independent of both secular and ecclesiastical control.[5] The network of priories in Normandy and England was already recognizably the *ordo beccensis* of later years. Herluin's precarious little community had achieved the security of a conventional Benedictine house.

Many of the patrons to whom this change was due came to Bec in October 1077 for the consecration of the new church. Gilbert Crispin has left a vivid account of the festivities: the crowds milling through the church so that the ceremony could

[1] Fauroux, p. 32, note 66; cf. no. 122. See also Orderic Vitalis, *Hist.Eccles.*iii (Chibnall II. 16–17).

[2] Appendix A5a. Conflans and Pontoise are on the map at the end of this book; Canchy is farther north. The French priories as a whole are discussed by Porée, i.383–442.

[3] M. Chibnall, *Select Documents of the English Lands of the Abbey of Bec* (London, 1951): Camden Soc. 3 ser.lxxiii), with references; cf. idem, 'The relations of St. Anselm with the English dependencies of the abbey of Bec 1079–1093', in *Spicilegium Beccense* (Bec/Paris 1959), i.521–30.

[4] See *Anselmi Epp.* 89; and for a graph of the expansion Appendix A5b.

[5] *De libertate beccensis ecclesiae* (Appendix A4b), *passim*. The author makes two claims: that Bec acknowledged no secular overlord except the duke himself; and that none of the early abbots of Bec had recognized the jurisdiction of the archbishops of Rouen. This *de facto* exemption was insecure by comparison with the clear legal independence of St. Étienne, Caen (see Ch. V).

scarcely take place; Lanfranc himself consecrating the high
altar; Herluin, who was by then over eighty, anxiously super-
vising the hospitality; the king and queen apologizing for their
absence.[1] It is the charter that was drawn up on this occasion,
reviewing most of the endowments since the beginning, which
allows us to see in detail the patrons who had established Bec.[2]
They are still grouped around the familiar strong-points of
Brionne and Vernon. Baldwin and Richard fitz Gilbert are
there, with the Crispins and other dependants; William of
Vernon allows the monks transport of goods at Vernon, and
confirms the gifts of his own men in the area. The other patrons
are sometimes well-known figures such as Roger of Beaumont
or Hugh of Grantmesnil; but these were less central to the
affairs of Bec. They wanted to have a stake there, as in Cormeilles, Lessay, St. Évroult and all the others—they would have
jumped at the notion of the unit trust. There was indeed good
financial reason to invest in Bec. The rights and property on the
Seine and the Eure, particularly at Rouen and near Paris, the
churches and tithes throughout Normandy and the *bourg* at
Bec itself, all had considerable potential for both the monastery
and its patrons.[3] The latter received a stiff price for their 'gifts',
perhaps even retaining a life-interest, while an astute abbot
could recoup his outlay with profit. Although the details are not
easy to recover from the formal language of a charter, there are
traces of such agreements at Bec itself, and abundant evidence
of similar transactions at Fécamp and St. Étienne, Caen.
Certainly Herluin did not build up so substantial a holding by
outright donations alone.[4]

In the long run the character of Bec was determined by its
patrons, from whose families the monks themselves often came.
It owed its security to the continuing generosity of these
local men and to the interest and protection of William the

[1] *V.H.*, pp. 105–7: 23 Oct. 1077. As John of Rouen was already incapacitated, 'the archbishop' (p. 107, line 3) must be Lanfranc.

[2] Porée i.645–9; cf. Fauroux, no. 98, pp. 253–4, and the map at the end of this book.

[3] Fauroux, no. 178.

[4] Fauroux, no. 98, pp. 251–3; cf. the tough financial bargaining that preceded certain donations to Fécamp in this period: L. Musset, 'La vie économique de l'abbaye de Fécamp sous l'abbatiat de Jean de Ravenne (1028–1078)', in *L'Abbaye bénédictine de Fécamp* (Fécamp, 1959), i.67–79.

Conqueror and his successors.[1] But within this familiar structure, which is to some degree typical of all the smaller houses of
eleventh-century Normandy, Lanfranc developed an outstanding school. Students came from both Normandy itself and
a wide area of Europe, bringing renown to Bec and contributing
to Anselm's decision to become a monk there. A school of this
kind could easily come to dominate the monastery, to the
detriment of the permanent community; yet it had no stability
as an institution: it depended entirely on Lanfranc's personal
ability as a teacher, and his freedom to exercise these skills.

iii. the school of Bec

Teaching was among Lanfranc's earliest duties as a monk: the
instruction of the child oblates—who were still an essential
section of any community—and perhaps other local children
who came to Bec for their education. It was a normal 'cloister'
school, aiming at fluency in Latin and a knowledge of the
monastic office: the level of instruction was elementary and the
range limited. Initially Lanfranc's school was only one aspect of
the improved organization of the community as a whole that
marked his priorate. What is not clear is when and why it grew
to be something more. According to Gilbert Crispin its impact
on the outside world was instantaneous:

Lanfranc's outstanding reputation quickly brought worldwide fame
to Bec and abbot Herluin. Clerks came flocking in, the sons of dukes,
the most distinguished masters of the west, while wealthy laymen and
many of high rank gave broad acres to Bec, to show their regard for
Lanfranc.[2]

But Gilbert was not there: it was ten years before he came to
Bec, and then as a child; he knew Lanfranc's school only in its
latest phase, when there is no doubt as to its reputation. In the
Vita Lanfranci another tradition is preserved: that to meet the
expenses of rebuilding the monastery *c.* 1060 Herluin allowed
Lanfranc to 'open' the school specifically as an expedient to

---

[1] Henry I, the empress Matilda (who was buried there) and Henry II were all
generous to Bec: see respectively Porée i.290–1, 377–9, 441 ff; i.292–6, 509–10;
i.381, 470, 488.

[2] 'Fama viri praeclarissima Beccum et abbatem Herluinum brevi per orbem
terrarum extulit. Accurrunt clerici, ducum filii, nominatissimi scholarum Latinit-
atis magistri; laici potentes, alta nobilitate viri multi pro ipsius amore multas eidem
ecclesiae terras contulere.' (*V.H.*, p. 97).

attract gifts.[1] The school was already in existence; but its pupils would now come from much farther afield. In other words the claustral school of Lanfranc's earlier years had become 'extra-claustral'; and it was then that its fame spread through the world. There is much to be said for this view. It is only in this last period *c.* 1059–63 that we have precise evidence of foreign students at Bec. Pope Nicholas II sent several of his junior clerics to Lanfranc for their education; and a former scholasticus of Bamberg remarked on the crowds of young Germans who were flocking to Lanfranc's lectures.[2] Again Anselm's decision to enter Bec, where Lanfranc's learning would eclipse his own, cannot be dated much before 1059.[3] The school of Bec had an international reputation for a few years at the end of Lanfranc's priorate, when he provided a quality and type of teaching that was exceptional for Normandy in his day. But it was essentially a short-term measure. It is not unlikely that Herluin's permission to 'open' the school ended when Lanfranc went to Caen; certainly the school was never established as an integral part of the monastery. The community itself was altered only accidentally, in that the most outstanding of all Lanfranc's pupils had become a monk there.

Anselm's relations with Lanfranc were not always easy, nor in the long run close: but there is no doubt that initially Anselm regarded him as a pattern of the monastic life and as far more deeply read than he was himself.[4] It was to Lanfranc that he owed the tools of argument for the *Proslogion* or the *Cur Deus Homo*, and probably also the familiarity with Augustine that was essential to his theology. But his cast of mind was radically different; and little of his mature work is in any sense a continuation of Lanfranc's own. Lanfranc had more in common with one of his Norman pupils, the monk Guitmund of La Croix-St.-Leofroy near Évreux. Guitmund became a master of repute, and later a bishop in South Italy.[5] His criticism of Berengar of

---

[1] 'Lanfrancus quoque licentia abbatis sui *iterum* scholam tenuit, et ea quae a scholasticis accipiebat abbati conferebat, abbas operariis dabat': *V.L.*, cap. 4.

[2] *J.L.*4446 (Nicholas II); Appendix A8a (the German pupils).

[3] *Vita Anselmi* i.5–6.

[4] R. W. Southern, *St. Anselm and his Biographer* (Cambridge, 1963), pp. 12–26: see also Ch. III, §i below.

[5] Orderic Vitalis, *Hist.Eccles.*iv (Chibnall II. 271 ff.); cf. *Anselmi Epp.* 19–20 and Ch. IV, §iii.

Tours, which was written ten years after Lanfranc's own, shows a better understanding of the philosophical issues in the debate and much less personal animus against Berengar. In his fundamental position however, the style of argument and the use of patristic authorities Guitmund's debt to Lanfranc is plain.

There is real and continuing doubt as to the most influential of all Lanfranc's pupils, bishop Ivo of Chartres. Robert of Torigny writes of him: 'When he was a young man he heard master Lanfranc, the prior of Bec, lecturing on sacred and profane texts in that famous school which he held at Bec.'[1] Though this is a plain statement, it is nowhere formally corroborated, and it is fairly late. On the other hand Ivo spent a number of years in Beauvais, a city which had strong links with Lanfranc's circle at Bec and Canterbury. He was teaching there when the monk Ernulf left St. Symphorien, Beauvais to be school-master at Christ Church.[2] The association continued under Anselm: the treasurer of Beauvais cathedral became a monk at Bec; and Anselm himself negotiated with the papacy on behalf of bishop Fulk and his proposed successor.[3] Ivo could well have belonged to this miscellaneous group of Beauvais men who had an interest in Bec. We might expect proof in Ivo's own writings, were there any surviving parallels with Lanfranc's. But Ivo's fragmentary notes on Exodus do not coincide with anything of Lanfranc's, though they are in a similar vein of commentary.[4] The obvious point of comparison is canon law.[5] Do Ivo's three great collections owe anything to Lanfranc's teaching at Bec? Certainly Bec had a copy of the abridgement of Pseudo-Isidore that may be Lanfranc's own; but that is the

---

[1] 'Hic dum esset juvenis audivit magistrum Lanfrancum, priorem Becci, de secularibus et divinis litteris tractantem in illa famosa scola quam Becci tenuit': *Chronicle*, s.a.1117.

[2] R. Sprandel, *Ivo von Chartres und seine Stellung in der Kirchengeschichte* (Stuttgart, 1962), p. 8. For Ernulf see below. Ch. VII, ii.

[3] *Anselmi Epp.* 117 (treasurer), 126 (Fulk), 272 (Fulk's successor). See also R. W. Southern and F. S. Schmitt, *Memorials of Saint Anselm* (London, 1969: *Auct.Brit. Med.Aev.*i), pp. 295–6.

[4] A twelfth-century English miscellany includes Ivo's exegesis of Exod.29: 2–3: MS. Oxford Bodl.Laud Misc.216, fol.2v (s.xii: Kirkstall, Can.Reg.). The Psalter-commentary attributed to Ivo is not his: B. Smalley, 'Master Ivo of Chartres', *Eng.Hist.Rev.* l (1935), 680–6.

[5] Migne, *P.L.*clxi; cf. Sprandel, op.cit., pp. 180–1.

sum total of the evidence.[1] Though Lanfranc occasionally quotes canon law, he never comments on it, as he might on a text taught in school. At a time when the great need in canon-law studies was for the rational arrangement of existing material and the elucidation of contradictions he was not responsible for any systematic collection, such as might have been the basis of Ivo's own. At most Lanfranc's instruction in the *artes* gave Ivo the tools with which to organize and clarify the study of canon law.

Anselm, Guitmund and Ivo died bishops. The majority of Lanfranc's pupils are known pre-eminently for their careers in government, and for their scholarship scarcely at all. Within the community William 'Bona Anima' succeeded Lanfranc as abbot of St. Étienne, Caen, and rose to be archbishop of Rouen. Two other monks of Bec found St. Étienne the road to promotion: Gundulf, prior of St. Étienne and bishop of Rochester, and Henry, prior of Christ Church and abbot of the Conqueror's foundation of Battle.[2] Lanfranc's own nephews both held office: Paul as abbot of St. Albans and Lanfranc the younger (amid a storm of criticism) as abbot of St. Wandrille.[3] Other Italians came to study without wishing to enter Bec. Nicholas II had sent pupils to Lanfranc; one south-Italian monk who came to hear Anselm ended his life as cardinal bishop of Tusculum.[4] The German students, on the other hand, are a shadowy company of which little is known. Lanfranc's writings circulated in Germany at an early date, but we do not know at whose instigation.[5] The most elusive of all are the men from France itself: it is exceedingly difficult to pin down anyone who came to Bec from the Île de France or Poitou or the Loire valley. Where the students at Bec can be known individually they are either Norman or Italian; and we must assume that the anonymous majority was similarly divided.

Why such a pattern developed is not so clear. Certainly there

[1] Now MS. Cambridge Trinity Coll. B.16.44: see Ch. VI, §ii.

[2] See respectively Ch. V, §i (William Bona Anima) and VI, §ii (Gundulf and Henry).

[3] See respectively Ch. VI, §ii (Paul) and *Anselmi Epp.* 137–8 (Lanfranc the younger).

[4] Eadmer, *Vita Anselmi* II. xxix, ed. Southern (London, 1962: Nelson's Med. Texts), p. 106, with references.

[5] R. B. C. Huygens, 'Bérenger de Tours, Lanfranc et Bernold de Constance', *Sacris Erudiri* xvi (1965), 362–4; cf. Ch. V, §i.

were political difficulties with Anjou; but it would be anachronistic to suppose that in themselves these prevented Angevin
students from coming to Bec. It may be argued that (like
Chartres in the time of Fulbert) Lanfranc's school prepared
men for office in the Church. The 'duke's sons', who so im-
pressed Gilbert Crispin, were destined in any case for ecclesiastical preferment; but public opinion was beginning to tell in
favour of literacy, as indeed common sense in an increasingly
complex world of canon law demanded it. Lower down the
social scale men hoped to make their fortunes in the bishop's
household: these are the forerunners of the ubiquitous *magistri*
of the twelfth century. For a few years the best training was to
be had at Bec. Other Norman schools had enjoyed a brief
distinction: Fécamp earliest of all, then in the 1030s and 1040s
Holy Trinity Rouen in the time of abbot Isembert, called
liberalis.[1] But Bec caught the market in the 1050s, when the area
under Norman control was expanding at an unprecedented
rate. Duke William's political and military success generated a
new demand for the trained administrator; the school of Bec
was a symptom of political sophistication and independence. For
a few years it provided the intelligentsia of Norman society:
then there were better schools at Caen or Bayeux or Rouen. In
the long term the monastery remained a centre of devotion
(modern—but not revolutionary) and an important land-
owner: it was a sound and successful house in the old Benedictine tradition.

[1] Isembert 'the German' (1033–*c*.1053) was a noted teacher of both the *artes* and
liturgical composition: his work survives in the latter only. See R. Heurtevent,
Durand de Troarn et les origines de l'hérésie bérengarienne (Paris, 1912), pp. 91–101, and
C. Hohler, 'The proper office of St. Nicholas . . .', *Medium Aevum* xxxvi (1967),
40–8.

III: Lanfranc the Scholar

i. the curriculum of Bec

We send you our beloved sons to cherish and instruct in dialectic and rhetoric . . . But if (as we have heard) you are taken up with the study of the Bible, even so we enjoin you to teach them.

Nicholas II to Lanfranc (1059–61)[1]

By the late 1050s Lanfranc was already known to be working on biblical commentary, though perhaps not to the exclusion of the study of the *artes*. Nicholas's observation is confirmed *c.* 1060 by abbot Williram of Ebersberg in Bavaria, who had himself been scholasticus of St. Michael's, Bamberg. Williram saw the students of southern Germany flocking westward to hear Lanfranc expounding the Bible: an unhappy change from the days when learning was to be had above all in the German schools.[2] Lanfranc was singled out as the master of the *artes* who was applying his skills to Christian doctrine: the method was familiar enough—the critical exposition of the meaning and structure of a text—but the material was new. The Psalter and the Pauline Epistles had become the set texts of Lanfranc's school. The *artes* were not superseded; on the contrary they were more necessary than ever: but the centre of the curriculum was the study of the Bible. Lanfranc's scholarly reputation today rests entirely on this new curriculum: on his percipience in having introduced it at Bec and on his skill as a commentator. It was the culmination of his teaching career. Of the more conventional academic work with which he was intermittently occupied *c.* 1030–60 only random fragments survive; yet even these illustrate how Lanfranc tackled a problem and the kind of questions that he asked.

His most enduring work was the correction of texts: the Old

---

[1] *J.L.*4446. Nicholas describes these young men rather ambiguously as 'hos . . . nostrae dilectionis filios imperatoris capellanos et nostros'; nothing further is known of them.

[2] Appendix A8a.

and New Testament and the writings of the Fathers; some of the liturgical manuscripts that he emended were still in use at Bec in the 1130s.[1] None of these corrected manuscripts has survived in the original; but several copies are known of the patristic texts which Lanfranc emended. Ambrose, *De Sacramentis* and *De Mysteriis* and Cassian, *Collations* i–xvii are all found with the colophon LANFRANCVS HVCVSQVE CORREXI: the text up to that point ('huc usque') had been prepared by Lanfranc for the scribe who made the fair copy.[2] As only the copy now survives, Lanfranc's emendations are not visible; they have been silently incorporated in the text. For the Ambrose however a modern editor has included the Lanfrancian recension in his apparatus, so it is possible to see just what changes Lanfranc made. Most scarcely affect the sense: 'popul*is*' for 'popul*o*', 'igitur' for 'ergo'.[3] A few however are substantial variants, here shown in italics:

Panis iste panis est ante verba sacramentorum; ubi accesserit consecratio, de pane fit *corpus* Christi.

And again:

Divino imperio virga Moyses tetigit aquas et se unda divisit, non utique secundum suae naturae *imperium*, sed secundum gratiam caelestis imperii.[4]

Although the *De Sacramentis* was a crucial text in the eucharistic controversy, the most critical passage of all, for which Lanfranc in his own *De corpore et sanguine Domini* even quotes an alternative reading, is here untouched.[5] Lanfranc's corrections are in no

---

[1] *V.L.*, cap.15; see also the *Chronicle* of Robert of Torigny, for many years a monk of Bec, s.a.1089.

[2] The only manuscript of the Ambrose is Le Mans B.Mun.15, fols. 123–41 (s.xii: St. Vincent, Le Mans). The Cassian manuscripts are Alençon B.Mun. 136 (s.xii in. St. Martin, Séez), Rouen B.Mun.535 (s.xi: Lyre) and a third, which was lost at the Revolution (L. Delisle, *Le Cabinet des manuscrits de la Bibliothèque Nationale*, Paris, 1874, ii.55). In no case is the colophon in Lanfranc's own hand.

[3] *De Sacramentis* iv.4.13; 15, ed. Faller: *Corp.Script.Eccles.Lat.* lxxiii (1955), pp.51–2.

[4] Ibid. iv.4.14 (caro Christi); 18 (naturae consuetudinem), ed.cit., pp. 52–4. Both emendations could well have originated as cross-references: 'caro Christi' refers to 'corpus esse Christi' and 'naturae consuetudinem' contrasts with 'caelestis imperii'.

[5] 'Si ergo tanta uis est in sermone domini Iesu, ut inciperent esse, quae non erant, quanto magis operatorius est, ut *sint*, quae erant, *et* in aliud commutentur': *De Sacramentis* iv.4.15 (ed.cit., p. 52); cf.*L.D.C.S.D.*, cap. 9 *ad fin.*, where the italicized words are omitted.

way tendentious: they are honest improvements, made in the light of such manuscripts (seemingly rather corrupt) as he had available. His edition of Cassian, which cannot be so easily checked, appears to be similar. But it has in addition four explanatory notes in the margin. For instance, one of abbot Isaac's discourses on prayer mentions the Anthropomorphites.[1] Lanfranc comments:

Anthropomorphites are so called because in their rustic simplicity they think that God has the human form which is described in the Bible; for *antropos* is the Greek for 'man'. They do not know the word of the Lord: 'God is a spirit'. He is incorporeal, neither divided into limbs nor measurable in bulk.

This is a straightforward but sufficient explanation, drawn from the most obvious of all sources, Isidore's *Etymologies* and St. John's Gospel.[2] In another fragment Lanfranc is deeply abstruse. He seems to be commenting on Isaiah's vision of the seraphim, who cry,

Holy, Holy, Holy, Lord God of Sabaoth!

St. Jerome notes that the Hebrew word for Lord has, as befits God (DEVS),

four letters, IOD HE IOD HE, that is IA twice over. When this pair of letters is doubled, it forms the ineffable and glorious Name of God.[3]

But an *ineffable* name is a contradiction in terms. Lanfranc proposed this solution:

The name of God is *ineffable*, in that the letters which are on the fourth 'grade' imply the existence of three grades below them, for which in this case there can be neither meaning nor a word to signify the meaning.[4]

---

[1] *Collationes* x.2, ed. Petschenig, *Corp.Script.Eccles.Lat.*xiii.2 (1886), p. 287.

[2] D'Achery, p. 252, quoting Isidore, *Etymologiae* VIII.v.32 (ed. Lindsay: Oxford, 1911) and John 4:24.

[3] *Epistolae* XVIIIA, ed. Hilberg: *Corp.Script.Eccles.Lat.* liv (1910), p. 84. Jerome cites an unusual (but admissible) form of the name of God: *iod he. iod he* for *iod he. vah he* (Jahweh).

[4] 'Nomen domini ineffabile, quia littere que quartum gradum tenent tres indicant esse primos; aput quos ergo tante rei non est (intellectus), nec uox esse potuit intellectum significans': MS. London B. L. Sloane 1580, fol. 16. See R. W. Hunt, 'Studies on Priscian in the eleventh and twelfth centuries', *Med.Renaiss.Stud.* i.2 (1943), 208; the emendation 'intellectus' is mine.

His note is preserved, in a corrupt form and out of context, in a late-twelfth-century commonplace book from Christ Church— no doubt simply out of piety towards Lanfranc. But it does show how the study of the Fathers could lead on to a problem of logic. Lanfranc is using a standard text of the *artes* (arguably the standard text of the day), the *De Decem Categoriis*. There the author explains that all words are classified 'by stages (*per gradus*), until everything that exists is included in a single term'[1] The first *gradus* includes individuals: *Socrates* or *Quare Times*. The second includes *man* or *horse*, and the third *animal* (*man* and *horse* equally). Finally comes οὐσία,

a certain infinite and all-inclusive name . . . beyond which nothing can be discovered or imagined.[2]

What is this οὐσία, the sole constituent of the fourth *gradus*? The Carolingian commentary on the *De Decem Categoriis* (which normally accompanies it in the manuscripts) cites John the Scot, who had distinguished four species in *Natura*: 'the uncreated creator; the created creator; the created and uncreating; the uncreated and uncreating'.[3]

The first of these ('quae creat et non creatur') is God.[4] The role here of all comprehending *Natura* is similar to that of οὐσία in the *De Decem Categoriis*; but the place of God in the scheme is left unsolved, for it can scarcely be allowed that He is a species of some greater genus. In terms of the *De Decem Categoriis* however a solution is possible: the Name of God can be identified with οὐσία, the ultimate term that is beyond utterance or comprehension.

The theological implications of this position were explored by Roscelin of Compiègne, who alleged that Lanfranc himself had

[1] Pseudo-Augustine, *Categoriae Decem*, ed. Minio-Paluello, *Aristoteles Latinus* I.v (Bruges/Paris, 1961), 133, lines 17–18.

[2] 'Ingenti quodam et capaci ad infinitum nomine omne quidquid est comprehendens dixit οὐσίαν, extra quam nec inueniri aliquid nec cogitari potest': ibid., p. 134, lines 17–19.

[3] 'Videtur mihi divisio naturae per quattuor differentias quattuor species recipere, quarum prima est in eam quae creat et non creatur, secunda in eam quae et creatur et creat, tertia in eam quae creatur et non creat, quarta quae nec creat nec creatur': *De Divisione Naturae* i, ed. Sheldon-Williams (Dublin, 1968), p. 36, lines 21–4. The commentary is unpublished: see e.g. MS. Cambridge Corpus Christi Coll. 206, pp. 24–39.

[4] Prima . . . in causa omnium quae sunt et quae non sunt intelligatur, quae deus est': *De Divisione Naturae*:, p. 38 lines 2–3; cf. 38, app., and pp. 5–9.

endorsed his opinions on the Trinity.[1] What is more interesting
is the entirely orthodox way in which Anselm developed the
same idea. The argument of the *Proslogion* runs beyond the
limits of contemporary theology: but it is initiated by a definition that is meant to be recognizable. Just as Socrates begins
with the current assumption that justice is 'rendering to every
man his due', Anselm sets out from familiar territory:

And indeed we believe that You are something
than which nothing greater can be thought.

Et quidem credimus te esse aliquid
quo nihil maius cogitari possit.[2]

This is the all-comprehending οὐσία of the *De Decem Categoriis*,
the fourth *gradus* 'extra quam nec inveniri aliquid nec cogitari
potest'. For Anselm too the basic texts of the *artes* were the
starting-point for higher things.

Lanfranc's most extensive criticism of the Fathers is his notes
on the *Moralia in Job* and the *De Civitate Dei*.[3] These are preserved at the end of the text to which they refer, as a detached
list in no discernible order. There is no system of reference, so
it is only by ingenuity and good luck that they can be related to
appropriate passages of Gregory and Augustine. Some are
apposite enough, others are only tangential to their text; and
for large tracts of both the *Moralia* and the *De Civitate Dei* there
are no notes at all. Are we to suppose that Lanfranc went
through these enormous texts commenting only on the few
passages to which the extant notes refer? Or are these the
fossilized remainder of a programme which cannot now be
recovered? The only explanation offered is at the end of the
notes on the *Moralia*, and it does not help much:

The notes that refer to the present volume are added here at the end,
lest inexperienced men should rashly attempt to use these words and
constructions without understanding them.[4]

---

[1] *Anselmi Epp.* 136, with references.

[2] *Proslogion* 2: *Anselmi Opera*, ed. Schmitt i (Seckau, 1938), 101; and cf. Lanfranc's
own phrase in *L.D.C.S.D.*, cap. 1: 'iurans per id *quod rebus omnibus incomparabiliter
maius est*'.

[3] For both series see M. T. Gibson, 'Lanfranc's notes on patristic texts', *Journ.
Theol.Stud.*n.s.xxii (1971), pp. 435–50.

[4] Ibid., p. 446, lines 150–2.

How could any reader (let alone the inexperienced) hope to find the appropriate note when he needed it? And if he did stumble on it, would he have a better understanding of Gregory or Augustine? The notes are a medley of the elementary and the recondite: simple points of grammar, etymological information, a reference to Boethian logic and a passage from the *Timaeus*, which is Lanfranc's sole quotation from the quadrivium. As a whole they are of a traditional type: common stumbling-blocks, whether in grammar, syntax or metre, are identified and explained. Any schoolmaster will build up a collection like this, adding his favourite recherché item of etymology or history. Such notes were traditionally attached to Virgil, Juvenal, Horace: the narrow range of classical poets studied so thoroughly that the student had long passages by heart. For the speech of Priam for instance, slain before his altar in Troy, the notes ranged from basic syntax to Epicurean philosophy:

> 'At *tibi pro scelere*,' *exclamat*, 'pro talibus ausis
> di, *si qua est* caelo pietas quae talia curet,
> persolvant *grates* dignas et praemia reddant
> debita, qui nati *coram me cernere* letum
> fecisti et patrios *foedasti funere* vultus.'[1]

A memorable phrase or incident in Virgil had become the vehicle for linguistic and antiquarian *minutiae*. It was indeed a radical experiment to replace the familiar classical poets with Gregory and Augustine, and one that must surely have proved unworkable. But it does indicate the direction in which Lanfranc was moving: he wished to exercise the skills of the *artes* on the texts of the Christian Church.

ii. the *artes*

Lanfranc's strength lay in the *artes*, in his command of the details of words and sentence-structure. For Guitmund of La Croix-St.-Leofroy, who had been his pupil at Bec, he was God's instrument in the renewal of the liberal arts; for the next generation he was a *dialecticus*, a master of argument.[2] Lanfranc

---

[1] *Aen.*ii.535–9; cf. the commentary of Servius, ed. Thilo (Leipzig, 1878), i.300–1. In the 1070s Anselm still regarded Virgil as an essential school text: *Anselmi Epp.* 64.

[2] Guitmund, *De corporis et sanguinis Christi veritate in Eucharistia* i (Migne, *P.L.* cxlix.1428B). Lanfranc the dialectician appears in Sigebert of Gembloux, *De Scriptoribus Ecclesiasticis*, cap. 155 (Migne, *P.L.*clx.582C) and William of Malmes-

was a first-class practitioner throughout the trivium, aware of new developments and ready to promote them.

The perennial task of the grammarian is to notice how and why language changes. Though he may hope to find certainty within a canon of accepted authors, he is always beset by alien borrowings, unfamiliar derivations and new fashions in accent. These problems had already exercised the Carolingians; and here Lanfranc follows them, providing similar answers to similar questions:

Job answered . . . How should a man be just with God . . . (who) maketh Arcturus, *Orion* and *Pleiades*, and the chambers of the south?

'Arcturum, Orion*as* et Hyad*as*': Lanfranc explains that the latter two are Greek accusatives, like 'rinocerot*a*'.[1] Other strange words have a historical origin:

Fugalia were sacrifices instituted in commemoration of Aeneas' flight (*fuga*) from Troy, as were *Phrygalia*; for he fled from *Phrygia*.[2]

A greater problem was the correct accentuation of Latin, especially Latin read in church. It appears in monastic anecdote: the obedient monk accepts correction, even when he is not in error; the proud man insists on singularity.[3] Although this difficulty was known to the Carolingians, it was growing more acute in the eleventh century, as French, Italian and Spanish emerged as written languages. For example *mulier* is stressed on the first syllable in Latin and the last in Old French (muillèr). Lanfranc's notes on the *Moralia* reflect this uncertainty:

The final *e* in *mulier* is short. In the *De Accentibus* however Priscian says that the oblique cases (e.g. *mulieris*) have the *e* long. But in the *Institutiones*, where he discusses third declension genitives, the final *e* remains short.[4]

---

[1] Gibson, 'Lanfranc's notes . . .', p. 443, lines 68–9: *Moralia* ix.11, commenting on Job 9:9.

[2] Ibid., p. 440, lines 28–9: *De Civ.Dei* ii.6.

[3] *V.L.*, cap.2. Berengar by contrast introduced novel pronunciations in the liturgy: R. B. C. Huyghens, 'Textes latins du xie au xiiie siècle', *Stud.Med.* viii (1967), 488, lines 395–9.

[4] Gibson, 'Lanfranc's notes . . .', p. 445, lines 132–7.

---

bury, *Gesta Pontificum* ii.74 (ed. Hamilton, p.150): see also *Miracula S. Nicholai*, cap. 7, p. 409.

Grammarians might argue and doubt; final authority lay with the practitioners. The classical poets were writing in a known metre to which the disputed word had to conform. Horace's

'Quis martem tunica: tect(um) *adamántina*[1]

was a plain ruling against the metrically intolerable *ádamantína*, that like a wounded snake drags its slow length along. Such authoritative examples had already been collected in the ninth century by Mico of St. Riquier; and it is from his or a similar collection that Lanfranc quotes Horace and Juvenal in his notes to the *Moralia* and the *De Civitate Dei*.[2] The collection of *exempla* was a standard work of reference for the practising writer and teacher.

The great innovation however in eleventh-century grammar was the renewed study of the *Institutiones* of Priscian. For the Carolingians Priscian had been one among several classical grammarians who were used as texts in school, and who all attracted some kind of commentary. For the *Institutiones* there is endless marginal annotation, varying widely from one manuscript to another and rarely even approaching a stable text. It is quite unspecialized: Priscian's illustrative quotations (a line of poetry or a fragment from a play) receive the same attention as the principles to which they refer, and the whole effect is turgid to a degree. Fundamental principles of language are buried in a heap of facts.[3] The masters of the eleventh century adopted the *Institutiones* as their central text (with perhaps the *Ars Maior* of Donatus in an ancillary role); and they began to furnish it with a comprehensive commentary. By *c.* 1050–70 several masters had worked independently on some part of the *Institutiones*, and their comments were being assembled in the collection known as the *Glosule*.[4] In following Priscian's text phrase by phrase the *Glosule* still introduces a good deal of

---

[1] *Carm.* I. vi. 13.

[2] See L. Traube, *Miconis Opus Prosodiacum* in *Poet.Lat.Aev.Carol.* (Berlin, 1892), iii.265–94; and S. A. Hurlbut, *Florilegium Prosodiacum* (Washington, 1932: privately printed); cf. idem, 'A fore-runner of Alexander de Villa-Dei', *Speculum* viii (1933), 258–63.

[3] Virtually none of this material has yet been published. A good example of the unspecialized gloss on the *Institutiones* is MS. Autun B.Mun.40* (s.ix med.: Tours).

[4] R. W. Hunt, 'Studies on Priscian in the eleventh and twelfth centuries', *Med.Renaiss.Stud.* i. 2 (1943), 194–231. In recent years other recensions of the *Glosule* have come to light, notably one that includes the work of Manegold.

trivial matter; and by the later twelfth century it in turn was giving way to the more systematic *summa*, which passed over Priscian's many *longueurs* and concentrated on essential problems. But for perhaps a century (1050–1150) the *Glosule*, in some shape or form, was the basic handbook to Priscian, comparable to the emerging *Gloss* on the Bible. Lanfranc's part in the construction of the *Glosule* is not yet clear. He is credited with an obscure note on the relation of Greek *digamma* (**F**) to Latin *v*.[1] Other masters contributed far more. Manegold of Lautenbach and Anselm of Laon made solid contributions to the *Glosule* themselves and have a better claim than Lanfranc to the equally important task of choosing excerpts from the work of other, unknown, masters. Anselm in particular had a school to satisfy that was larger and more permanent than Lanfranc's schools at Bec or Caen. At the same time one twelfth-century manuscript of the *Institutiones* from northern France has marginal notes that to some extent draw on the *Glosule*: and these notes are quite frequently marked *L* and occasionally LAN.[2] If both categories are really Lanfranc's work, then his contribution to the *Glosule* is increased, and he too can be reckoned among the founders of scholastic grammar. But much turns on the interpretation of *L*; we can say only that speculation of this kind may be vindicated in the future.

Grammar impinged on other disciplines, not always legitimately. One of the classic points of debate in the *Institutiones* is the status of the verb *to be*. Does it express the very existence of its subject, where an ordinary verb merely shows what the subject is doing? Some opinions preserved in the twelfth century at Chartres include an explanation proposed by Lanfranc:

The verb *to be* is active in relation to substances and passive in relation to accidents.
i.e. 'The man is . . .' or 'The donkey is . . .' (active);
but 'Whiteness is . . .' (passive).
The basis for the distinction is this: that accidents do not exist independently, but only in substances.[3]

[1] Priscian, *Institutiones* i.12, ed. Hertz (Leipzig, 1885), i.11 (=Keil, *Grammatici Latini* ii). Lanfranc commented, '*u* ea figura erat *affinis digamma cognatione soni*, id est sui nominis': Hunt, op.cit., p. 206, app.

[2] MS. Harvard lat.44, first noticed by Dr. Klibansky. For Lanfranc's copy of the *text* of the *Institutiones* see below, p. 181, n. 3.

[3] MS. Chartres B.Mun.209, fol.86v, now destroyed: Hunt, op.cit., pp. 224–5.

Here the grammatical status of active and passive is determined by an appeal to logic: substances are active and accidents passive. Another early master plunged deeper still, asserting a comparable relationship between God and the creation: 'God is . . .' (active); but 'A created thing is . . .' (passive). That the theological dimension of the verb *to be* was a real problem can be seen in the biblical *Gloss* itself. Anselm of Laon—most sober and moderate of scholars—comments on the opening of St. John's Gospel, 'In the beginning *was* the Word':

> The verb *to be* is used in two senses. Sometimes it expresses movement in time, on the analogy of other verbs. But at other times it expresses the being (*substantia*) of whatever it refers to, with no temporal connotation whatever; that is why it is called the verb substantive. So here: 'In the beginning *was* the Word' is, as to say, 'In the Father the Son is', for *was* is not used with a temporal but a supra-temporal meaning.[1]

Even a subject that is quintessentially theological can be approached by way of grammar. Or the key may be found in logic. Augustine refers contemptuously to 'the World-soul and its parts', which the pagan believed to be gods. In his commentary on this passage Lanfranc resorts at once to the organization of species and genera:

> Infinites can have no genera above them: they are linked (as genus to species) only with what is below. So God, eternal and unchangeable, is linked with the *anima mundi* and its parts, which to the pagan are gods also.[2]

The whole structure of the universe, creator and created, is subject to the laws of logic. This is heady stuff, a threat both to Christian orthodoxy and to the constructive development of logic and grammar.

---

[1] '*In principio erat verbum.* Anselmus. Sum verbum duplicem habet significationem. Aliquando enim temporales motus secundum analogiam aliorum verborum declarat. Aliquando substantia uniuscuisque rei de quo predicatur sine ullo temporali motu designat; ideo et substantivum vocatur. Tale est quod dicitur: In principio *erat* verbum quasi in patre subsistit filius. Non enim pro tempore sed supra ponitur *erat*' (MS. Oxford Bodleian Lyell 1, fol. 4), quoting John the Scot, *in Prologum Euang. Johannis* cap. vi (Migne, *P.L.* cxxi. 268B; critical edition by E. Jeauneau, *Sources Chrét.* cli (1969), 226–8. The best printed edition of the *Gloss* is Gadolus, *Biblia Latina* (Venice, 1495: I.C.23278).

[2] Gibson, 'Lanfranc's notes . . .', p. 441, lines 49–54; cf. the discussion of the *nomen domini* above.

In the study of logic proper Lanfranc is known only as the author of a *Dialectica*, now lost. It is recorded in the later eleventh century at St. Aper, Toul, a house with an excellent modern library.[1] By *c.* 1100 that title would imply a complete exposition of the *logica vetus*, as Garland attempted *c.* 1080 and Abelard achieved with greater success *c.* 1120.[2] Did Lanfranc then compose the earliest *Dialectica* of all? I rather doubt it. He is familiar with the *logica vetus*; but at the same time he still uses the *De Decem Categoriis*, a text that is fundamentally irreconcilable with Boethian logic.[3] Both Garland and Abelard recognized it as an outsider: they gave it no consideration, and it was never used by serious logicians again. If Lanfranc was still prepared to accept the *De Decem Categoriis*, it is almost impossible to see him as a pioneer in the study of the *logica vetus*.

A rather better case can be made for his contribution to rhetoric. Independent commentary on Cicero's *De inventione* and the *Ad Herennium*, which were to be the basic texts of twelfth-century rhetoric, seems to have begun *c.* 1030–40 in South Germany and Italy. Both were discussed by Manegold in the 1060s; and by the end of the century they were well established.[4] The chance survival of one Lanfrancian opinion for each suggests that he too was involved in the early commentary. Neither fragment is of any value in itself. At *De inventione* i.48.89, the list of ways in which an argument can be faulted, a twelfth-century commentator remarks: 'Lanfranc thinks that this can be omitted; for it is all contained in the previous discussion. But his opinion cannot be accepted'.[5] There perhaps Lanfranc did have a case; but in another instance he is the object of ridicule, and justifiably so. In the *Ad Herennium* ii.26.42 Ajax is claiming the armour of Hector:

---

[1] G. Becker, *Catalogi Bibliothecarum Antiqui* (Bonn, 1885), no. 68, item 250: 'Lantfrancus de dialectica'. The 'Questiones Lantfranci' (ibid., no. 54, item 6) were probably theological: cf. Appendix D.

[2] L. M. de Rijk, *Garlandus Compotista, Dialectica* (Assen, 1959); idem, *Petrus Abaelardus, Dialectica* (Assen, 1956).

[3] See pp. 42–3 above.

[4] M. Dickey, 'Some commentaries on the *De Inventione* and the *Ad Herennium* of the eleventh and early twelfth centuries', *Med.Renaiss.Stud.* vi (1968), 1–41.

[5] 'Lanfrancus superfluum hoc iudicat. dicit enim hec omnia in superioribus contineri reprehensionibus. Non est autem fides habenda verbis illius': MS. Hereford Cathedral P.1.iv, fol.17v (s.xii[1]: English).

Let it be said plainly (aperte fatur *dictio*)—understand this:
if we want to take Troy (*potiri si studeamus Pergamum*), the man who has already achieved much orders the armour to be given to him—and I am he.
I have the right to enjoy my brother's armour, and I adjudge it to myself, both as his kinsman and as his equal in valour.

It is a difficult speech to construe; for Ajax is hammering at his audience with a succession of short clauses illogically arranged, which is indeed quoted in the *Ad Herennium* as an example of confused argument. One small error in his text (the *d* of *d*ictio broken into *cl*itio) led Lanfranc into desperate surgery. He is said to have explained that '*Clitio* was a soldier, as were *Studemus* and *Pergamus*. And so,' the later commentator continues, 'misled by his ignorance of history, he construed thus:

Clitio speaks and orders the armour to be given to one man; Studemus orders . . . Pergamus orders . . .
"But," said Ajax, "it is mine."

He had expunged the words *potiri si*.'[1] The worst part of this disaster is the rendering of Troy as an otherwise unknown soldier, Pergamus. Lanfranc was up against a new text, which here defeated him; and his explanation survived only as a warning to later students. His rhetorical commentaries were quickly superseded, or incorporated anonymously in other men's work. But this should not lead us to believe that Lanfranc was a bad or an inconsiderable rhetorician. He expounded the new rhetoric at least a decade before Manegold, *modernorum magister magistrorum*, who wrote the first surviving commentaries on both the *De inventione* and the *Ad Herennium*. Lanfranc is among the pioneers, whose success is measured by the very commentaries that superseded their own. In his own work rhetoric was always the basic tool, whether for scholarship or in due course for the duties of public life.

iii. the Bible

I know a man in France, who used to be a very eminent dialectician; now he has turned to the learning of the Church, and has taxed the wits of many by his subtle exegesis of the Psalter and the Pauline Epistles. (Williram of Ebersberg *c*.1060)

---

[1] R. W. Hunt, 'Studies on Priscian . . .', pp. 207–8; cf. C. Calboli, *Rhetorica ad C. Herennium* (Bologna, 1969), pp. 130 and 248.

In his later years at Bec—*c.* 1055 onwards—Lanfranc turned his mind to the study of the Bible, making a particular name for himself in the exegesis of the Psalter and the Pauline Epistles. It was a traditional pair of texts: the Psalms were prophetic of the dispensation to come; and St. Paul and especially the author of Hebrews[1] often draw on the Psalms. The theme was continued and developed by the Latin Fathers. Augustine, for instance, preaching on the verse—

'The Lord said unto my Lord: Sit thou on my right hand, until I make thine enemies thy footstool'—

turns at once to Paul:

Christ sits at the right hand of God. It is a wonderful mystery, hidden so that we may believe it, removed so that we may hope for it. *For we are saved by hope. But hope that is seen is not hope; for what a man seeth, why doth he yet hope for?*

What does Paul mean? It is by hope that we are saved. *If we hope for that which we see not, then do we with patience wait for it* . . . Our righteousness is by faith and by faith our hearts are cleansed, that we may see what we have believed . . . etc.[2]

Carolingian commentators follow the same high-road: in the school of Auxerre the Psalter and the Pauline Epistles were expounded as though each reflected and elucidated the other.[3] Lanfranc was the heir of a long-established tradition, and one that even in his own day was by no means exhausted. New manuscripts were being copied of the patristic and Carolingian commentators; and new commentaries on the same ample scale were still being constructed: the great Pauline commentary of Bruno the Carthusian was written only a few years before Lanfranc's death.[4] So the state of biblical exegesis was quite different from that of commentaries on the *artes*. Whereas there Lanfranc had been a pioneer, whose work was necessarily superseded and forgotten, as a commentator on the Bible he was

---

[1] Lanfranc and most of his contemporaries and successors in the twelfth century regarded Hebrews as Pauline. All further references in this chapter are therefore to the *fourteen* Epistles, including Hebrews.

[2] Augustine, *Enarrationes in Psalmos* 109.8, expounding Ps.109:1 (A.V.110): *Corp.Christ Ser.Lat.*xl.1607–8; cf. Rom.8:24–5.

[3] For the current discussion of the school of Auxerre see R. Quadri, 'Aimone di Auxerre alla luce dei *Collectanea* di Heiric di Auxerre', *Italia Med.Uman.*vi (1963), 1–48 and idem, *I 'Collectanea' di Eirico di Auxerre* (Freiburg, 1966: *Spicil.Friburg*, xi).

[4] Migne, *P.L.* cliii.11A–566C: see A. Stoelen, 'Les commentaires scripturaires attribués à Bruno le Chartreux', *Rech.Théol.Anc.Med.*xxv (1958), 177–247.

working in a recognized genre, which in one specific respect he was able to improve. Lanfranc brought his skill as a rhetorician and a student of the *artes* to bear on the problems of Pauline commentary; he evolved a more rigorous, tighter criticism of the Bible, drastically abbreviated in comparison with main-stream Carolingian work, with a more effective and lucid arrangement on the page. Even here however he had contem-porary models, and colleagues from whom he could learn.

The earliest Psalter-commentary of the period is the work of Bruno, bishop of Würzburg (1034–45). In 1045 Bruno accom-panied Henry III to Hungary, where he was an early casualty of a state reception: the emperor was holding court in an upper hall (a *vetus solarium*), when the floor caved in, and Bruno was fatally injured. So we have a memorable *terminus ad quem* for the first scholastic commentary on the Psalms: it belongs specifically to the decade before Lanfranc began to teach in Bec.[1] The material of Bruno's work is essentially Cassiodorus' *Expositio Psalmorum*, a more academic commentary than the sermons of Augustine just quoted: Cassiodorus was ready to elucidate the rhetorical structure of a Psalm, or the etymology of a strange word. Bruno goes further in the same direction, reducing his original to the main issues, simply stated and answered. The Psalmist writes—

I was glad when they said unto me: We will go into the house of the Lord.
Our feet shall stand in thy gates: O Jerusalem.
Jerusalem is built as a city: that is at unity in itself.
For thither the tribes go up, even the tribes of the Lord . . .[2]

Bruno concentrates on three questions. Who is addressing the Psalmist? What gives Jerusalem its unity? Who are the 'tribes' concerned? His answers (or his rendering of Cassiodorus' answers) are brief enough to be accommodated in the margin of the Psalter itself: the work was envisaged from the first as a gloss rather than an independent commentary. It survives in four splendid manuscripts from Tegernsee in Bavaria, all written

---

[1] Hermann of Reichenau, *Chronicle*, s.a.1045: *Mon.Ger.Hist.Script.* v.125; cf. Manitius ii.71–4.
[2] Ps.121:1–4 (A.V.122): Migne, *P.L.*cxlii.464D–5D; cf. Cassiodorus, *Expositio Psalmorum* cxxi.1–4 (*Corp.Christ.Ser.Lat.*xcviii.1149–52).

within a generation of Bruno's death.[1] They are in the tradition of the Carolingian presentation text, expensively illustrated in scarlet and gold; but they are at the same time precursors of the glossed Bible of the twelfth century. While Bruno added virtually nothing to the substance of Psalter-commentary, his choice of the rhetorician Cassiodorus and his reduction of the scale of his comment to the proportions of the glossed page foreshadow to a marked degree the new commentaries of Lanfranc and his successors.

Lanfranc's own commentary survives in two fragments quoted by Herbert of Bosham in his edition of the Great Gloss of Peter Lombard. Psalm 13 includes a passage that is an amalgam of Ps.5:11 + Ps.139:4 + Ps.10:7 + Is.59:7–8 + Ps.35:2; it does not appear as such in the original Hebrew:

> In hoc psalmo.v. sunt versus qui in hebreo non sunt.[2]

Lanfranc knew no Hebrew; he is presumably referring to Jerome's translation *iuxta hebraicam veritatem*.[3] But his instinct is right: to establish his text before discussing it, so far as his linguistic and critical resources allow. Again at Ps.17:30— 'With the help of my God I shall leap over the wall (*murum*)'— Lanfranc offers as an alternative 'the enemy's rampart', *parietem inimici*, an echo of the Pauline 'middle wall of partition'.[4] The Pauline reference is certainly deliberate: throughout his work Lanfranc has an eye for the cognate phrase from which, as here, a significant theological parallel can be drawn. As to Lanfranc's place in Psalter-commentary as a whole, we can see only that a little of the material was worked into the definitive exegesis of the mid-twelfth century. More may well be found; but at the moment Lanfranc is only one figure in an established tradition. He brought a sharp critical eye to the text, more critical perhaps than his predecessors: but the

[1] MSS. Munich StaatsB.Clm 18121, Oxford Bodleian Rawl.G.163, Laud lat.96, Vatican Rossiana 184: see O.Pächt and J. J. G. Alexander, *Illuminated Manuscripts in the Bodleian Library Oxford* i (Oxford, 1966), nos. 33–4 and C. E. Eder, 'Die Schule des Klosters Tegernsee im frühen Mittelalter im Spiegel der Tegernseer HSS', *Stud.Mitt. Gesch.Benediktiner-Ordens* lxxxiii (1972), 92–106.

[2] Ps.13:3² (A.V.14:5–7): Lanfranc's comment is quoted by B. Smalley, 'La *Glossa Ordinaria*: quelques prédécesseurs d'Anselme de Laon', *Rech.Théol.Anc.Méd.* ix (1937), 375, with references.

[3] J. N. D. Kelly, *Jerome: His Life, Writings and Controversies* (London, 1975), pp. 158 ff.

[4] Smalley, loc.cit.; cf.Eph.2:14.

character and proportions of scholastic commentary on the Psalter had already been established in the work of Bruno of Würzburg.

The other wing of the diptych is the Pauline Epistles. Here again Lanfranc had a German forerunner, the historian and poet Hermann of Reichenau, who died in 1054.[1] Hermann's glosses on the Pauline Epistles survive in one manuscript, now in St. Gall; and they have a marked resemblance in form, (not in content) to the more successful commentary that Lanfranc produced *c.* 1055–60. Like Bruno of Würzburg Hermann had turned away from the inordinately long commentaries of the Carolingians. He cites Augustine, Ambrose and Jerome often, but briefly; and he complements their theology with his own interpretation. For instance Paul writes, 'First, I thank my God through Jesus Christ for you all, that your faith is spoken of *throughout the whole world.*' (Rom.1:8).

HERMANN: 'The whole world' (*universo mundo*) means here heaven and earth, throughout which the angels may be held to declare the faith of the Roman Christians; for 'there shall be joy in heaven over one sinner that repenteth' (Luke 15:7). The Apostle says, 'Are they not all ministering spirits?' etc. (Heb.1:14). There is no doubt that their faith will be declared on earth; for when the mistress of all the world (*totius orbis*) submits in faith to the heavenly Bridegroom, that can never be concealed.[2]

Lanfranc may not have known Hermann's commentary, there is no evidence that he did; but the formula that he himself adopted is in many respects similar: a balance of patristic and modern comment within the compass of a marginal gloss.

With Lanfranc's commentary on Paul we leave the wide ocean of fragments for terra firma. The text survives in a relatively stable form in a number of manuscripts, none from Bec itself but several which are closely dependent on a Bec original.[3] The best of these is a late-eleventh-century book

---

[1] Manitius ii.756–77; cf. p. 52, n.1.

[2] MS. St Gall StiftsB.64, p.14 (s.xi: S.German). I am greatly indebted to Professor Bischoff for advice on this manuscript.

[3] M. T. Gibson, 'Lanfranc's *Commentary on the Pauline Epistles*', *Journ.Theol.Stud.* N.S.xxii (1971), 86–112. Anselm lent a Bec manuscript to Chaise-Dieu in Auvergne (*Anselmi Epp.* 70:? cf. ultimately MS. Paris B.N.lat.2875) and to Christ Church, Canterbury (ibid. 66: cf. the St. Augustine's, Rochester and Worcester manuscripts discussed in 'Lanfranc's *Commentary* . . .').

from St. Augustine's, Canterbury. Like the St. Gall manuscript of Hermann's commentary it is laid out as the Pauline text with a marginal gloss; brief notes or verbal equivalents may be interlinear. The book was prepared for a gloss from the outset, with wide ruling for the main text and closer ruling for the glosses in the outer margin only; there is a narrow column between text and gloss for the reference-signs that relate each gloss to a specific phrase. The gloss script is smaller than the text script, with more abbreviations, and there is almost no decoration. This is effectively the format of the glossed Pauline Epistles as that was to remain throughout the twelfth century. Its visual simplicity is in sharp contrast to the magnificence of earlier glossed books of the Bible: Bruno's commentary or the Carolingian commentaries that are occasionally laid out as a marginal gloss.[1] But the technical gain was so great that the new format is virtually inseparable from the new type of commentary which it expressed. The reader had before him at appropriate points on the same page both practical help in construing the Latin and theological or historical notes on the meaning of the text. Lanfranc took the latter, as Hermann had, from the Fathers, and provided the former himself. Here, for instance, is a typically concentrated passage from Paul's letter to the Church at Rome (Rom.3:4–10):

 . . . Let God be *true*, but every man a liar; as it is written,
That thou mightest be *justified* in thy sayings,
and mightest overcome when thou art judged. (Ps.51:4).
But if our unrighteousness commend the righteousness of God,
5 what shall we say?
Is God unrighteous who taketh vengeance? (I speak as a man)
God forbid: for then how shall God judge the world?
For if the truth of God hath more abounded through my lie unto
his glory; why yet am I also judged as a sinner?
10 And not rather, (as we be slanderously reported, and as some
affirm that we say,) Let us do evil that good may come?
whose damnation is just.
What then? Are we better than they?
No, in no wise: for we have *before proved* both Jews and Gentiles,
15 that they are all under sin; As it is written,
There is none righteous, no, not one. (Ps.14:3)

[1] See e.g. MSS. Cambridge Corpus Christi Coll.272 (Psalter) and Munich StaatsB.Clm 14345 (Pauline Epp.: see exhibition catalogue *Karl der Grosse*, Aachen, 1965, no. 472).

Lanfranc directed the student first to the truth and justice of God (lines 1–2):

This is a proof that God is true:
for justice in [his] sayings is truth.[1]

To spell out the syllogism—

God is just in his sayings;
But just sayings are truth,
Therefore God is true.

No doubt this kind of argument helped to direct St. Anselm to the more profound investigations of the *De Veritate*. Lanfranc then turns to Paul's parenthetical proposition that man's wickedness contributes to and increases the righteousness of God (lines 4–11):

Paul appears to have given the reason why 'all men are liars' (Ps.116:11). Note that he calls wickedness a lie. He puts forward this argument on behalf of those who have misunderstood the whole issue.[2]

In other words, Lanfranc has brought out the elements of disputation in his text: the proposition represents the thought of Paul's opponents. Finally he draws attention to 'we have before proved etc.' (line 14). The proof is straightforward:

It is as though Paul were to say,
We who are equal cannot be more excellent.

But where does Paul actually say this? Nowhere in the surviving text, but 'no doubt in some sermon which he preached to the people'.[3] Historically the explanation is plausible enough. An earlier passage in the same discussion may indicate the level and character of Lanfranc's exegesis. Paul writes (Rom.2:1):

Therefore thou art inexcusable, O man,
whosoever thou art that judgest;
for wherein thou judgest another, thou condemnest thyself;
for thou that judgest doest the same things.

---

[1] 'Probatio quod Deus verax est: iustitia enim sermonum est veritas': D'Achery, p.13, no. 5 (Migne, *P.L.*cl.115B).

[2] 'Hoc ideo subinfert: quia dicens, *ut iustificeris in sermonibus tuis*. Visus est causam reddidisse, cur omnis homo esset mendax. Et vocat iniquitatem mendacium' (no. 7); 'Iterum hoc subinfert ex persona male intelligentium' (no 9): D'Achery, loc.cit.

[3] 'Quasi diceret; Qui pares praecellentiores esse non possumus. Nec hoc superius in hac Epistola dixit: sed credendum est, in sermone quem ad populum habebat eum dixisse': D'Achery, p. 14, no. 13 (Migne, *P.L.*cl.116A).

LANFRANC: This is an invective against rulers. Paul says:
> Since all who commit and agree to (wickedness) shall
> perish, so also shall those who judge others, if they
> are enmeshed in the same sin.[1]

Lanfranc's explanation is again syllogistic:

All who sin shall perish.
The rulers are enmeshed in sin;
therefore they too shall perish.

The syllogism is implicit in the Pauline text, but Lanfranc
brings it into the open. In other passages he shows how one
statement can balance another. Paul exclaimed to the Church
at Corinth (I Cor.9:15):

It were better for me to die,
than
that any man should make my glorying void.

LANFRANC: If I had preached in the hope of a reward from you,
> *I should have no glory;*
> That is, I die eternally.
> For to die temporally is an evil, but less of an evil than to
> die eternally. Paul says this 'equipollently':
> *It were better for me to die.*[2]

'Equipollency' was not yet an exact technical term as Abelard
uses it. For Lanfranc it sometimes, as here, indicates balance,
sometimes strict logical equivalence.[3] But in principle Lanfranc's intention is clear: to unravel the complexities of St.
Paul's argument in terms of such basic knowledge of the *artes*
as could be assumed in his audience.

The doctrinal element in his commentary is patristic.
Approximately two-thirds of all the notes are labelled
'Augustine' or 'Ambrose'; and it is here that the theology of St.
Paul is clarified and developed. Now Augustine wrote no

---

[1] 'Invectio in Rectores. Dicit enim: Cum omnes facientes et consentientes
sunt perituri; etiam et hi qui alios iudicant, si eodem peccato tenentur impliciti':
D'Achery, p. 10, no. 1 (Migne, *P.L.*cl.110B).

[2] 'Non ideo, inquit, evangelizavi ut quid a vobis accipere velim. Nam si propter
hoc evangelizavero, non mihi gloria, id est moriar aeternaliter. Nam malum est
mori temporaliter; sed minus malum quam aeternaliter mori: et hoc est quod dicit
aequipollenter; Bonum est enim mihi magis mori': D'Achery, p. 63, no. 13 (Migne,
P.L. cl.185BC); cf. the similar comment on I Cor. 8:8.

[3] *L.D.C.S.D.*, cap.7: see Ch. IV, §iii.

commentary on the Pauline Epistles as a whole,[1] although of
course he refers to Paul very frequently throughout his writings.
The 'Augustine' glosses in Lanfranc's commentary are drawn
from a wide range of his work, so wide that we may wonder at
the extent of Lanfranc's knowledge and the profound resources
of the Bec library. But Lanfranc's skill lay elsewhere. His
'Augustine' glosses are drawn verbatim from the great Carolingian *Collectaneum* of Florus of Lyons.[2] The cathedral library at
Lyons was rich in early manuscripts of St. Augustine (at least
two of the sixth century and several of the seventh); so Florus
could provide more and better quotations than the most
diligent scholar could excavate for himself. At II Thess. 2, for
example, Florus quotes passages from *De Civitate Dei* xx, from
Augustine's letter to bishop Hesychius and from his homily on
Psalm 105. He adds nothing whatever of his own, but still the
Augustinian commentary on that single chapter of St. Paul
takes up six columns of a folio manuscript; the complete
commentary is usually divided into two large volumes.[3] All this
material Lanfranc has drastically abbreviated. The excerpt
from the *De Civitate Dei* is reduced to three short fragments, the
letter to Hesychius to twenty-three words and the third passage
omitted altogether.[4] The actual wording is altered hardly at all:
Lanfranc's technique is pure scissors-and-paste. Of course much
is lost by such methods; but the result is at least manageable:
many of the crucial passages of Augustine remain and there is
still room for the complementary viewpoint of 'Ambrose'.

Here again there was no commentary by St. Ambrose of
Milan, but Carolingian scholarship had supplied the deficiency.
During the ninth century two commentaries circulated under
the name of Ambrose:

---

[1] The exception is Galatians, for which Augustine wrote a full *Expositio:Corp.
Script.Eccles.Lat.*lxxxiv, (1971).

[2] Migne,*P.L.*cxix.279A–420B (summary list of texts only): see further A. Wilmart,
'Sommaire de l'exposition de Florus sur les Épîtres', *Rev.Bén.* xxxviii (1926),
205–16; C. Charlier, 'La compilation augustinienne de Florus sur l'Apôtre', ibid.
lvii (1947), 132–86; and (for the Lyons manuscripts) S. Tafel, 'The Lyons Scriptorium', in W. M. Lindsay, *Palaeographia Latina* iv (1925), 40–62. In the case of
Galatians Lanfranc used Augustine's own *Expositio* direct.

[3] MS. Oxford Bodley 317, fol.129vb–131rb (s.xii[1]: Christ Church, Canterbury).
This manuscript contains II Cor.–Heb.; the companion volume (Rom.–I Cor.) is
Cambridge Trinity Coll. B.4.5.

[4] D'Achery, pp. 180–1, nos. 3–5, 8, 14 (Migne, *P.L.*cl.342A–3B; 344AB).

(1) Rom.–Philemon   Ambrosiaster[1]
       Heb.   the Latin version of John Chrysostom[2]
(2) Rom.–2 Cor.   Ambrosiaster
       Gal.–Philemon   the Latin version of Theodore of Mopsuestia
       Heb.   the Latin Chrysostom

Lanfranc had an 'Ambrose' of the second type, including Theodore of Mopsuestia as well as Chrysostom. He treated it in the same way as his 'Augustine': verbatim quotation severely abridged.[3] He had adopted the teaching of (as he thought) two great and orthodox Latin Fathers and reduced it to the proportions of a marginal gloss. But with the 'Ambrose' he had done rather more. The three components of his 'Ambrose' (Ambrosiaster, Theodore and Chrysostom) belong to an exegetical tradition which Ambrose himself would scarcely have accepted, the so-called school of Antioch. Their critical treatment of the text, with the emphasis on a literal interpretation rather than an allegorical, had in the long run been eclipsed by a more thoroughgoing allegorical tradition, partly because several Antiochene exegetes had been indicted for heresy.[4] Yet 'Ambrose' remained, sheltering authors of the alternative tradition and maintaining the principle that the Bible too was a text in a historical setting, with the same kind of linguistic and syntactical puzzles as the *Aeneid* or the *Satires* of Juvenal. In choosing 'Ambrose' and Augustine as the patristic elements in his commentary Lanfranc achieved a balance of the two major aspects of Antique exegesis, the literal and the allegorical. He could not have done so had his 'Ambrose' been genuine; but error itself led him in the right direction. Taken as a whole his commentary had two constituents that were to persist in Pauline exegesis throughout the twelfth century: the right 'mix' of patristic quotations and the pervasive use of the *artes* to explain

[1] *Ambrosiastri qui dicitur Commentarius in Epistulas Paulinas: Corp.Script.Eccles.Lat.* lxxxi (1966–9) 3 vols. The name 'Ambrosiaster' was coined by Erasmus.

[2] Migne, *P.L.*c.1031D–84B; cf. E. Riggenbach, '*Die älteste lateinischen Kommentare zum Hebräerbrief* (Leipzig, 1907), pp. 18–20; 228–9=*Forsch. Gesch. Neutest. Kanons*, ed. Zahn, VIII.i.

[3] H. B. Swete, *Theodori Episcopi Mopsuesteni in Epp.Pauli Commentarii* (Cambridge, 1880–2), i.l, *et passim*; cf. A. Souter, *The Earliest Latin Commentaries on the Epistles of St. Paul* (Oxford, 1927), p. 53.

[4] M. L. W. Laistner, 'Antiochene exegesis in western Europe during the Middle Ages', *Harvard Theol.Rev.* xl (1947), 19–23.

the text and bring it to life. Grammar, logic and rhetoric remain servants however; the philosophical concepts to which they lead are never applied to the Bible. Here Lanfranc knew the dangers and took no risks.

Lanfranc's commentary had an immediate success: it circulated widely and was still being copied well into the twelfth century.[1] What is more important, it was taken up in the schools at Laon and Paris. The masters of Laon, Anselm (more correctly *Ansellus*) and his brother Ralph, were the popularizers of eleventh-century learning: they take the role played by Auxerre two centuries before. They seem to have had little original genius as scholars; they founded no lasting academic tradition in Laon itself: but momentarily they were able to bring together the disparate experiments of their contemporaries and their immediate predecessors in both the *artes* and the study of the Bible and present these as a coherent and useful curriculum.[2] For a generation *c.* 1080–1100 Laon was the centre of French scholarship. Even after that much of the material that had been gathered at Laon remained in use at Paris: so the scattered resources of eleventh-century learning ultimately reached the twelfth-century schools. Lanfranc's commentary provided the model for the Laon commentary on the Pauline Epistles, called from its opening phrase *Pro altercatione*.[3] The layout of the page is similar, and a significant number of individual glosses reappear, both patristic and 'modern'; some are quoted verbatim, others show through in a modified or extended form. Again the purpose is the same: the rhetorical exposition of Paul, strengthened by patristic theology. No new

---

[1] At least two adaptations were made: a northern French commentary (MS. Paris B.N.lat.12267) and a commentary found in Metz and Tegernsee (MSS. Berlin (E) Deutsche StaatsB. Phill.1650 and Munich StaatsB.Clm.18530a). See respectively B. Smalley, 'La *Glossa Ordinaria*: quelques prédécesseurs d'Anselme de Laon', *Rech.Théol.Anc.Méd.*ix (1937), 386–8, and C. E. Eder, 'Die Schule des Klosters Tegernsee . . .', *Stud.Mitt.Gesch.Benediktinerordens* lxxxiii (1972), 113–14.

[2] The *floruit* of the school of Laon is discussed by R. W. Southern, *St.Anselm and his Biographer* (Cambridge, 1963), pp. 357–61. There is scarce but reliable evidence for the teaching of the *artes* at Laon in master Anselm's glosses on grammar and rhetoric: R. W. Hunt, 'Studies on Priscian in the eleventh and twelfth centuries', *Med.Renaiss.Stud.* i. 2 (1943), 207 app., 209–10.

[3] The commentary *Pro altercatione*, which survives in some scores of manuscripts (on the most conservative reckoning), has never been edited: Migne's text (*P.L.* cxiv.469A–670D) is wholly misleading. I have used MS. Oxford Bodleian Auct. D.I.13 (s.xii. med.? Winchester) throughout.

ingredient has been added; yet the *Pro altercatione* remained the standard commentary on the Pauline Epistles until the middle of the twelfth century, and then made a substantial and acknowledged contribution to the definitive commentary of Peter Lombard.[1] The effective formula for Pauline exegesis had proved to be the materials and method proposed in Lanfranc's commentary.

iv. the new learning

'Cur Deus homo?' (St. Anselm of Canterbury)

St. Anselm's answer was essentially his own, but the traditional argument from which he began had been formulated in the school of Laon.[2] Was the incarnation of Christ the only possible means of Man's salvation? Had God no other resource? In practical terms it might have been argued that this scarcely mattered: the incarnation was a historical fact. But the Laon masters, like St. Anselm, were interested not in the common-sense solution but in the abstract coherence of a fundamental doctrine; what was logically necessary was unassailably true. Other problems—theological, legal and moral—received similar treatment. What is meant by the 'will' of God? How should we understand 'Love thy neighbour'? Should a child oblate who does not wish to remain in his monastery be allowed to leave? The questions continue, profound or trivial, seemingly without end; and they are a new departure in western scholarship. The material is overwhelmingly patristic: a long series of excerpts from Gregory and Augustine, Hilary, Jerome, Ambrose and Bede is followed by a brief comment by the master, Anselm of Laon or another.[3] His conclusion is often tentative; it may add little and solve nothing; nevertheless the modern scholar is pitting his wits against antiquity, choosing, arranging, reconciling, even rejecting the opinions (*sententiae*) of the Fathers. And his scope is limitless. The very title of one of the

---

[1] The *Pro altercatione* was expanded by Gilbert de la Porrée to form the 'media glosatura', and Gilbert's work in turn revised by Peter Lombard: B. Smalley, 'Les commentaires bibliques de l'époque romane: glose ordinaire et gloses périmées', *Cahiers Civil. Méd.* iv (1961), 16.

[2] Southern, *St. Anselm*, loc.cit.

[3] O. Lottin, *Psychologie et morale aux xiie et xiiie siècles* (Gembloux, 1959), v.32-4; 65; 67. Dom Lottin has omitted the patristic material, quoting only the conclusions by modern masters.

early sentence-collections, *Liber Pancrisis*, shows what its compiler had in mind:

Here begins the *Liber Pancrisis*, which means *All Gold*; for it contains these golden sentences or questions of the holy fathers Augustine, Jerome, Ambrose, Gregory, Isidore, Bede and the modern masters William, bishop of Châlons, Ivo, bishop of Chartres, and Anselm (of Laon) and his brother Ralph.

Question 1: the nature of God.[1]

In principle here was a systematic account of God and the universe, beginning with the creation and continuing in an orderly manner until the Last Judgement. If these ambitions were not fulfilled, if in practice every kind of miscellaneous question crowds in, until neither sympathy nor ingenuity can see any pattern whatever, the ideal is still beyond doubt. What these early masters are attempting is the rational and comprehensive arrangement of patristic and modern *sententiae* such as was ultimately achieved in the *summa* of the twelfth and thirteenth centuries. In the hands of Abelard, Peter Lombard and Aquinas the jumble of sentence-literature proved to be the material of scholastic theology.[2]

For Lanfranc all this was very dangerous ground. The monastic scholar should know the Fathers, and in normal circumstances that would suffice; he was not expected to outdo the Fathers at their own game. 'Altiora te ne quaesieris' (Ecclus. 3:22) was the only safe principle in a question of doctrine. It is fundamental to Lanfranc's only excursion into theology proper, his debate with Berengar of Tours.

---

[1] MS. London B. L. Harley 3098, fol.1: cf.Lottin, op. cit., p.11.

[2] The development towards the *summa* can be seen in the *Sic et Non* of Peter Abelard (Migne, *P.L.*clxxviii.1339A–1610B); cf. his references to the *sententiarum collationes* that took place at Laon: *Historia calamitatum* 3 (Migne, loc.cit. 124A).

IV: The Dispute with Berengar of Tours

i. the historical circumstances

In the summer and autumn of 1049 pope Leo IX went on an extended progress through Lorraine and eastern France, holding synods in early October at Rheims and a fortnight later at Mainz, turning south through the Vosges to Reichenau in Advent and Verona for Christmas; he was in Rome for another synod just after Easter. The pattern in 1050 was similar, though less ambitious: Vercelli in September, back through the French Jura to Besançon in early October, and up the eastern margin of France to his own see of Toul at the end of the month.[1] Leo travelled with a full papal entourage, such as few of his predecessors had taken across the Alps; and his passage was marked by dramatic incidents and scenes of enthusiasm. He was a master of the memorable gesture. At the consecration of Besançon cathedral he displayed to the crowd the arm of St. Stephen, 'splintered by the stones that had killed him'; the relics were placed beneath a most beautiful circular altar-stone of rose-coloured marble, engraved with the Chi-Ro monogram and the eagle of St. John.[2] At Rheims he preached in the open air to seemingly endless crowds; for two days litanies and processions built up to the translation of St. Remigius and the consecration of the new abbey church.[3] The enthusiasm carried over to the papal council held there immediately afterwards: two bishops were deposed for simony; the archbishop of Rheims himself only just avoided censure, and the archbishop of Besançon, attempting to defend one of the guilty men, was silenced by the ever-watchful patron Remigius. At once Leo

---

[1] *J.L.* 4167–242.

[2] *J.L.* 4249: Migne, *P.L.*cxliii.668BC. The altar-stone is in the north-west chapel of the nave in the present cathedral: see C. Fohlen, *Histoire de Besançon des origines à la fin du xvie siècle* (Paris, 1964), pp. 265–8.

[3] *Historia dedicationis ecclesiae S. Remigii*, caps. 10 ff: Migne, *P.L.*cxlii. 1424A–38A.

welcomed the miracle—'Adhuc vivit beatus Remigius'; he regarded the miraculous as neither dubious nor unexpected. It was Leo's great strength that he believed in such local cults and also recognized that the excitement they generated gave impetus to a papal council and validated its decisions.

The council of Rheims was a focus for the discontents of northern France as a whole. Five Norman bishops attended, out of real concern for the good of the Church (if we may judge by the synod recently held at Rouen), but equally to look after the political interests of Normandy.[1] Duke William's projected marriage alliance with Flanders was condemned, but at the same time Geoffrey Martel, count of Anjou, his rival to the south, was threatened with excommunication. Geoffrey had already annexed Tours (1044) and—what affected Normandy more closely—was about to take over Maine, the border county between Normandy and the Loire valley. Hugh IV of Maine was a child, and the effective ruler his godfather Gervase, bishop of Le Mans.[2] In 1048 Geoffrey had seized Gervase and thrown him into prison; now at Rheims he was excommunicated until he released the bishop. There can be little doubt that the Norman contingent supported this move, for Gervase's cause was ecclesiastically impeccable and politically expedient. Soon afterwards he was welcomed at the court of duke William, whence by a route that is now entirely obscure he emerged in 1055 as archbishop of Rheims. Count Geoffrey had lost that round; and although he continued his pressure on Maine during the 1050s, control of the area passed increasingly to William of Normandy.

For Berengar these events cast long shadows.[3] He belonged to a family of canons of St. Martin's, Tours, men with substantial hereditary prebends and the prospect of office in the abbey; but *c.* 1040 he accepted political reality and found employment in

[1] Geoffrey of Coutances, Ivo of Séez, Herbert of Lisieux, Hugh of Bayeux, and Hugh of Avranches: ibid., col. 1431A. For archbishop Mauger's synod of Rouen see Ch. V, §ii below.

[2] R.. Latouche, *Histoire du comté du Maine pendant le x*e *et le xi*e *siècle* (Paris 1910: *Bibl.Éc.Hautes Études* 183), pp. 26–30; cf. *Actus Pontificum Cenomannis in urbe degentium* xxxi, ed. Busson and Ledru (Le Mans, 1902: *Soc.Archives Hist.Maine*), pp. 366–7.

[3] For Berengar's career and the history of Anjou as a whole at this time see L. Halphen's classic study, *Le Comté d'Anjou au xi*e *siècle* (Paris, 1906); cf. further O. Guillot, *Le Comte d'Anjou et son entourage au xi*e *siècle* (Paris, 1972), i. 419–20, ii.75–6.

Angers with Fulk Nerra, count of Anjou. Throughout the 1040s the choice was well justified, as Geoffrey Martel moved into Vendôme and Tours and threatened Le Mans. As Angers became the capital of the lower Loire valley Berengar was securely placed at the centre of patronage. Like Lanfranc he was a master of the liberal arts and an exponent of the Bible, but being a professional teacher (rather than the monk who only exceptionally opened a school) he built up a unique reputation. Manner and matter were alike impressive. His dignified and arresting gestures, the odd pronunciation he affected for familiar words, the involution of his rhetorical style: all this combined with real scholarly originality to attract crowds of students. He was also the count's letter-writer, devising a brilliant, if untenable, justification for his treatment of bishop Gervase. Count Geoffrey had acted in defence of the jurisdiction with which God had entrusted him and for the maintenance of peace and order; it was the bishop who had confused the affairs of God with secular politics.[1] Berengar added lustre to count Geoffrey's court; he rose to be archdeacon and treasurer of Angers cathedral and he had every prospect of a bishopric. But after the council of Rheims Geoffrey Martel's position was significantly less secure, and it declined further throughout the 1050s; Normandy by contrast was stronger than it had been for a generation. Although Berengar remained in Anjou until the 1060s, the count's protection was markedly less effective just when he needed it most.

By the summer of 1049 Berengar was being widely criticized for the novelty of his teaching. He was said to maintain that the Eucharist was not the body and blood of Christ, that baptism and marriage were mere ceremonies of no importance and (although this he denied) that episcopal authority was not conveyed by the pastoral staff.[2] It was the publicity that Berengar gave to his opinions as much as their actual content that caused

[1] C. Erdmann and N. Fickermann, *Briefsammlungen der Zeit Heinrichs IV* (Weimar, 1950), no. 84.

[2] Theoduin of Liège, *Letter to Henry I of France*, 1049/50 (the first three opinions): Migne, *P.L.*cxlvi.1439B–42C. For Berengar's denial of the last opinion see his own letter to Ascelin of Chartres: D'Achery (*V.L.* pagination), p.24B (Migne, *P.L.*cl. 66C) and critical edition now by R. B. C. Huygens, 'Les lettres de Bérenger de Tours et d'Ascelin de Chartres', in *Litterae Textuales: Essays Presented to G. I. Lieftinck* ii. 16–22.

alarm. Here was a brilliant and persuasive speaker who expounded the Christian mysteries to a miscellaneous audience that carried his teaching across France. 'By your arguments,' expostulated the bishop of Langres, 'the Eucharist that is our common strength and support is turned to a general and public evil.'[1] Berengar's irresponsibility was more scandalous than his errors. The earliest reaction came from Chartres, where Berengar himself had studied in the time of Fulbert. Berengar had an acrimonious debate with the dean of the cathedral, Ascelin, and other local scholars probably in the autumn of 1049.[2] This encounter may have convinced him that he needed allies, for soon afterwards he tried to engage the support of Lanfranc, his esteemed colleague and dear friend:[3]

A report has reached me, brother Lanfranc, from Ingelran of Chartres which, dear friend, I cannot but bring to your attention. It is this: that you disapprove of John the Scot's opinions on the Eucharist, and indeed consider them heretical, where he differs from that fellow Paschasius, whose opinions you have adopted. If this be so, brother, you dishonour your own intelligence—the intelligence with which God has abundantly endowed you—by reaching a hasty conclusion. You are not yet so expert in the study of Scripture nor have you had much discussion with men of greater experience. So now, brother, inexperienced as you are in these matters, I should like to discuss them with you, if the opportunity arise, in the presence of whatever fit judges or audience you please. Until then do not take offence at my assertion:

If you think John the Scot a heretic, whose propositions on the Eucharist we uphold, then you must consider Ambrose, Jerome, and Augustine heretical, not to mention the rest.

We wish you health and sobriety in the Lord.

The letter is perhaps a shade patronizing in tone: but it does imply almost inescapably that Lanfranc and Berengar were more than casual acquaintances. Berengar was an established scholar when Lanfranc came to France, and Lanfranc admitted

---

[1] 'Haec communis virtus, haec publica fortitudo, commune et publicum malum sit': Migne, *P.L.*cxlii. 1327C.

[2] Berengar, op.cit. (p. 65, n. 2); Ascelin, *Letter to Berengar*: D'Achery (*V.L.* pagination), pp. 24–5 (Migne, *P.L.*cl 67A–68D).

[3] D'Achery (*V.L.* pagination,) p. 22CD (=Migne, *P.L.*cl. 63CD), re-edited by R. B. C. Huygens, 'Textes latins du xie au xiiie siècle', *Stud.Med.* viii (1967), 451–9.

to having heard his lectures on logic—although he had not found them profitable.[1] We may well speculate that the link between the two scholars was closer still, close enough to explain some of the bitterness in their subsequent controversy. Lanfranc was not in Bec when the letter arrived, so it was sent after him, very probably to the council of Rheims, where it gave rise to the rumour that Lanfranc himself was tarred with heresy.[2] As with other business that could not be summarily concluded, Leo IX postponed full discussion of Berengar's teaching until the annual Easter synod:[3] in the intervening months books could be read and advice taken. Lanfranc had joined the papal entourage by the time it reached Remiremont in the Vosges (14 November),[4] and in April 1050 he attended the synod in Rome. There he vindicated his orthodoxy unopposed; Berengar did not appear. Leo seems to have envisaged a public debate between the two scholars, for when he summoned Berengar again to meet him at Vercelli, as he travelled north in September, he asked Lanfranc to remain at court until this second synod. But in the event the king of France would not tolerate papal interference at this level,[5] so Lanfranc never displayed his skill. The synod of Vercelli condemned Berengar's teaching, and there for the moment Leo let the matter rest.

Lanfranc's first encounter with Berengar after the dispute began was in the late autumn of 1050. Duke William summoned scholars from the whole of Normandy to a court at Brionne, a few miles south of Bec, and Berengar came with a retinue of supporters.[6] But although on Berengar's own testimony Lanfranc was present at Brionne, he was not one of the main protagonists in the debate that followed. Throughout the 1050s Norman orthodoxy was upheld by the great ducal monastery of

---

[1] Guitmund of La Croix-St.-Leofroy, *De corporis et sanguinis Christi veritate* i: Migne, *P.L.*cxlix. 1428BC; cf. *Miracula S. Nicholai*, cap.7.

[2] As the letter ultimately fell into the hands of a *clericus* of Rheims (*L.D.C.S.D.*, cap.4), it is a fair guess, but only a guess, that Lanfranc was at the papal council there. Heresy of some kind was on the agenda: *Hist.dedic.eccles.S.Remigii*, cap.14: Migne, *P.L.* cxlii.1431C.

[3] For Leo's synods see *L.D.C.S.D.*, cap.4, corroborated by *D.S.C.*, pp. 33–48.

[4] *Lanfranci Epp.*13: consecration of Remiremont (dioc.Toul).

[5] *D.S.C.*, p. 16; cf. Henry I's disapproval of the council of Rheims: *Hist.dedic. eccles.S.Remigii*, cap.9 (Migne, *P.L.*cxlii.1422C–3D).

[6] Durand, *Liber de corpore et sanguine Christi* IX. xxxiii: Migne, *P.L.* cxlix.1422A; *D.S.C.*, p. 12.

Fécamp, first by abbot John in the final book of his *Confessio Fidei*, then in a treatise directed specifically at Berengar by Durand, the abbot's cross-bearer,[1] finally in the eucharistic confession made by one of the synods of archbishop Maurilius, himself a monk of Fécamp.[2] The only other Norman participant at this time was the abbot of Préaux, who had a discussion with Berengar in 1050.[3] Elsewhere the debate continued: at Liège, Paris, Poitiers,[4] and outstandingly in Chartres. 'The profound and acute thinker of the age', bishop Fulbert, 'in doctrine and way of life a pupil of the pupils of Christ',[5] had left a group of students, some in Chartres some scattered, who now rallied to exhort Berengar to sobriety and restraint. Unlike the monks of Fécamp these men had known him as an academic colleague; they write not in condemnation but in grieved surprise. 'O in cunctis aliis reverentissime vir!' exclaimed Hugh of Langres.[6] He was followed by Ascelin, dean of Chartres, and Adelmann, scholasticus in the cathedral at Speyer, one of the great churches of the Salian emperors. Adelmann's exposition was answered with a contemptuous epigram from Horace: 'The mountains groan in travail—and there comes forth a mouse.'[7] It is well seen how Berengar made enemies, irrespective of his eucharistic

---

[1] John of Fécamp, *Confessio Fidei* iv (Migne, *P.L.* ci. 1085D–98D); see J. Leclercq and J.-P. Bonnes, *Un Maître de la vie spirituelle au xie siècle: Jean de Fécamp* (Paris, 1946), pp. 31–44. Durand, op.cit. (Migne, *P.L.* cxlix, 1375D–1424B): see R. Heurtevent, *Durand de Troarn et les origines de l'hérésie bérengarienne* (Paris, 1912): cf. A. Wilmart, 'Distiques d'Hincmar sur l'Eucharistie?', *Rev.Bén.* xl (1928), 87, app.

[2] Migne, *P.L.* cxliii.1382D–3B, from a Rouen sacramentary. The text cannot be precisely dated, but it is probably earlier than the papal formula of 1059 (see below).

[3] Durand, op.cit., col. 1421D; cf. C. Erdmann and N. Fickermann, *Briefsamm-lungen der Zeit Heinrichs IV* (Weimar, 1950), no. 98. (Durand's chronology is untenable.)

[4] Theoduin of Liège, *Letter to Henry* I: Migne, *P.L.* cxlvi. 1439B–42C (Liège); Durand, op.cit., cols. 1422C–4A and Theoduin, op.cit. (Paris); C. Erdmann and N. Fickermann, op.cit., no. 88 (Poitiers). For the royal synod in Paris see further J. de Montclos, *Lanfranc et Bérenger: la controverse eucharistique du xie siècle* (Louvain, 1971: *Spic.Sacr.Lovan.*37), pp. 109–14.

[5] 'Fulbertus Carnotensis episcopus, nostri temporis sagax et acer philosophus, sed fide vita moribusque discipulorum Christi discipulus': Durand, op.cit., col. 1405B. Note the play on 'servus servorum dei'.

[6] Hugh of Langres, *Letter to Berengar*: Migne, *P.L.*cxlii.1328B. For Ascelin see p. 66, n. 2; for Adelmann see now R. B. C. Huygens, 'Textes latins du xie au xiiie siècle', *Stud.Med.* viii (1967), 459–89.

Cf. Horace, *De arte poetica* 139: de Montclos, op.cit., pp. 129–30.

doctrine; but during the 1050s he still had support in many quarters. His own bishop, Eusebius Bruno of Angers, was loyal; he had a friend at the French court and a helpful critic in Paulinus of Metz.[1] Even Rome was anxious rather than hostile: at the council of Tours in 1054 the legate Hildebrand accepted —as an interim solution—a very simple compromise formula proposed by Berengar himself.[2] Among the *dramatis personae* of this crucial decade when Berengar and his opponents adopted and clarified their varied positions, only Lanfranc is missing. He wrote nothing; he received no letters: he had no lot nor part with the disputants—and this in the most glorious years of the school of Bec.

The turning-point in the controversy was the intervention of pope Nicholas II. Berengar was summoned to the Easter council of 1059, and there finally he appeared in person.[3] In a plenary session of the council his writings were burnt and he himself accepted on oath a eucharistic confession drawn up by cardinal Humbert. The news of Berengar's recantation and the eucharistic formula to which he had sworn were circulated 'to all the cities of Italy, France and Germany, wherever Berengar's false doctrine had been current before'. In this way Lanfranc learned the details of the affair,[4] which he was to use later on with fine dramatic effect:

Your works were examined and condemned at Rome by Nicholas of blessed memory, supreme pontiff of all Christendom, and by 113 bishops. So bowing low—yet with pride in your heart—you lit the fire and in full view of the Council threw onto it your books of false doctrine and swore to the true faith.[5]

[1] Theoduin, op.cit. Eusebius Bruno withdrew his support in the early 1060s, probably after the synod of Angers (April 1062): see Erdmann and Fickermann, op.cit., no. 86, with references. For Berengar's friend at court see ibid., no. 88, and for Paulinus (who was also writing on behalf of Siegfried of Gorze) see E. Martène and U. Durand, *Thesaurus Novus Anecdotorum* (Paris, 1717), i. 196BD.

[2] *D.S.C.*, p. 52. Bernold of Constance, who purports to describe the synod of Tours, confuses (a) the oaths of 1054 and 1059 and (b) the anathema in cap.xv (*rectius* xi) of the First Council of Ephesus with the eucharistic profession of the same council: text in R.B.C. Huygens, 'Bérenger de Tours, Lanfranc et Bernold de Constance', *Sacris Erudiri* xvi (1965), 380–1.

[3] *L.D.C.S.D.*, caps. 1–2; *J.L.*4399.

[4] Nicholas' letter to Lanfranc (*J.L.*4446) clearly implies that Lanfranc had not visited Rome in the first months of Nicholas' pontificate (Jan.–April 1059); cf. de Montclos, op.cit., pp. 43–4 app.

[5] *L.D.C.S.D.*, cap. 1.

Arius had returned and was again confounded: if the heresy was different, the response of the Church was unchanged. As Arius had been defeated at Nicaea, so Nicholas' council, with its ranks of bishops, saw itself in the great tradition. Contemporary manuscript illumination showing the theologian confounding the heretic had a direct relevance:[1] Augustine had exposed the fallacies of Manichee and Donatist, now his mantle fell on cardinal Humbert. The 1059 council was to a great extent Humbert's work; and Humbert himself was the secretary, legate and biographer of Leo IX, a man who for many was still the ideal pope. Loyalty to Leo's memory (in addition to his formal cult) was a moving force in the thought and legislation of the papal court: Humbert brought to the council the weight of Leo's prestige as well as his own. It was formidable opposition: yet it had curiously little immediate effect.

When Berengar returned to France, he repudiated his oath, as taken under duress, and resumed his discussion of the Eucharist. The fragments of his first surviving treatise are seasoned with disparaging remarks about Nicholas II and Humbert, 'the absurd Burgundian'.[2] The mills of God ground slowly: by July 1061 Nicholas and Humbert were dead, and there had been no response to Berengar's intransigence. Alexander II, who became pope in October 1061, was an outsider, uncommitted to Humbert's settlement. Now at last Lanfranc returned to the fray. His treatise *On the body and blood of the Lord* was written *c.* 1063, when he was already abbot of St. Étienne, Caen. He defends the 1059 settlement against Berengar's attack and expounds the philosophical and patristic basis of orthodoxy. It is something of a puzzle why he intervened at all, and why he was moved to do so as late as 1063. He was becoming prominent in Norman politics, and no doubt shared the continuing mistrust of Anjou. But primarily Lanfranc seems to have acted out of loyalty to Humbert and Leo IX: his experience of Leo's court in 1050 had stayed with him. *The Liber de corpore et sanguine Domini* opens not with an exposition of the Eucharist, nor even with Berengar's

---

[1] J. J. G. Alexander, *Norman Illumination at Mont St. Michel 966–1100* (Oxford, 1970), pp. 100–2; cf. Durand, op.cit., col. 1393A.

[2] *L.D.C.S.D.*, cap.2.

own treatise of *c.* 1060, but with the 1059 council, its 113 bishops and Nicholas 'of blessed memory, supreme pontiff of all Christendom'.[1]

Yet the root of the controversy was elsewhere, in a real shift of Christian belief and practice.

ii. the doctrinal issue

Hoc est corpus meum, quod pro vobis tradetur: hoc facite in meam commemorationem.

I Cor. 11:24 (Vulgate).

St. Paul's words are the crux of the Eucharist: the celebrant consecrates the bread on the altar, and thereafter the bread *is* the body of Christ. Receiving this consecrated bread the faithful participate in the life of Christ and thereby constitute the true Church: 'We being many are one bread, and one body: for we are all partakers of that one bread' (I Cor.10.17). Traditionally the ceremony culminates here; and theological discussion has equally centred on the words: 'This is my body'. But the tradition, though venerable, is not patristic. For Ambrose and Augustine (as for many of their followers today) the Eucharist was the act of the group as a whole rather than an exercise of power by the priest alone. Their attitude is very clear in the sermons that St. Ambrose preached in Easter Week, immediately after the baptism of the catechumens on the night before Easter.[2] They had gone down into the great font in the *basilica noua*; they had been immersed and anointed and finally—in white clothing like the saints in the Apocalypse—they had entered the church itself for the Eucharist on Easter Day. Participation in the Eucharist is the logical corollary of baptism. The candidate has been removed from the context of his old life and brought into the land of the living. What more natural than that he should join his fellows there in the eucharistic meal? The Eucharist expresses the freedom of the new community. It expresses too the sacrifice of Christ which supersedes the sacrifices of the Jewish covenant. But whether contrasted with the evil and transience of the world, or contrasted

[1] Ibid., cap.1.
[2] Ambrose, *De Sacramentis* i-vi, ed. Faller: *Corp.Script.Eccles.Lat.*lxxiii (1955).

with the old covenant, the Eucharist was seen as a complete and varied act of worship. The technical problem of *how* the bread and wine were, or became, or signified, the body and blood of Christ received little attention. It was scarcely relevant; and should the question be asked there was sufficient explanation in the limitless power of God. 'You saw,' said Ambrose, 'bread, being carried up to the altar.
"But I brought that bread here myself," you will say: "It's just plain bread."
No!' comes the reply, 'once consecrated, the bread becomes the flesh of Christ . . . It is Christ's own words that make the sacrament, the words by which all things were made: the heavens, the earth, the sea and all living creatures . . .
If the words of Christ have such power that
things which did not exist should come into being,
have they not the power that
things which did exist shall continue in being and be changed into something else?'[1]

This passage has a central place in later controversy, but it is by no means central to Ambrose's preaching. For him the traumatic experience was baptism, whereby the Christian was irrevocably separated from the world: 'you were dead, now you are alive; old and now young again; buried with Christ (figuratively, in the baptismal water), and sharing in his resurrection'.[2] In this ceremony of initiation the candidate crosses over from the dirt and darkness of the human condition into the light of the redeemed.[3]

A generation later Augustine expounded a fundamental eucharistic text in his sermons on St. John's Gospel: 'Except ye eat the flesh of the son of man, and drink his blood, ye have no life in you' (John 6:53). In principle he holds to the position of Ambrose, that the Eucharist is the common meal of the redeemed; but his discussion of baptism is elsewhere, and whereas no doubt in his own mind the two are linked, they are not so

---

[1] Ibid. iv.14–15. The latter part runs: 'Si ergo tanta vis est in sermone domini Iesu, ut inciperent esse, quae non erant, quanto magis operatorius est, ut sint, quae erant, et in aliud commutentur' (p. 52, lines 20–3).

[2] Ibid. ii.19; iv.7; ii.23.

[3] Ibid. iv.5; cf. ii.23 ('humana conditio') and iii.15 ('lumen sacramentorum').

presented to the congregation. He develops the moral and figurative aspects of the rite, as Ambrose does; but Ambrose is using metaphor and Old Testament parallels to elucidate the actions of the liturgy: Augustine expounds the Eucharist in the context of trinitarian theology.[1] The Eucharist unites the faithful in the society of the true Church; as Christ lives because of the Father, they participate in the life of Christ. So the Eucharist found its place in Christian doctrine, not as a difficult or contentious issue, but almost without argument.

Ambrose could still envisage the apostolic Church, set over against the world; there was a real gulf between any Christian, layman or cleric, and the secular society which he had renounced. Even in the late fourth century this distinction was breaking down: with infant baptism the ceremony of initiation lost its emotional impact,[2] and when society as a whole was formally Christian the eucharistic meal was no longer the activity which patently defined the Church. Another and equally radical change was beginning in northern Europe, where the cults displaced by Christianity were more limited and alien than the religions of the late Empire; especially in a situation of mass conversion Christians were liable to find in their new religion not enlightenment but magic. The magic was there, and now for some time it was to have the upper hand. The eucharistic meal, in which the whole Christian community had participated (with different functions, but essentially as equals), became far more esoteric. It was a sacerdotal activity in which the laity, though present, seldom took an active part; and the end-products, so to speak, were the consecrated elements. These were intrinsically sacred. The bread was utterly different from its former state, and miraculously shown to be so, whether as a fragment of flesh on the altar or in the vision of a child on the altar at the moment of consecration.[3] The consecrated bread became a touchstone distinguishing Jew from

---

[1] Augustine, *Tractatus in Iohannem* xxvi.15–19: *Corp.Christ.Ser.Lat.*xxxvi (1954), 267–9.

[2] For the changing attitude to baptism see J. D. C. Fisher, *Christian Initiation: Baptism in the Medieval West* (London, 1965).

[3] B. Colgrave, *The Earliest Life of Gregory the Great, by an Anonymous Monk of Whitby* (Lawrence, 1968), Ch.20; K. Strecker, *Miracula Nynie Episcopi* (Berlin, 1923: *Mon.Ger.Poet.lat.aev.Carol.* IV.ii.957–9), quoted by Paschasius, *De corpore et sanguine Domini* xiv. 120–68.

Christian, a form of ordeal, even a form of ordeal that could be delegated.[1] The barbarians had surely prevailed.

At the same time it was the needs of the mission-field that first showed up the deficiencies of eucharistic theology, indeed the absence of any patristic discussion more rigorous than Ambrose's sermons. Paschasius Radbertus, the scholasticus at Corbie, was asked *c.* 830 to send a comprehensive exposition of the Eucharist to the newly founded daughter-house of Corvey in Saxony.[2] Corbie had a remarkable library, and Paschasius was a learned and critical scholar: he produced a book that was fundamental to eucharistic thought for 300 years. The *De corpore et sanguine Christi* is based on a first-hand knowledge of the Fathers—Ambrose, Augustine, Hilary, Jerome—yet it takes cognizance of eucharistic practice as Paschasius himself knew it. Baptism and the Eucharist were no longer two sides of the one coin; the baptized community was no longer set in opposition to the state; the gulf lay now between the multitude of ordinary Christians and the single priest officiating at the altar. Further, and harder to understand, Ambrose's resurrection theology was receiving less attention than the events of Good Friday: the actual sacrifice of Christ on the cross. Given this new situation Paschasius cannot but emphasize the role of the priest and the change in the elements at consecration: 'In the power of the Spirit the body and blood of Christ are made by his own words from the material of bread and wine.' Again, later:

The material of the bread and wine are really changed inwardly to the flesh and blood of Christ, so that after consecration they are truly held to be the true flesh and blood of Christ.[3]

If the consecrated elements are not, truly and objectively, the body and blood of Christ, the whole exercise is pointless:

---

[1] The ordeal by reception of the Host persisted into the twelfth century. For the detection of the Jew see the miracle of Syrus, first bishop of Pavia, added to Paschasius, *De corpore et sanguine Domini* vi. 55–67ff. (see next note); for the truth-ordeal see for instance *Vita Leonis IX* ii.5 (Migne, *P.L.*cxliii.493B), where the bishop of Speyer who failed was reputedly paralysed.

[2] Paschasius, *De corpore et sanguine Domini,* ed. Paul, *Corp.Christ.Cont.Med.* xvi (1969), pp. vii–viii, 3–7, and *passim.*

[3] 'Corpus Christi et sanguis virtute Spiritus in verbo ipsius ex pane vinique substantia efficitur' (op.cit. iv. 38–9); 'Substantia panis et vini in Christi carnem et sanguinem efficaciter interius commutatur, ita ut deinceps post consecrationem iam vera Christi caro et sanguis veraciter credatur' (op.cit. viii. 64–7).

Paschasius is already in the dilemma, unknown to Ambrose, which was to persist throughout the Middle Ages.

The *De corpore et sanguine Domini* was no doubt well received by the Saxon public for whom it was designed. When it was presented some years later to Charles the Bald, the reaction of the court intelligentsia was very mixed.[1] Taken out of context (as I have just quoted them), the Paschasian definitions seemed to allow the crudely physical interpretation of the Eucharist that was already implied in the eucharistic miracles of popular belief. Even though Paschasius' argument is consistently directed towards the spiritual reception of the body and blood of Christ, even though he formally excludes the view that the consecrated elements were digested like ordinary food,[2] the individual phrase could still be misinterpreted. Hincmar stood with Paschasius. But many scholars were doubtful, including John the Scot; and their hesitations were expressed by Ratramnus, one of the younger monks in Corbie itself. Ratramnus' treatise on the Eucharist is no rival to Paschasius' book as a whole, and does not pretend to be; but on the specific question of whether the elements are changed at consecration it is philosophically clear cut:

The body and blood of Christ which are received in the mouths of the faithful are in their outward appearance images. But by the power of the divine word their invisible status is truly the body and blood of Christ. As visible created objects they feed the body, but in virtue of their more powerful status they feed and sanctify the minds of the faithful.[3]

The consecrated bread and wine are material symbols of spiritual truth: the image or 'figure' of the reality beyond. Ratramnus cited in his support the postcommunion prayer:

---

[1] As abbot of Corbie Paschasius sent his book to Charles in 843-4 (op.cit., p. x). The best account of the theological reaction is still J. Geiselmann, *Die Eucharistielehre der Vorscholastik* (Paderborn, 1926), pp.144-218.

[2] Paschasius, op.cit., xx. 45-50.

[3] 'Corpus et sanguis Christi quae fidelium ore . . . percipiuntur figurae s(i)nt secundum speciem visibilem. At vero secundum invisibilem substantiam, id est divini potentiam verbi, corpus et sanguis vere Christi existunt. Unde secundum visibilem creaturam corpus pascunt, iuxta vero potentioris virtutem substantiae mentes fidelium et pascunt et sanctificant': Ratramnus, *De corpore et sanguine Domini*, ed. Bakhuizen van den Brink 2nd edn. (Amsterdam/London, 1974), cap. xlix. Ratramnus was writing *c.* 844, or a few years later (ed.cit., p. 28).

Lord we pray that your sacraments may reach fulfilment in us, that what we now enact in an outward form we may receive in truth.[1]

Here was a text, known to every priest, that balanced the material against the spiritual, the figure against the reality, the bread against the body of Christ. The elements suffered no physical change, but the value and efficacy of the sacrament was not thereby reduced. Paschasius in turn defended his position in an open letter,[2] and to the credit of all concerned there was no heresy-hunt. In effect the Carolingians had posed a new set of questions, that turned on the meaning of a 'sacrament'. Ambrose had used the word quite generally of the mysteries, the holy things, which the believer approached at baptism: 'You whose heart was blind before have begun to see the light of the sacraments.'[3] To Augustine the term did require explanation:

The sacrifice that we see is a sacrament of the unseen sacrifice: it is a sign of the holy,

or, in a dangerous simplification which was not Augustine's own,

A sacrament is a sign of the holy.[4]

This famous definition marked out the area of later controversy. As a sign points to something other than itself, the sacrament and the thing signified are different; and the latter is the more important. So the consecrated bread points to the body of Christ: as Paschasius argued, the bread is not only what it appears to be but also the body of Christ; alternatively, as Ratramnus argued, the bread is an image or figure of the *res*, the thing itself.

---

[1] 'Perficiant in nobis domine quesumus tua sacramenta quod continent, ut quae nunc specie gerimus rerum veritate capiamus': ibid., cap.lxxxviii; cf. *Sacramentarium Gregorianum*, ed. Lietzmann (Münster-i.W.,1921), p.95, no.166, 8. Ascelin of Chartres attributes this prayer to Gregory the Great: D'Achery (*V.L.* pagination), p.25B.

[2] *Letter to Fredugard of S. Riquier* (*c.* 856): ed. Paul, *Corp.Christ.Cont.Med.* xvi (1969), 135–59; 169–73.

[3] 'Qui ante corde videbaris esse caecatus, coepisti lumen sacramentorum videre': *De Sacramentis* iii.15, ed. Faller: *Corp.Script.Eccles.Lat.* lxxiii (1955), 45.

[4] 'Sacrificium ergo visibile invisibilis sacrificii sacramentum, id est sacrum signum est': *De Civitate Dei* x.5: ed. Hoffmann, *Corp.Script.Eccles.Lat.* xl (1899), 452; cf. Geiselmann, *Die Eucharistielehre der Vorscholastik* (Paderborn, 1926), pp. 293–4.

The antithesis of material and spiritual, the transient and the eternal, fits readily to most forms of Platonism: the physical object reflects or leads to the spiritual reality beyond. This way of thought still seemed reasonable to Fulbert in the early eleventh century. Round his communion cup at Chartres there was a long inscription summing up the traditional eucharistic faith:

The sacrament passes, but the strength which it conveys and the grace mediated remain for ever. Many take part in the sacrament, but few are joined together in love. He who loves the Lord unreservedly comes to the sacrament in the right way. The new commandment is love, the new testament the promise of the kingdom of heaven; this sacrament of unity is the pledge of our inheritance.

Here is the patristic high-road which all could accept: Berengar himself, who presumably knew the actual chalice, was to quote the inscription in full to his critics from Chartres.[1] In a brief treatise on the Eucharist Fulbert's language is more technical:

What appeared as the *substance of bread and wine* without
is now the body and blood of Christ within . . .
Earthly material transcending the level of its nature and origin [is]
changed into the *substance of Christ*.[2]

He strays here onto uncertain ground, for the *substantia panis et vini* cannot be reconciled with both the *terrena materies* and the *substantia Christi*: what seems to be precise terminology is irretrievably confused. Fulbert's difficulty arises from his interest in modern scholarship. As the *logica vetus* was mastered in the schools of Europe from the late tenth century onwards, the straight antithesis of image and reality, *figura* and *res*,

---

[1] 'Sacramentum quidem transitorium est, virtus vero, quę per ipsum operatur, et gratia, qua insinuatur, eterna. Participatio sacramenti multorum est, paucorum communio caritatis. Qui Dominum pure diligit, bene ad sacramentum accedit. Mandatum novum caritas; testamentum novum promissio regni celorum; pignus hereditatis, id est sacramentum communionis': C. Erdmann and N. Fickermann, *Briefsammlungen der Zeit Heinrichs IV* (Weimar, 1950), no. 88, p. 154.

[2] 'Quae substantia panis et vini apparebat exterius, iam corpus Christi et sanguis fit interius . . . Terrena materies, naturae et generis sui meritum transcendens, in Christi substantiam commutetur': Migne, *P.L.*cxli.202C; 203C. Although Migne prints this treatise among Fulbert's letters (no. 5), the manuscript tradition is quite separate; the ascription to Fulbert is confirmed by Durand of Fécamp, *De corpore et sanguine Christi* xx (Migne, *P.L.*cxlix. 1405B–6A).

seemed less valid. Reality for Aristotle lay primarily in the individual concrete object; perhaps the validity of a sacrament should be defined in terms of the physical object itself (bread, wine, water, oil) rather than the non-physical reality to which it referred. 'Hoc est corpus meum': this bread is itself, intrinsically, the body of Christ. Fulbert's wish to define the Eucharist in these Aristotelian terms rather than from the traditional Platonist standpoint led him to assert that the *earthly material* was changed into the *substance of Christ*. In so doing he had moved much closer to Paschasius, whose doctrine of the Eucharist matched, or could be seen as matching, Aristotelian logic as the doctrine of Ratramnus did not. The unlikely alliance of Paschasius and Aristotle set the direction of eucharistic theology in the eleventh century, without of course solving the myriad difficulties of its exact expression.

The scholars who first wrestled seriously with the implications of the *logica vetus* for traditional theology were Fulbert's pupils, and pre-eminent among them Berengar of Tours. Initially he seems to have been concerned with sacraments in general: baptism, marriage and episcopal investiture presented close parallels with the Eucharist. How could a material object represent, or in some sense be, an invisible object or a spiritual truth? If it was an image or figure, had it any intrinsic value? The Eucharist was peculiarly vulnerable to such questions, and Berengar quickly got the reputation of a heretic. The words of consecration added a new mental label to the bread, they did not change it; the body of Christ on the altar was a figment of the imagination.[1] But if that were so, the truth was inaccessible:

If still in images we see,
When shall we grasp reality?

The fears of many were voiced in that epigram of Peter the Deacon.[2] To Berengar the confusion of image and reality that was encouraged by a half-understood Aristotelianism and apparently already perpetrated by Paschasius was a more immediate threat to the faith. He appealed to the ancient

---

[1] Hugh of Langres, *Letter to Berengar*: Migne, *P.L.*cxlii. 1327B; Durand, op.cit., col.1393A.

[2] 'Si adhuc in figura sumus,/quando rem tenebimus?: *D.S.C.*, p. 43. Peter the Deacon was a leading figure at the council of Rheims: *Historia dedicationis ecclesiae S. Remigii* (Migne, *P.L.* cxlii.1431BC and cf. p. 63, no. 3 above).

tradition of Gregory the Great and Ratramnus, with its clear distinction between what is 'enacted in an image' and what is 'received in truth'. That alone would scarcely have given offence. But it is all too characteristic of Berengar that he attributed Ratramnus' treatise to the one author calculated to flutter ecclesiastical dovecotes, John Scotus Erigena.[1] Though never formally condemned, John the Scot was always suspect, for his incomprehensible cleverness and his commitment to a Greek scholarly tradition that was otherwise unknown in the west. Berengar certainly owed nothing to Greek learning, nor indeed to the genuine works of John the Scot: it seems to have been a simple error of ascription. It is more significant that in following Ratramnus Berengar found the consensus of scholarly opinion against him; Paschasius had a measure of support that he had never known in his lifetime. The rest of Berengar's early teaching can only be inferred in the most fragmentary way from the reactions of his critics. Perhaps in these lost writings he did go far beyond Ratramnus, but we can only postulate that he did: from the evidence that survives Berengar's original position can still be expressed in the traditional words of the liturgy.

Berengar's real contribution to eucharistic theology was in forcing his critics to clarify their own views. Among Fulbert's pupils Hugh of Langres was ready to argue that—

If the nature and being of the bread and wine fundamentally remain after consecration, nothing can be held to have been altered . . . So you have this choice:
either you change the nature of the bread entirely,
or you do not dare to call it the body of Christ.
If you were to say that the bread retains its own nature, and yet is not powerless as a sacrament, you would be speaking against reason: if you maintain its nature, you are still removing its inherent qualities. But so long as a thing retains its own nature it cannot lose the qualities inherent in its nature.[2]

---

[1] J. de Montclos, *Lanfranc et Bérenger: la controverse eucharistique du xie siècle* (Louvain, 1971: *Spic.Sacr.Lovan.* 37), p. 49, with references.

[2] 'Namque si panis et vini natura et essentia reali principalitate post consecrationem persistunt, translatum nihil potest intelligi . . . Quapropter necesse est ut aut panem omnino a sua natura deiicias, aut ipsum Christi corpus dicere non praesumas. Quod si forte dixeris et suam naturam retinere et tamen non esse impotens sacramentum, contra rationem loqueris: si cui naturam conferes inhaerentia tollis. Omnes enim res, dum in sua natura consistunt, ab inhaerentibus naturae non recedunt': *Letter to Berengar*, ed.cit., 1327 AD, slightly simplified in translation.

Hugh's position is founded on the wholehearted acceptance of Aristotle's *Categories* that eventually produced the classic eucharistic formula of the twelfth century. In addition his treatise owes its form to the practical rhetoric of the schools: 'you will object', 'but I reply'; Hugh has already adopted some of the simple machinery of scholastic analysis that marks Lanfranc's commentary on the Pauline Epistles. But he believed that the last word lay with the Fathers, particularly Ambrose:

Cease then to be Error's knight, doing battle with a heavenly mystery; and remember that the will of God and the word of God are above the whole of nature. He has the power to create; believe also that he has the power to change . . . For with God to will is to do.[1]

On similar lines the dean of Chartres maintained that the natural order was inseparable from the will of God:

You accuse me of over-riding the laws of nature. I reply that nature is nothing other than the will of God . . .[2] For him, to will is to do.

Berengar's critics in the early days were unanimous here, but the position proved hard to defend. If the natural world had some autonomy, however relative, then either its laws were incessantly broken by the Eucharist or the eucharistic conversion should be explicable in terms of these laws. The theologian choosing the latter alternative was committed still more deeply to Aristotle.

These scholarly arguments took some time to reach Rome: indeed the papacy showed little academic initiative before the 1070s. In 1054 at the synod of Tours Hildebrand accepted the simple assertion that 'the bread and wine on the altar after consecration are the body and blood of Christ.'[3] Berengar himself had drafted this formula and was ready to confirm it on oath without reservation. But the problem remained: in what sense were the consecrated elements really Christ? It was not enough for the bread to *be a sacrament of* the body of Christ; it must *be* the body of Christ, absolutely. Either the bread and wine were fundamentally changed or (so it seemed) they were a mockery: image and reality were now directly opposed. Whatever the difficulties for the theologian, the plain man's choice could not

[1] Ibid. 1328CD.
[2] *Letter to Berengar:* D'Achery (*V.L.* pagination), p. 25D (=Migne, *P.L.* cl.67D).
[3] *D.S.C.*, p. 52.

be in doubt; and five years later cardinal Humbert swung to the other extreme from the conservative and innocuous definition of 1054. His formula expresses with brutal clarity the most straightforward solution of all:

I believe that the bread and wine which are laid on the altar are after consecration not only a sacrament but also the true body and blood of our lord Jesus Christ, and they are physically taken up and broken in the hands of the priest and crushed by the teeth of the faithful, not only sacramentally but in truth.[1]

The tentative and qualified definitions, the silence before a mystery, are thrust aside: it is a blunt assertion that the Eucharist is 'real'. Humbert was never a half-measures man; but his formula still seems extraordinarily crude. Yet he found it, as he thought, in one of Augustine's sermons on St. John: 'The man who is not in Christ and Christ in him certainly does not eat his flesh and drink his blood.' Augustine's meaning is plain, and far from Humbert's; but by the eighth century the passage had acquired an explanatory gloss—'even if he physically and visibly crush with his teeth the sacrament of the body and blood of Christ'.[2] The way was open for Humbert's simple statement of the plain truth. His formula cannot be ignored. It was circulated widely by Nicholas II as the official papal and indeed Christian position, and as such it was quoted by Ivo of Chartres and passed into Gratian's *Decretum*.[3] Yet it could not but embarrass the world of learning; and although Lanfranc undertook its defence as a conciliar edict, neither he nor his successors attempted its justification as theology.

iii. the *Liber de corpore et sanguine Domini*

Lanfranc, a Catholic by the mercy of God, to Berengar, the adversary of the Catholic Church. (*L.D.C.S.D.*, cap. 1)

---

[1] 'Profiteor ... eam fidem tenere ... scilicet panem et vinum quae in altari ponuntur post consecrationem non solum sacramentum sed etiam verum corpus et sanguinem domini nostri Iesu Christi esse, et sensualiter non solum sacramento sed in veritate manibus sacerdotum tractari frangi et fidelium dentibus atteri': *L.D.C.S.D.*, cap. 2.

[2] *Tractatus in Iohannem* xxvi. 18: *Corp.Christ.Ser.Lat.* xxxvi. 268 and app., expounding John 6:56. See L. Hödl, 'Die *Confessio Berengarii* von 1059', *Scholastik* xxxvii (1962), 370–94.

[3] A. Friedberg, *Corpus Iuris Canonici* (Leipzig, 1879), i.1328–9: *Decretum* III *De Consecratione dist.* II. xlii, with references.

There were two sides to the eucharistic formula of 1059. Theologically it was at best primitive, but legally it was impregnable. What Leo IX had begun Nicholas II completed, and that not in isolation but with the support of a council that was in size and scope almost ecumenical. (Humbert at least had no doubt that the Greek Church fell within the jurisdiction of Rome; and here Lanfranc seems to have agreed with him. He thought in terms of 'the universal Church', 'the Church throughout all the world', with no reservation that the Greeks, if consulted, might have the right to differ.) Against this monolithic institution with its divine authority stood the arch-deacon of Angers and the rabble that followed him: in defiance of the papal edict and the unanimous faith of the Church.[1] 'You would have us believe', Lanfranc concludes—in a passage that could readily be applied to the Spiritual Franciscans—

that the Gospel was preached to all nations, the world believed, the Church was founded, grew and prospered—but by the blind folly of men it later went astray and perished, and in us alone and those who follow us does the holy Church remain on earth.

The true Church is hidden and the Roman Church, that flourishing and increasingly wealthy institution, is its false image: 'the church of the malignant . . . the see of Satan'.[2] It may seem an excessive reaction. But for Lanfranc the funda-mental marks of the Church were unity and peace: not in a future eschatological state only, but here on earth. In the words of the Psalmist—'Jerusalem is built as a city that is at unity in itself . . . Pray for the peace of Jerusalem: they shall prosper that love thee' (Ps. 122:3,6). One single heretic was too many, rather as in Anselmian theology the slightest imperfection was no less lamentable than the greatest.[3] Here essentially is what Lanfranc is defending: not the 1059 settlement in itself but the universal authority of the contemporary Church (summed up in pope and council) which reflected and guaranteed its peace and unity.

The historic Church—the Church in time rather than in

---

[1] *L.D.C.S.D.*, caps. 1–2: note that the passage 'Ad haec Gregorii septimi tempore . . . ab ea recesserant' (cap. 2) is a later interpolation.

[2] *L.D.C.S.D.*, caps. 22–3; cap. 16.

[3] R. W. Southern, *St. Anselm and his Biographer* (Cambridge, 1963), pp. 103–4.

space—was represented by the Fathers. The central text still comes from Ambrose. Christ can create from nothing; he has also the power—

> that things which do exist should continue in being and be changed into something else.

Lanfranc had edited the *De Sacramentis* at Bec; so he was able to cite a variant reading and its relation to a passage in the *De Mysteriis*.[1] He had a precise knowledge of his most important source, however interpreted. The supporting material is largely (and possibly wholly) Carolingian. Paschasius' treatise had attracted a string of proof-texts, at Corbie itself in the ninth century, then a century later in the work of Heriger of Lobbes. A former *scholasticus* in Liège, Heriger wrote a brief treatise on the Eucharist, summarizing the Carolingian debate and certain more recent opinions, and increasing the Corbie proof-texts to twenty-one.[2] Lanfranc draws freely on both collections, but especially the latter. Eighteen of his patristic quotations coincide with Heriger's, some exactly, others with a line added or removed. Gregory, Augustine, Ambrose, Leo the Great, the First Council of Ephesus: they were all to hand in Heriger's *catena*. Lanfranc treated them just as he had Florus' *Collectaneum* for his commentary on Paul: intelligently used, both Florus and Heriger saved a great deal of work. He checked his references, but where possible he used material that was already to hand.[3] It is only in the final pages of the *Liber de corpore et sanguine Domini* that Lanfranc's choice of quotations seems to be original,[4] and there he is no longer arguing a case; he is heaping

---

[1] *L.D.C.S.D.*, cap. 9: Ambrose, *De Sacramentis* iv.15, *De Mysteriis* ix.52, ed. Faller (*Corp.Script.Eccles.Lat.* lxxiii: 1955), pp. 52 and 112.

[2] For the nine Corbie proof-texts see Paschasius, *De corpore et sanguine Domini*, ed. Paul, *Corp.Christ.Cont.Med.* xvi (1969), 162–9. For Heriger's *Exaggeratio* (i.e. the 'enlargement' of the Corbie *catena*) see Ratramnus, *De corpore et sanguine Domini*, ed. Bakhuizen van den Brink, 2nd edn. (Amsterdam/London, 1974), pp. 29–32; cf. pp. 6–7.

[3] Lanfranc cites, sometimes more than once, Corbie nos. III, VI and Heriger nos. 4, 5, 7, 10, 12, 13, cf. no. 8. He abbreviates e.g. Corbie no. VI, and expands e.g. Heriger no. 12. The quotation (cap. 10) from *Passio Andreae* 6 may have been suggested by the *Dicta Herigeri*: Migne, *P.L.*cxxxix.187C.

[4] *L.D.C.S.D.*, caps. 19–23. The unidentified quotations in caps. 1–18 are: Gregory the Great to Justin (cap.13); Augustine, *De catechizandis rudibus* (caps. 13, 17, 20); Gregory the Great to Savinus (cap.17); Ambrose to Irenaeus (cap.18); Augustine *in Psalmos* xlv and lxv (cap.18).

text upon text to show the overwhelming doctrinal unanimity of the Fathers.

Beyond the scholars and intellectuals was the whole body of the faithful; and they too declared the mind of the Church. Popular belief throughout the centuries had been reinforced by eucharistic miracles, nor were these discounted by the learned:[1] Lanfranc himself told of an incident in his boyhood when a priest had found real flesh and blood on the altar during Mass, and the visibly converted elements had been sealed as relics within the altar.[2] The only difference here was that the elements were *seen* to be converted; the miracle itself was repeated at every celebration of the Eucharist. The miraculous continually impinged on normal life—as can be seen in the safeguards lest the power so released should be misapplied. In Lanfranc's own *Constitutions* the measures enjoined if the consecrated bread were lost or the wine spilt go well beyond the maintenance of good order.[3] A detached Lanfrancian note, that circulated in England, shows his attitude more clearly still:

The priest should not leave any other bread or wine on the altar during Mass, lest his blessing should pass by accident to the bread and wine that is adjacent, as Isaac's blessing passed to Jacob. Isaac blessed Jacob, but he thought he was blessing Esau.[4]

The power might escape, and go wrong. Given the comprehensive authority of the universal Church, present and historic, the intelligentsia and the simple believers, it may well be asked why Lanfranc went further. Might he not have followed Theoduin of Liège, who regarded the whole matter as already settled? Heretics were heretics, and they had no right to a hearing. Lanfranc is in fact closer to Theoduin's position than may at first appear.

The *Liber de corpore et sanguine Domini* is cast as a dialogue

[1] *L.D.C.S.D.*, caps. 17; 19.

[2] Guitmund of La Croix-St.-Leofroy, *De corporis et sanguinis Christi veritate* ii: Migne, *P.L.*cxlix.1449D–50A.

[3] *Constitutions*, pp. 90–2.

[4] 'Nec super altare ullo modo remaneat panis vel vinum infra missam preter illa que sacrabit sacerdos, ne forte transeat benedictio sacerdotis ad panem que (sic)a regione est, vel ad vinum: sicut transivit benedictio Ysaac super Iacob. Ysaac namque benedixit Iacob, et tamen putabat se benedicere Esau. Hoc exemplum protulit de hoc Lanfrancus': MS. Oxford Bodleian Barlow 37, fol.48v (s.xii[1]: English); cf. MS. Durham Cath.Lib.B.IV.24, fol. 126, where the passage is added (s.xii[1]) to the St. Carilef manuscript of Lanfranc's *Constitutions*.

between Lanfranc and Berengar, in lieu perhaps of the personal confrontation that had been projected since 1050, but had never taken place.[1] Berengar's contribution consists of excerpts from his lost treatise of *c.* 1060; Lanfranc provides the replies. Of course Lanfranc has chosen the excerpts in the first place: his fundamental skill, as always, was in presenting material to make a case. Here he misses nothing. 'I was always ready to meet you, but you hadn't the nerve to face educated critics.' 'You bought your way out of trouble.' 'You manipulate your sources; you are congenitally inaccurate.' 'You are incapable of constructing a valid syllogism; you are indifferent to truth, perjured, irreverent and finally trivial.'[2] Morally dishonourable and logically inconsistent, Berengar could scarcely be doctrinally sound. Like Anselm of Besate, but here in a 'live' argument, Lanfranc sets his opponent's words and actions in the worst possible light, so that they stand self-condemned.[3] Frivolous though it may appear now, it was the accepted rhetorical practice of the time, and not without effect. Berengar's intellectual insolvency is established in three brief passages of arms, which also illustrate Lanfranc's own methods of disputation:[4]

BERENGAR: The light shineth in the darkness, and the darkness comprehended it not (John 1:5).

LANFRANC: In the darkness of this world the light of faith illumines what we can see through a glass darkly (I Cor. 13:12), if God reveals it. But your clouded intellect cannot perceive this light; for in thinking itself uniquely wise it has lost itself in futile hypotheses and become foolish in the sight of God (Rom.1:21–2).

Lanfranc's answer here is a tissue of Pauline phrases brought together by the argument of Rom. 1:18–25. It is a master-stroke that he does not actually quote Paul's conclusion: 'they have changed *the truth of God* into a lie' (Rom. 1:25). But the reader will supply it, especially when he sees the second exchange:

---

[1] There is no record that Lanfranc and Berengar met or corresponded after the ducal court at Brionne (autumn 1050); cf. p. 67, n. 6 above.

[2] See e.g. *L.D.C.S.D.*, cap. 1 (cowardice and triviality); cap. 2 (irreverence and corruption); cap. 3 (indifference to truth); caps. 4–5 (perjury); cap. 7 (incompetence in logic); cap. 9 (manipulation of sources); cap. 10 (inaccuracy); cap. 20 (bribery).

[3] See above, pp. 13–14.

[4] *L.D.C.S.D.*, cap.3.

BERENGAR: The enemy of *the truth* affirms the truth, whether he will or no.

LANFRANC: The man who affirms the truth, willingly or otherwise, you hold to be an enemy of the truth. But whoever affirms the truth does so either intentionally or not: there is no halfway position. So you will have it that everyone who affirms the truth is an enemy of the truth. But that is intolerable. The Truth himself uses a very different name for those who acknowledge him: Now I call you not servants but friends (John 15:15).

In reversing Berengar's proposition—'The enemy is an affirmer' to 'The affirmer is an enemy' Lanfranc is guilty of sharp practice by his own standards as much as ours. In the final exchange he returns to exegesis:

BERENGAR: The Burgundian perishes by his own sword, like Goliath.

LANFRANC: You call yourself David and Humbert Goliath. You would do well to call yourself Goliath, for you are the most arrogant of men, and you will perish by what you think, write and say, as though by your own sword. It is Humbert who is David . . . fighting for the Church with the shield of faith and the sword of the spirit which is the word of God (Eph. 6:16–17).

The Pauline 'armour of God' is referred to David's victory over Goliath, who signifies the arrogance of heretics; perverting Scripture they are finally defeated with their own weapons:

When David had overcome Goliath, he killed him with his own sword, as the saints defeat the heretics with the same words and texts with which the heretics themselves attack.[1]

Lanfranc is professing the same strategy: Berengar's own most cherished texts will be turned against him. Throughout these exchanges Lanfranc appears as the exegete, fluent in the cross-references and multiple significance of Scripture. Even his logic in the second passage depends on a gospel text, and designedly so; for the *Liber de corpore et sanguine Domini* is not primarily a doctrinal thesis, but an exposition of Scripture and tradition clarified (where unavoidable) in the terms of contemporary

[1] Angelomus of Luxeuil, *Enarrationes in Libros Regum* I. xvii (I Sam.17: 49–51): Migne, *P.L.*cxv.313BC, abridged. Angelomus' commentary is the basis of the twelfth-century *Gloss* on I Sam. 17:40. David killed Goliath with a stone and then beheaded him with his own sword.

philosophy. Lanfranc is reluctant to enter the arena of the *artes* at all, and he does so only to show that there too he can win.

Berengar's initial error is to propose not statements but concealed questions. But proof must begin from what is already established; so his argument is rotten at the foundation.[1] Having discredited Berengar at a deliberately simple level of logic, Lanfranc's next move is more subtle—and more dubious:

BERENGAR: *Non* constare poterit affirmatio *omnis*, parte subruta.[2]

> If a part were to be removed, the affirmation *as a whole* would *not* stand.

LANFRANC [taking two words out of context]:

> The form *non omnis* is a PARTICULAR NEGATIVE (Not every A is B).
>
> The form *nulla* is the UNIVERSAL NEGATIVE (No A is B).
>
> Your statements (i) 'The bread and wine are only sacraments' and (ii) 'The bread and wine are only the body and blood of Christ' are both affirmations.
>
> But your PARTICULAR NEGATIVE (*non omnis*) need not apply to either (i) or (ii). Had you written *nulla*, it would be a different matter:
>
> *Nulla* affirmatio constare poterit, parte subruta.
>
> 'Panis et vinum solummodo sunt sacramenta' est affirmatio.
>
> 'Panis et vinum solummodo sunt sacramenta' non constare poterit, parte subruta.
>
> As it is, you have constructed an invalid syllogism.

It is useless to point out that the 'particular negative' is of Lanfranc's own making; and that in any case Berengar is probably referring to neither (i) nor (ii) but to the words of consecration, 'Hoc est corpus meum.' As a debating-point it was sufficient; and any but the most exacting reader would credit Lanfranc with victory. Indeed it was a stylish victory, that depended not on the routine progression of a syllogism but on one of the newer tricks of logic. In the study of Christian doctrine, Lanfranc writes,

---

[1] 'His duobus vitiosissimis principiis totam argumentationem tuam identidem repetendo ad finem usque contexis': *L.D.C.S.D.*, cap.7; cf. caps. 6–7 as a whole.

[2] *L.D.C.S.D.*, cap. 7.

I have no desire to propose logical problems or to solve them. Even if the subject-matter is such that it can be more clearly explained by dialectic, so far as possible I conceal this art by *equipollency of propositions*, lest I seem to put more trust in art than in truth and the authority of the holy Fathers.[1]

Here Berengar's original proposition is replaced by what is alleged to be its exact equivalent; the crux of Lanfranc's case is the substitution of the one for the other.[2] Like the heretics of old, Berengar is vanquished with his own weapons.

Happily Lanfranc does not continue in this vein. In the discussion of a sacred subject the logical word-game was not enough: what is held by faith should also be explored in faith or, to use a Pauline expression, 'secundum rationem fidei' (Rom. 12:6). The tag is not Lanfranc's; but it was widely used by his contemporaries (including Berengar), and it exactly expresses the tension they felt between faith and logic.[3] No one doubted the validity of logic as a way to truth: yet patristic opinion had as much force as the most watertight syllogism. But it should at least be possible to discuss the truth of faith according to its own terms of reference: not apprehended mystically nor accepted blindly but analysed, within the given framework

---

[1] 'In tractatu divinarum litterarum nec proponere nec ad propositas respondere cuperem dialecticas quaestiones vel earum solutiones. Et si quando materia disputandi talis est, ut huius artis regulis valeat enucleatius explicari, in quantum possum per aequipollentias propositionum tego artem, ne videar magis arte quam veritate sanctorumque patrum auctoritate confidere': *L.D.C.S.D.*, cap. 7, reading 'huius artis regul*is*' with MS. London B. L. Royal 5 A.XV and other early manuscripts. See further p. 57, nn. 2–3, above.

[2] 'Equipollency' had been a technical term in Antiquity, and was to become so once more: see Ps.-Apuleius, περὶ ἑρμηνίας, ed. Thomas (Leipzig, 1908: Tbnr), p. 181; Abbo of Fleury, *Syllogismorum Categoricorum et Hypotheticorum Enodatio*, ed. van de Vyver (Bruges, 1966), pp. 41–2; Garlandus, *Dialectica* vi, ed. de Rijk (Assen, 1959), pp. 131–5; Abelard, *Dialectica* ii, ed. de Rijk (Assen, 1956), 191–2.

[3] St. Paul's original meaning is quite different: 'according to the proportion of your faith' (A.V.); 'to the limit of your vision' (Philipps). For the eleventh-century use of the term see e.g. Durand of Fécamp, *De corpore et sanguine Christi* iv: 'sanctorum patrum dicta nonulla subteximus quae . . . ad rationem fidei roborandam satis . . . idonea' (Migne, *P.L.* cxlix. 1384C). Other examples are Adelmann of Liège, *Letter to Berengar*, ed. Huygens, 'Textes latins du xiᵉ au xiiiᵉ siècle', *Stud.Med.* viii (1967), 478, line 74; Anastasius, *De corpore et sanguine Domini* (Migne, *P.L.* cxlix.433D); Berengar, *D.S.C.*, pp. 94, 176, and Letter 83 (ed.cit., p. 65, n. 1 above), p. 137. Paschasius sees an absolute contrast (as the later scholars do not) between *humana ratio* and *ratio fidei*: *De corpore et sanguine Domini*, ed.cit., (p. 74, n. 2 above), i. 165–70.

of dogma. This is outstandingly Anselm's achievement in his *Meditatio de ratione fidei* (his early title for the *Monologion*); and to a lesser degree it is Lanfranc's when, having eventually cleared all the ground, he essays a positive eucharistic confession:[1]

> The material objects on the Lord's Table which God sanctifies through the priest are by the agency of God's power indefinably, wondrously, in a way beyond our understanding, converted to the body of Christ in their being. Their outward appearance and certain other qualities remain unchanged, so that those who receive them are not shocked by the naked flesh and blood, and so that believers may receive the greater rewards of faith ...
>
> What we receive is the very body which was born of the Virgin, and yet it is not. It *is*, in respect of its being and the characteristics and power of its true nature; it *is not*, if you look at the outward appearance of the bread and wine.

In essentials Lanfranc is still—as he would wish to be—close to Ambrose. By the power of God the eucharistic elements are changed into what they had not been before—and really so, not just 'in a manner of speaking'. Precisely how the change is effected is beyond our comprehension. Lanfranc's language is more technical: *terrena substantia, essentia, species, proprietas naturae* reflect the eucharistic prayer and discussion of the intervening six centuries. One crucial phrase comes from the liturgy for Christmas Day—'As he who was born a man shone forth as God, so may this *material object* endow us with what is divine.'[2]

---

[1] 'Credimus igitur *terrenas substantias,* quae in mensa dominica per sacerdotale mysterium divinitus sanctificantur, ineffabiliter, incomprehensibiliter, mirabiliter, operante superna potentia, *converti in essentiam dominici corporis, reservatis* ipsarum rerum *speciebus* et quibusdam aliis qualitatibus, ne percipientes cruda et cruenta horrerent, et ut credentes fidei praemia ampliora perciperent; [ipso tamen dominico corpore existente in caelestibus ad dexteram Patris, immortali inviolato integro, incontaminato, illaeso: ut vere dici possit,] et ipsum corpus quod de Virgine sumptum est nos sumere, et tamen non ipsum. Ipsum quidem *quantum ad essentiam veraeque naturae proprietatem atque virtutem*; non ipsum autem si spectes panis vinique *speciem,* [ceteraque superius comprehensa]': *L.D.C.S.D.,* cap. 18. I have not translated the words in square brackets.

[2] '[Munera nostra quesumus domine nativitatis hodierne mysteriis apta proveniant, ut] sicut homo genitus idem refulsit deus, sic nobis haec *terrena substantia* conferat quod divinum est': *Sacramentarium Gregorianum,* ed. Lietzmann (Münster-i.-W., 1921), p. 11, no. 7, 4, quoted in *D.S.C.,* p. 283. See also the eleventh-century addition to Paschasius, *De corpore et sanguine Domini,* ed.cit. xxi. 298–302; Hugh of Langres, *Letter to Berengar* (Migne, *P.L.*cxlii. 1330B); and Durand, *De corpore et sanguine Christi* ii (Migne, *P.L.*cxlix. 1380A).

Terrena substantia is the visible, material bread; and in principle (though not invariably)[1] Lanfranc keeps to the ancient usage. For the invisible 'being' of the eucharistic elements, in contrast with their outward appearance, he follows his immediate predecessors: Hugh of Langres and Durand of Fécamp. The change affects the *natura et essentia* of the bread and wine (Hugh); the elements become the body and blood of Christ 'secundum naturae proprietatem' or 'per proprietatem naturalis veritatis integerrimam' (Durand).[2] These words are free from liturgical overtones; and *essentia* in particular is a good equivalent for *substantia* in the Aristotelian sense of the fundamental nature of an object, as distinct from its perceptible characteristics. In proposing that the eucharistic change affects the elements in their *essentia*, while 'their outward appearance and other qualities remain unchanged', Lanfranc has in effect put forward the theory of transsubstantiation: the substance changes, the accidents remain. But his language is still hesitant and experimental. Earlier in the treatise he clarifies *essentia* in three different ways: 'in pristinis essentiis' (cap. 5), 'in principalibus essentiis' (caps. 7–8), 'secundum interiorem essentiam' (cap. 9). Although none of these is incompatible, a single agreed phrase would be more convincing. This is not the stable language of eucharistic theology; it is still the jargon of contemporary scholarship, tools caught up for a specific purpose and as quickly laid aside. Its limitations can be seen in a comparable argument advanced by cardinal Humbert. Here a bishop's consecrated status is linked to his temporalities as substance to accidents; the estates 'are contained by and contain the episcopal dignity, just as a subject so contains its accidents that these very accidents define the subject'.[3] Striking though the

---

[1] Lanfranc is inconsistent in his use of *substantia*: 'panem et vinum . . . inter sacrandum . . . in substantiam carnis et sanguinis commutari' (cap. 8); cf. his summary of Berengar's position, 'panem vinumque . . . inter consecrandum quantum ad substantiam immobilia [*sic*] permanere' (cap. 22).

[2] Hugh of Langres, op.cit., col.1327AB; Durand, op.cit., vii (col. 1411C); iv (col.1387C).

[3] 'Continet autem episcopalis dignitas res Deo sacratas, continetur quoque ab eis, immo in eis, utputa et ipsa a Deo consecrata, ac si quodlibet subiectum sic sua accidentia contineat, ut id quoque ab ipsis principalius contineatur': *Adversus simoniacos* III.ii: *Mon.Ger.Hist.Libelli de Lite* (Hanover, 1891), i. 200, lines 20–2; cf. lines 20–31. It is possible that Lanfranc was indebted to Humbert's analogy, but much more likely that he adapted a current scholastic formula independently.

analogy may be, it is never fully worked out; it is merely an impressive device. In the same way Lanfranc's more elaborate terminology is little more than display, easily detached from his main argument.

Aristotle's concept of substance might be the philosophical key to the Eucharist, but Lanfranc still put his trust in the Fathers; over half his treatise is patristic quotation.[1] It is here that his real contribution lies. The *Liber de corpore et sanguine Domini* offered a thorough yet convenient summary of patristic thought; Lanfranc continually reiterated that sure guidance could be found nowhere else. Much that Paschasius had believed was set aside, particularly the concept of eucharistic union with Christ: flesh of his flesh and bone of his bone, our bodies are spiritually united with his.[2] Edifying metaphor though this might be, it implied a personal identification with Christ that was ultimately heretical, and Lanfranc cut it out. In returning, so far as he could, to the original purity of the Fathers, he prepared the way for the definitive modern formula of transsubstantiation. Here, as in so many respects, Lanfranc saw the Promised Land from afar off.

iv. the outcome of the controversy

As a reply to Berengar that could be placed on the most ortho- dox shelves, a eucharistic treatise founded four-square on the Fathers, Lanfranc's book was widely accepted throughout northern Europe: it became a standard component of any manuscript entitled 'De corpore et sanguine Domini';[3] Ivo of Chartres included excerpts in his *Decretum*.[4] The recipient of the

---

[1] Lanfranc's treatise is like any sentence-collection in its high proportion of patristic texts, rather tentatively elaborated by the modern master. See O. Lottin, *Psychologie et morale aux xii*[e] *et xiii*[e] *siècles* (Gembloux, 1959), v.18 (list of manuscripts) and *passim*. (Lottin prints *only* the 'modern' additions.)

[2] Paschasius, *De corpore et sanguine Domini*, ed. Paul, *Corp.Christ.Cont.Med.* xvi (1969), XIX: 'Carn[i] quidem [nostrae] caro [Christi] spiritaliter conviscerata' (lines 12–13); 'ex ipso per ipsum refecti convisceremur in Christo' (line 58); 'in ipso concorporati inveniuntur' (lines 70–1). For the last cf. Durand, op.cit. xv (col.1398C).

[3] Lanfranc supplied the polemicist Bernold of Constance with much of the patristic and historical material for his account of the controversy (1088). See Bernold, *De veritate corporis et sanguinis Domini*; cf. R. B. C. Huygens, 'Bérenger de Tours, Lanfranc et Bernold de Constance', *Sacris Erudiri* xvi (1965), 355–87.

[4] Ivo, *Decretum* ii.9 (*L.D.C.S.D.*, caps. 9–23: excerpts), ii.10 (*L.D.C.S.D.*, cap.2: 1059 oath). Ivo may have studied at Bec: see above, pp. 36–7.

treatise took it very seriously indeed. The so-called *De Sacra Coena* is a phrase-by-phrase reply to the *Liber de corpore et sanguine Domini*: precept upon precept, line upon line.[1] In long parenthetical diatribes and with unimaginable repetition Berengar heaps scorn on his opponent, demolishing his arguments or overwhelming them with an avalanche of words. Yet Berengar had a case, and he had something to say: his eucharistic faith was a great deal more complex than Lanfranc would allow. For instance it was simply not true that he understood the Eucharist as merely the memorial of Christ's passion.[2] Berengar too relied on the *De Sacramentis*, interpreting the crucial text in a way that Ambrose would perhaps have found more acceptable than eleventh-century orthodoxy.[3] The best indication of his fundamental belief, beyond the exigencies of debate, is a fragment from his treatise of *c.* 1060:

The eucharistic sacrifice has two constituents, the sacrament, which is visible, and that to which the sacrament refers (the *res sacramenti*), which is invisible. The latter is the body of Christ. If it were before our eyes it would be visible, but being exalted into heaven and sitting at the right hand of the Father 'until the time of the restoration of all things' . . . it cannot be summoned down from heaven, as the person of Christ consists of God and man.[4]

It is a reasonable position, that does not preclude the belief that Christ is present in the sacrament. In the *De Sacra Coena* itself Berengar repeatedly contrasts the bread and wine as objects in themselves (the *sacramentum*) with the power or spiritual benefit

---

[1] For the text of *D.S.C.* see R. B. C. Huygens, 'À propos de Bérenger et son traité de l'Eucharistie', *Rev.Bén.* lxxvi (1966), 133–9. Berengar wrote the book *c.*1065–73, when he was probably back in Tours: see the reference to Hildebrand, who 'adhuc superest' (p. 49).

[2] 'Tu credis . . . Christi carnem et sanguinem propterea vocari quod in memoriam crucifixae carnis et de latere effusi sanguinis in ecclesia celebrentur, ut dominicam passionem per hoc admoniti semper recolamus, et recolentes carnem nostram cum vitiis et concupiscentiis incessanter crucifigamus': *L.D.C.S.D.*, cap. 22.

[3] *L.D.C.S.D.*, cap.9; cf. *D.S.C.*, pp. 180–2.

[4] 'Sacrificium . . . ecclesiae duobus constat, duobus conficitur: visibili et invisibili, sacramento et re sacramenti. Quae tamen res (id est Christi corpus) si esset prae oculis, visibilis esset; sed elevata in caelum sedensque ad dexteram Patris "usque in tempora restitutionis omnium", quod scribit apostolus Petrus (Acts 3:21), caelo devocari non poterit, sicut Christi persona Deo constat et homine': *L.D.C.S.D.*, cap. 10 (punctuation mine).

which they convey (the *res sacramenti*): 'their appearance is material, their fruit spiritual'.[1] Lanfranc's error is to insist that the external appearance (the *species*) of the bread and wine is physically combined with the *res sacramenti*: the sacrament is no longer a 'sign' pointing beyond itself. At the same time Berengar and Lanfranc were not diametrically opposed. They had far more in common than either would admit, and in the end of the day Zachary of Besançon said as much:

There are not a few—indeed they are plentiful, but unobtrusive— who are of the same opinion as the condemned Berengar, yet they condemn him as the Church does. This was his crime: in rejecting the verbal formula of the Church, he caused scandal by his own plain speech.[2]

Berengar may not have been a more learned man than Lanfranc, but his range was wider. He could certainly see the problem of the Eucharist in terms of logic: if the words 'Hoc est corpus meum' remove the substance of the bread and wine, then the subject *hoc* is destroyed by its own predicate.[3] Berengar escapes from his verbal dilemma into the doctrinal impasse that the words of consecration effect no substantial change. He would seem to be on more promising ground when he turns to physics. The eucharistic conversion proposed by his opponents is 'a change in the nature of the bread and wine' (Durand), 'a material change' (Lanfranc) or as Berengar himself put it the 'corruption' of one physical object as it becomes another:[4] this is the language of Chalcidius and Macrobius as much as the *logica vetus*. Berengar is at least as interested in the work of the *physici* as he is in the logicians. With the growing academic competence in the quadrivium, in which Berengar himself may

---

[1] *D.S.C.*, p. 166 (quoting Augustine). Fr. Häring has argued in a notable study that Berengar was attempting a very much more precise definition of a sacrament than his contemporaries would accept: 'Berengar's definitions of *Sacramentum* and their influence on medieval sacramentology', *Medieval Studies* x (1948), 109–46, particularly 111–12.

[2] *In Vnum ex Quattuor* iv (Migne, *P.L.*clxxvi.508B), composed at Laon *c.* 1150.

[3] *D.S.C.*, pp. 107–8; cf. p. 87, n. 2 above. See R. W. Southern, 'Lanfranc of Bec and Berengar of Tours', in *Studies in Medieval History presented to F. M. Powicke*, ed. R. W. Hunt *et al.* (Oxford, 1948), pp. 45–6.

[4] Durand, op.cit., cols.1380A, 1397C, 1405A; Lanfranc, *L.D.C.S.D.*, cap.5; Berengar, *D.S.C.*, pp. 94, 161–2.

have played a minor part,[1] 'the nature of physical reality'[2] might well seem a better frame of reference in which to consider the Eucharist. But this approach raised a question that nearly everyone saw to be intractable. What was the physical effect of consecration? Is the holy measurable? Although a few rash spirits did essay an answer,[3] Berengar did not: for most scholars this was the limit of inquiry. When neither physics nor logic could offer a eucharistic definition that was generally valid, it was not blind conservatism that made men cling to the Fathers.

The definitive settlement, for Lanfranc's lifetime, arose from papal necessity rather than academic progress. Gregory VII was no theologian, and he had disregarded Berengar for the most legally productive years of his pontificate. But in the spring of 1078 he was reminded of Berengar (in what terms we do not know) by Hugh of Cluny, and in November Berengar himself was examined at Rome. The inquiry revealed considerable uncertainty in the papal court; the matter was deferred for three months; finally at the pre-Lent synod of 1079 Gregory promulgated a new formula. Berengar accepted it, though unwillingly, and withdrew to an edifying retirement as a hermit near Tours.[4] We cannot turn aside to examine these events in detail, but we may well wonder at the unheralded burst of activity. It seems likely that Gregory was under pressure to confirm that he himself was orthodox. In June 1080 the rebel German bishops at the synod of Brixen alleged *inter alia* that

---

[1] A certain Berengar (who may well have been the archdeacon of Angers) encouraged Hermann of Reichenau to write his treatise on the astrolabe, and himself described how to construct one: N. Bubnov, *Gerberti Opera Mathematica* (Berlin, 1899), pp. 113–14, xx–xxii. For Berengar's medical skill see Letter 97, ed.cit. p. 65, n. 1 above.

[2] See e.g. Hugh of Langres, *Letter to Berengar*: 'Rerum existentium . . . naturam si bene perspiceres' (Migne, *P.L.*cxlii.1326D), and for the outlook of the *physici* in general T. Gregory, *Platonismo medievale* (Rome, 1958).

[3] See e.g. the Norman Anonymous (*c.*1100) on the effects of consecration: *Tractatus* iv, ed. Boehmer (*Mon.Ger.Hist. Libelli de Lite* (Hanover, 1897), iii. 664).

[4] Gregory, *Registrum* v.21 (to Hugh of Cluny); vi.17a (1079 synod): ed. Caspar (Berlin, 1923), ii.384; 425–7. See M. T. Gibson, 'The case of Berengar of Tours', *Studies in Church History* vii (1971), 61–8; R. B. C. Huygens, Bérenger de Tours . . .' (op.cit. p. 91, n. 3 above), pp. 355–403. For Berengar's last years see A. J. Macdonald, *Berengar and the Reform of Sacramental Doctrine* (London, 1930), pp. 198–209.

Gregory sympathized with Berengar's eucharistic opinions.[1] As heresy was the one crime for which a pope could be deposed, it may well be that the abbot of Cluny had given Gregory a timely hint. Whatever the circumstances, the formula of 1079 was considerably more sophisticated than Humbert's original:

I believe . . . that the bread and wine on the altar . . . *are changed in their substance ('substantialiter converti')* into the true . . . flesh and blood of Jesus Christ . . . After consecration they are the true body of Christ born of the Virgin . . . and the blood of Christ which flowed from his side, not symbolically and as a sacrament but *in their real nature and true being.*[2]

The break-through here is *substantialiter,* a new technical term which indicated Aristotelian substance without the risk of confusion with *substantia* in its traditional sense. At the same time a traditional and cherished formula is retained: 'in proprietate naturae et veritate substantiae'.

The oath of 1079 was the work of Alberic, monk of Monte Cassino, who reputedly withdrew from the council to think, and returned a week later with the formula as we have it.[3] But it reflects a great deal more than Alberic's personal invention. Durand of Fécamp had experimented with *substantialiter* as early as the 1050s;[4] and it was brought into regular use by Lanfranc's pupil Guitmund, monk of La Croix-St.-Leofroy. Guitmund's study *De corporis et sanguinis Christi veritate* is the first attempt to assess Berengar's arguments constructively and

---

[1] *Mon.Ger.Hist.Constitutiones* (Hanover, 1893), i.119, lines 39–40. Egilbert, archbishop-elect of Trier, made a similar accusation: 'En verus pontifex et iustus sacerdos, qui . . . dubitat, si illud, quod sumitur in dominica mensa, sit verum corpus et sanguis Christi' (P. Jaffé, *Bibl.Rer.Germ.* (Berlin, 1869), v, no. 61).

[2] 'Ego Beringarius corde credo et ore confiteor panem et vinum, quę ponuntur in altari, per mysterium sacrę orationis et verba nostri Redemptoris *substantialiter converti* in veram et propriam vivificatricem carnem et sanguinem Iesu Christi domini nostri et post consecrationem esse verum Christi corpus quod natum est de Virgine et quod pro salute mundi oblatum in cruce pependit et quod sedet ad dexteram Patris, et verum sanguinem Christi, qui de latere eius effusus est, non tamen per signum et virtutem sacramenti, sed *in proprietate nature et veritate substantie:*' Gregory VII, *Registrum* vi.17a, ed.cit., ii.426–7 (abridged in translation).

[3] P. Meyvaert, 'Bérenger de Tours contre Albéric du Mont-Cassin', *Rev.Bén.* lxx (1960), 324–32, with references.

[4] Durand, op.cit., cols. 1386D; 1405A.

to see the problem of the Eucharist as a whole.[1] It was written *c.* 1073–5, and was presumably known to the synod of Poitiers (1075), which declared that the bread and wine were—

transformed in their substance (substantialiter transmutatum) into the true body and blood of Christ: that same body which was born of the Virgin . . . and that same blood which flowed from his side.

The verbal coincidence here with the formula of 1079 is too close to be fortuitous.[2] In sum, a consensus of scholarly opinion was emerging in the 1070s, not without cross-currents and certainly not repudiating earlier discussion, but effectively committed to the Aristotelian concept of substance and accidents in defining the Eucharist. Throughout the twelfth century this commitment increased *pari passu* with the command of Aristotle, until ultimately the full doctrine of transsubstantiation was enunciated by Innocent III.[3] Logic prevailed over physics—perhaps to the impoverishment of eucharistic thought; and the various cognate issues of baptism, marriage and investiture which had clustered round the problem of the Eucharist were set aside. For the first time eucharistic theology was clearly delimited, with a precise relation to secular learning and a specific place in modern surveys of theology and canon law. Abelard and his contemporaries had in this respect a far simpler task than Durand, Lanfranc, Guitmund and Berengar himself.

Lanfranc's contribution to this complex history is easily exaggerated. In the 1050s, when Berengar was a real threat to the faith, he did nothing; it was Humbert who gave a dogmatic answer, however crude. Nor did the formula that ultimately emerged owe much to Lanfranc exclusively; his own distinctive phraseology 'in principalibus essentiis' or 'secundum interiorem

---

[1] Migne, *P.L.*cxlix. 1427A–94D. See Geiselmann, op.cit., (p. 76, n. 4 above), pp. 375–96, and the illuminating note in H. Jorissen, *Die Entfaltung der Transsubstantiationslehre bis zum Beginn der Hochscholastik* (Münster–i.-W., 1965), pp. 147–8.

[2] R. Somerville, 'The case against Berengar of Tours: a new text', *Studi Gregoriani* ix (1972), 53–75 (text p. 68). The author could well have been a local scholasticus: the schools of Poitiers had a long tradition and a distinguished future in the twelfth century.

[3] Innocent proposed the doctrine in 1202 and again at the Fourth Lateran Council: A. Friedberg, *Corpus Iuris Canonici* (Leipzig, 1881), ii.637; 5. See Jorissen, op.cit., pp. 6–8, with further references.

essentiam' never won acceptance.[1] Lanfranc made one funda- ɔ
mental point at the right time: that without a sound patristic
basis the theologian was lost. Beyond that he did little to clarify
the technical problems of eucharistic definition. What he did
see clearly, and strove to defend, was the peace and unity of the
Church. It was in his vision of the Church universal, agreed and
authoritative in doctrine, that Lanfranc best understood 'the
body of Christ'.

[1] §iii above. Whether Lanfranc ever learned of the 1079 formula is open to doubt:
it was not added to his own canon law book at Canterbury. See Z. N. Brooke, *The
English Church and the Papacy* (Cambridge, 1931), p. 233.

V: Caen 1063–1070

i. St. Étienne, Caen

I am reminded of the emperor Theodosius, who when he went into battle against the tyrants was fortified by the inspired utterances of the monk John, who lived in the Egyptian desert. As he chose John out of all his monks, because by his obedience he had received the gift of prophecy, so William chose Lanfranc, a man filled with the Holy Ghost in word and deed. (*Gesta Guillelmi* i. 52)

To William of Poitiers, who was a court chaplain in the 1060s, duke William's extraordinary political and military success in these years called for a lofty antique parallel: Theodosius the Great campaigning against the usurpers Maximus and Eugenius.[1] It is a strained comparison, but not quite ridiculous, given that William both established control of Normandy itself and campaigned with spectacular success elsewhere. What is more curious is Lanfranc's role as the prophetic monk. There were bishops in Normandy—Odo of Bayeux, Geoffrey of Coutances—energetic, wealthy, not simoniacal, who gave William solid support in his enterprises, on a scale that Lanfranc could never have matched. John of Fécamp was as good an administrator and a more notable man of prayer, in what had traditionally been the family monastery of the dukes of Normandy. Again, it comes as something of a surprise in Lanfranc's life that the prior of Bec, who has not put his name to a single surviving charter, should at a stroke be transformed into the unique figure in Norman politics, and should remain such for the rest of his life. Part at least of the explanation lies in his position as abbot of St. Étienne, Caen.

By 1063 ducal control of Normandy extended far beyond the Risle valley, which had been the effective frontier of the 1040s. William's victory at Mortemer (1054) had confirmed his access to the land west of the Seine basin, the upland country beyond

---

[1] Cf. Augustine, *De Civitate Dei* v. 26.

Bayeux known today as the *bocage*.[1] But a battle is nothing: what
William needed was a centre of administration that commanded
the south and west as well as his original territory in Rouen and
north of the Seine. The Romans had chosen Bayeux; and
William too must have had its strategic value in mind when he
gave the bishopric to his half-brother Odo in 1049. But as a base
for government Caen was better still. Built on the narrow strip
of limestone that divides Lower Normandy from the *bocage*
Caen looked towards Brittany and the west without losing
touch with the Seine valley. It commanded the routes inland to
Le Mans and Chartres and an increasing share of the traffic on
the Orne and the Dives. Caen was more convenient even than
Bayeux; Coutances and Avranches were strategically out of the
question, and Fécamp similarly too remote in the north. It had
already emerged as a trading centre *c.* 1025: Richard III
included in his wife's dowry the *villa* of Caen, with its churches,
toll, fair and market; and over the decades that followed
Fécamp, St. Wandrille and St. Ouen all began to acquire
property in the area.[2] These were still minor investments, but
they were symptomatic; they help to explain the choice of Caen
for William's council in 1047 to proclaim the *treuga dei* after
Val-ès-Dunes.[3] By 1060 William had built a stone castle at
Caen and founded the abbey of Holy Trinity (the Abbaye-aux-
Dames) to the east of the castle and by 1063 St. Étienne (the
Abbaye-aux-Hommes) to the west.[4] The abbeys dominated the
new city; and their first loyalty was to William and the ducal
house. St. Étienne in particular replaced Fécamp as William's
family monastery, providing a supply of literate men and written
documents, a means of control over a complex of estates, a
source of ready cash, a community to pray for the duke and

---

[1] William's reasons for developing Caen are discussed in a brief but illuminating
article by J.-F. Lemarignier, 'L'origine de Lille et de Caen', *Rev.Moyen Âge Lat.* iv
(1948), 191–6; cf. M. de Boüard, 'De la Neustrie carolingienne à la Normandie
féodale: continuité ou discontinuité?', *Bull.Inst.Hist.Res.*xxviii (1955), 1–14.

[2] Lemarignier, op.cit., p. 194, with references; cf. *Fauroux*, nos. 58, 34, 52, 70.
See further L. Musset, 'Actes inédits du xie siècle', *Bull.Soc.Antiq.Norm.* lviii (1965),
119–26.

[3] M. de Boüard, 'Sur les origines de la trêve de Dieu en Normandie', *Annal.
Norm.* ix (1959), 169–89.

[4] Musset, pp. 13–15; no. 2, 4. Traces of William's great hall have been discovered
to the east of the *aula* of Henry I, which still stands: M. de Boüard, 'La salle dite de
l'échiquier, au château de Caen', *Med.Archaeol.* ix (1965), 67–8.

finally an impressive mausoleum. Whoever was abbot of St. Étienne had the ear of the duke, and a unique position in his government.

Lanfranc was abbot for seven years, the first crucial period in the establishment of the monastery. Its initial endowment was in and around Caen, and in the valleys of the Orne and the Dives, probably a more compact group of estates than the scattered resources of Bec. This centralization was achieved not by the casual munificence of benefactors but by steady policy. Lanfranc himself bought, acquired or exchanged a long list of property; and his successors continued in the same way.[1] St. Étienne was founded in an area that had already been built on and parcelled out to many owners, and the early transactions often concern land within Caen itself: for example Lanfranc's purchase of six *iugera* of water-meadow, or his exchange of eight *iugera* immediately in front of St. Étienne for an equal amount in another part of the city.[2] The abbey benefited from the rising value of urban property, from the trade in leather and cloth and from the export of building-stone. The traffic was both local and regional, and increasingly after the Conquest it extended across the Channel.[3] The merchants of Caen were not yet trading on the scale of those of Rouen, but still they used and required liquid cash: St. Étienne thus had both a rising income from tolls and the opportunity to lend money. By abbot William's time (1070–9) the house was already fairly deeply involved in cash transactions.[4] It is in the 1070s that specific documentation begins: but it is clear that Lanfranc had already set his abbey on this course a decade earlier. For William the Conqueror St. Étienne was a much needed extension of his patronage in central Normandy. Whereas the mainstay of Bec had been one

---

[1] Musset, no. 20; cf. 14.

[2] At the Conqueror's funeral one such owner dramatically reasserted his claim to the actual piece of ground in which the body was being interred: Orderic Vitalis, *Hist.Eccles.* vii (Chibnall, IV. 106–7).

[3] Musset, pp. 44–7. For the English estates of Holy Trinity and St. Étienne see D. J. A. Matthew, *The Norman Monasteries and their English Possessions* (Oxford, 1962), pp. 30–1.

[4] Musset, *passim*; cf. idem, 'La vie économique de l'abbaye de Fécamp sous l'abbatiat de Jean de Ravenne (1028–1078)', in *L'Abbaye bénédictine de Fécamp* (Fécamp, 1959), i. 67–79 and, more generally, idem, 'Les conditions financières d'une réussite architecturale: les grandes églises romanes de Normandie', in *Mélanges R. Crozet* (Poitiers, 1966), i. 307–13.

local family, the counts of Brionne, and its associates, the patrons of St. Étienne reflect not only the immediate locality but the ducal court. William himself was a major patron, and as duke he ratified other men's gifts, so establishing his own authority over the property confirmed.[1] In this respect Holy Trinity was as valuable as St. Étienne: the abbess Matilda held the same type of property in the same areas (within Normandy) as Lanfranc. Like Fulk Nerra's abbeys in Anjou and Geoffrey Martel's foundation in 1040 of Holy Trinity, Vendôme, the new houses at Caen stiffened the duke's control of an area in which his direct power was still recent and limited.

Both abbeys were symbols of ducal authority, and from the first they were conceived in the grand manner. The nearest parallel is Jumièges, the greatest architectural achievement to survive from the 1060s, but in certain technical points the Caen churches are more advanced: the 'hollow wall', which had been a tentative expedient at Jumièges, was adopted as an integral feature of St. Étienne. For the St. Étienne west front—twin towers set on a 'westwork'—the model may well have been the original Norman façade of Bayeux cathedral.[2] Much of Lanfranc's work still stands. The choir was rebuilt in the thirteenth century, but the nave is Lanfranc's, subject to modifications at the triforium level by his immediate successors.[3] He was no doubt less involved in the actual construction than he had been at Bec, but the cathedral at Canterbury (1070–7) is sufficient proof that Lanfranc understood the design of the abbey churches of Caen. There too the elaborate western façade and spacious nave matched the function of the church:

[1] Musset, *passim*. The patrons of Bec are not significant patrons of St. Étienne: except for Hugh of Grantmesnil (Musset, no. 6) they appear only to witness other men's donations.

[2] T. S. R. Boase, *English Art 1100–1216* (Oxford, 1953), pp. 3–5; cf. J. Bony, 'La technique normande du mur épais à l'époque romane', *Bulletin Monumental* xcviii (1939), 156–63. The west front is discussed by J. Philip McAleer in an unpublished Ph.D.thesis for the University of London (Courtauld Institute) 1963: 'The Romanesque Church Façade in Britain', pp. 43–60.

[3] J. Merlet, 'L'église St. Étienne de Caen (Calvados)', *Les Monuments historiques de la France* (1968), 62–4, pls. 81–6; for the choir see E. G. Carlson, 'Excavations at St. Étienne, Caen (1969)', *Gesta: International Centre of Medieval Art* X.i (1971), 23–30. There is a useful account of St. Étienne, with excellent photographs, in L. Musset, *Normandie romane* (Pierre-qui-Vire, 1967), i. 51–61, 111; pls. 1–21. See also R. Liess, *Der frühromanische Kirchenbau des elften Jahrhunderts in der Normandie* (Munich, 1967), pp. 183–201, with references.

to accommodate crowds on the great festivals and to manifest the prestige of the community and its cult. Yet St. Étienne, far more than Christ Church, Canterbury, was inextricably involved in ducal affairs. During William's lifetime the abbey had acquired a fragment of the arm and the blood of their patron Stephen; but the more significant relics (briefly though they were held) were the crown, lance and sceptre of England.[1] On his deathbed William presented his greatest trophies to the abbey in which he was to be buried, as the queen had been buried at Holy Trinity. St. Étienne was the focus of piety at once for and towards the ducal house: on the one hand a personal monastery for the dukes themselves, such as would be founded by any great Norman family, and on the other a mausoleum comparable, on however small a scale, with the royal mausoleum of the Salian kings at Speyer.

It need scarcely be said that St. Étienne was a gate to preferment. Whether men had followed Lanfranc from Bec or come directly as novices to St. Étienne, they went on to office elsewhere, sometimes the episcopate, frequently the government of a Norman or English abbey. Most were lifelong monks; but for two archdeacons Caen proved to be a crucial stage in their career. William Bona Anima, archdeacon of Rouen, entered Bec *c.* 1060, and became Lanfranc's prior and successor at St. Étienne, whence he was promoted in 1079 to the see of Rouen itself; William de Rots, monk of St. Étienne and a former archdeacon of Bayeux, went on to be abbot of Fécamp.[2] St. Étienne was a road to higher things. As such it attracted benefactors like Roger of Montgomery, donor of a little commercial enclave on the Dives;[3] and by their common interest these baronial patrons were brought closer to the duke, in whose hands patronage ultimately lay. It is the recurring pattern of endowment and preferment: at Bamberg and Speyer, at Chartres; at Fécamp, briefly at Bec itself and now at St. Étienne, Caen.

In every case the centre of patronage has a school, both in the sense of a group of *alumni* who in later years remember their

---

[1] Musset, nos. 30 (relics of Stephen) and 24 (regalia).

[2] Orderic Vitalis, *Hist.Eccles.* iii–v: Chibnall, II. 254–5, III. 22–5 (William Bona Anima); II. 150–1, 292–5 (William de Rots). Caen remained a centre of preferment well into the twelfth century: C. Hippeau, *L'Abbaye de St. Étienne de Caen, 1066–1790* (Caen, 1855), pp. 55–9.

[3] Trun (dép. Orne: ch.-lieu de canton): Musset, no. 1.

common origin and in the specific sense of a scholastic institution, however ephemeral. St. Étienne is no exception. Lanfranc's reputation as a master at Bec encouraged men to follow him to Caen, where he continued to teach in person. As Nicholas II had sent his chaplains to Bec, the kinsmen of pope Alexander were entrusted to Lanfranc at St. Étienne.[1] By then it seems likely that Lanfranc was more interested in biblical commentary than in the *artes* for their own sake; but the only indication of his curriculum at Caen is an unexpected rubric found in several German manuscripts of the *De corpore et sanguine Domini* The book is attributed to Lanfranc, abbot of Caen, writing 'by the inspiration of the Holy Ghost and at the request of his pupil Theodoric, canon of Paderborn'.[2] If we assume, as I think we must, that the treatise was written within a year or so of the death of cardinal Humbert (May 1061), then it was almost certainly already finished when Lanfranc went to Caen. Possibly he expounded the proof-texts in school; at any rate the rubric is evidence of the rapid distribution of the *De corpore et sanguine Domini* east of the Rhine, even if we discount Theodoric's claim to be humanly speaking its only begetter. Theodoric himself wrote a commentary on the Lord's Prayer, which to a remarkable degree retains the stamp of the *artes*. For instance 'Pater noster *qui es*' gives rise to a discussion of how God 'is':

The being of God is prior to all being; so in saying *qui es* we mean specifically 'God'. His being is indivisible, whereas man is compounded of body and soul, and will dissolve again into these elements. We are right then to begin with God's being and existence, rather than to say with the Fool, 'Non est Deus.'[3]

Though Theodoric was writing in the late 1070s, he could well be indebted here to his studies with Lanfranc. But precisely what he studied, and whether he also studied elsewhere we do not know.

As a formal institution the school at St. Étienne is even less

---

[1] *J.L.* 4669; cf. *Lanfranci Epp.* 1.

[2] R. B. C. Huygens, 'Bérenger de Tours, Lanfranc et Bernold de Constance', *Sacris Erudiri* xvi (1965), 362–4.

[3] Migne, *P.L.* cxlvii. 334AC, abridged. Theodoric was writing in memory of Imad, bishop of Paderborn (1051–76); i.e. Imad has died fairly recently. See further A. Hauck, *Kirchengeschichte Deutschlands* 6th edn., iii (Berlin/Leipzig, 1952), 966–7.

substantial than the school of Bec: after Lanfranc's departure in 1070 it ceased to exist.[1] Where Caen differs from Bec is in the resources of the city. Among the parishioners of Holy Trinity *c.* 1085 was Gerald *scolarius*; later the *scholasticus* Gilbert appears as witness to a charter.[2] These are mere names, but others among the clergy of Caen achieved spectacular preferment. The priest Roger became bishop of Salisbury and justiciar of England; and Arnulf the grammarian, tutor to William the Conqueror's daughter Cecilia, went on the First Crusade and died patriarch of Jerusalem: that he was also a competent teacher may be inferred from the *Gesta Tancredi*, written in honour of the founder of Edessa, by Arnulf's pupil Ralph, again 'of Caen'.[3] Finally *c.* 1080–90 Theobald of Étampes, writing to Margaret of Scotland in the hope of a situation, assumed the grandiose style *doctor cadumensis*.[4] Though Lanfranc was the queen's spiritual adviser, there is no reason to think that he gave Theobald his support or that Theobald ever went to Scotland. Indeed the style that Theobald used later on, *magister Oxinfordie*, suggests that he went straight from Caen to England; he was not the man to overlook the felicities of *doctor Scottorum* or *magister Caledonie*. But the title is significant none the less; for the epithet *cadumensis* must mean not Theobald's birthplace but the city where he taught. He had come from Étampes to the city of

[1] The library of St. Étienne has vanished almost completely: only a missal survives from the eleventh century (MS. Montpellier B.Fac. Médec. 314) and a scattered handful of books from the twelfth century (MSS. Cambridge Emmanuel Coll. 29, Paris B.N. lat. 1930, nouv.acq. lat. 1590 and Vat.Reg.lat.703B). Certain early twelfth-century additions to the *Gesta Normannorum Ducum* are attributed to a monk of St. Étienne, Caen: J. Marx, *Guillaume de Jumièges* (Rouen/Paris, 1914: *Soc.Hist.Norm.*), pp. xxii–xxv.

[2] For Gerald see Musset, no. 17bis. *Gislebertus et Alveredus scholastici* witness an agreement of 1092/1110 between St. Étienne and Fécamp; the former is presumably the witness from Caen: see E. Deville, *Notices sur quelques MSS normands conservés à la bibliothèque S. Geneviève* (Évreux, 1905), iv. 37, summarizing the lost cartulary of St. Étienne, fol. 49.

[3] William of Newburgh, *Historia Rerum Anglicarum*, I. vi, ed. Howlett (London, 1884: Rolls Ser.), i. 36 (Roger as *sacerdos admodum tenuis* at Caen); London B. L. Harley Roll A.3, no. 4 (early preferment at Avranches): cited by E. J. Kealey, *Roger of Salisbury* (California/London, 1972), p. 5. For Arnulf and Ralph see respectively L. Bréhier, 'Arnoul de Rohez', in *Dict.Hist.Géog.Ecclés.* iv. 619–21, and H. Glaesener, 'Raoul de Caen: historien et écrivain', *Rev.Hist.Ecclés.* xlvi (1951), 16–21.

[4] Migne, *P.L.* clxiii.765A and 759–76 *passim*: see Rashdall, *The Universities of Europe in the Middle Ages*, ed. F. M. Powicke and A. B. Emden (Oxford, 1936), iii. 16–18.

Arnulf and the *scholastici* Gilbert and Gerald. For the eleventh century there is very seldom better evidence than this: we may take it that by *c.* 1080 there was a school in Caen, presided over perhaps by Arnulf and attracting young men like Theobald, Ralph and Roger.[1] But it has no continuity as an institution with Lanfranc's school at St. Étienne.

ii. the Norman Church

When Lanfranc arrived in Normandy prestige, wealth, learning and spiritual excellence were to be found in the monasteries rather than the episcopate. The great foreign abbots—John of Fruttuaria at Fécamp, Suppo of Fruttuaria at Mont-St.-Michel, Isembard Teutonicus at Holy Trinity, Rouen—kept Norman monasticism in touch with the Church as a whole. Their customaries were written in the light of experience in Burgundy and Northern Italy: Fonte Avellana and Vallombrosa as well as Fruttuaria itself and William of Volpiano's colony at Dijon; their liturgical and musical innovations drew as easily on Reichenau as on Cluny or Limoges.[2] At the same time Normandy was not the passive recipient of monastic colonization; the great monastic houses were supported, like the rest of the Norman Church, by the new families who were climbing to power. But the monks had an independence that the secular clergy had lost. Although they could have onerous military and financial obligations, they were free from ecclesiastical jurisdiction beyond the walls of their own community: neither the diocesan bishop nor any other abbot nor the pope had any effective power of intervention. Western canonists came to regard this as unsatisfactory; but fundamentally the situation reflected not a lack of organization in the Church but the absence of ducal authority throughout much of Normandy. Power lay with the great families, and one aspect of that power was the control of episcopal appointments: the house of Bellême, for instance, operating in the no-man's-land between

---

[1] For a useful survey of the evidence see R. Foreville, 'L'école de Caen au xie siècle et les origines normandes de l'université d'Oxford', in *Études médiévales . . . A. Fliche* (Montpellier, 1952), pp. 81–100. The association with Oxford depends solely on Theobald of Étampes.

[2] See the forthcoming volumes of Hallinger, *Corpus Consuetudinum Monasticarum* (Siegburg 1963—), and for Isembert C. Hohler, 'The proper office of St. Nicholas . . .', *Medium Aevum* xxxvi (1967), 40–8.

Normandy and Maine, had in their gift the sees of Le Mans, Séez and even Tours.[1] On the feudal chess-board bishops were indispensable. *Ipso facto* then, from William's point of view, the exertion of ducal authority included placing his own candidates in these privately owned sees. Indeed he might well begin with the bishops, where the weight of canon law was in his favour. As the political turning-point for William was *c.* 1050, in the aftermath of Val-ès-Dunes, so virtually to the year came a radical change in the episcopate.[2] Évreux fell vacant in 1046, Coutances in 1048, Bayeux and Lisieux in 1049. Two of the new bishops, Odo of Bayeux and Geoffrey of Coutances, were to dominate the Norman Church for a generation. They were still Norman aristocrats, but unlike their predecessors they had a common loyalty, or at least duty, to duke William. Perhaps for this reason the bishops as a whole were better able to act as a group with common objectives: they re-established episcopal authority within their dioceses, they built cathedrals, they reorganized their finances, their lands and their cathedral chapters. Suddenly the episcopate became respectable, even zealous; and by 1070 the Norman Church was structurally up to date and morally reputable to a degree that had been inconceivable in 1042. William's control of his bishops was not only crucial to his own authority; it proved to be the essential prerequisite for the reform of his Church. At the same time the monasteries began to lose their dominance, not by any dramatic attack on their privileges but by the mere restoration of the episcopate. To see this transfer of power was valuable experience for a future archbishop of Canterbury.

The first sign of the new era is a council held at Rouen by archbishop Mauger in or before 1049.[3] Mauger was the duke's uncle and nephew to the previous (murdered) archbishop, a survivor from the harsh times of William's minority. Within a few years Mauger himself was deposed by a papal legate; and he has often been presented since as the archreprobate, symbolic of the old order that was happily passing. Could such a

---

[1] J. Boussard, 'La seigneurie de Bellême aux xe et xie siècles', in *Mélanges* ... *L. Halphen* (Paris, 1951), pp. 43–54.

[2] D. C. Douglas, 'The Norman episcopate before the Norman Conquest', *Camb.Hist.Journ.* xiii (1957), 101–15.

[3] F. Pommeraye, *Sanctae Rotomagensis Ecclesiae Concilia* (Rouen, 1677), pp. 65–8 (=Mansi, *Concilia* xix.751A–4A).

man possibly have chaired the first, and in many ways seminal, reforming synod? But this paradox seems to be the creation of later historians. Mauger's crimes may have been scarlet, but they are never defined: William of Poitiers makes the conventional assumption that he despoiled his church, William of Malmesbury the unlikely guess that he had condemned the duke's marriage as uncanonical. We should surely remember that Mauger was deposed after a baronial revolt, in which his loyalty to the duke had been very suspect.[1] He was a rebel whom William (warned by Geoffrey Martel's experience with the bishop of Le Mans) took the trouble to remove canonically. Mauger's political errors have no bearing on his capacity for ecclesiastical reform. The canons of his council include no manifest anachronisms, indeed they correspond very accurately to the evils of the day: simony and office-seeking, the alienation of church property, the sale of the sacraments. As legislation they seem unexceptionable, whether or not they could be enforced. At the least Mauger's council is a declaration of principle: when William's own bishops took office, reform was already in the air.

During the 1050s Lanfranc was still only prior of Bec, conceivably an adviser to his diocesan in Rouen, but not himself an agent of change. He was an attentive back-bencher in the councils of the Church. In 1063 he became an active participant and, if we are to believe William of Poitiers, a kind of ducal representative set on his 'watchtower' of St. Étienne.[2] It is more certain that in these years Lanfranc was able to observe the duties and the hazards of an archbishop's position, first from Maurilius (1055–67) and then from his successor John of St. Philbert, erstwhile bishop of Avranches. They were very different men. Maurilius was a monk of exceptionally wide experience, with a monk's interest in liturgy and in building; he was quick to formulate a eucharistic profession against Berengar of

---

[1] William of Poitiers, *Gesta Guillelmi* i.53; William of Malmesbury, *Gesta Regum* iii. 267 (ed. Stubbs, ii. 327). But see Orderic's deathbed speech of William the Conqueror: 'Proteruum quoque presulem qui nec Deo deuotus nec michi fidus erat de pontificali sede per decretum papae deposui' (*Hist.Eccles.* vii, ed. Chibnall IV.84–5). Mauger's brother William, count of Arques, had led the revolt of 1054.

[2] 'Illi [Lanfranco] consulta animae suae, illi speculam quandam, unde ordinibus ecclesiasticis per omnen Normanniam prospiceretur, commisit: *Gesta Guillelmi* i. 52.

Tours.[1] His legislation is intelligent and moderate: clergy shall
not bear arms nor act as stewards and administrators for
wealthy laymen; if priests or deacons, they shall not be married;
those in minor orders shall be dissuaded from marriage, but not
forcibly.[2] Lanfranc was to be concerned with several of these
questions in England. Maurilius was sympathetically remembered in his own cathedral and he was by no means an unsatisfactory archbishop; but he had been brought in to replace
Mauger when no candidate from the aristocracy could have
been admitted, and he was always necessarily the duke's man.
With archbishop John Rouen returned to normal. The son of
Ralph d'Ivry, *vicomte* of the Cotentin, and himself a landholder
in his own right, John combined reforming zeal with a deter-
mination to rule his province. For the first time the Norman
Church is seen as a strictly episcopal organization under the
central jurisdiction of Rouen. John extended his own effective
authority by the use of archdeacons; and unlike Maurilius he
was prepared to join issue with the monastic establishment. His
assertion of the archbishop's right to visit St. Ouen (his most
powerful neighbour in Rouen itself) was only the most notorious
of several attempts to limit monastic immunity.[3] His legislation
includes canons on simony, marriage discipline, and the pastoral
care of the laity, topics that were becoming familiar, though not
always accepted: John was stoned in his own cathedral for his
ruling on clerical marriage.[4] At the same time he was positively

---

[1] *Acta Archiepiscoporum Rothomagensium*, ed. Mabillon, *Vetera Analecta* (Paris,
1723), p. 224 (Migne, *P.L.* cxlvii. 279A–80A). cf. M. de Boüard, 'Notes et hypo-
thèses sur Maurille moine de Fécamp, et son élection au siège métropolitain de
Rouen', in *L'Abbaye bénédictine de Fécamp* (Fécamp, 1959), i. 81–92; for the eucharistic profession see G. Bessin, *Concilia Rotomagensis Provinciae* (Rouen, 1717), p. 49.

[2] Maurilius held four councils: Caen (1061), Rouen (1063), Lisieux (1064) and
Lillebonne (1066). *Acta* survive for Caen and Lisieux: see respectively Pommeraye,
op.cit., pp. 71–2 (Mansi, *Concilia* xix. 937C–40A) and L. Delisle, 'Canons du
Concile tenu à Lisieux en 1064', *Journ.Savants* (1901), 517; the latter reflects
decisions taken at Rouen the previous year.

[3] Even as bishop of Avranches John had clarified the archidiaconal rights of the
abbot of Mont-St.-Michel (*Gallia Christiana* xi. 475CD; cf. J.-F. Lemarignier,
*Étude sur les privilèges d'exemption et de juridiction ecclésiastique des abbayes normandes des
origines à 1140* (Paris, 1937), pp. 158–60. See also canons 2 and 14 of the council of
Rouen (1072): Pommeraye, op.cit., pp. 87–9 (Mansi, *Concilia* xx. 36BC; 38BC).
John's struggle with St. Ouen is graphically described in *Acta Archiepisc.*, ed.cit.,
pp. 224–6 (Migne, *P.L.* cxlvii. 9B–14A); cf. Lemarignier, op.cit., pp. 155–6, app.

[4] John held councils in 1070, 1072, and 1074, the first probably in Rouen, the
two latter, for which *acta* survive, certainly so: Pommeraye, pp. 84–90; 94–6 (Mansi,

interested in the organization of a cathedral, as distinct from a monastery; while he was still at Avranches he sent to Maurilius his *De officiis ecclesiasticis*, which is a serious discussion of the liturgical life of a secular chapter.[1] John was the archbishop whom Lanfranc knew best. His letters to John in the 1070s show a mutual regard that can only have been established in Normandy the decade before.[2] John was a pattern to follow, and a warning: we hear of no violent confrontations in Lanfranc's councils in England.

While he was in Caen however Lanfranc's prime concern was for the rights, the prosperity and above all the independence of St. Étienne. If monastic exemption was under fire from the episcopate, a papal privilege was coming to prove stronger than a bishop. In 1068 Lanfranc secured a bull from Alexander II that granted exemption from the bishop of Bayeux; and a decade later the abbot, again at the bishop's expense, secured archidiaconal jurisdiction both within Caen and in a number of parishes elsewhere in the diocese.[3] Odo was laying up trouble for Lanfranc in England; but as diocesan of St. Étienne he conceded far more than Lanfranc was to think proper when he was a bishop himself. Lanfranc appears at St. Étienne as one of the great foreign abbots, who were effectively independent of any local bishop, but he is among the last of the kind: by the 1060s such freedom could be established only with papal help. It might even be argued that in St. Étienne the papacy had a unique foothold in Normandy: the house depended on Rome for its liberty and indeed for its existence. Had not Nicholas II agreed to recognize the duke's marriage on condition that he and Matilda built two abbeys in Caen, St. Étienne and Holy Trinity? We have already seen that even if this settlement was reached, it was not negotiated personally by Lanfranc at the council of 1059.[4] Indeed the evidence for the agreement is surprisingly late. It is mentioned neither in Alexander II's

---

[1] R. Delamare, *Le 'De Officiis Ecclesiasticis' de Jean d'Avranches* (Paris, 1923); incomplete text in Migne, *P.L.* cxlvii. 27B–62D. See further A. Morey and C. N. L. Brooke, *Gilbert Foliot and his Letters* (Cambridge, 1965), pp. 189 and 196.

[2] *Lanfranci Epp.* 13–17.

[3] *J.L.* 4644 (see further Lemarignier, op.cit., pp. 143–6, 160–76); Musset, no. 13.

[4] See above, p. 69, n. 4.

Concilia xx. 7A; 33D–40C; 397C–9E). For the riot over clerical marriage see Orderic Vitalis, *Hist.Eccles.* iv (Chibnall, II, 200–1).

exemption privilege nor (what is more) in the ducal foundation charter for either Holy Trinity or St. Étienne. Even a phrase in the proemium such as 'moved by conjugal affection' or a circumlocutory reference to the papacy would meet the case: but there is nothing.[1] The story is first told by Orderic Vitalis in the early twelfth century; for William of Malmesbury it is current but unattested; it appears again in the *Vita Lanfranci* and, with embellishment, in the *Roman de Rou*:

> Before their union was allowed
> A hundred prebends they endowed:
> A hundred poor men clothed and fed,
> To sick and crippled gave their bread
> At Cherbourg and at Rouen,
> At Bayeux too, no less than Caen—
> These pious gifts are with us still
> As founded by the ducal will.
>
> In Caen at last their work to crown
> Two abbeys rose within the town:
> Two monasteries side by side,
> That should for monks and nuns provide.[2]

Whatever the bargain struck over William's marriage, it did not imply a continuing papal interest in St. Étienne while Lanfranc was abbot.

Lanfranc's relations with the papacy were sympathetic rather than close. He was on friendly terms with Leo IX, Nicholas II and Alexander II; but he was in no sense a Norman emissary to the *curia* or a local papal legate.[3] He rarely travelled to Rome: after his long stay in 1050, he did not return until 1067. Even then, although he was indeed on official business (the transfer of the bishop of Avranches to Rouen), he was not alone; he was assisted by that grey eminence among papal legates, bishop Ermenfrid of Sion.[4] What made papal influence a reality

---

[1] Musset, nos. 2 and 4.

[2] Orderic, *Interpolations in William of Jumièges*, 'Gesta Normannorum Ducum' xxvi, ed. Marx (Paris, 1914), pp. 181–2; cf. *Gesta Regum* iii. 267 (ed. Stubbs, ii. 327), *Vita Lanfranci*, cap. 3, and Wace, *Roman de Rou*, lines 4525–40, ed. Holden (Paris, 1971: Soc.Anc.Textes Franc.), ii.55–6.

[3] John of Fécamp describes himself as a papal legate in a letter to Leo IX: 'mihi uestrae fidelitatis nuncio, immo (immisso: Migne) ipsius Petri apostolorum principis legatione functo' (Migne, *P.L.* cxliii. 798B).

[4] *J.L.* 4643; cf. *Acta Archiepisc.*, ed.cit., p. 224 (Migne, *P.L.* cxlvii. 279A).

in the 1060s was the active presence of such legates, rather than any special relationship with St. Étienne or with Lanfranc himself.[1]

iii. the conquest of England

The duke enlisted the help of the pope in his enterprise, and received a standard . . . as a sign of St. Peter's approval. (*Gesta Guillelmi* ii.3)

Duke William set out on his English expedition with a title to legitimacy from Alexander II, and when he was victorious he repaid the pope with the banner of the defeated king Harold.[2] In the same way Nicholas II had achieved a *modus vivendi* with the Normans in southern Italy, establishing Richard of Capua and Robert Guiscard as papal vassals; Alexander II himself had just sent a similar banner to the Patarene leader Erlembald of Milan.[3] These were more than gestures of approval; they cast the pope in the role of feudal overlord and imposed on the recipient obligations, hazily defined but accepted as serious and binding: in 1084 for instance, when Gregory VII was besieged in Castel Sant' Angelo, Guiscard came to his rescue. For William the Conqueror the relationship brought immediate tactical advantage: the English magnates had plausible grounds to support him, and the higher ecclesiastics were virtually obliged to do so. Alexander's banner was the secular equivalent of the pallium. At the same time William's fundamental claim to England was as the legitimate successor of Edward the Confessor: Harold Godwinson was the interloper, William the legal heir. Whatever the truth of this claim, it too was plausible, enabling those hostile to the house of Godwin to adhere to William and giving others, uncommitted or realist or turncoat, an excuse for following their own interest.

On Christmas Day 1066 William was crowned in Westminster Abbey, Edward's foundation and the place of his burial a year before. His crown, lance and sceptre were the Anglo-Saxon regalia, the crown embellished with an arc such as

---

[1] T. Schieffer, *Die päpstlichen Legaten in Frankreich . . . 870–1130* (Berlin, 1935: Hist.Stud. 263), pp. 53–129.

[2] 'Memorabile quoque vexillum Heraldi, hominis armati imaginem intextam habens ex auro purissimo, quo spolio pro munere eiusdem apostolici benignitate sibi misso par redderet': *Gesta Guillelmi* ii. 31.

[3] P. Kehr, 'Die Belehnungen der süditalienischen Normannenfürsten durch die Päpste (1059–1192)', *Abhand. Preuss.Akad.Wissensch.* (1934), i.3–52, especially p.9; cf. C. Erdmann, *Die Entstehung des Kreuzzugsgedankens* (Stuttgart, 1935), pp. 172–5, 129.

Conrad II had added to the imperial crown of Otto the Great.[1] The parallel was certainly deliberate. The Anglo-Saxon kings whom William succeeded (as the Salian Conrad replaced the Saxons in Germany) had an ancient and continuing claim to *imperium* over the whole of Britain and the islands adjoining. From the eighth century at latest they had styled themselves *rex Britanniae, apice totius Albionis sublimatus, totius Britanniae basileus*.[2] William himself already ruled Normandy and Maine and claimed the overlordship of Brittany; now as heir of the Anglo-Saxon *imperium* his jurisdiction extended unimaginably far: he was *basileus* over many kingdoms, a latter-day *bretwalda*.[3] Such claims far outran William's actual resources, and it would be easy to dismiss them as dreams. Yet they are the most characteristic dreams of eleventh-century monarchs. Cnut's empire in Britain and Scandinavia, Henry III's in Germany, Italy and Eastern Europe, Gregory VII's vision of dominance over the West, and indeed further still: all these were to some extent dreams. It has been called an era of 'large principles and small fields of action';[4] that is not to say that the ideas were less important, or less real, to contemporaries than the limited power that they could exercise in practice. William the Conqueror's *imperium* not only had a long ancestry, in the empire of Constantine, Theodosius and Justinian;[5] it was a commonplace of eleventh-century politics. In justifying his rule in England William and his advisers displayed an inspired eclecticism, moving at one moment towards feudal dependence on the pope, at the next towards the vague but ancient role of

---

[1] *Carmen de Hastingae Proelio*, lines 763–78, ed. Morton and Muntz (London, 1972: Oxford Medieval Texts), pp. 48–51; cf. P. Schramm, *Herrschaftszeichen und Staatssymbolik* (Stuttgart, 1955: *Mon.Ger.Schrift.* XIII), ii. 393–4.

[2] E. John, *Orbis Britanniae* (Leicester, 1966), pp. 1–63. The titles quoted are respectively Aethelbald of Mercia, Athelstan, and Edgar: P. H. Sawyer, *Anglo-Saxon Charters* (London, 1968), nos. 89, 421, 824. See further D. C. Douglas, *William the Conqueror* (London, 1964), pp. 247–64. The hagiographer Goscelin, reflecting conventional opinion *c.* 1080, uses similar styles for Edgar, *Anglici orbis basileus*, and Cnut, *regnorum basileus*: *Vita Edithae*, ed. Wilmart, *Anal. Bolland.* lvi (1938), 39, and *Translatio Mildrethae*, MS. London B.L. Cotton Vespasian B. xx, fol. 173v. See also Osbern, *Vita S. Dunstani*, pp. 71, 90, 105, and Eadmer, *De reliquiis S. Audoeni*, p. 364, line 86.

[3] See already the foundation charter of Holy Trinity, Caen: 'convenientes *imperii nostri* excellentissimi pontifices' (18 June 1066: Musset, no. 2).

[4] R. W. Southern, *The Making of the Middle Ages* (London, 1953), p. 36.

[5] See e.g. William of Poitiers, *Gesta Guillelmi* i. 52; ii. 39–41.

the *bretwalda*. Either was probably more acceptable to the
English than a simple claim to be king of England by right of
conquest.

Initially William was accepted by the Anglo-Saxon establishment, lay and ecclesiastical. Very possibly they had no option;
many would receive him with reservations: but formally he had
complete recognition as king. The archbishops of Canterbury
and York both came to his coronation, Ealdred of York anoint-
ing him and Stigand assisting.[1] For his part William did not set
out to expropriate the English on principle. The lay aristocracy
lost a great deal; many heads of families were dead or in exile:
but the social stratum immediately below (the property-holding
citizen of London, for instance) survived and prospered.[2] In the
same way the ecclesiastical establishment at first continued
intact: Stigand and Ealdred remained in power, and their
bishops with them. Indeed they were now the major representatives of the old order, and the principal hope of those who
wished to see it restored. By the autumn of 1067 the formal
unanimity of William's coronation was gone, and there were
revolts throughout England, culminating in bitter fighting in
Yorkshire and the north and scattered but persistent resistance
in the Isle of Ely and parts of East Anglia. Manifestly the
bishops were involved. William concluded, as he had in Normandy twenty years earlier, that ecclesiastical appointments
must be in his own hand. Again as in an exactly parallel
Norman situation he called on a papal legate to carry out an
essentially political decision according to canon law.

In the spring of 1070 bishop Ermenfrid of Sion and other
papal emissaries assisted William in the overhaul of the English
episcopate.[3] Ermenfrid had long experience in Norman affairs

---

[1] 'Illius et dextram sustentat metropolita;/Ad leuam graditur alter honore pari':
Carmen de Hastingae Proelio, lines 803–4 (ed.cit., pp. 50–1). Ealdred anointed
William, but Stigand (who is reputed to have anointed Harold) was also present.

[2] See e.g. *c.*1080 Eadmer Anhaende of London (D. C. Douglas, *The 'Domesday Monachorum' of Christ Church, Canterbury*, London, 1944, pp. 58–60) and a
generation later the prosperous Anglo-Saxon 'middle class' to which Christina of
Markyate belonged (C. H. Talbot, *Christina of Markyate*, Oxford, 1959, pp.10–12
and *passim*).

[3] D. Wilkins, *Concilia Magnae Britanniae* (London, 1737), i. 322–3; 356: see
further Orderic Vitalis, *Hist.Eccles.* iv (ed. Chibnall, pp. xxxii–xxxiv) and H. E. J.
Cowdrey, 'Bishop Ermenfrid of Sion and the penitential ordinance following the
battle of Hastings', *Journ.Eccles.Hist.* xx (1969), 225–42.

and some knowledge of England: he had brought archbishop
Ealdred his pallium in 1062. In a council at Winchester in
Easter week archbishop Stigand was formally deposed. There
were good canonical grounds for doing so: he held the see of
Winchester in plurality; he had intruded into Canterbury
against the legal occupant; he had received his pallium from
Benedict X. All these points could have been made however in
1066, or indeed on Ermenfrid's earlier visit in 1062. When we
see the other depositions at Winchester—Aethelmaer, bishop of
Elmham, and Aethelric, bishop of Selsey—and remember the
flight of abbot Aethelsige of St. Augustine's at about the same
time, we cannot but think that archbishop Stigand's whole
connection was being extirpated root and branch for its part in
the recent rebellion.[1] Archbishop Ealdred had just died (September 1069); he kept his reputation but he was replaced not,
as traditionally, by the bishop of Worcester, but by a reliable
and indeed distinguished Norman, Thomas of Bayeux. The one
other deposition is obscure in its timing, but not in the reasons
behind it: bishop Aethelwine of Durham, who was already
outlawed, was seemingly not deposed until 1071.[2] But the
principle is clear. The only bishops who were deposed were
those involved in the recent revolts; otherwise William was
content to wait for the death of an incumbent and then replace
him with his own candidate. With few exceptions this is true of
the English abbots also.[3] The first new appointments were made
at a second council in Windsor at Whitsun: Thomas of Bayeux
to York, the King's chaplains Walkelin and Herfast to Winchester and Elmham, and the Anglo-Saxon Stigand to Selsey.

[1] Stigand and his brother Aethelmaer successively held the see of Elmham; the
family had property in the area: see F. Barlow, *The English Church 1000-1066*
(London, 1963), pp. 192, 217 and (for an excellent discussion of Stigand's deposition), pp. 302–10. Stigand witnessed a royal charter as late as 13 Apr. 1069;
Bishop–Chaplais, pl. xxviii.

[2] J. Le Neve, *Fasti Ecclesiae Anglicanae 1066–1300*, ed. D. E. Greenway (London,
1971), ii. 29. Aethelwine was the brother of the deposed bishop of Selsey: *A.S.
Chron.D*, s.a. 1069.

[3] Abbot Godric of Winchcombe was deposed in 1066, abbot Ealdred of Abingdon
in 1071 (for assisting bishop Aethelwine), abbot Wulfric of New Minster, Winchester, in April 1072 and abbot Geoffrey of Westminster in 1072–6. Brihtric was
moved from Malmesbury to Burton (1066–7), and *c.* 1070 two abbots in Stigand's
connection fled from their monasteries (St. Albans and St. Augustine's, Canterbury): Knowles-Brooke-London ad loc. For Lanfranc's depositions in 1084–5 see
below, Ch. VI, §ii.

The principal vacancy that remained was Canterbury itself. The business was again entrusted to Ermenfrid of Sion, who held a council in Normandy to declare the King's choice of the abbot of St. Étienne as his new archbishop.[1] Lanfranc was known and trusted, and he had no family connection to divide his loyalty: the parallel with Maurilius, brought in by Ermenfrid in 1055 to replace the treasonable archbishop of Rouen, scarcely needs further emphasis. Lanfranc was horrified at the proposal: neither as a monk nor a scholar had he any future in England, and he was already stricken in years; he was in his late fifties, if not older. But he had no choice. The King invested him on 15 August, and a fortnight later he was in Canterbury.[2]

On Sunday 29 August 1070, the feast of the Beheading of St. John the Baptist, Lanfranc was received in Canterbury, consecrated archbishop and enthroned.[3] The ceremony was performed by eight bishops: from the old regime London, Rochester, Sherborne and Wells, together with the four bishops who had been appointed since the Conquest, Dorchester (1067), Winchester, Elmham and Selsey. Only Exeter, Hereford and Worcester were absent; Leofric was the most remote, Walter reputedly the least diligent, while Wulfstan of Worcester had a prior loyalty to the archbishop of York. It was a very respectable tally of English bishops, with no external assistance. The papal legates who had so dominated the scene earlier in the year, deposing Stigand, proposing Lanfranc and even consecrating the bishop of Winchester, had all left England by mid-August 1070; they took no part in Lanfranc's consecration. Throughout his archiepiscopate only one was to return, for one specific issue. Lanfranc may not have wished to be isolated in this way, but again the choice was not his. In practice he had to work with a dozen episcopal colleagues, who were apparently co-operative, and the King.

[1] *Lanfranci Epp.* 1; cf. Orderic Vitalis, *Hist. Eccles.* iv (ed. Chibnall, II. 252–3).
[2] *Florentii Wigorniensis Chronicon*, ed. Thorpe (London, 1849), ii. 7; cf. *Acta Lanfranci*, p. 287: 'eligentibus eum senioribus eiusdem ecclesiae, cum episcopis et principibus, clero et populo Angliae, *in curia regis*' (my italics).
[3] *Scriptum Lanfranci*, p. 165.

VI: England 1070–1089

i. the primacy

We have delegated to archbishop Lanfranc such personal and apostolic authority in the conduct and settlement of these disputes that any decision of his (so long as it is just) can be considered as firm and binding as if the settlement had been made in our own presence.   (Alexander II to William the Conqueror)[1]

IF the papal legates had departed, Alexander II was ready to delegate some of their power to Lanfranc himself, not *ex officio* as the archbishops of Canterbury were to exercise it later on, but as a personal honour that added greatly to his status in England. It was a natural arrangement for Alexander, who had sent students to Lanfranc at Bec and Caen,[2] and extremely useful to Lanfranc in his first years in Canterbury. At the same time a legate's powers were of limited duration and imprecise: Alexander's support, however wholehearted, would not of itself give Lanfranc security. Like all his predecessors he had to rely on the King, who was a law unto himself, and on his bishops. By participating in his consecration the majority of Lanfranc's suffragans had already declared their goodwill, but not their formal obedience. That was normally expressed when each bishop was himself consecrated. During the ceremony he made a public profession of obedience to his metropolitan, an act comparable with feudal homage and comparably binding. Although it was primarily the liturgical recitation that validated the oath, from time to time in some provinces written professions were presented at the ceremony and kept as a record. For instance Fulbert's profession has survived, as do other professions of the tenth and eleventh centuries from both Sens and Besançon.[3] At Canterbury Lanfranc found a series of such

---

[1] *J.L.* 4695: autumn 1071.

[2] *Lanfranci Epp.* 1.

[3] G. Waitz, 'Obedienzerklärungen burgundischer und französischer Bischöfe', *Neues Archiv* iii (1878), 195–202.

professions running from Lichfield (once the prospective metropolitan of Mercia) to the forged profession of Ealdwulf of York (995):[1]

While I live, I shall unhesitatingly obey your commands, and always submit in humble obedience to you, archbishop Aethelheard and to your successors for ever. Although others may have acted differently in the past, I shall always be obedient to the see where I received this honour and where all the glorious bishops of our nation have received it in the past.

It is right too that I and all my fellow-bishops should look to the episcopal see of St. Augustine, which the worthy archbishop Aethelheard now rules, and to the city of Canterbury, from which by St. Gregory's command office in the Church comes to us all.[2]

The weakness of this Canterbury series is in the tenth century, where there is only one profession (to archbishop Oda) besides the forgery just quoted; but all in all it is a sufficiently convincing archive on which to assert the archbishop's metropolitan rights within his own province. Forgery apart, what the early professions do not support is any formal primacy of the archbishop of Canterbury over the province of York.

The first consecration that Lanfranc was called on to perform brought up this very issue. Thomas of Bayeux, who had been chosen as archbishop of York at the Whitsun council, came in the autumn of 1070 to be consecrated at Canterbury.[3] Encouraged perhaps by the Ealdwulf forgery,[4] Lanfranc demanded a written profession of obedience; there was a furious argument, and Thomas departed unconsecrated. He was clearly within his rights: there was absolutely no precedent for an archbishop of York recognizing the jurisdiction of Canterbury, beyond the archbishop's right to consecrate him. (Some archbishops of York had in fact been consecrated as bishops of Worcester

---

[1] M. Richter, *Canterbury Professions* (London, 1973: Canterbury and York Soc. lxvii), nos. 1–30: none survives in the original. I am grateful to Dr. Richter for his generous help.

[2] Richter, no. 1: the forgery is based on a late eighth-century profession by Eadulf, bishop of Lindsey.

[3] The account that follows is based on the so-called *Scriptum Lanfranci*: H. Boehmer, *Die Fälschungen Erzbischof Lanfranks von Canterbury* (Leipzig, 1902), pp. 165–7. See Appendix A 13a.

[4] The earliest manuscript of the Ealdwulf forgery (Richter, no. 1) is London B. L. Cotton Cleopatra E.i (1121–3), but the forgery itself seems to me to be at least fifty years older: see further Appendix C.

within the province of Canterbury, and then translated as consecrated bishops to York: but Lanfranc never invoked this
✓ argument.) The King's first reaction was to support Thomas;
but Lanfranc prevailed on him to refer the dispute to Rome,
where both archbishops were going for their pallia the following
year. Meanwhile Thomas professed obedience to Lanfranc
personally, not to his successors, and was duly consecrated. As
much the younger man, Thomas was likely to outlive the con-
sequences of his oath: even so, it proved to be the thin edge of
the wedge. Lanfranc went on to secure written professions from
Wulfstan of Worcester, Remigius of Dorchester and Herfast of
Thetford. Wulfstan had been consecrated in 1062 by Ealdred
of York, but had not professed obedience to him; Remigius had
been consecrated in 1067 by Stigand, and had professed
obedience; Herfast had been consecrated in the interregnum,
we do not know by whom, and was now professing obedience
for the first time.[1] In their professions all three bishops (even
Herfast) rehearse the iniquities of Lanfranc's predecessor, yet by
the autumn of 1070 that was hardly the main issue. Stigand was
gone. What was still undecided was the proper allegiance of two
of these bishoprics (Worcester and Dorchester) and of the vacant
see of Lichfield. All were claimed by Canterbury, but Worcester
especially had a long and close alliance with York. There is
little reason to think that Lanfranc secured a renewal of
obedience from other bishops—Walkelin, for example:[2]
Wulfstan and Remigius were the two that mattered.

In the autumn of 1071 Lanfranc and Thomas travelled to
Rome—together: personally they seem to have remained on
friendly terms.[3] Each received his pallium (Lanfranc with
special marks of papal condescension) and Alexander II heard
the case. Now the substance of the dispute was brought into the
open. Archbishop Thomas claimed not only the independence
✓ of his own see but jurisdiction over Worcester, Dorchester and

---

[1] Richter, nos. 31–3; see further F. Barlow, *The English Church 1000–1066*
(London, 1963), pp. 302–10. Herfast's predecessor, Aethelmaer, was deposed at
Easter 1070: see above. pp. 113, n.3, 114, n.4.

[2] Appendix A13b.

[3] *Lanfranci Epp.* 9–11; Thomas is said to have been Lanfranc's pupil (Appendix
A 19b). The *Acta Lanfranci* (Appendix A 14a) places the journey in the second year
of Lanfranc's archiepiscopate, i.e. after 29 Aug. 1071. The party also included
Remigius of Dorchester (Richter, no. 32) and Baldwin, abbot of Bury St. Edmunds
(*J.L.* 4692): see further § iv below.

Lichfield. When these three are included in the province of York, it covers a sizeable area of England; without them York is reduced to one suffragan (Durham) and insubstantial claims in Scotland and the Isles. In terms of status and power these border bishoprics meant far more to archbishop Thomas than his profession of obedience. He could hold his own synods and consecrate his own bishops—in short he could run his own province—if the border bishoprics were his. Where right lay was another question. The primacy itself might have been judged by the pope, for Gregory the Great had in principle defined that it should alternate between the archbishops of London and York according to seniority of consecration. Predictably enough Lanfranc argued that Gregory's definition was irrelevant to Canterbury and Thomas that York had parity with the other archbishop, wherever he had his see. But on the border bishoprics Alexander II had no guidance whatever; the problem went beyond specifically ecclesiastical matters, such as attendance at synods, to affect episcopal estates and jurisdiction and the service owed to the King. Here the dispute touched the interests of William the Conqueror so nearly that Alexander referred it back for settlement in England. At the same time he granted legatine powers to his lector Hubert and (specifically in respect of the border sees) to Lanfranc himself.[1] At Easter 1072 an agreement was reached in the royal chapel in Winchester castle. Only those immediately concerned were present: the King and Queen, the papal legate, the two archbishops, the bishops of Winchester (as host), Worcester and Dorchester (as the disputed sees) and Thetford (lately the royal chancellor).[2] Archbishop Thomas was required to make a new profession of obedience to Lanfranc and his successors, absolutely;[3] and all three border bishoprics were adjudged to Canterbury. The lion's share seemed to have gone to Lanfranc. At Whitsun the judgement was confirmed in the royal court at Windsor, witnessed by a long list of bishops and abbots and sent in multiple copies round the kingdom.[3] Then Hubert returned

[1] For Hubert see next note. Lanfranc's legatine powers are defined in *J.L.* 4695 (cf. p. 116, n.1 above).

[2] T. A. M. Bishop and P. Chaplais, *Facsimiles of English Royal Writs to A.D. 1100* (Oxford, 1957), no. xxix. Herfast was replaced as chancellor by Osmund of Salisbury in 1070: yet it is hard to see in what other capacity he is witnessing here.

[3] Richter, no. 34.

to Rome with the text of the agreement and, we may conjecture, the covering letter which Lanfranc wrote to Alexander II.

It is Lanfranc's letter which shows what had been settled by
the royal constitution and what had not.[1] The decision on the
border sees was final; but the obedience of York was little more
than provisional. Thomas swore obedience to Lanfranc and his
√ successors: *Thomas's* successors were free. If the dispute was not
to be renewed with every consecration of an archbishop of York,
Lanfranc had to convert his temporary advantage into an outright declaration of primacy. The discussions in England had
cleared the ground: what he now sought was a papal privilege,
based on the evidence that had already satisfied William the
Conqueror. His prime source was Bede. Throughout the *Historia
Ecclesiastica* the archbishops of Canterbury exercise pastoral
responsibility over the whole of Britain. The northern bishops
come or send representatives to archbishop Theodore's council
of Hertford and he himself travels in the north, even reconsecrat-
√ ing the church at Lindisfarne in honour of St. Peter.[2] This was
convincing testimony, and it was supplemented for more recent
times by the episcopal professions and the records of councils.
Most impressive of all was the series of papal privileges to the
same effect: Gregory the Great, Boniface, Honorius, Vitalian,
Sergius, a later Gregory, Leo and Leo IX all gave unanimous
√ witness to the primacy of Canterbury. If today we know that the
evidence of Bede stops short just when it would be telling and
that the roll-call of papal privileges is a list of forgeries, Lanfranc
√ and his contemporaries did not:[3] there is no doubt that Lanfranc
himself thought his petition well founded. But he was too
sanguine, or too late, in asking for a new privilege. The reply
that survives is from archdeacon Hildebrand, to whom Lanfranc
had sent an ancillary note.[4] Hildebrand indicates almost curtly
that it is without precedent for such a privilege to be granted in
the petitioner's absence: until Lanfranc appears personally in
Rome there can be no progress. Alexander's reply is lost; it may

[1] *Lanfranci Epp.* 3.
[2] Bede, *Historia Ecclesiastica* iv.2 and 5; iii.25, ed. Colgrave and Mynors (Oxford,
1969: Oxford Med.Texts), pp. 332; 348–52; 294. Of course Theodore's jurisdiction
did not extend to the Celtic west; but both Bede and Lanfranc were vague on this
point.
[3] For the origin and date of the forged privileges see Ch. VII §ii, and Appendix C.
[4] *Lanfranci Epp.* 5–6.

have been at this juncture that he invited Lanfranc to spend Christmas 1072 at the papal court.[1] But Lanfranc never returned to Rome, and he pressed his petition no further. There was little point in doing so if Hildebrand was against it. In the words of a contemporary epigram—

To live at Rome's your hope? Then from the roof-tops say, 'Beyond our lord the pope the pope's lord I obey!'[2]

Lanfranc had a shrewd sense of when to stop. ✓

To our minds the substantive gain was the disputed bishoprics, without which the archbishop of York could not develop a viable province. Yet Lanfranc was not crudely concerned to defeat York. Fundamentally the primacy was not the administrative control of a neighbouring province (summoning to synods, enforcing laws), but a general hegemony over Britain, Ireland and the northern Isles: the ecclesiastical counterpart of ↶ William the Conqueror's claims to be *rex Britanniae, totius Britanniae basileus*.[3] The royal constitution of 1072 described Lanfranc as *prima(s) totius Britanniae*, and he continued to use that title, discreetly but resolutely, for the rest of his life. Thomas of York was let off lightly: in 1072 he professed obedience to 'Lanfranc, archbishop of Canterbury and (his) successors', with no mention of the primacy.[4] But the other bishops whom Lanfranc consecrated recognized him unambiguously as *Britanniarum primas*[5] or (exceptionally) *totius Britannicę regionis primas* and *primas totius Britannicę insulę*.[6] Most of these were ↗

[1] *Lanfranci Epp.* 1.

[2] 'Vivere vis Romae, clara depromito voce:/Plus domino papae quam domno pareo papae': M. Lokrantz, *L'opera poetica di S. Pier Damiani* (Stockholm, 1964), p. 55 (no. xvii); cf. p. 68 (no. lxxix).

[3] See above, p. 112, nn. 2 and 3; and cf. further the illuminating remarks of D. Bethell, 'English monks and Irish reform in the eleventh and twelfth centuries', *Hist. Studies* viii (1971), 129–33.

[4] Richter, no. 34; cf. *Lanfranci Epp. 3*: 'rogavit [Thomas] enim regem ut me rogaret quatinus . . . aliqua quae mei essent iuris studio ei caritatis concederem.'

[5] *Britanniarum primas*: the bishops of Dublin, London, Rochester, Salisbury, Hereford, Chichester, Wells (Richter, nos. 36–41, 46–7). The profession of John of Wells (no. 47) is an original.

[6] *Totius Brittannicę regionis primas*: Osbern of Exeter (no. 35). *Primas totius Britannicę insulę*: Maurice of London (no. 44). The only evidence that the title was used before Whitsun 1072 is the profession of Osbern of Exeter (no. 35); but it is possible that Osbern was consecrated between Easter and Whitsun 1072 and/or that his profession was later interpolated to match the others. After Whitsun 1072 the title is omitted by Donngus of Dublin, William of Thetford and Robert of Chester (nos. 42–3, 45: the two latter are originals).

bishops within the province of Canterbury, who owed duty to Lanfranc as their metropolitan in any case; to accept the new title cost them nothing. Yet in doing so they gave it currency, converting the traditional assumption that Canterbury was the principal see in the kingdom into the precise language that might one day support a claim at Rome. Beyond his own province Lanfranc was formally recognized only in Dublin: in the greater part of Ireland, in Scotland and the Isles and even in Wales neither Canterbury nor York had more than a vague and intermittent influence. Both Lanfranc and Thomas now tried to define this influence more clearly.

Although York had close trading links with the Norse kingdom of Dublin, the ecclesiastical associations of Ireland in the eleventh century were with the south of England, and here Dublin followed suit. In the 1020s Dunan, bishop of Dublin, is thought to have been consecrated at Canterbury;[1] in 1074 Patrick, a monk of Worcester, was consecrated by Lanfranc in St. Paul's, London, at the petition of the clergy and people of Dublin. Why the Dubliners were so zealous for the Canterbury connection can be seen from the terms of Patrick's profession:

I, Patrick, bishop-elect of the metropolis of Dublin in Ireland, offer my written profession to you . . . Lanfranc, primate of Britain and archbishop of Canterbury, promising all due obedience to you and your successors.[2]

In what sense Dublin was a 'metropolis' is difficult to know. By 1074 the kingdom of Dublin was a diminishing enclave that had just submitted to Toirrdelbach ua Briain, king of Munster. When Toirrdelbach was recognized by the northern king Maelsechlainn and the abbot of Armagh in 1079, he became overlord of the whole of Ireland and the only real arbiter of the Irish Church.[3] Although he confirmed bishop Patrick's appoint-

[1] The main evidence is *Lanfranci Epp.* 37 ('*more antecessorum nostrorum*'), which does not amount to much: but see further A. Gwynn, 'The origins of the see of Dublin', *Irish Eccles. Rec.* (1941), 107–12.

[2] Richter, no. 36: 'Ego Patricius ad regendam *Dublinam metropolem Hibernie*, electus antistes etc.' Note that the city, not the bishop himself, is 'metropolitan'; cf. *Lanfranci Epp.* 36–7. See further A. Gwynn, *The Writings of Bishop Patrick 1074–84* (Dublin, 1955: *Script.Lat.Hibern.*i) pp. 1–7.

[3] For political and ecclesiastical affairs in Ireland see A. Gwynn and D. Gleason, *A History of the Diocese of Killaloe* (Dublin, 1962), pp. 90–120; J. A. Watt, *The Church and the Two Nations in Medieval Ireland* (Cambridge, 1970), pp. 5–12; F. J. Byrne, *Irish Kings and High-Kings* (London, 1973), pp. 165–201 *et passim*.

ment, Dublin was not, and could not be, the dominant see in Ireland. The centres of power in the Church were still Armagh, Tuam and (with the ascendancy of Munster) above all Cashel. Yet Lanfranc's support was worth something to Dublin. The kingdom had the external recognition so badly needed if it was to survive at all, and Lanfranc himself had an entry into Irish ecclesiastical affairs. He encouraged king Guthric in his devotion to Rome, at the same time expressing Gregory VII's anxiety over the extraordinary marriage customs of the Irish:

> There are said to be men in your kingdom who marry within their own kindred, or that of their deceased wives; others desert their wives as and when they please; they even traffic them for other men's wives in exchange.
> See that you correct this . . .[1]

It was good advice, from a distance: bishop Patrick was not for instance required to attend synods in England, nor is there any evidence that he actively promulgated reform in Dublin.[2] When he was drowned ten years later crossing the Irish Sea, the Canterbury connection continued, with the approval of Toirrdelbach himself. The Irish monk Donngus, who had been sent for his education to Canterbury, was consecrated by Lanfranc in 1085. He too professed obedience, but in markedly less exuberant terms than Patrick had done:

> I, Donatus, bishop-elect of the church of Dublin, which is in Ireland, promise canonical obedience to you and your successors, O Lanfranc archbishop of the church of Canterbury.'[3]

It was clearer by now where power in the Irish Church really lay.

For Toirrdelbach himself the association with Canterbury

---

[1] *Lanfranci Epp.* 37; cf. Gregory VII, *Epp. Vagantes*, ed. Cowdrey (Oxford, 1972: Oxford Med. Texts), no. 1 (*J.L.*4801: *Lanfranci Epp.* 40). Lanfranc's phrase 'pretiosum sanctae Romanae ecclesiae filium' in *Ep.* 37 echoes Gregory's description of William the Conqueror: 'carissimum et unicum filium sanctae Romanae ecclesiae' (*J.L.* 4803: 20 Nov. 1073).

[2] Watt, op.cit., p. 218; Patrick was an attractive Latin versifier, sole witness to the latinity of Worcester in the mid-eleventh century: Gwynn, *The Writings of Bishop Patrick*, pp. 102–5 and *passim*.

[3] Richter, no. 42. Patrick's profession is modified at three points: *Dublinensis ęcclesię* (not *Dublinam metropolem*); *quę in Hibernia sita est* (not the deliberately ambiguous *Hibernię*); the title *Britanniarum primas* is omitted. For Donngus himself see the *Annals of St. Mary's, Dublin*, ed. Gilbert, *Chartularies of St. Mary's Abbey, Dublin* (London, 1884: Rolls Ser.), pp. 250–1.

and Worcester suited his aspirations as high-king, without in any way limiting his freedom of action. Like any dominant ruler of the time he was ready to tighten up the government of the Church and its social legislation; and in Domnall Ua h-Énna he had an outstanding bishop of Munster, learned and interested in the Church abroad. That Lanfranc in turn understood the situation in Ireland may be doubted: he addressed 'the magnificent Toirrdelbach' in much the same way as 'the glorious Guthric', passing on to both equally the papal criticism of their marriage customs.[1] But to Toirrdelbach he added further counsel of his own:

I am told—
  (i) that bishops are consecrated by one bishop without assistance;
  (ii) that many bishops are ordained to villages and small towns;
  (iii) that children are baptized without the use of consecrated chrism;
  (iv) that bishops are conferring holy orders for money.

These practices are universally condemned: in the Bible, in canon law, and in the teaching of the Fathers.[2] Such specific comments surely reflect specific questions from Toirrdelbach on points of canon law; and they match an equally specific theological ruling given to bishop Domnall:

If baptized children die before they receive communion, we do not in any sense believe (God forbid!) that they will be damned . . .
An unbaptized child in danger of death may, if there is no priest available, be canonically baptized by a lay believer . . .[3]

This is the stuff of which conciliar legislation is made, whether or not Toirrdelbach himself ever held a council. Gregory VII hoped that he would. With rare tact he wrote to Toirrdelbach promising open-ended support: 'If I can ever be of assistance, do not hesitate to let me know'.[4] But the hard evidence comes from

---

[1] *Lanfranci Epp.* 37–8.

[2] *Lanfranci Epp.* 38. The earliest *acta* to survive from an Irish synod are those of Cashel (1101): Gwynn and Gleason, op.cit., pp. 111–12. There is little significant coincidence, but cf. Cashel (i) simony and (viii) forbidden degrees of marriage.

[3] *Lanfranci Epp.* 33. For the practice of giving children the consecrated Host as soon as they were baptized see *The Stowe Missal*, ed. Warner (London, 1915: Henry Bradshaw Soc. xxxii), ii. 32; cf. F. J. Byrne, 'The Stowe Missal' in *Great Books of Ireland: Thomas Davis Lectures 1964* (Dublin, 1967), pp. 38–50.

[4] 'Si qua vero negotia penes vos emerserint quae nostro digna videantur auxilio, incunctanter ad nos dirigere studete, et quod iuste postulaveritis Deo auxiliante impetrabitis': Gregory VII, *Epp.Vagantes*, ed.cit., no. 57 (*J.L.* 5059).

the reign of Muirchertach (1086–1119), Toirrdelbach's son and successor. Then synods were held, a papal legate was appointed, and the hill of Cashel itself passed to the bishops of Munster; provinces were set up on the continental model based on Cashel, Tuam, Armagh and, eventually, Dublin. Toirrdelbach had set these changes in motion, as David to Muirchertach's Solomon; but it was not until Anselm's time that the effects were felt in Canterbury. For Lanfranc only Dublin was accessible and comprehensible: in the lands beyond he knew little and made no claims, even as *primas Britanniarum.*

Relations with Scotland and the Isles were on a different basis altogether. Jurisdiction there had been clearly adjudged to York, if York could establish it.[1] In the mid-eleventh century the Orkneys were being supplied with bishops from Bremen, the old mission-station for Scandinavia and the northern Isles.[2] But archbishop Thomas was lucky: less than a year after the council of Winchester earl Paul of the Orkneys sent him a bishop to be consecrated at York. Lanfranc instructed Wulfstan and Peter (recently confirmed as his own suffragans) to assist Thomas, without prejudice to their allegiance or to Thomas's jurisdiction over the Orkneys.[3] In March 1073 bishop Ralph professed obedience to Thomas, and his successors followed him: Roger (1100–8) and Ralph Nowell (1109–14).[4] With Lanfranc's co-operation Thomas had not only acquired another suffragan but had made a significant move in the clarification of the northern provinces. The quasi-primatial jurisdiction of Bremen was being replaced by direct and perhaps more effective

[1] 'Subiectionem vero Dunelmensis hoc est Lindisfarnensis episcopi atque omnium regionum a terminis Licifeldensis episcopii et Humbrę magni fluvii usque ad extremos Scotię fines ... Cantuariensis metropolitanus Eboracensi archiepiscopo eiusque successoribus in perpetuum obtinere concessit': royal writ of 1072, ed. Bishop–Chaplais, no. xxix. For Eadmer's ill-conceived attempt to submit to Canterbury when he was bishop of St. Andrews see R. W. Southern, *St. Anselm and his Biographer* (Cambridge, 1963), p. 236.

[2] In the period 1043–72 the three (probably successive) bishops consecrated by archbishop Adalbert of Bremen were Thorulf, John and Adalbert: Adam of Bremen, *Gesta Hammaburgensis Ecclesiae Pontificum* IV.xxxv and III.lxxvii, ed. Schmeidler (Hanover, 1917: Mon Ger.Hist. in usum schol.), pp. 271 and 224. See D. E. R. Watt, *Fasti Eccles.Scotic.Med.Aev.* (Edinburgh, 1969: *Scot.Rec.Soc.* N.S.l), pp. 247–8.

[3] *Lanfranci Epp.* 11–12.

[4] Watt, *Fasti*, pp. 248–9; for Ralph's profession see *Chronica Pontificum Ecclesiae Eboracensis*, ed. Raine, *The Historians of the Church of York* (London, 1886: Rolls Ser.), ii.363.

control, in the Orkneys by York (and later Nidaros) and in Scandinavia by the local sees of Lund, Nidaros and Upsala. Of archbishop Thomas's relations with the Scottish mainland we are quite ignorant. There the leading ecclesiastic of the 1070s was Fothad, bishop of St. Andrews, who was to be seen retrospectively as metropolitan of Scotland. But historically Fothad was only the personal leader of a group of Scottish bishops, whose dioceses were ill defined and who were in some ways more like the Irish episcopate than the English. Technically then it was for archbishop Thomas to establish relations with Fothad or, following the example of St. Cuthbert and in conjunction with the bishop of Durham, to encourage monastic colonization along the Tweed, at Melrose or Jedburgh. This was the pattern that eventually did emerge, in the second and third decades of the twelfth century.[1] But Thomas himself did nothing: here he left the initiative entirely to Lanfranc.

Whereas the Anglo-Saxon kings never exercised jurisdiction in Ireland, they were from time to time overlords of the kings of Scotland. In 1059 Malcolm Canmore did homage to Edward the Confessor, and in 1072 William the Conqueror came as far north as Abernethy to receive homage from him again.[2] Whether William was regarded as the latterday *bretwalda* for Scotland as a whole or simply as the king receiving homage for lands held in England was never clear. Either way, William the Conqueror's impressive appearance on the edge of the Highland Line meant nothing in terms of practical politics; the ceremonies merely renewed the association of the English and Scottish courts. The figure who linked the two definitively was Edgar Atheling's sister Margaret, who in 1057 had returned to England from the German-dominated court of Hungary, and had finally married Malcolm Canmore in 1070.[3] We may conjecture that she had been betrothed in 1059, when Malcolm came south to do homage, and that first Harold's accession, then the Conquest

---

[1] G. W. S. Barrow, *The Kingdom of the Scots* (London, 1973), caps. 5–6. By *c.*1125 it was asserted in York that Fothad had professed obedience to archbishop Thomas (Hugh the Chanter, s.a.1109: cf.Watt, *Fasti*, p. 290); but this is very hard to credit.

[2] *A. S. Chron. DE*, s.a. 1072: see further R. L. G. Ritchie, *The Normans in Scotland* (Edinburgh, 1954), pp. 385–8; 7–8; 29–30.

[3] *A. S. Chron. D*, s.a. 1067; cf. Turgot, *Vita S. Margaretae Scotorum Reginae*, ed. Hodgson Hinde (1867: Surtees Soc.li), pp. 234–54. See further Ritchie, op.cit., pp. 8–11; 24.

itself, had delayed the marriage. To allow the king of Scotland to marry into the Anglo-Saxon royal house was a major decision: William the Conqueror set a limit to his military commitments in the north and gained a potential ally, at the risk of Margaret's children returning to claim his crown. But Margaret's own loyalty was not in doubt; and it seems to have been confirmed by her recognition of Lanfranc as her spiritual adviser. Here was a permanent link with the English court and (if we may speculate) a channel of information for William the Conqueror on Scottish affairs.

Queen Margaret had grown up in the serious and demanding piety of the Empress Agnes and her circle. Generous patrons of monastic houses and drawing on the monastic liturgy for their own devotion, these great ladies also looked to the monks for personal spiritual direction. Peter Damian and John of Fécamp sent the Empress letters of exhortation and instruction on prayer which are far from platitudinous; they were themselves exploring the frontiers of devotion, and writing to Agnes made them define and clarify their thought.[1] Such mentors were an established (and obviously necessary) element in the court piety that in her narrower and remote sphere Queen Margaret still tried to maintain. She had little help from Lanfranc, if we may judge by his one surviving letter:[2]

In the brief span of a letter I cannot hope to unfold the joy with which you flooded my heart when I read your letter to me, O queen beloved of God. With what holy cheer the words flowed on, inspired as they were by the Holy Spirit! What you had written was uttered through you, rather than by you: by your mouth of a truth He spoke, who said to his disciples,

'Learn of me, for I am meek and lowly in heart.' It is by this yoke of Christ that you, who are born of a royal line, educated as befits a queen, and nobly joined to a noble king, are choosing me as your father—a man of no account, of neither birth nor worth, ensnared in sin: and you ask me to treat you as my spiritual daughter. I am not as you believe me; but may I be so because of your belief. Do not be

---

[1] A. Wilmart, 'Une lettre de S. Pierre Damien à l'impératrice Agnès', *Rev.Bén.* xliv (1932), 125–46; J. Leclercq and J.-P. Bonnes, *Un Maître de la vie spirituelle au xie siècle: Jean de Fécamp* (Paris, 1946), pp. 211–17, cf. 44–5. St. Anselm, writing to William the Conqueror's daughter Adelaide (1071) and the empress Matilda (1104) is another exponent of the genre.

[2] *Lanfranci Epp.* 61.

under any misapprehension: pray for me that I may be fit to pray to God for you as a father prays, and to have my prayer for you answered. Let there be a mutual exchange between us of prayers and good works. It is little that I contribute, but I know that I shall receive far more. From now on let me be your father and be you my child.

Given that he may never have met the queen, Lanfranc is too near the brink of mere flattery. Even if he draws back (as I think he does), he had neither experience nor talent in this type of direction.

In its public aspect the queen's piety took the form of elaborate, ritualized, works of charity[1] and (like her continental counterparts) monastic patronage. Holy Trinity, Dunfermline was the first regular Benedictine house in Scotland, founded by the queen as her personal chapel and family mausoleum and inaugurated by three monks from Christ Church, Canterbury.[2] Here Lanfranc knew what he was doing. Lavishly endowed with property, furnishings and plate, linked in confraternity with Christ Church and deliberately sharing its other name of Holy Trinity, the new house at Dunfermline was a firm basis for the influence of Canterbury in the far north. Towards the end of Lanfranc's archiepiscopate a similar link may have been envisaged with Christ Church, Dublin, where monks were established *c.* 1085–9.[3] But whereas the monastic community there was in direct contact with the bishop (forming in effect a monastic chapter), the monks of Dunfermline were never at the centre of ecclesiastical government. No foreign monks were imposed on existing houses, as they had been in England, nor did any of these native communities adopt the queen's monasticism of their own accord: Holy Trinity, Dunfermline, remained an exotic import. Queen Margaret came nearer to influencing the Scottish Church by her patronage of St. Andrews: she presented a great silver crucifix, and provided a hostel for pilgrims crossing the

[1] Turgot, *Vita S. Margaretae*, pp. 247–9.

[2] Barrow, op.cit. (above, p. 126 n. 1), pp. 193–8: see *Lanfranci Epp.* 61.

[3] Anselm's criticism of bishop Samuel of Dublin implies that Lanfranc gave books and ornaments to bishop Donngus for Christ Church, Dublin, and that monks were established there by either Donngus or his predecessor: *Anselmi Epp.* 277–8); cf. A. Gwynn, *The Writings of Bishop Patrick 1074–84* (Dublin, 1955: *Script.Lat.Hib.*i), p. 7. As a monk of Christ Church, Canterbury, Donngus seems to me the more likely candidate.

Tay.[1] Finally she was given to summoning church councils. Like William the Conqueror in Normandy and England, and like the high-kings of Ireland, the queen (in the words of her biographer) 'ordered councils to be held at frequent intervals'.[2] There she criticized and confuted the native clergy—presumably Fothad and his colleagues, though no one is named. They err in their reckoning of Lent; they do not receive communion at Easter;[3] in some areas the liturgy is barbarously divergent; they work on Sundays; and (inevitably) their marriage customs are inadmissible. Whether the native clergy listened, and whether indeed the queen's set speeches represent the modernizing views of the early twelfth century rather than her own, we cannot judge; there is scarcely any evidence beyond her biography.[4] But there is curiously little coincidence with Lanfranc's advice to Toirrdelbach. Marriage customs were a universal headache; otherwise Queen Margaret's reforms do not touch the power-structure of the Church, as the proposals to Toirrdelbach and Lanfranc's own legislation in England in nearly all cases do. As the royal saint whom twelfth-century kings could invoke in their dealings with the Church, the queen did have real influence on ecclesiastical change in the next generation. But in her own day there was neither widespread reform nor any serious contact with the Church outside Scotland. In the capacity of primate and archbishop, Lanfranc had achieved no more than Thomas of York.

Holy Trinity, Dunfermline and Christ Church, Dublin, in their different ways, kept Lanfranc in touch with areas in which William the Conqueror's jurisdiction was at best honorific. They had no parallel in Wales, where the Norman Conquest was a political fact. Whether by direct military onslaught, or by acquiring allies among the native princes, or by exerting

---

[1] Turgot, *Vita S. Margaretae*, pp. 239 (the crucifix: cf. below, p. 164, n. 3) and 247.

[2] Ibid., pp. 243–5.

[3] The point at issue is curiously close to Berengar's dispute with the clergy of Chartres in 1050: *Letter to Ascelin* and Ascelin's reply (D'Achery, *V.L.* pagination, pp.24D–5A = Migne, *P.L.*cl.66A–7B).

[4] Judging by Paschal II's advice to Turgot, bishop of St. Andrews, and others, the issues debated at queen Margaret's councils were still alive in 1112/14: D. Bethell, 'Two letters of pope Paschal II to Scotland', *Scot.Hist.Rev.*xlix (1970), 33–45. It is perhaps over-sceptical to propose that Paschal's advice gave Turgot material for the *Vita S. Margaretae*.

pressure through the monasteries on the Welsh Marches, or by
establishing a bishop at Chester, William envisaged direct
intervention in Wales. In 1081 he travelled to St. David's to
receive homage from the Welsh princes, as in 1072 he had
received Malcom Canmore's in Scotland. But the Welsh were
accessible compared with the Scots; their homage was more
than ceremonial. Similarly the archbishop of Canterbury was
not the reassuringly distant ally who was occasionally invoked
in Dunfermline or Dublin but another potential overlord. The
meeting at St. David's was the last attempt to establish relations
with William the Conqueror that would salvage some independence for the Welsh Church. The clergy of St. David's rose
to the occasion with claims that more than equalled the primacy
of Canterbury.[1] St. David's was 'the metropolis of the whole
country of the Britons', and the saint himself 'archbishop of the
entire Britannic race', with wide jurisdiction in Ireland into
the bargain. Subsequently other archbishops emerged from
the shadows to defend ancient liberties in Herefordshire and
Gloucestershire;[2] their claims had still less historical foundation
or hope of fulfilment. What is remarkable in all cases is the
instinctive resort to a legendary predecessor to justify a claim
that is effectively novel. Here it may well be thought that legal
right could be found with neither party: that the archbishop of
Canterbury's primacy was essentially no better founded than
the jurisdiction of his celebrated *confrères*, the archbishops of St.
David's, Llandaff and Caerleon-on-Usk.

For Lanfranc and William the Conqueror the primacy was
not only a precise legal concept; it asserted the unity of the
Norman Church in Britain. Throughout his reign William was
challenged time and again by disaffected groups in Yorkshire,
East Anglia, Kent or the West of England. Had any of these
succeeded, England could easily have relapsed into a land of
great earldoms, each with its regional Church. Alternatively if
rebels were to find help abroad, some foreign adventurer might
persuade a fully independent archbishop of York to crown him

---

[1] Rhigyfarch, *Life of St. David*, ed. J. W. James (Cardiff, 1967), especially cap.
53; discussed by N. K. Chadwick, 'Intellectual Life in West Wales in the last days
of the Celtic Church', in *Studies in the Early British Church*, ed. N. K. Chadwick *et.al.*
(Cambridge, 1958), pp. 121–82.
[2] C. N. L. Brooke, 'The archbishops of St. David's, Llandaff and Caerleon-on-
Usk', in *Studies in the Early British Church*, ed.cit., pp. 201–42.

King of England.[1] Here the primacy had a practical meaning: irrespective of a bishop's duty to his immediate metropolitan, all bishops owed (so to speak) liege homage to Canterbury. The principle could even in special circumstances apply to an abbot. When Alexander II confirmed the exemption of Bury St Edmunds from the bishop of Elmham (Thetford), he safeguarded the rights of 'the primatial bishop', here Canterbury.[2] Lanfranc could not be described as abbot Baldwin's metropolitan; but he was still his primate. The title did duty in a range of situations, that were not always strictly compatible in law or logic. But Lanfranc was neither inflexible in demanding the title nor over-confident in its efficacy. Such detachment was less easy for his successors, who finding the road (as they thought) open hastened along it rather too eagerly.

ii. papal relations

(a) You are aware ... that, since first the name of Christ was preached there, the kingdom of the English has been *in the care and wardship of the prince of the apostles*, until members of an evil head ... abrogated God's treaty and turned aside the English from the right way ...

(b) As you well know, while the English did remain faithful they sent to the apostolic see *an annual tribute* as evidence of their loyalty and devotion. Part of the money was consigned to the Roman pontiff, and part to the community of the church of St. Mary, which is known as the 'Schola Anglorum'. (Fragments of a letter of Alexander II to William the Conqueror.)[3]

The payment of Peter's Pence, to which Alexander II here refers, and which he no doubt went on to request from William, had been thoroughly established in England since at least the early tenth century.[4] Athelstan and his successors extended it

---

[1] Lanfranc made this point at once: Hugh the Chanter, s.a. 1070.

[2] *J.L.*4692; cf. J.-F. Lemarignier, *Étude sur les privilèges d'exemption et de juridiction ecclésiastique des abbayes normandes ... jusqu'en 1140* (Paris, 1937), p. 147: see p. 149, n. 3 below. It is characteristic of the fluid terminology of the second half of the eleventh century that *primas* also meant simply 'magnate': e.g. Geoffrey of Coutances is 'unus de primatibus Anglorum' (Bishop–Chaplais, pl. xxix).

[3] J.L. 4757. The italicized phrases are, respectively: *sub apostolorum principis manu et tutela* and *annuam pensionem*.

[4] W. E. Lunt, *Financial Relations of the Papacy with England to 1327* (Cambridge, Mass., 1939), i.3–30. It is abundantly clear from the evidence here assembled that in the tenth and eleventh centuries Peter's Pence was a royal tax rather than an ecclesiastical.

into the territory that they recovered from Danish rule; they
provided for its collection and legislated against those who
evaded payment. Imposed by the King and sent to Rome as
royal alms, it was an ancient and valued link with the papacy,
as Alexander II said. What is debatable is the association of
Peter's Pence with a papal wardship that derived ultimately
from Gregory the Great's mission to Kent—the idea that
Peter's Pence implied papal jurisdiction over England, indeed,
if the term 'tribute-money' is taken strictly, a proprietary right
such as a lord exercised over his estates.[1] There is no evidence
that Alexander pressed the point so far. William had invaded
England under a papal banner: this undefined recognition
of his authority perhaps encouraged Alexander to explore a
little further. It was the cloud no bigger than a man's hand,
which grew menacing only in the later years of Lanfranc's
archiepiscopate.

Alexander's practical negotiations with England were conducted by that veteran campaigner, Ermenfrid of Sion, who
held councils at Winchester and Windsor in the spring of 1070.[2]
The see of Canterbury was rendered vacant, York filled,
Winchester filled and the candidate consecrated: it was his last
and most spectacular intervention in the affairs of William the
Conqueror. At the same time Ermenfrid and his assistants, the
cardinal-priests Peter and John Minutus, drew up canons of
reform: condemning simony, securing Church property, providing for more effective ecclesiastical government and for the
liturgically correct celebration of the Eucharist.[3] While the
King and his magnates may have contributed to these councils
and even disputed details of legislation, essentially Ermenfrid
had a clear field, such as no papal legate would ever have again.
By the late autumn both archbishops were consecrated and
active, and the initiative in ecclesiastical government passed to
England. But there were still frequent, even hectic, exchanges

---

[1] Ibid., pp. 42–6: cf. Thietmar of Merseburg there cited, p. 44.

[2] Ch. V, §iii above: see further H. E. J. Cowdrey, 'Bishop Ermenfrid of Sion and
the penitential ordinance following the battle of Hastings', *Journ.Eccles.Hist.*xx
(1969), 225–42. Dr. Cowdrey's proposal that Ermenfrid was active only at the
second council (Whitsun, at Windsor), and even then as the King's man, seems
inherently improbable and very difficult of proof.

[3] D. Wilkins, *Concilia Magnae Britanniae* (London, 1737), i.322–3, 365: cf.
C. N. L. Brooke, 'Archbishop Lanfranc, the English bishops and the council of
London of 1075', *Studia Gratiana* xii (1967), 58.

with Rome: 'The matter is too urgent for me to await the return of the messengers whom I have just sent back to you', exclaimed Lanfranc, requesting immediate attention to the resignation of the bishop of Sherborne and the consecration of the bishop of Lichfield.[1] Two cathedral communities sought and obtained papal confirmation of their monastic status, and in the autumn of 1071 abbot Baldwin of Bury St. Edmunds travelled to Rome in person to secure a comprehensive privilege for his house.[2] On the same occasion both archbishops received their pallia and Remigius of Dorchester, who had been consecrated by Stigand, was at Lanfranc's intervention reinstated by the pope.[3] Lanfranc himself brought back a letter of commendation to William the Conqueror, asking that with Lanfranc's help the King re-examine the case of the bishop of Selsey, who had been perhaps over-hastily deposed by the papal legates the year before.[4] In the spring of 1072 another of Ermenfrid's assistants, the *lector* Hubert, witnessed the primacy agreement and may have helped also to draw up further reforming canons;[5] the legate was a witness now to the decisions of others, but still an accepted and valued participant. All in all, there is abundant evidence that in these early years of Lanfranc's archiepiscopate bishops, monastic envoys and papal legates moved freely and frequently between England and Rome. It is true that Lanfranc himself refused an invitation to spend Christmas 1072 at the papal court, but that was scarcely recalcitrance in a man who had been in Rome the previous autumn. He said that he was over-whelmed with work; and we may believe him.[6]

The change came with Gregory VII, though not at once. Soon after his consecration (30 June 1073) the pope wrote to Lanfranc very much in the style of the initial plea for sympathy

---

[1] *Lanfranci Epp.*2. In the event the bishop of Sherborne stayed on, and Lichfield remained vacant for another two years.

[2] *J.L.* 4761–3; 4692.

[3] *J.L.* 4693 was presumably given to Thomas on this occasion; cf. p. 118, n. 3 above. For Remigius see his own profession (Richter, no. 32: Appendix A 13b); contrast the story in Eadmer, *Historia Novorum*, pp. 10–12.

[4] *J.L.*4695, reinforced later by *J.L.*4762 to Lanfranc; cf. *Florentii Wigorniensis Chronicon*, ed. Thorpe (London, 1848), ii.6.

[5] Bishop–Chaplais no. xxix: for the *acta* see p. 143, nn. 1–6 below. Hubert first appears with Ermenfrid at the Norman assembly (summer 1070) in which Lanfranc was chosen as archbishop.

[6] *Lanfranci Epp.* 1: for the work-load see further *Epp.* 16, 43 and 50.

and support that he had sent round Europe the day after his election: 'You will have heard how the office was forced upon me, and with what burdens I am now oppressed . . . The bearer of this letter, whom we both love as a son, will tell you the whole story'. Almost as an afterthought the pope condemns the immoral marriage customs of the Irish.[1] Apart from the suggestion (it is no more) that Canterbury was responsible for the whole of the British Isles, he is expressing generalized goodwill; the relationship with Alexander II shall continue. If Gregory's other early letters are much more businesslike, reaffirming the privileges of Bury St. Edmunds and St. Étienne, Caen, here too he is continuing the work of his predecessor.[2] In the case of St. Étienne the cardinal-priests Peter and John Minutus reappear as legates (spring 1074); but, like Hubert, they take no independent action. After that there is a sharp decline in both legates and letters, but still no active friction. Neither the political drama at Rome nor the innovations of papal synods seems to have involved or disturbed the English Church. These peaceful years ended in the autumn of 1076. From September 1076 until the spring of 1078 Gregory endeavoured to replace Juhel, bishop of Dol with his own candidate—a Breton abbot who having come to Rome on his own affairs was amazed to receive this uncovenanted honour.[3] In 1078 he sent legates to depose archbishop John of Rouen, now incapacitated; and a year later the province was assigned to the primatial jurisdiction of Lyons.[4] Next archbishop John's successor, the upright and experienced William Bona Anima, was under censure for failing to visit Rome or to cooperate with Gregory's legates in France.[5] By the spring of 1080 these legates had suspended bishop Arnold of Le Mans; the following year virtually the entire Norman episcopate was under censure.[6] While depositions of this kind were usually temporary, they were seriously disruptive of

---

[1] Gregory VII, *Epistolae Vagantes* 1, ed. Cowdrey (Oxford, 1972: Oxford Med. Texts), pp. 2–5; cf. Gregory VII, *Registrum* i. 1–4 (23–8 Apr. 1073).

[2] *Reg.*i.31 (20 Nov. 1073: Bury); i.70 (4 Apr. 1074: St. Étienne); see also *Reg.* i.34 (2 Dec. 1073: Remigius of Lincoln).

[3] *Epp.Vag.*16: 'abbatem, qui cum ob alias causas quas explicare prolixum est ad nos venisset, pontificatus onus ex insperato subire compulsus est.' (cf.*Reg.*iv.4–5: 27 Sept. 1076); *Reg.*iv.17 (31 Mar. 1077); ibid.v.22–3 (22 May, 1078).

[4] Ibid.v.19 (4 Apr. 1078); vi.34–5 (20 Apr. 1079).

[5] Ibid. ix.1 (spring 1081).

[6] Ibid.vii.22–3 (24 Apr. 1080); ix.5 (1081).

government, both in Normandy and what might be termed the Norman empire, Brittany and Maine. William the Conqueror, being ready to negotiate, recovered much: but he had learned caution by the time Gregory turned his attention to England.

In the autumn of 1079 the pope made a determined effort to get both English and Norman representation at his forthcoming Lenten synod (March 1080). Bishops were legally obliged to attend, he wrote eloquently: a heathen king would not have stood in their way.[1] A heathen king was at less risk. William refused to allow any of his clergy to go to the synod, and he maintained the embargo for the rest of his reign: while letters and legates might still enter England (though more rarely), there was to be no traffic the other way. Just as attendance at a metropolitan synod was one of the few specific criteria of a suffragan's allegiance to his archbishop, so bishops attending a papal synod were reaffirming their personal allegiance to the pope. Secular and spiritual jurisdiction were easily confused, and indeed could not be fully separated; once in Rome a bishop could well take a personal oath of loyalty, without sufficiently defining its nature or limits. That this was not an idle fear may be judged from the legation of Hubert the subdeacon in the spring of 1080.[2] Hubert came to England with elaborate letters of introduction and, as Z. N. Brooke has argued, the personal authority to negotiate further. He requested payment of the arrears of Peter's Pence and asked that the king do fealty to the pope for England. William agreed to the former without argument and refused the latter: there was, he said, no precedent for papal jurisdiction of this kind. If, as seems virtually certain, Gregory linked the two demands, inferring a right of jurisdiction from the payment of *census*,[3] William did not, nor would he

---

[1] Ibid.vii.1 (23 Sept. 1079); cf.vi.30 (25 Mar. 1079).

[2] Ibid.vii.23, 25–6 (24 Apr. and 8 May 1080); *Lanfranci Epp.* 7–8: see Z.N. Brooke's illuminating discussion, *The English Church and the Papacy* (Cambridge, 1931), pp. 139–44. For Hubert's movements 1077–80, idem, 'Pope Gregory VII's demand for fealty from William the Conqueror', *Eng.Hist.Rev.* xxvi (1911), 227–31. If, as is generally assumed, Hubert the subdeacon is the Hubert *lector* of 1070–2 (p. 133, n. 5 above), he was a man known to William the Conqueror and apparently trusted: 'filium nostrum et fidelem communem' (*Reg.*vii.26; see also *Epp.Vag.*34 to Anselm, *ad fin.*).

[3] Cardinal Deusdedit, whose canon law collection was finished by 1087, classified Peter's Pence as payment signifying proprietary right: W. von Glanvell, *Die Kanonessammlung des Kardinals Deusdedit* (Paderborn, 1905), p. 378. This opinion

argue the point. That the acknowledgement of spiritual authority can and must be irrespective of secular jurisdiction may not have been self-evident in 1080; but the formal difficulty that holding land by an oath of homage excludes holding it by the payment of *census* can scarcely have been overlooked. But these difficulties are technical. William had already seen Gregory claim jurisdiction in Normandy on any pretext or none: give him an inch, and he would take an ell.

William's refusal caused no breach with Rome, perhaps because Gregory could not afford one. The year 1080 was the climacteric in his dealings with the emperor: thereafter he was under increasing military pressure from Henry IV and at the same time losing support to the antipope Clement III. In these later years his relations with England are marked by determined goodwill, whatever the provocation. In 1081 a papal legate intervened in Maine to make peace between William and Fulk Rechin; the next year Gregory himself wrote in support of William's candidate for the see of Le Mans.[1] At this level papal assistance was still worth something. But when Gregory again tried to bring Lanfranc to Rome and he refused to go, the threatened suspension was not put into effect.[2] Even the imprisonment of bishop Odo of Bayeux in the same year elicited only a sorrowful rebuke: 'You have acted unworthily, putting worldly considerations before the law of God and having insufficient regard for the honour due to a priest.'[3] Gregory could do better than that. The papal initiatives of 1076–80 had given way to an alliance in which the politically stronger partner was the king. By 1085 even that had been dissolved by William, unilaterally. As Lanfranc wrote to the Clementine cardinal Hugo Candidus,

Our island has not yet renounced Gregory nor decided whether she owes obedience to Clement. When we have considered both sides

---

[1] Orderic Vitalis, *Hist.Eccles.* iv (ed.Chibnall, II. 310–11), with references; Gregory VII, *Epp. Vag.* 48.

[2] Gregory VII, *Reg.*ix.20 (May/June 1082). Z. N. Brooke's slightly hesitant assumption (op.cit., p. 232) that Lanfranc did go to Rome in 1082 is based on the spurious *J.L.*5256: W. Holtzmann, *Papsturkunden in England* ii (Berlin, 1935), no. 2; p. 138. n. 4 below.

[3] *Reg.*ix.37 (winter 1083): contrast the much stronger letter to archbishop Hugh of Lyons on the same subject (*Epp.Vag.*53).

---

was incorporated a century later into the *Liber Censuum* ed. Fabre and Duchesne, *Bibl.Éc.Franc. Athènes Rome* (Paris, 1910), i.345, 355.

(if we ever do), we shall be able to see more clearly what is to be done.[1]

Gregory was still pope, until the King and his advisers had made up their minds.

Judgement was suspended for the rest of Lanfranc's life; yet there are grounds for thinking that communications were opened with the antipope, and kept open. The masterly neutrality of the letter to Hugo is in reply to Hugo's own letter, brought to England by Lanfranc's messengers.[2] Unless they were casually intercepted on the way (and that we may doubt), Lanfranc had already written to Hugo, or conceivably to the antipope himself. Clement certainly wrote to Lanfranc, two letters which are commonly dated in or after 1085, but need not be so late, and a third after September 1087.[3] It is a familiar enough theme: that Lanfranc should give Clement his personal support and advice in Rome—the Church of God being battered by so great a tempest—and that he should restore the payment of Peter's Pence. Clement needed the money, and still more the recognition. Peter's Pence had a sharper political edge than in the days of Alexander and Gregory, and this Clement understood. We enjoin you, he wrote,

to spur on the English King *to give St. Peter honour and due reverence* and to pay the [customary] *money from his kingdom*.[4]

Here the 'honour and reverence due to St. Peter' echoes Gregory's blunt demand for fealty, to which the definitive reply had already been given. What was more ominous was Clement's brief reference to a claim to land by St. Mary, Wilton. While it

---

[1] *Lanfranci Epp.* 59.

[2] Ibid.: 'Literas tuas·quas mihi per portitorem mearum misisti . . .' Lanfranc might have encountered Hugo Candidus at the papal court in 1050 or even (*Lanfranci Epp.* 13) at Remiremont in 1049, for Hugo belonged to that area: F. Lerner, *Hugo Candidus* (Munich/Berlin, 1931: *Hist.Zeitschr.* Beiheft 22), pp. 7–8; above, p. 67, n. 4.

[3] F. Liebermann, 'Lanfranc and the antipope', *Eng.Hist.Rev.*xvi (1901), 328–32; further discussion by P. Kehr, 'Zur Geschichte Wiberts von Ravenna (ClemensIII)', *S.B. Preuss. Akad. Wissensch.* (1921), 356–60. Letters 1 and 2 were sent from Rome, where Clement was established in the spring of 1084, and where possibly he had access to the papal archives. Letter 3 was written after the death of William the Conqueror.

[4] Letter 2: 'Unde volumus et fraterne premonemus, ut cum rege anglico *de honore sancti Petri et debita reverentia ac de pecunia regni sui* multum agas ac consulas' (Liebermann, op.cit., p. 331); cf. Letter 3 (p. 332).

was not surprising that a refuge of the Anglo-Saxon aristocracy should turn to the pope who was acknowledged by the German court, the formal appeal from England to Rome was a new development which Lanfranc can scarcely have welcomed.[1] Whatever his response, he kept the letters carefully, adding them to the canon law book which he had given to Christ Church a decade earlier.[2] Slight though these are, they constitute Lanfranc's sole dealings with the papacy (however defined) from *c.* 1083, when contract with Gregory was lost, until after the death of Victor III. Eventually in the spring of 1088 another Gregorian pope wrote to Lanfranc. The bark of Peter has narrowly escaped shipwreck, and still the seas run high; the bearer of this letter will tell you all.[3] Urban II was writing in exactly the vein of Gregory VII in 1073 and Clement III *c.* 1085: an exploratory letter seeking support in dangerous times. Like Clement he asked for Peter's Pence, echoing Alexander II's argument that the Roman see had transmitted the faith to England; Urban too needed the recognition as much as the funds. The cardinal subdeacon Roger was sent to deliver the letter and negotiate with Lanfranc and William Rufus. But it is not at all clear that he was ever admitted to England. Hugo Candidus had been discouraged from coming as the legate of Clement III;[4] Roger seems to have been no more welcome as the legate of Urban II. Caution and disengagement could go no further.

Given Lanfranc's influence with William Rufus, it is certain that he approved this policy of 'Wait and see'; but whether his theoretical conception of papal authority changed in any way is another question. If it seems that Lanfranc and the King became isolationist in principle, that is to read back (as Eadmer is

---

[1] Letter 3: 'Tuę pręterea caritati mandamus, quatinus inclito principi uestro suggeratis, ut pro amore Dei et beatorum apostolorum Petri et Pauli terram, quam cenobium sancte Mariae Wiltonensis ęcclesię tempore patris sui amisit, ei restituat' (p. 332). Lanfranc is not known to have had any personal interest in Wilton, except as the recipient of Goscelin's *Life of St. Edith* (App. D, p. 244). In the autumn of 1088 the bishop of Durham appealed to Urban II; but the case was judged by William Rufus and the bishop exiled, without reference to the pope: p. 160, n. 3 below; Appendix A 19a.

[2] MS. Cambridge Trinity Coll.B.16.44, pp.405–6: cf. p. 139, n. 1 below.

[3] *J.L.* 5351.

[4] 'Non laudo ut in anglicam terram venias, nisi a rege Anglorum licentiam veniendi prius accipias': *Lanfranci Epp.* 59.

inclined to do) from the later disputes of the time of Anselm. In the 1080s Gregory VII was at once extremist and weak; and William the Conqueror, still more William Rufus, responded pragmatically. Clement III held Rome; he had the support of the emperor and a number of cardinals: it was far from clear that the Gregorian line would prevail. Even Urban II, scholar of Rheims and prior of Cluny, who might well have won Lanfranc's approval personally, still looked politically unconvincing in his foothold at Terracina. There was good reason not to get involved, nor even to prefer either claimant openly.

But it was one thing to lie low during the uncertainties of a schism, quite another to doubt that papal authority was theoretically necessary in the universal Church; and here Lanfranc never departed from the position expressed in the *Liber de corpore et sanguine Domini*. His belief in the unity of the Church is confirmed by his zeal for canon law. Z. N. Brooke has shown that the collection of councils and papal decretals that Lanfranc acquired from Bec was then circulated widely throughout England.[1] We may postulate a copy in the hands of every bishop, and those abbots, such as Gloucester and Westminster, who were most involved in conciliar legislation; and the source of these books is unquestionably Christ Church, Canterbury. The collection is a peculiar version of Pseudo-Isidore: the abridged Decretals followed by a mixed text of the Councils. Whether or not Lanfranc was himself the compiler, he would have approved of the principles on which it was made: by the elimination of nearly all the pastoral material in the Decretals Pseudo-Isidore has been greatly reduced in bulk without loss of the legal essentials.[2] We seem to see the hand that cut down those unmanageable Carolingian commentaries on the Pauline Epistles. Certainly Lanfranc used the collection, finding in it nearly every canonistic quotation for his own archiepiscopal letters.[3] As a textbook of canon law Pseudo-Isidore, whether

---

[1] MS. Cambridge Trinity Coll.B.16.44: see Z. N. Brooke, *The English Church and the Papacy* (Cambridge, 1931), Ch. 5, N. R. Ker, *English Manuscripts in the Century after the Norman Conquest* (Oxford, 1960), pls. 4–5, and below, p. 180, n. 1.

[2] H. Fuhrmann, *Einfluss u. Verbreitung der pseudoisidorischen Fälschungen* (Stuttgart, 1973: *Mon.Ger.Hist.Schriften* XXIV), ii.421; cf. Brooke, p. 62. Pseudo-Isidorean studies have been placed on a new footing by Professor Fuhrmann's work (3 vols. 1972–4).

[3] Brooke, op.cit., pp. 68–9.

complete or abridged, chose itself, for it was the one collection generally available in eleventh-century Europe: what was universally recognized in the western Church was the best (indeed the only possible) lawbook for use in England. It has been termed papalist, by ninth-century standards or in comparison with Burchard's *Decretum* perhaps justly. But it is not Gregorian: it provides no more than the raw material for the *Dictatus Papae*. What it did provide was common ground for contemporary discussion both at the papal court and in the provinces. Lanfranc presumably knew this, but he seems to have been unaware of the modern collections in which that discussion was expressed. There is no evidence that the *Collection in Seventy-Four Titles* reached England in his time; the other new collections emerged only in the 1080s and Ivo's *Panormia* a decade later still. These are all systematic, organized however imperfectly according to their subject-matter, whereas Pseudo-Isidore keeps to the chronological order of popes and councils.[1] Lanfranc found the old arrangement satisfactory enough, but it scarcely outlived him. It is not that he deliberately affected the antique, but that in the study of canon law, as in so many other respects, he is just on the Carolingian side of the watershed.

iii. councils and colleagues

On one of the great festivals when the King wore his crown, as he was sitting at dinner in his royal garments and diadem with Lanfranc at his side, a court jester, seeing how the King shone with gold and precious stones, cried out in the great hall . . . 'Behold, I see God!'[2]

'Ecce Deum video.' Although the fool was whipped for his blasphemy, he had come dangerously near the truth: that William the Conqueror was the vicegerent, if not the image, of God in England. He ruled the Church, as he ruled his secular magnates, generally with equity, taking advice, but always

---

[1] Fuhrmann, op.cit., ii. 486–544. Burchard's *Decretum* (c. 1010), which was already systematic, may have been available to Lanfranc at Christ Church (MS. London B. L. Cotton Claudius C.VI: s.xi, reached Christ Church at an unknown date); but it had no known influence on his work, nor further circulation by his agency.

[2] *V.L.*, cap. 13, translating 'quidam scurra' as a jester, who could readily be whipped, rather than a courtier, who could not. See further P. Corbett, 'The Scurra', *Latomus* cxlv (1976), 23–31.

having the final word. This is not to say that Lanfranc and his fellow-bishops were weak men who toadied to the King. Given the military exigencies of the 1070s, to accept an English see or abbey was to accept absolute royal control; the only alternative was the choice attributed to Guitmund of La Croix-St. Leofroy: to refuse the spoils of war and ultimately to leave William's dominions altogether.[1] Ecclesiastical government was insepar- able from royal; and ecclesiastics are often to be found doing the King's business rather than their own. That is a platitude, yet it is still true. Lanfranc's control of the English Church can never quite be detached from the King's control of England as a whole.

Like his Anglo-Saxon predecessors William the Conqueror appeared in full royal state at Christmas, Easter and Whitsun, normally at the royal castles of Gloucester, Winchester and Windsor.[2] He could keep the great feasts at Gloucester abbey and Winchester cathedral: for Whitsun he may have gone to Westminster or St. Paul's. For his magnates, both lay and ecclesiastical, these were regular opportunities to show loyalty and do business. There need have been no written summons: it was a vassal's self-evident duty and interest to attend. Far- reaching decisions might emerge, outstandingly the proposals for the Domesday Survey that were considered at the Christmas court of 1085. But no *acta* survive, nor even a comprehensive list of courts held. What we have is an echo of the royal courts in the ecclesiastical councils that were held at the same time. While these are distinct assemblies, it is clear that the bishops and abbots who were already at court would attend the council,[3] that business could be initiated in the royal assembly and con- firmed in the ecclesiastical. At Easter 1072 for instance, at the council of Winchester, Lanfranc deposed the abbot of the principal local monastery, New Minster.[4] We cannot believe that he did so irrespective of the King's wishes, nor would the

---

[1] Orderic, *Hist.Eccles.* iv, ed. Chibnall II. 270–81.

[2] Winchester in particular was a major royal residence: H. M. Colvin, *The History of the King's Works* (London, 1963), ii.854–5; cf.i.37 (Gloucester) and ii.864–5 (Windsor), with references.

[3] The only formal summons to survive is a *legatine* letter requiring bishop Wulfstan to attend the council of Winchester, 1070: R.R. Darlington, *The 'Vita Wulfstani' of William of Malmesbury* (London, 1928: Camden Soc. 3 ser.xl), pp. 189–90.

[4] *Acta Lanfranci*, p. 288.

King remove an abbot unilaterally: here the ecclesiastical
council was a distinct and necessary aspect of the royal court.
William of Malmesbury sums up the situation in one of the
many legends of Glastonbury. When bishop Giso of Wells
delated the abbots of Muchelney and Athelney to Lanfranc's
council of 1081, they refused to acknowledge any superior but
the abbot of Glastonbury, by whom alone and in whose chapter-
house they could be judged:

Lanfranc (ready to support a Canterbury man), 'I would not wish to
impoverish Dunstan's nurse.'
William the Conqueror, 'I would rather not distress the Lord's mother.'

The archbishop gave a lead, but it was the King who concluded the matter: jurisdiction went to St. Mary the Virgin,
Glastonbury.[1]

Lanfranc held seven councils: in 1072 at Winchester and
Windsor, in 1075 at St. Paul's, London, in 1076 again at
Winchester, in 1077–8 in London, in the New Year of 1081 at
Gloucester and in the winter of 1085–6 again at Gloucester.[2]
Little is known of the last three beyond a bare notice in the
Acta Lanfranci and the Glastonbury anecdote. But the recent
discovery of further *acta* for Easter 1072 warns us to be cautious;
much may have been lost or never formally recorded.[3] The
surviving legislation falls within a span of four years, 1072–6. It
corresponds to similar activity in Normandy by archbishop
John of Rouen (dep. 1078), and it reflects some of the pre-
occupations of the reformers in Rome. But the Norman influence is much the stronger.

At Easter 1072 in the castle chapel at Winchester the King,
the papal legate and a few chosen magnates settled the primacy
dispute between Canterbury and York. Their decision is
preserved in a royal writ.[4] But when Lanfranc 'made many
regulations about the conduct of Christian worship'[5] he may
have done so in a larger gathering, perhaps in the cathedral

---

[1] *De Antiquitate Glastoniensis Ecclesiae*: Migne, *P.L.*clxxix. 1729AD.
[2] Appendix A.12.
[3] M. Brett, 'A collection of Anglo-Norman councils', *Journ.Eccles.Hist.* xxvi
(1975), 301–8. See particularly pp. 305–6: the random survival of much provincial
legislation and even of the fundamental papal *acta* of Clermont, 1095.
[4] *Reg.*i.64: Bishop–Chaplais, pl.xxix.
[5] 'Multa . . . de Christianae religionis culta servanda instituit': *Acta Lanfranci*,
p. 288.

itself. Several of the *acta* are indeed precisely liturgical: the adjustment of two feast-days, and the confirmation of the second Ember Day at a fixed point in June.[1] This last provision was not only complex but disputed, for current papal opinion regarded the first two Ember Days as movable.[2] Lanfranc summarized Anglo-Norman practice in a mnemonic:

> The first fast falls as March begins;
> The next the second week of June;
> The third the third week of September;
> The last the *third* week in December—
> Never the fourth, for it must give way
> To the greater feast of Christmas Day.[3]

Although even in Latin these verses are of no literary merit, they do show Lanfranc unexpectedly at odds with Rome on an issue that nearly fell within canon law. The rest of the legislation is pastoral and disciplinary, ranging from the familiar condemnation of simony to a problem that the Conquest may have exacerbated: the unattached clergy and monks who were drifting from one diocese or monastery to another.[4] The King's interest was remembered too, in a treason law similar to the legatine provision of 1070 and in the devotional support of both clergy and laity:

Let every priest say three masses for the King, those in minor orders say a psalter and the laity give sevenfold alms, that all may by their alms assist the poor.[5]

Where the *Regularis Concordia* had envisaged monastic prayers for the royal family,[6] Lanfranc's council now called on the secular clergy and their parishioners.

In 1075, while William the Conqueror was campaigning in

---

[1] Brett, p. 308: canons 11, 14, 12.

[2] A. Molien, 'Les Quatre-Temps', in *Dict. Théol. Cath.* (Paris, 1937), xiii.1452–3; G. G. Willis, *Essays in Early Roman Liturgy* (London, 1964: Alcuin Club xlvi), pp. 49–97, with references. Anglo-Saxon practice seems to have followed the Roman usage that the first two fasts moved with Easter and Whitsun.

[3] Walther, no. 5057: Latin text in Appendix D; cf. Rouen 1072, canon 8 (Orderic, *Hist. Eccles.* iv, ed. Chibnall II. 288–9).

[4] Brett, pp. 307–8. The unattached clergy were a continuing problem: see the councils of Windsor, 1070 (canon 3), London 1075 (canon 4), Winchester 1076 (canon 3) and *Lanfranci Epp.* 24.

[5] Brett, p.308, canon 9.

[6] *Regularis Concordia*, ed. Symons (London, 1953: Nelson's Med. Classics), pp. 13, 14, 16, etc.

France, the principal council of the reign was held in St. Paul's cathedral.[1] Thomas of York attended, as did every English bishop with the exception of Walcher of Durham (who was fully occupied on the northern frontier) and over twenty abbots; bishop Geoffrey of Coutances was there as a major landholder and, it may be thought, the King's representative.[2] Protocol having been settled in so notable a gathering, the principal business was to recognize the transfer of three sees: Sherborne, Selsey and Lichfield. Hermann of Sherborne, who had already moved from Ramsbury in 1058, moved nearly definitively to Old Sarum, on the hill above Salisbury. The other two broke with long tradition: St. Wilfrid's see of Selsey was transferred to Chichester, a few miles to the north; Chad's see of Lichfield, the would-be archbishopric of Mercia, went to Chester in the far north-west. Still other transfers were in process: Dorchester to Lincoln, Elmham to Norwich, and in the long term Wells to Bath. More astonishing than the number is the apparent casualness with which a bishop would move, and go on moving, until he found the right site. The formal justification was legal:

Following the decrees of popes Damasus and Leo and also the councils of Sardis and Laodicaea, which prohibit the existence of episcopal sees in small townships, by the generosity of the King and the authority of the synod three . . . bishops were permitted to move from townships to cities.[3]

The principle had already been invoked by Leo IX, when he urged Edward the Confessor to transfer the see of Crediton to Exeter.[4] But the authority in 1075 was rather pointedly not papal: it was a conciliar judgement founded on traditional canon law. The other measures range from curiously random fragments of monastic customary, which no doubt reflect some particular crises of the moment, to further provisions for the laity: familiar legislation on the degrees of kinship and a very

---

[1] D. Wilkins, *Concilia Magnae Britanniae* (London, 1737), i. 363–4: see C. N. L. Brooke, 'Archbishop Lanfranc, the English bishops, and the council of London of 1075', *Studia Gratiana* xii (1967), 41–59, with references.

[2] He witnesses as 'unus de Anglicç terrę primatibus': cf. p. 158 n. 1 below.

[3] London 1075, canon 4.

[4] *J.L.*4208 (1049): 'Leofricus episcopus sine civitate sedem pontificalem tenet . . . Praecipimus atque rogamus ut adiutorium praebeas ut a Cridionensi villula ad civitatem Exoniam sedem episcopalem possit mutare.'

specific prohibition of white magic—'The bones of dead animals must not be hung up anywhere as a charm against cattle-disease.'[1] The council of Easter 1076, the last for which *acta* survive, covers some of the same ground.[2] It is astonishing to find the case of Aethelric of Selsey only now being concluded, whether with compensation to Aethelric (if he was still alive) we do not know.[3] But the business otherwise is routine: the discipline of the lower clergy, the restriction of the extra-claustral activity of monks, the pastoral care of the laity. By now the council was a recognized forum for publicizing and even debating[4] the mandates of ecclesiastical government. It may have afforded Lanfranc an opportunity to guide his colleagues; but what is far clearer is the freedom of the episcopate from metropolitan direction at any other time. A bishop was lord in his diocese, having the entire pastoral oversight of clergy, monks and laity. Occasionally Lanfranc could offer support; but without a specific invitation he rarely intervened *qua* metropolitan.

He was exceptionally fortunate in the archbishop of York. Thomas of Bayeux had been one of bishop Odo's young men, sent (according to York tradition) to Lanfranc himself for his education.[5] At Canterbury he was regarded as an intelligent and hard-working man, whose mistakes arose from inexperience or bad advice.[6] He does not seem to have quarrelled with the decision on the primacy; certainly by the autumn of 1072 he was writing to Lanfranc in terms that the most sensitive primate must have approved:

To the most reverend and holy Lanfranc, archbishop of Canterbury, supreme pastor of all Britain, his vassal Thomas, who is also, unless it seem presumptuous to his holiness, archbishop of the church of York . . .

[1] London 1075, canon 8: ne ossa mortuorum animalium quasi pro uitanda animalium peste alicubi suspendantur. The more general condemnation of sooth-saying and divination in the same canon would be aimed at the laity also.

[2] Wilkins, op.cit. i. 367: see Appendix A12. below.

[3] Winchester 1076, canon 1. Aethelric had been deposed at Easter 1070; cf. p. 114 above.

[4] London 1075, canon 6, indicates that questions could be put from the floor.

[5] Hugh the Chanter, *History*, ed. Johnson (London, 1961: Nelson's Med.Texts), p.2. Thomas rose to be treasurer of Bayeux cathedral; for Odo and the 'Bayeux connection' see p. 156, n. 4 below.

[6] *Scriptum Lanfranci*, p. 165 (Appendix A13a); Hugh the Chanter, op.cit., p. 2.

Lanfranc responded with equal cordiality, sending the bishops of Worcester and Lichfield to assist in the consecration of Ralph, bishop of the Orkneys.[1] Thomas attended the council of 1075 and probably others; more convincing still, the archbishops could co-operate in strictly pastoral affairs: divorce law and the reception of a penitent from a Norman diocese. There are those, Lanfranc wrote, who suffer by separation, because their friendship is based on worldly advantage; those who are united in Christian love cannot be divided by bodily absence and the mere interposition of space.[2] Even so short a flight is rare in Lanfranc's correspondence: in Thomas he had a man who spoke his language and whom he could trust.

Lanfranc's good understanding with Thomas of York did much to stabilize the three border-bishoprics. Each had legal and administrative difficulties, for which Lanfranc acquired responsibility when he vindicated the jurisdiction of Canterbury in 1072. At Worcester he had only to assist Wulfstan to recover the estates that had been absorbed by York when Ealdred of Worcester became archbishop.[3] Wulfstan himself was an extremely capable diocesan, systematic in his pastoral duties and an effective administrator. We may suppose that he was consulted over bishop Patrick's appointment to Dublin in 1074; he was still Lanfranc's ally in quelling the magnatial revolt of 1088. In his ready support for William the Conqueror and Rufus and his commitment to monasticism, strictly ordered and sufficiently financed, Wulfstan could well have been Lanfranc's most congenial colleague. Wulftstan in turn seems to have trusted Lanfranc. He consigned to him his special protégé, the monk Nicholas, to learn the practice of the monastic life; on a more public stage Lanfranc's confidence is already obvious *c.* 1070–2 when he gives Wulfstan the custody of the vacant see of Lichfield.[4] There the diocesan administration was

---

[1] *Lanfranci Epp.* 11–12; cf. p. 125 above. Bishop Ralph was consecrated in York on 3 Mar. 1073.

[2] Ibid. 9–10: 'quaelibet localis intercapedo' (*Ep.*10).

[3] William of Malmesbury, *Vita Wulfstani* ii.l, ed. Darlington (London, 1928: Camden Soc. 3 ser. xl), pp. 24–6, cf. xxix-xxxi; Hugh the Chanter, op.cit., p. 11: 'molimine et instinctu Lanfranci archiepiscopi'.

[4] *Vita Wulfstani* iii.17; ii.l, ed.cit., pp. 56–7 (Nicholas), 26 (Lichfield). Nicholas maintained the association with Canterbury when he himself was prior of Worcester (1116–24): R. W. Southern, *St. Anselm and his Biographer* (Cambridge, 1963), p. 283n., with references.

inchoate and the financial problems acute. Bishop Peter, a man of whom personally little is known, was consecrated in the autumn of 1072. Finding the diocese still ravaged after William the Conqueror's harrying three years before,[1] he initiated the transfer to Chester that was confirmed in 1075; it was perhaps in the interim that he tried to take over the property of St. Peter's, Coventry. He descended on the abbey with a great retinue, broke into the strong-boxes in the monks' dormitory, pulled down houses in the precinct for their building-material and as a final insult remained to enjoy monastic hospitality for a week. Lanfranc's reaction was curiously muted.[2] Although rebuking Peter for the invasion, he imposed no ecclesiastical censure; the bishop seems to have withdrawn with his authority unimpaired. Here we can have only half the story; in the case of Dorchester there is rather more. Like Lichfield, this was a secular see in some administrative and legal disarray. Bishop Remigius had been almoner of Fécamp, in itself a position of financial responsibility, and from the first a strong supporter of the Conquest. He had been rewarded with Dorchester in 1067: so speedily as to be convicted later of at least technical irregularity in his consecration.[3] Remigius was unique among the English bishops in being a monk in a secular see: a monk who could not in practice maintain his profession. The criticism that he attracted was due in part perhaps to this ambiguous status, but more probably to his determined rule in a vast and undergoverned diocese. In 1072 he transferred his see to Lincoln,[4] and presumably at that point clarified its northern boundary with York.[5] He too hoped to profit by the wealth of one of the great Anglo-Saxon abbeys, here Ely. He acquired some of what was argued to be Ely land and laid claim to episcopal customs

---

[1] The devastation is vividly described by a chronicler in Evesham, who had seen the refugees coming south: *Chronicon abbatiae de Evesham*, ed. Macray (London, 1863: Rolls Ser.), pp. 90–1.

[2] *Lanfranci Epp.* 29. Peter's successor did indeed transfer the see from Chester to Coventry in 1102.

[3] William of Malmesbury, *Gesta Pontificum* i.42, iv.177, ed. Hamilton (London, 1870: Rolls Ser.), pp. 66, 312; Richter, no. 32: cf. F. Barlow, *The English Church 1000–1066* (London, 1963), pp. 302–10.

[4] Bishop–Chaplais no. 14.

[5] *J.L.*4695: 'Item sibi [sc.Lanfranco] negotium de discernenda lite quae inter archiepiscopum Eboracensem et episcopum Dorcacestrensem *de pertinentia diocesis eorum* est . . . commendavimus'; cf. *Lanfranci Epp.* 11.

within the abbey itself and its jurisdiction: the dispute crystall-
ized in the 1080s when the bishop claimed, and eventually
exercised, the right to consecrate abbot Symeon.[1] Although only
the monastic side of the case has survived, it is reasonably clear
that Remigius increased his revenues and that he maintained
the essential point that Ely was not exempt. Faced with the
same problem as Peter of Lichfield, he had shown considerably
more finesse. To both Lanfranc gave his support where at all
possible: to Peter for his transfer to Chester, to Remigius when
his consecration was called in question and in his anxiety (in
circumstances that we cannot now recover) that William
the Conqueror was giving credence to his detractors.[2]
What Lanfranc could not offer was complete support in
all circumstances, for in any territorial dispute he himself
was liable to be sent in by the King as a royal justice. In
Remigius' case little was lost, but in the classic dispute of
this type Lanfranc did finally give judgement against his own
suffragan.

The most publicized case of his archiepiscopate, though not
strategically the most dangerous, concerned the East Anglian
see of Elmham. Crowded between Remigius' diocese and the
coast, Elmham was isolated and under-endowed; before the
Conquest it had been a satellite see of Canterbury, and probably
viable as such. When Aethelmaer of Elmham was deposed,
along with archbishop Stigand his brother, at Easter 1070, the
see was given to Herfast, the King's chancellor. Herfast's
thoughts turned at once to the royal abbey of Bury St. Edmunds,
generously endowed and giving better access to the south.[3]
Unlike Coventry and Ely however Bury had a comprehensive
privilege of exemption from pope Alexander II. In any dispute
immediate jurisdiction lay not with the diocesan bishop
(Elmham), but with the 'primate'. The formula was very
similar to the privilege which Lanfranc himself had negotiated
for St. Étienne: direct appeal to Canterbury, as St. Étienne to

---

[1] *Liber Eliensis* ii.118–27, ed. Blake (London, 1962: Camden Soc. 3 ser.xcii),
pp. 200–7, with references: see below, pp. 157–8.

[2] See p. 133 above (Remigius' consecration) and *Lanfranci Epp.*58 (his detractors).

[3] For the basic chronology see Hermann the archdeacon, *De miraculis S. Edmundi*
caps. 25–9, ed. Arnold, *Memorials of St. Edmund's Abbey* (London, 1890: Rolls Ser.),
i. 60–7.

Rouen.[1] Prima facie then Lanfranc had an absolute mandate to protect Bury on terms that he had already welcomed in Normandy. If reinforcement were necessary, he was a personal friend of abbot Baldwin.[2] On the other hand, now that he was an archbishop himself, he disliked the exempt abbey on principle; and Bury was no exception.[3] By 1072 Herfast was contemplating a move to Thetford, on the Norfolk–Suffolk border, south of Elmham and more of a commercial centre; but his pressure on Bury continued. Finally in the autumn of 1073, in response to a sharp note from Gregory VII,[4] Lanfranc did dispatch a primatial rebuke to Herfast:

Were you to devote less time to gambling and games of chance, to read the Bible for a change and to learn some canon law . . . you would cease to argue with your mother church . . . No reasonable man can think that your rash claim falls outside my jurisdiction, since by the mercy of God the whole island of Britain is known to constitute the one jurisdiction of our one church.[5]

Fine words; but they make no reference to the primatial relationship with Bury, which was central to the privilege, nor are the protagonists summoned to any ecclesiastical tribunal of Lanfranc's own. Over the next few years there were two royal inquiries, in the second of which Lanfranc himself took part; and finally at Easter 1081 the case was concluded in a royal assembly, held presumably at Winchester. On each occasion judgement was given in favour of Bury St. Edmunds, the decision of 1081 being confirmed a few months later in a royal charter.[6] Lanfranc fully accepted this procedure. Since Herfast's accession over a decade earlier he had regarded the invasion of Bury as a dispute over property rather than the violation of a

---

[1] *J.L.*4692 (Bury); 4644 (St. Étienne: cf. p. 109, n. 3 above).

[2] *Lanfranci Epp.* 18 and 42.

[3] Eadmer, *Historia Novorum*, pp. 132–3. See Z. N. Brooke, *The English Church and the Papacy* (Cambridge, 1931), pp. 130–1; and *contra* J.-F. Lemarignier, *Étude sur les privilèges d'exemption et de juridiction ecclésiastique des abbayes normandes des origines à 1140* (Paris, 1937), pp. 143–50. Given the similarity between the two bulls (*J.L.*4644 and 4692), Lemarignier is committed to seeing Lanfranc as 'partisan du rattachement de Bury à Rome' (p. 149), despite his reluctance to invoke the Bury bull against Herfast (p. 150).

[4] Gregory VII, *Reg.*i.31 (20 Nov. 1073).

[5] *Lanfranci Epp.*23: '. . . cum per misericordiam Dei totam hanc quam vocant britannicam insulam unam unius nostrae ecclesiae constet esse parrochiam'.

[6] *Reg.*i.137; cf. D. C. Douglas, *Feudal Documents from the Abbey of Bury St Edmunds* (London, 1932: Rec. Social Econ. Hist.viii), pp. 50–5.

papal privilege. His celebrated advice a year later to judge Odo of Bayeux not as a bishop but as earl of Kent was no sudden political device:[1] it expressed the archbishop's consistent attitude towards the lawsuits of his own suffragans.

Where Lanfranc could be of positive value as a metropolitan was in his command of canon law. Ecclesiastical business at diocesan level was becoming more clearly demarcated from royal, and at the same time more technical. Herfast himself, who was proficient enough in secular law, was glad to draw on Lanfranc's experience as a canonist; there is no hint here of personal tension between them.[2] Hugh of London received sound advice as he embarked on his episcopate; his successor Maurice had practical encouragement in bringing two quarrelling nuns to reason.[3] A matrimonial case in the diocese of Chichester had attracted attention in Rome; and once more Lanfranc came to the bishop's assistance.[4] Finally Walcher of Durham was bluntly advised that a man who had been living as a monk, though unprofessed, must remain a monk: 'compelle intrare'.[5] Only that handful of cases has survived: there is nothing from Walkelin of Winchester, Osbern of Exeter, Osmund of Salisbury, all active and gifted bishops. If Lanfranc's advice is not consistently felicitous, it is clear and practical. In international terms he was by no means a leading canonist, but he knew quite enough for the type of *insolubilia* that would otherwise have gone to Rome. Here once more 'the lawyer of Pavia' had mastered his brief.

iv. the King

God sends no greater mercy on earth than . . . when he commits the kingdoms of this world to the rule of good kings. Thence peace dawns and discord is hushed . . . (Lanfranc to Toirrdelbach, king of Munster)

---

[1] William of Malmesbury, *Gesta Regum* iv. 306, ed. Stubbs (London, 1889: Rolls Ser.), ii. 361.

[2] *Lanfranci Epp.* 21–2. William of Malmesbury's story that Lanfranc had convicted Herfast of crass ignorance when he visited Bec is irreconcilable with Herfast's position as chancellor 1068–72: *Gesta Pontificum* ii. 74, ed.cit., pp. 150–1. Lanfranc himself regarded Herfast as ignorant of the studies appropriate to a bishop, which is a different matter: *Lanfranci Epp.* 23 and cf. 33 *ad fin.*

[3] *Lanfranci Epp.* 24 (bishop Hugh) and 31 (bishop Maurice).

[4] Ibid. 28: 'cum uiro suo maneat' is the crucial phrase.

[5] Ibid. 26.

While the King lives, we have peace of a kind; but after his death we expect to have neither peace nor any other benefit. (Lanfranc to Alexander II)[1]

Lanfranc came to England when the first shock of the Norman invasion was over, and the political situation was becoming in consequence extremely unstable. In 1069–70 there had been sustained English resistance in Yorkshire and the Midlands; in 1075 there was to be a dangerous alliance of the Norman earls of Hereford and Norfolk and the Anglo-Saxon earl of Huntingdon. In such circumstances the archbishop of Canterbury lived in two worlds: the legal and pastoral problems of the English Church and the legal and military exigencies of royal government. As a tenant-in-chief Lanfranc had not only to administer the estates and revenues of his see; he was expected to act in any capacity on behalf of William the Conqueror in and beyond Kent. His participation in local affairs was assumed, and on several occasions he was cast for a notable part elsewhere. Although Lanfranc came to Canterbury with only seven years' experience as an ecclesiastical magnate, he grasped these essentials rather quickly.

Archbishop Stigand had controlled a great barony in southern and eastern England: the estates of Christ Church and Winchester, his own family holdings, and the further estates controlled indirectly through his patronage of St. Augustine's, Canterbury, Glastonbury and Ely;[2] at the same time he enjoyed the protection and support of the house of Godwin. Whatever the criticisms of his pastoral record, Stigand had been a magnificent archbishop, with ample financial resources and for many years political security. He had weathered the Conquest; directly or indirectly he retained his monastic patronage and the control of Winchester and Elmham. But we do not know the price he paid for survival. He may well have admitted new tenants to Christ Church or bought support with rights and revenues. Dean Godric of Christ Church is known to have appropriated some land;[3] and other monks may have followed

[1] Ibid. 38 and 1.

[2] F. Barlow, *The English Church 1000–1066* (London, 1963), pp. 76–81, with references; *Liber Eliensis*, ed.cit. ii. 103; cf. p. 114. n. 1 above.

[3] D. C. Douglas, 'Odo, Lanfranc and the Domesday Survey', in *Historical Essays in honour of James Tait*, ed. J. G. Edwards *et al.* (Manchester, 1933), p. 52; cf. App. A14b,2.

his example. What is certain is that the moment Stigand fell, the estates of the see could readily be alienated; his tenants had to find a new patron, and they were unlikely to look to Godric the dean. The situation was no doubt steadied within a few months by Lanfranc's arrival. But assuming no further losses after August 1070, over two dozen estates, large or small, were already gone: enough to cause financial strain to an archbishop who did not have Stigand's ancillary sources of revenue. To recover them Lanfranc had to prove his title at law; and he took at least ten years to do so completely. In 1072 at a shire court on Penenden Heath near Maidstone, he vindicated his judicial privileges as archbishop in Kent and recovered six Christ Church estates from Odo of Bayeux and his tenants and Hugh de Montfort.[1] Although only a handful of villages was actually retrieved at Penenden Heath, this court became a symbol of all Lanfranc's subsequent litigation: the exhaustive inquiry into ancient rights, the prince-bishop Odo vanquished by the lawyer-monk. In practice most of the negotiations were conducted with less ceremony; some business was certainly delegated to the courts of individual hundreds.[2] Lanfranc recovered the property of his see by slow, hard bargaining. 'Every day I endure so many troubles and vexations ... I suffer such injury and distress, hardness of heart, greed and dishonesty':[3] it may be thought that some part of these tribulations arose from the long battle to recover the endowments of Christ Church.

The Christ Church lands lay substantially in Kent and Sussex, with two great holdings north of the Thames in Middlesex. Beyond that there was some property in Essex and Suffolk and outlying groups in Surrey, Hertfordshire, Buckinghamshire and Oxfordshire.[4] Lanfranc took care to protect his rights and property in London and the Kentish ports of Dover and Sandwich.[5] Inland he acquired (or recovered) a small property

---

[1] J. Le Patourel, 'The reports of the trial on Penenden Heath', in *Studies in Medieval History presented to F. M. Powicke*, ed. R. W. Hunt *et al.* (Oxford, 1948), pp. 15–26; cf. App. A 14b,1.

[2] Douglas, op.cit., p. 52; F. R. H. Du Boulay, *The Lordship of Canterbury* (London, 1966), pp. 36–43, the indispensable study for the discussion that follows.

[3] *Lanfranci Epp.* 1.

[4] *Domesday Book* i. 3–5: see comprehensively Du Boulay, op.cit., pp. 43–7.

[5] For London see Douglas, op.cit., pp. 58–63, with references; cf. *Reg.*i.265 (Harrow) and *Reg.* ii. 532 (confirmation to Anselm of rights established by Lan-

in western Kent by exchange with Odo of Bayeux and illegally annexed on his own account some Westminster lands in Hertfordshire.[1] The privileges in London and Sandwich in particular were to prove a sound commercial investment. The total resources of the see are recorded in Domesday Book and, at greater length, in the cognate survey known as *Domesday Monachorum*.[2] Both incorporate earlier material, some of it no doubt assembled by Lanfranc. Indeed one section of *Domesday Monachorum* has the rubric:

This was the usage before the arrival of the lord archbishop Lanfranc.[3]

A stranger trying to understand a new diocese, a methodical man who had already begun to set in order the estates of St. Étienne, a magnate establishing his claim to disputed property: there was sufficient reason for Lanfranc to make a survey of the resources of Christ Church. A concern for estate records and the maintenance of archives was the hallmark of the progressive bishop: Wulfstan of Worcester and Giso of Wells undertook such inquiries; and among the abbots characteristically Baldwin, a monk of St. Denis, made a thorough overhaul of the records of Bury St. Edmunds.[4] If Lanfranc too produced the archetype of *Domesday Monachorum*, he was in good company. The shadow on the picture is our ignorance of what, if anything, had already been attempted by Stigand. It is generally assumed that he did nothing, that Lanfranc had to rely on oral testimony rather than any pre-existing surveys. But considering the broad acres, monastic and episcopal, that Stigand

---

[1] *Sir Christopher Hatton's Book of Seals*, ed. Loyd and Stenton (Oxford, 1950: Northants Rec.Soc.xv), no. 431; cf. Du Boulay, op.cit., p. 390 WITTERSHAM, with references. The Westminster lands are noted by F. E. Harmer, *Anglo-Saxon Writs* (Manchester, 1952), p. 502; Du Boulay, p. 37, n. 1.

[2] D. C. Douglas, *The 'Domesday Monachorum' of Christ Church Canterbury* (London, 1944).

[3] 'Hęc est institutio antiqua ante aduentum domini Lanfranci archiepiscopi': *Domesday Monachorum*, ed.cit., p. 79.

[4] For Worcester see *Hemming's Cartulary*, discussed by N. R. Ker, in *Studies . . . presented to F. M. Powicke*, pp. 49–75. For Wells see the *De primordiis episcopatus Somersetensis*, ed. Hunter in *Ecclesiastical Documents* (London, 1840: Camden Soc.), pp. 15–20. For Bury see D. C. Douglas, *Feudal Documents from the Abbey of Bury St. Edmunds* (London, 1932), pp. 1–44.

---

franc). For Dover see *Reg.i.*176; for Sandwich ibid., 101–2 (grants by bishop Odo) and Du Boulay, op.cit., p. 35, with references.

controlled, such a conclusion is not inescapable. Lanfranc's task may have been rather to convert Anglo-Saxon records into Latin.[1]

By the time of the Domesday Survey the property of Christ Church could be divided in three: the lands of the archbishop, the lands enfeoffed to the archbishop's knights and the lands of the community. A quota of sixty knights was due to the King, all of whom were a charge on the archbishop rather than the monks.[2] Lanfranc fulfilled this service in the normal way, by enfeoffing tenants who could guarantee the provision of knights. The majority were Norman, identifiable sometimes as dependants of Bec or the new foundations at Caen.[3] Some had already been established by Odo of Bayeux; many could not be dislodged: so it was in recognition of ineluctable fact that Lanfranc created nearly a hundred knights' fees rather than the required minimum of sixty. By this device he retained formal control of land that was otherwise effectively lost. The families that he recognized were to settle in as the gentry of Kent; a number can still be identified with certainty in the time of Thomas Becket.[4] Eventually there was cachet in an English ancestry: by the 1180s the monks of Canterbury could see the whole class of *milites archiepiscopi* as Anglo-Saxon *threngs* to whom Lanfranc had given confirmation of tenure and a new name.[5] For the monks themselves he defined more exactly the *terrae monachorum* and the revenues due to specific functionaries: to the cellarer *ad victum* or the chamberlain *ad vestitum*.[6] Here Lanfranc showed no special originality: it was the record of these decisions in Domesday Book

---

[1] For the question of Anglo-Saxon records *vis-a-vis* Norman see further J. Campbell, 'Observations on English government from the tenth to the twelfth century', *Trans.Roy.Hist.Soc.*, 5th ser. xxv (1975), 39–54, especially 48–51.

[2] Du Boulay, op.cit., pp. 52–65, with references.

[3] Du Boulay, pp. 54–65, 92–9, 330–92, with references; *Domesday Monachorum* ed.cit., pp. 36–73, 105.

[4] H. M. Colvin, 'A list of the archbishop of Canterbury's tenants by knight-service in the reign of Henry II', *Kent Records* xviii (1964), 1–40. Compare the establishment of the feudal tenants of Durham: H. S. Offler, *Rannulf Flambard as bishop of Durham (1099–1128)* (Durham, 1971: Durham Cathedral Lecture), pp. 11–12.

[5] *Epp. Cantuarienses*, ed. Stubbs (London, 1865: Rolls Ser.: *Chron.Mem.Richard I* vol.ii), p. 225; cf. Du Boulay. op.cit., p. 79.

[6] Du Boulay, pp. 18–22, with references (division of lands); R. W. Southern, *St. Anselm and his Biographer* (Cambridge, 1963), pp. 256–60 and *Lanfranci Epp.* 54 (revenues).

that made them, for good or ill, the norm for the future. Even in his own time Lanfranc was compared with his great predecessor archbishop Dunstan, zealous for the welfare of his monks and the endowments of Christ Church. During the lawsuit on Penenden Heath it was Dunstan who came to encourage him; when Lanfranc was ill, he saw Dunstan riding out with his retinue, and in struggling to kiss his foot in the stirrup he was restored to health.[1] These were miracles appropriate to an admired archbishop, and yet at the same time wishful thinking. The political and tenurial power of Stigand, that to a great extent reflected Dunstan's own, had dissolved in 1070. Lanfranc had the see of Canterbury, and nothing more: the far-flung 'connection' of earlier days was gone.

His principal ally was the bishop of Rochester, both suffragan and feudal tenant. In 1077 he was able to appoint to this satellite see the perfect coadjutant. Gundulf of Rochester first appears as a monk of Bec in the 1050s, by his name presumably Italian and conceivably related to Anselm.[2] As sacrist of Bec and prior of St. Étienne he developed a talent for organization that was invaluable to Lanfranc in the early years at Christ Church and in the problems that he faced at Rochester himself. He found an undistinguished secular see, its estates and revenues at risk and its buildings inadequate; and over thirty years he established a monastic chapter, observant and suitably housed, began to reconstruct his cathedral and made the basic lists and surveys that underlie the cartulary of *c.*1120, the *Textus Roffensis*. Lanfranc gave Gundulf every support. He spoke for the lost Rochester estates as well as his own at Penenden Heath and thereafter.[3] He provided vestments and liturgical plate without stint: twenty-five copes, two gilt candelabra, a silver shrine for the relics of Paulinus of York.[4] Gundulf in turn was an utterly reliable, and effective, colleague, the prop of Lanfranc's

---

[1] Osbern, *Miracula S. Dunstani* 18; 20, ed. Stubbs, *Memorials of St. Dunstan* (London, 1874: Rolls Ser.), pp. 143–4; 151–2. For Dunstan's own plea at Erith, which has remarkable similarities to Penenden Heath, see Du Boulay, pp. 33–5.

[2] R. A. L. Smith, 'The place of Gundulf in the Anglo-Norman Church', *Eng. Hist.Rev.*lviii (1943), 257–72, with references; and see below, p. 175, n. 3. Anselm's father was called Gundulf also.

[3] Du Boulay, pp. 83–4; 37–8: cf. *Textus Roffensis* fol. 170v–3, ed. Sawyer, *Early English MSS in Facsimile* XI (Copenhagen, 1962), vol. ii.

[4] J. Thorpe, *Registrum Roffense* (London, 1769), p. 120; cf. Lanfranc's *obit*, lines 35–9. The candelabra were repeatedly pawned in hard times: Thorpe, p. 123.

old age in England. In 1088 he resisted the rebels in Kent, and after Lanfranc's death it was again Gundulf who maintained the archbishop's rights, at whatever cost, against St. Augustine's.[1] Beyond Kent Lanfranc still had influence in St. Albans, a section of Stigand's patronage which now went to Lanfranc's nephew Paul.[2] On a lesser stage Paul enacted his uncle's part at Canterbury, stabilizing the endowments and bringing stone and tiles from the ruins of Verulamium to reconstruct the abbey church. Lanfranc's help ranged from 1,000 marks for the building fund to the provision of books to be copied in the new scriptorium; his own *Constitutions* for Christ Church were quickly imposed on the community at St. Albans.[3] That is the sum of Lanfranc's 'connection' in England, and even in Normandy his support was limited: Bec was a respectable house of the second rank and St. Étienne scarcely established. Beside the massive resources of Odo of Bayeux or Geoffrey of Coutances it was not enough.[4]

His very isolation recommended Lanfranc to William the Conqueror. He could only be the King's man; he could safely be left in charge. In 1075 the alliance of the earls of Hereford and Norfolk with Waltheof, earl of Huntingdon, was the last serious opportunity for an English rising.[5] In William's absence abroad it was Lanfranc who had the over-all direction of Wulfstan and Aethelwig holding the line of the Severn and the bishops of Bayeux and Coutances with Richard fitz Gilbert and William of Warenne containing the eastern rebels within Norfolk and Cambridgeshire. When the revolt was totally subdued, Lanfranc sent a succinct report to the King:

[1] See respectively p. 160, n. 2 and p. 189, n. 1 below.
[2] *Gesta Abbatum S.Albani*, ed. Riley (London, 1867: Rolls Ser.), i.51–64. For Stigand see Knowles–Brooke–London, pp. 65–6, with references.
[3] *Gesta Abbatum* i. 54, 58; note the allocation of specific revenues to the scriptorium (ibid. 57–8). The St. Albans manuscript of the *Constitutions* was thought to be in Lanfranc's own hand: *Gesta Abbatum* i. 61, 58–9; cf. Appendix D.
[4] For Odo see most recently D. R. Bates, 'The character and career of Odo, bishop of Bayeux (1049/50–1097)', *Speculum* l (1975), 1–20, with references. Some of the ramifications of the Bayeux cathedral chapter are discussed by C. N. L. Brooke, 'Gregorian reform in action: clerical marriage in England 1050–1200', in *Medieval Church and Society* (London, 1971), pp. 86–7. For Geoffrey see above all J. Le Patourel, 'Geoffrey of Montbray, bishop of Coutances, 1049–93', *Eng.Hist.Rev.* lix (1944), 129–61.
[5] D. C. Douglas, *William the Conqueror* (London, 1964), pp. 231–3, with references.

Norwich castle has fallen and its defenders have sworn to leave England within forty days. The mercenaries who served the traitor Ralph have begged a similar indulgence. The castle itself is occupied by Geoffrey of Coutances, William of Warenne and Robert Malet, with 300 heavily armed men, slingers and many siege-engineers. By God's mercy the clamour of war has entirely ceased on English soil.[1]

For a moment Lanfranc was 'the protector of England'.[2] But for a moment only: he had no continuing office nor any guarantee that William the Conqueror would listen to him. It was on his advice that earl Waltheof threw himself on the King's mercy, only to be imprisoned and executed:[3] we cannot suppose that Lanfranc knowingly sent the man to his death.

Lanfranc was at court relatively seldom (judging at least by his appearance in witness-lists),[4] but he is often found on the king's business in various parts of England. As a local magnate he received royal writs confirming property to Cluny and hunting-rights to Battle Abbey;[5] beyond his own lordship he confirmed rights and property for instance to Abingdon and St. Paul's.[6] But his role is best defined in two protracted legal battles in East Anglia. In the later 1070s he held a shire court at Bury St. Edmunds to determine the claims of Herfast of Thetford against abbot Baldwin,[7] and during the 1080s he endeavoured to clarify the lands and rights of Ely, particularly with regard to the bishop of Lincoln.[8] Though the protagonists are

---

[1] *Lanfranci Epp.* 35 (slightly abridged); cf. 34, 25.

[2] *V.L.*, cap.15: 'princeps et custos Angliae'.

[3] *Florentii Wigorniensis Chronicon*, ed. Thorpe (London, 1849), ii. 10–12; *A. S. Chron.D*, s.a. 1075–6: cf. Douglas, loc.cit.

[4] Appendix A11a.

[5] *Reg.*i.179 (Cluny); 260 (Battle): see Appendix A11ab. Although Battle was founded in 1067, it hung fire for ten years or more, and Lanfranc never took any active part in its establishment; cf. C. N. L. Brooke, 'Princes and kings as patrons of monasteries: Normandy and England', in *Il monachesimo e la riforma ecclesiastica (1049–1122): La Mendola 1968* (Milan, 1972), pp. 133–5, corroborated by E. Searle, *Lordship and Community: Battle Abbey and its Banlieu* (Toronto, 1974) pp. 21–7.

[6] *Reg.*i. 49, 200 (Abingdon); i.111, 274 and Gibbs, *Early Charters of St. Paul's*, no. 12 (St. Paul's). See further Appendix A 11.

[7] Pp. 148 n.3–149 n.6 above. See Herman the archdeacon, *De miraculis S. Edmundi* cap. 25–9, ed. Arnold, *Memorials of St. Edmund's Abbey* (London 1890: Rolls Ser.), i.60–7 and D. C. Douglas, *Feudal Documents from the Abbey of Bury St. Edmunds* (London, 1932), pp. lxiii, app., and 50–6; cf. *Lanfranci Epp.* 19.

[8] P. 148 n. 1 above. See *Liber Eliensis* ii. 120–7, pp. 203–7, 426–32, and (with significant differences of chronology) E. Miller, 'The Ely land pleas in the reign of William I', *Eng.Hist.Rev.* lxii (1947), 438–56. According to *Liber Eliensis* ii. 135 there were royal inquiries into the Ely lands (a) under abbot Thurstan, *ob.*1072–3 and

clerics, Lanfranc's jurisdiction here is royal: he is specifically the King's 'justice'. As his own lawsuit had been heard on Penenden Heath by Geoffrey of Coutances *in loco regis*,[1] so he now heard similar disputes in the shire court and—what was no less important—enforced the decision afterwards. Odo of Bayeux held a similar inquiry at Evesham, where the new abbot was refusing to recognize military tenants already established on his estates; a series of lay magnates investigated the endowments of Ely; others again were involved in the dispute at Bury St. Edmunds.[2] All these are civil cases that for some reason fell outside the competence of the local courts. Lanfranc and the other magnates who took part, clerical and lay, had *ad hoc* authority from the King to resolve them; there was no permanent office of 'King's justice'. But for the duration of the plea the justice exercised real power, sometimes alone, often shared with other magnates; it was the traditional and appropriate way for the tenant-in-chief to participate in royal government.

As a justice Lanfranc was not singled out beyond his colleagues. Although theoretically the *placita* of his childhood in North Italy are similar to those of Anglo-Saxon England, and parallels may be found between Anglo-Saxon law and Lombard, there is little reason to believe that continental law, verbally or in principle, was ever applied to the English disputes.[3] The essential qualification for a justice was not technical expertise but social position: if Lanfranc knew more law than

---

[1] J. Le Patourel, 'The reports of the trial on Penenden Heath', in *Studies in Medieval History presented to F. M. Powicke* (Oxford, 1948), ed. R. W. Hunt *et al.*, p. 23: 'qui in loco regis fuit et iustitiam illam tenuit'. For Geoffrey's other *placita* see Le Patourel, 'Geoffrey of Montbray' (p. 156 n. 4 above), pp. 148–9.

[2] The subsequent development of the king's 'justice' is discussed by F. West, *The Justiciarship in England 1066–1232* (Cambridge, 1966), pp. 1–30. For the Evesham plea see *Chronicon Abbatiae de Evesham*, ed. Macray (London, 1863: Rolls Ser.), pp. 96–7, and for Odo's resolution of a dispute between Gundulf of Rochester and the sheriff of Cambridge see *Textus Roffensis*, fols. 175–6v, ed.cit. (p. 155, n. 3 above.)

[3] Above, p. 4 n. 4, p. 5 n. 1: cf. D. M. Stenton, *English Justice 1066–1215* (Philadelphia, 1964), pp. 6–21, with references. MS. Oxford Bodleian Laud Misc. 742 is a complete text of the *Lombarda*, with some glosses, copied *c.*1120 in Bury St. Edmunds, no doubt at the instigation of the Italian abbot, Anselm of S. Saba.

(b) under abbot Symeon *acc.*1082. The latter consisted of a shire court at Kentford (ibid. ii. 116–17), in which Lanfranc was not involved, a second shire court held by Lanfranc and others at an unknown place (ibid. ii. 120–1) and additional negotiations in which Lanfranc again took part (ibid. ii. 122–7).

Odo of Bayeux and Geoffrey of Coutances, they had far more land. What could well be argued is that Lanfranc had a specific area of jurisdiction. The pleas at Ely and Bury St. Edmunds are matched by an interest in the Fenland abbeys. When abbot Aelsi of Ramsey, after years in the wilderness, was restored to the King's favour *c.* 1080, his possession was confirmed in a writ to Lanfranc, who later assisted in the recovery of further monastic rights and property.[1] Conversely it was by Lanfranc's decision that Fulcard of Thorney and Wulfketel of Crowland were deposed at Christmas 1085.[2] Although he certainly did intervene elsewhere, Lanfranc seems to have had a special interest in East Anglia. The area as a whole coincides with none of the later Domesday circuits: Huntingdon/Lincoln (VI), Cambridge (III) and Suffolk (VII).[3] Yet whenever the circuits were devised, the actual material of the inquest was already shaped by the King's justices, in whose footsteps the Domesday commissioners were to travel from one shire court to the next.

Lanfranc was not a commissioner himself; he took no part in the survey beyond sending in his own returns for Christ Church.[4] It might be thought that his years were telling at last. But in the autumn of 1087 he was back in politics. On 9 September William the Conqueror died on campaign in France, leaving Normandy to his eldest son Robert and England to William Rufus. Such a division of the inheritance, however just, was immeasurably inconvenient to anyone who held lands on both sides of the Channel. The old King, foreseeing revolt, had sent a letter to Lanfranc designating Rufus as his heir in England.[5] Lanfranc crowned the new King just before Michaelmas and remained his loyal adherent in the power-struggle that

---

[1] *Reg.*i. 177 (confirmation of Aelsi's possession of Ramsey) and 296, *Cartularium monasterii de Rameseia*, ed. Hart and Lyons (London, 1884: Rolls Ser.), i. 233. For Aelsi himself see R. W. Southern, 'The English origins of the *Miracles of the Virgin*', *Med.Renaiss.Stud.* iv (1958), 194–8.

[2] F. Barlow, *The Life of King Edward* (London, 1962: Nelson's Med.Texts), p.lii (Thorney); *A.L.*, p. 290 (Crowland): cf. Knowles–Brooke–London, pp. 74 and 42 respectively.

[3] V. H. Galbraith, *The Making of Domesday Book* (Oxford, 1961), pp. 7–8, with references.

[4] *Lanfranci Epp.* 54: see Appendix D5.

[5] Orderic Vitalis, *Hist.Eccles.* vii, viii, ed. Chibnall, vol. IV, pp. 96, 110; cf. ibid. x, vol. V, p. 202. For Lanfranc's supposed authorship of a new *ordo* for Rufus' coronation see Appendix D.

exploded the following spring. Odo of Bayeux, newly released by the Conqueror's deathbed amnesty, led a rising in Kent; Geoffrey of Coutances and Robert de Mowbray rebelled in the West Country; they were joined by other magnates in the Midlands, East Anglia and as far north as Durham.[1] It seems amazing that Rufus survived. But the revolt was a bid for power by a few great men with much to lose, commanding neither intense local loyalty nor foreign aid. It was defeated by the old guard of 1075—by Wulfstan, who defended Worcester 'like a second Moses rebuking the children of Israel',[2] by Lanfranc and Gundulf in Kent and by the King's own generalship. Much depended on the recovery of Kent. The castles of Tunbridge, Pevensey and Rochester were besieged in turn by the King's troops, and when finally Rochester fell the revolt was called off. Odo of Bayeux returned to Normandy for good, but Geoffrey of Coutances and most of the other magnates involved made their peace quickly and without apparent cost. The notable exception was the bishop of Durham. Perhaps as a monk and a native of Maine William of St. Carilef lacked family support; for whatever reason he stood to lose his office. For a while he staved off the inevitable, but in November 1088 he was brought before the King at Salisbury.[3] He proved a tenacious disputant: as a bishop he was not subject to a lay tribunal; as a feudal tenant he could not be tried until he was repossessed of the temporalities of Durham. A debate of this kind was Lanfranc's home territory. As he had defeated Berengar in the literary forum of the *De corpore et sanguine Domini*, so here, only a few months before his death, he won an assured victory:

The bishop must do justice to the King
before he demands justice for himself.

Then a sudden hatchet-blow:

Whatever *we* do will be just.

[1] *A. S. Chron.*, s.a.1088; *Florentii Wigorniensis Chronicon*, ed. Thorpe (London, 1849), ii.21–6; *Textus Roffensis*, fols. 173v–4, ed.cit. (p. 155, n. 3 above); William of Malmesbury, *Gesta Regum* iv. 306, ed. Stubbs (London, 1889: Rolls Ser.), ii.360–3; Orderic Vitalis, *Historia Ecclesiastica* viii, ed.cit. IV. 121–35, with references.

[2] *Flor.Wigorn.*ii.25: 'quodammodo alter Moyses parat se viriliter staturus pro populo et civitate sua'.

[3] *De iniusta vexatione Willelmi episcopi*, ed. Arnold, *Symeonis Monachi Opera Omnia* (London, 1882: Rolls Ser.), i.179–91: see Appendix A19a.

Then a return to principle:

We judge you not as a bishop but as a vassal,
as we judged Odo of Bayeux before the King's father.

When the bishop tried to keep Durham castle, arguing that it was on the King's safe-conduct that he had left it, Lanfranc finally swung the court against him:

If the bishop refuses to resign the castle, the King may justly take it; by his original breach of faith and by accusing the King's magnates of deceit the bishop has lost the safe-conduct which he here invokes.

Enthusiastic applause in court—

'Seize the bishop,' shouted Rufus' barons. 'The old bloodhound's right!'[1]

---

[1] 'Tunc Radulphus Piperellus et omnes laici unanimiter conclamantes dixerunt, "Capite eum, capite eum, bene enim loquitur iste vetulus ligaminarius (*lyam-hound*)"': ibid., p. 187.

VII: Canterbury 1070-1089

i. the cathedral

LANFRANC's first duty at Canterbury was to restore the fabric of √his cathedral after the great fire of 1067. The Christ Church historians are eloquent of this disaster: the choir was in ruins, the monks huddled into the nave for their attenuated office; the tombs of the saints lay exposed to wind and rain. Worse still, the archives were destroyed: the immemorial title-deeds to the lands and privileges of Christ Church were reduced to a few illegible scraps of parchment.[1] Perhaps the monks exaggerated a little. Lanfranc was enthroned in the old cathedral, however ruinous; and a considerable quantity of pre-Conquest charters is extant even now. Not everything went up in flames, either in the cathedral proper or in the monastic buildings.[2] The real difficulty was the character of the old cathedral itself. Eadmer, who had known it as a boy, describes it as in several respects a conscious imitation of St. Peter's in Rome.[3] Of course it was much smaller; but like old St. Peter's it had the raised sanctuary above a ring-crypt, then the *schola* for the choir (perhaps

---

[1] *Lanfranci Epp.* 3; cf. Eadmer, *Vita Bregwini* (Migne, *P.L.* clix.758A; new edition by B. W. Scholz, *Traditio* xxii, 1966, 144).

[2] The dormitory, refectory and cloisters were still habitable. Essential repairs were put in hand at once, and later in Lanfranc's archiepiscopate there was extensive rebuilding: Lanfranc's *obit*, lines 9–12; cf. Osbern, *Miracula S. Dunstani*, cap.16. Traces of Lanfranc's dormitory and infirmary may still be seen: R. Willis, *The architectural history of the conventual buildings of the monastery of Christ Church in Canterbury* (London, 1869), pp. 21–9; 47–59 (figs. 5–6). Willis recorded the remains of Lanfranc's dormitory (148′ x 78′), uncovered in 1860 and destroyed in 1867 (fig. 2).

[3] *De reliquiis S.Audoeni*, pp. 364–6: see H. M. Taylor, 'The Anglo-Saxon cathedral church at Canterbury', *Archaeol.Journ.*cxxvi (1969), 101–30, with a comprehensive discussion of earlier literature. Criticisms of Dr. Taylor's position ibid. cxxvii (1970), 196–210, and *Archaeol.Cantiana* lxxxiv (1969), 175–84, do not seem to me to be convincing. The site of the throne is confirmed in an eleventh-century *ordo* for the reception of an archbishop: D. H. Turner, *The Claudius Pontificals* (London, 1971: Henry Bradshaw Soc. xcvii), pp. xxxvii–xxxviii; *Anglo-Saxon Chronicle*, s.a. 1051. The first capitular seal of Christ Church shows the old cathedral: *Cat. Seals British Museum* i, no. 1368, pl.IX. Here and in the chapter as a whole I am indebted to the advice of Dr. Nicholas Brooks.

surrounded by a low wall, such as can be seen today in Santa Sabina). The church was entered by doors north and south of the *schola*; in the west end stood the original main altar, with the archbishop's throne behind. Internally the organization was almost exclusively related to the saints. Wilfrid was in the easternmost altar, with Fursey, the Irish hermit, in the crypt below him; archbishops Oda and Elphege on either side of the high altar; Dunstan buried deep beneath his memorial pyramid west of the high altar and east of the choir; and the Frankish virgin Austroberta in the western apse. The saints filled the • church, not the great saints of all Christendom, but the heroes of the Anglo-Saxon past. Local cults in an archaic building, they had little chance of survival, irrespective of the obvious damage done by the fire. Lanfranc dismantled the old cathedral to its foundations and built a considerably longer modern church in its place:[1] a short triapsidal choir, transepts to the west of that, and an impressive nave of seven bays ending in twin towers with gilded pinnacles. The great tower was over the crossing; it had golden cherubim on its pinnacle, visible from a great distance to the traveller as he came into Canterbury.[2] In many ways the design was based on St. Étienne, Caen, which was still under construction in the 1070s; but Christ Church had one technical development of real importance.[3] Whereas the western towers of St. Étienne are still recognizably the Carolingian 'westwork', a distinct unit built against the end of the nave, those at Christ Church were tied in to the last bay of the north and south nave aisles. This integration of nave and west front was a crucial step towards vaulting the nave itself in stone. It is characteristic of Lanfranc that he looked towards this ° further achievement without living to see it. His cathedral was completed in 1077; but in that it was pioneering it was soon altered.[4] Prior Ernulf, the schoolmaster in Lanfranc's day, doubled the length of the choir; prior Conrad added stained glass, sculpture

---

[1] Eadmer, *Vita Bregwini*, ed.cit., col. 758BC and Gervase, *Tractatus de combustione et reparatione Cantuariensis ecclesiae*, pp. 9–11: Taylor, op.cit., p. 117.

[2] Osbern, *Miracula*, cap. 22: see the second capitular seal (*Cat. Seals British Museum* i, no. 1369, pl.IX).

[3] J. Philip McAleer, 'The Romanesque Church Façade in Britain' (1963: unpublished Ph.D thesis for the Courtauld Institute, London); cf. p. 101, n. 2 above.

[4] Gervase, op.cit., pp. 12–16.

and a splendid painted ceiling; and the new choir was consecrated by archbishop William in 1130. The cathedral had become an ornate Romanesque building, narrow for its length, and technically inferior to Winchester or Norwich. The next major fire, in 1174, was an opportunity to build the present Gothic choir with its corona to the east for the shrine of Becket; subsequently the nave too was rebuilt in the new style. Prior Goldston replaced the south-west tower *c.* 1400; but its neighbour stood until 1834, when it was rebuilt to match Goldston's.[1] Lanfranc's cathedral was never accepted as definitive. It was intelligently designed and effective to the eye, but alterations began almost at once, and continued until scarcely a stone now remains of the original building.

Within the church the *confessio* was gone; and the eye was drawn instead to a great crucifix, with Mary and John on either side, set on a beam across the east of the nave.[2] Stigand had given such a group to his other cathedral of Winchester and to Ely, and a 'great cross' to St. Augustine's, Canterbury; archbishop Ealdred gave a cross 'of German work' to Beverley minster; and a resourceful abbot of Bury St. Edmunds in the same period took the exact measurements of the Volto Santo of Lucca and had it reproduced to scale by his own craftsmen at home.[3] These wonders have all vanished; they are the early expression of a devotion that was to find its way into every parish church, growing banal through repetition. In the 1070s however such crucifixes were unfamiliar in Normandy and France: they could be found in the Rhineland, where perhaps they originated, northern Italy and England. The crucifix in Lanfranc's cathedral was English, with a difference. Above it were two cherubim, one on either side, as the cherubim that

[1] Lanfranc's tower was 113 feet high: Willis (1845), p. 64. The most accurate record is a water-colour executed in 1832 by J. C. Buckler for the Society of Antiquaries, to whom I am indebted for permission to reproduce it. For a view of the west front as a whole see W. Woolnoth, *A Graphical Illustration of the Metropolitan Cathedral Church of Canterbury* (London, 1816), pl.6, opp.p.51.

[2] Gervase, op.cit., p. 10.

[3] P. H. Brieger, 'England's contribution to the origin and development of the triumphal cross', *Medieval Studies* iv (1942), 85–96; cf. F. Barlow, *The English Church 1000–1066* (London, 1963), pp. 21 and 79. For similar crucifixes from Cologne and (?) Werden *c.* 1060 see *Rhein und Maas: Kunst und Kultur 800–1400* (Cologne, 1972), i.191–2. None of the English crucifixes has survived, apart from a fragment (s.xii ²⁄₄) at South Cerney, Glos.: G. Zarnecki, 'The Chichester reliefs', *Archaeol. Jour.* cx (1953), 117, pl. xxviB.

watched over the ark of the covenant. They were complemented by the cherubim on the central tower, who guarded the ark-like nave of Christ Church itself. Bede explains that these cherubim are the Old Testament and the New; and the covering of the ark is the mercy of Christ: as the ark was sprinkled with blood on the Day of Atonement, so Christ's blood is the new and perfect atonement for his people.[1] The cherubim are a permanent reminder of where the new law touches the old. Their flight symbolizes the understanding and exposition of the faith:

As from age to age our knowledge grows, they preach Christ's redemption and give it ceaseless honour, their wings spread as for flight. Just as the spoken word flies through the air from the speaker's mouth to the heart of the listener, so the cherubim spread their wings as though they were about to fly.

The figure would appeal to a grammarian, one of whose classic problems was to determine how the word spoken reached the hearer's brain.[2] Eastward of the crucifix was the high altar, and finally the archbishop's throne. Westward was a vast gold *corona* suspended from the roof of the nave: the circle of candles was fully lit only on great festivals like Christmas and Easter.[3] From the relative capacity of nave and choir it would seem that the liturgical round was performed west of the crucifix, where the *schola* had been in the old cathedral. Certainly the crucifix itself was a focus of the liturgy in Holy Week, and of the major processions entering by the west door.[4] Lanfranc himself was buried 'ante crucifixum', a second Dunstan in the midst of his monks.[5]

Lanfranc's cathedral concentrated the attention on the

---

[1] Bede, *De Tabernaculo* i.501–92, ed. Hurst, *Corp.Christ.Script.Lat.*cxixA (1969), pp. 17–20, commenting Exod.25:17. Cherubim are found with crucifixes in early Irish art, but otherwise nowhere before the thirteenth century. There is a good Irish example in MS. Durham Cathedral A.II.17, fol. 38₃v: R. A. B. Mynors, *Durham Cathedral Manuscripts* (Oxford, 1939), pl. 3.

[2] *De Tabernaculo* i.586–92; cf. Priscian, *Institutiones* i.1.

[3] Gervase, op.cit., p. 9; cf. *Constitutions*, p. 58.

[4] *Constitutions*, pp. 25, 46–7; cf. Willis (1845), pp. 70–1.

[5] i.e. west of the crucifix: Orderic, *Hist.Eccles.* viii (Chibnall IV.170); Eadmer, *Vita Anselmi*, pp. 145–6, app. When the choir was rebuilt, Lanfranc was moved first to the Trinity Chapel and then, when that was replaced by the shrine of Becket, to the chapel of St. Martin in the north choir transept, where a simple inscription of the late twelfth century may still be seen on the wall: Gervase, op.cit., pp. 16 and 26).

universal Christian doctrines of the Incarnation, the Redemption and the Eucharist, rather than on the local saints of England; but there is no reason to believe that he despised the Anglo-Saxon saints as such. During the building operations the saints and archbishops who had been buried in the old church were reinterred in the western apse; when the apse itself was pulled down they were moved again, with due ceremony, into the refectory, until they could be established in the cathedral once more.[1] This kind of scrupulosity (if it is no more) is not comparable with the wholesale destruction of Anglo-Saxon antiquity that took place for example at St. Albans, where the tomb of King Offa himself was destroyed and his bones scattered.[2] The exclusive devotion of Christ Church to the English saints was ended; but the saints themselves were still held in honour.

'Our Bezaleel', wrote the hagiographer Goscelin, commending himself to Lanfranc *c.* 1080.[3] As Bezaleel had made the ark of the covenant, its cherubim, the golden vessels and the rich hangings, so Lanfranc had adorned Christ Church. He had provided gold and silver plate for the liturgy and vestments, heavy with gold thread and embroidered with dragons and strange birds; there was a great processional cope with silver bells round the fringe and a topaz clasp set with amethysts.[4] If such conspicuous wealth now seems at best vulgarity, out of key with Lanfranc's earlier life at Bec, it should be remembered that he was furnishing a cathedral. Ceremony and magnificence were required of him as archbishop. At the procession through the city on Palm Sunday for instance, with its liturgical stations outside the gates and at the cathedral door, the more splendid the vestments the better; even the little silver bells were not out of place.[5] Queen Margaret of Scotland, who honoured the poor to excess, took the same view: she owed it to her position to keep

---

[1] Osbern, *Miracula S. Dunstani*, caps. 17 and 19 (removals to the west end and the refectory); Eadmer, *Vita Bregwini*, col. 758C (definitive removal).

[2] *Gesta Abbatum*, ed. Riley (London, 1867: Rolls Series), i.62.

[3] A. Wilmart, 'La légende de Ste Édith en prose et vers par le moine Goscelin', *Anal.Bolland.*lvi (1938), 34; cf.Exod.37:1–9.

[4] Lanfranc's *obit*, lines 3–6. The vestments are described in prior Eastry's inventory of 1321, ed. J. Wickham Legg and W. H. St. John Hope, *Inventories of Christ Church, Canterbury* (London, 1902), pp. 50–7. Later in the fourteenth century several were burnt to recover the gold (ibid., p. 13).

[5] *Constitutions*, pp. 22–6.

up a magnificent court.[1] In later years a more intellectual defence would be called for, such as Suger offered for St. Denis:

> Praise not the gold that men have wrought,
> But to its meaning raise your thought.
> The only gold that truly shines
> Is what gives light within your minds,
> To show the true light, Christ—the door
> Of that real world we'd lost before.[2]

But in the England of William the Conqueror no such apologia was needed.

ii. the community

When Lanfranc arrived in Canterbury, the dominant monastic community was without question St. Augustine's. The house had prospered throughout the century, and significantly its abbots had kept in touch with the outside world. Wulfric attended the council of Rheims, and may on the same occasion have visited St. Bénigne, Dijon, which seems to have been the model for his great rotunda.[3] His successor Aethelsige (1061–70) obtained from Alexander II the right to wear the mitre and sandals of a primatial abbot. Leo IX had granted a similar privilege to St. Boniface's house of Fulda, so presumably Alexander was ready to see St. Augustine's as founded by the apostle of England.[4] Nor was it simply a title of honour. The ambitions of St. Augustine's are summed up in a series of charters and privileges that emphasize the complete liberty of the house from all jurisdiction, secular or ecclesiastical.[5] The abbot represents Rome in England, he is the archbishop's

[1] Turgot, *Vita Margaretae*, ed. Hodgson Hinde (Durham, 1867: Surtees Soc.li), p. 242.

[2] Suger, *De rebus in administratione sua gestis* 27: Migne, *P.L.*clxxxvi. 1229A (freely translated).

[3] A. W. Clapham, *English Romanesque Architecture before the Conquest* (Oxford, 1930), pp. 149–52; cf. Anselm of Rheims, *Historia dedicationis ecclesiae S. Remigii*: Migne, *P.L.*cxlii.1431B. The other English participants at Rheims were Duduc, bishop of Wells, and Aelfwine, abbot of Ramsey.

[4] *J.L.*4541; cf.4170 (Leo IX to Fulda).

[5] W. Levison, *England and the Continent in the Eighth Century* (Oxford, 1946), pp. 181–206. St. Médard, Soissons, and St. Ouen, Rouen, claimed a similar status in this period as the 'apostolic' foundations of Gallia and Neustria respectively (ibid., pp. 211–16).

equal; his house is the *mater primaria* of all the English monasteries. These documents, purporting to be of the seventh and tenth centuries, are all forgeries of the eleventh, but the claims which they embody were not invented overnight. However unreasonable, they were the established convictions of the community, reinforced by the presence in St. Augustine's of the founders of Kentish Christianity: Augustine himself and succeeding archbishops, King Ethelbert and others of his line, including (since 1035) the wonder-working relics of St. Mildred of Thanet.[1] From the beginning St. Augustine's had been the saint's own monastery. Its 'primatial' status was reinforced by Stigand, who made the abbey one of the centres of his ecclesiastical lordship, openly preferring it to the cathedral.[2] This was the more demoralizing for the community at Christ Church in that it had been equally neglected by Stigand's predecessors, Eadsige (1035–50) and Robert of Jumièges (1051–2).[3] Men like dean Godric were left in charge, competent enough perhaps, but unknown and powerless outside Canterbury. In the struggle for estates and revenue, and more insidiously for prestige, the community at Christ Church was on the defensive; the storms of the Conquest threatened it with erosion of privilege or even dissolution. But in the spring of 1070 there was a sudden lull; for Aethelsige of St. Augustine's had fled the country and Stigand was deposed.[4] For a few months both communities were thrown on their own resources.

It was probably at this point that the community at Christ Church assembled a dossier of privileges for the new archbishop. Their fundamental claim was to monastic status, implied by Bede and assumed since the time of Dunstan, but nowhere formally confirmed. What was needed was a papal letter. Like St. Augustine's in similar circumstances, Christ Church too became the subject of a letter from Boniface IV to King

[1] Goscelin, *Translatio S. Mildrethe* (B.H.L.5960): MS. London B. L. Cotton Vespasian B.xx, fol. 178. For these disputed relics see further. Ch. VII, § iv.

[2] Stigand's *obit* appears in the St. Augustine's martyrology: MS. London B. L. Cotton Vitellius C.xii, fol. 120. In his time the abbot of St. Augustine's is said to have held (in rotation with Glastonbury and Ely) the office of royal 'chancellor' in England: F. Barlow, *The English Church 1000–1066* (London, 1963), pp. 125–6.

[3] Eadsige became incapacitated in 1044; his duties were performed by abbot Siward of Abingdon as *chorepiscopus* (1044–8): *Anglo-Saxon Chronicle*, s.a.1044.

[4] The dates given for Aethelwige's flight range from 1067 to 1070 (Knowles–Brooke–London, pp. 35–6); 1070 is the most reasonable.

Ethelbert establishing monks perpetually in his cathedral. The papal concession is limited and specific:

We grant that you may set up in the monastery in Canterbury which St. Augustine dedicated to the Saviour a house of monks living according to a rule, so that the archbishops (being themselves monks) may live with monks.[1]

There is nothing here to compare with the dreams of greatness at St. Augustine's: the claims to an ancient primacy recently fortified by Alexander II. The primatial claims of Christ Church turned on the archbishop. They are embodied in nine forged privileges, that answer the St. Augustine's forgeries in their own language.[2] Boniface V writes to archbishop Justus, Vitalian to archbishop Theodore, Sergius I to the kings of Mercia and Northumbria, Leo III to archbishop Aethelheard. The names vary but the doctrine is one: the primacy of the archbishop of Canterbury over all Britain. The archbishop was *ex officio* head of the monastic community; and an abbot like that could look the abbot of St. Augustine's in the eye. Implausible though the claims of both sides may appear now, within the local feuds of Canterbury they were taken seriously: one forgery fed another. Lanfranc as ever walked circumspectly. Whatever its earlier status, Christ Church had in fact been monastic since the time of Dunstan. So the monastic privilege of Boniface IV was sent for confirmation to Rome.[3] The primacy on the other hand was still a live issue, and one that concerned William the Conqueror as much as Alexander II. It was only in the spring of 1072, after William had ruled in favour of Canterbury, that Lanfranc petitioned Alexander for a privilege confirming his primacy over York. His case rested on the decision of the royal council and historically on Bede's account of archbishop Theodore; but he ended with an unmistakable, if summary, reference to the forged privileges.[4] He never quoted the actual text, and when he

---

[1] *J.L.* 1998; cf. Bede, *Historia Ecclesiastica* i.26,33. The text is also printed by H. Boehmer, *Die Fälschungen Erzbischof Lanfranks von Canterbury* (Leipzig, 1902), no. I.

[2] See Appendix C.

[3] *J.L.*4761 (=*Lanfranci Epp.*4).

[4] *Lanfranci Epp.*3: 'Vltimum quasi robur totiusque causae firmamentum prolata sunt antecessorum uestrorum Gregorii, Bonifacii, Honorii, Vitaliani, Sergii, item Gregorii, Leonis item ultimi Leonis priuilegia atque scripta quae Dorobernensis ecclesiae praesulibus . . . sunt data aut transmissa.'

encountered resistance at Rome he did not press the matter further. For half a century after 1072 the forged privileges were almost forgotten. Their value was in any case symbolic. They expressed the community's confidence in its Anglo-Saxon past: in Augustine and Ethelbert, in Wulfred and the others who had consolidated the estates, in Dunstan, who had renewed the monastic way of life. Lanfranc could scarcely ignore the privileges, whatever he thought of their authenticity.

The same piety towards the founding fathers marks the pre-Conquest liturgy of Christ Church. Archbishop Dunstan had established monasticism on the most admired continental lines, expressed (or thought to be expressed) in the *Regularis Concordia*. By the mid-eleventh century he was regarded at Christ Church as its author, and the monks took a proprietary interest in what might be called 'the rule of St. Dunstan'.[1] Miracles took place at his tomb: the blind and the lame were cured and the proud brought low. A church was dedicated to him in the city; and the 'Dunstan bell' hung in the south-west tower of Lanfranc's new cathedral.[2] Few would remember Dunstan personally; but a monk in his sixties would have known archbishop Elphege, a hero of quite a different sort. Honourable but undistinguished in life, he was killed by Danish raiders in 1012 and quickly regarded as a saint. His feast (19 April) and Dunstan's (19 May) were the real singularities in the Christ Church liturgy.[3] In

---

[1] Anselm assumes that Dunstan is the author: *Anselmi Epp.* 39. One of the two surviving manuscripts, and probably the other, was at Christ Church in the mid-eleventh century: N. R. Ker, *Catalogue of Manuscripts containing Anglo-Saxon* (Oxford, 1957), nos. 155 and 186.

[2] Osbern, *Miracula S. Dunstani* and Eadmer, *Miracula S. Dunstani, passim.* For St. Dunstan's church outside the West Gate see the St. Gregory's foundation charter (Appendix A10a) and W. Urry, *Canterbury under the Angevin Kings* (London, 1967), map 1a. The Dunstan bell is mentioned c.1080 by Goscelin, *Vita S. Edithae*, ed. Wilmart, *Anal.Bolland.* lvi (1938), p. 38; cf. Osbern, op.cit., p. 138.

[3] The main evidence for the pre-Conquest liturgy of Christ Church is the kalendar in MS. London B. L. Arundel 155, which can be dated to 1012–23: F. Wormald, *English Benedictine Kalendars pre-1100* (London, 1933: Henry Bradshaw Soc.lxxii), no. 13. The case for ascribing MS. London B. L. Add. 37517, the 'Bosworth Psalter' (pre-1012: Wormald, no. 5), to Christ Church also is well argued by P. M. Korhammer, 'The origin of the Bosworth Psalter', *Anglo-Saxon England* ii (1973), 173–87. Gasquet and Bishop, in their pioneering analysis of the Bosworth Psalter, assumed that Arundel 155 was a post-Conquest text reflecting the practice of Christ Church *after* (as they argued) Lanfranc had wielded his knife on the old Anglo-Saxon kalendar: *The Bosworth Psalter* (London, 1908), pp. 27–42.

other respects it had remained conservative, even in the face of continental innovation. The new feasts of the Virgin, the Conception and the Presentation, which had gained acceptance at Winchester and Glastonbury and perhaps elsewhere, were making virtually no headway at Christ Church: the established liturgy was still in essentials that of Dunstan and Aelfric.[1] It seems to have been perfectly acceptable to Lanfranc, apart from the two great local feasts. Initially both Dunstan and Elphege were removed from the kalendar. No question was raised as to their holiness of life or the authenticity of their remains:[2] but they had been canonized by local acclamation alone, and by 1070 that was scarcely enough. During his year in Rome Lanfranc had witnessed the elevation of Gerard of Toul to universal recognition as a saint; and the solemnity of the process, initiated by the pope and confirmed by a papal bull, inevitably cast doubt on the credentials of other modern saints who had been accepted more casually.[3]

Although in principle Lanfranc was on firm ground in suspending the cults of Elphege and Dunstan, he did not make his work at Christ Church easier by doing so; and in practice he was allowing both by *c.* 1080. The case of Elphege was submitted to Anselm, who argued that in refusing to jeopardize his people Elphege had died for justice. Witness to justice being *ipso facto* witness to truth, Elphege was a martyr and eligible for veneration. Lanfranc gave way fairly gracefully, commissioning a hymn in Elphege's honour and allotting him a feast of the second rank.[4] His attitude to Dunstan is more puzzling. No

[1] The earliest solid evidence outside Winchester is for Worcester, Exeter, and St. Augustine's, Canterbury, all in the later eleventh century: E. Bishop, 'On the origins of the feast of the conception of the blessed Virgin Mary', *Liturgica Historica* (Oxford, 1918), pp. 238–59; S. J. P. van Dijk, 'The origin of the Latin feast of the conception of the blessed Virgin Mary', *Dublin Review* ccviii (1954), 251–67; 428–42. MS. London B. L. Harley 2892 (s.xi[1]: Christ Church) has a benediction for the Conception of the Virgin (ed. Woolley, *The Canterbury Benedictional*, London, 1917, pp. 118–19: Henry Bradshaw Soc.li); what is lacking is clear evidence in the Christ Church kalendars (*pace* Woolley, the Conception is not found in the Bosworth Psalter).

[2] Lanfranc had the reliquaries opened and their contents listed: Eadmer, *De reliquiis S. Audoeni*, p. 367, lines 195–9. But he took no such risks as his former chaplain, Walter of Evesham, who tested the relics of his church by passing them through fire: *Chronicon abbatiae de Evesham*, ed. Macray (London 1863: Rolls Series), pp. 335–7; see also Eadmer, *De reliquiis*, p. 362, lines 31–2.

[3] *J.L.*4219; see Ch. IV § i. above.

[4] Eadmer, *Vita Anselmi* I.xxx, pp. 50–4; cf. *Constitutions*, p. 59.

feast of Dunstan is envisaged in the *Constitutions*.[1] Yet Dunstan was the dominant saint in Christ Church, the centre of popular devotion, even the pattern archbishop with whom Lanfranc himself was compared. The hagiographer Goscelin, dedicating a book to Lanfranc *c.* 1080, addresses him as 'the vicar of Dunstan'.[2] Now Dunstan was nothing to Goscelin: had the flattery not been appropriate, he would not have used it. Lanfranc's hesitation went beyond legal caution to theological disquiet over the cult of Dunstan as such. He recognized— better than some of his more reckless Norman colleagues—the strength of the old devotion. At the same time it was peripheral to the faith and alien to his own convictions and experience. So for a few years at least Lanfranc hung fire on Dunstan, neither eradicating the cult nor formally admitting it. He was unwilling that the tomb of Dunstan should be the emotional centre of his church. But he did not leave the house swept and garnished. The dedication of the new cathedral was the occasion of a ceremony which both drew in the populace and reaffirmed the central doctrine of Christianity. It was Palm Sunday, 1077.[3] Setting out from a church outside the city wall, a procession carrying palms and a shrine with a consecrated Host made its way slowly towards Canterbury. It halted at one of the gates to reenact Christ's entry into Jerusalem. The monks sang —

> Gloria laus et honor tibi sit,
> Rex Christe redemptor;

and the children, posted above the gate, replied—

> Israel es tu rex,
> Davidis et inclita proles.

The cathedral bells began to ring as the procession arrived in the city; it stopped again at the west door and finally moved into the nave, to the foot of the great crucifix. At the dedication of Lanfranc's cathedral the translation of relics was thus replaced by the Palm Sunday procession; the Host itself was carried in as

---

[1] *Constitutions*, pp. 55–65. It is just possible that 'the feast of the house' (p. 55) was the feast of Dunstan rather than (as we might expect) the feast of the Trinity.

[2] *Vita Edithae*, ed.cit., p. 38.

[3] *Constitutions*, pp. 22–6; 151–2. For the date see Appendix A 15b. The Palm Sunday procession in the Canterbury Benedictional (p. 171, n.1 above) differs from Lanfranc's in two essentials: it is directed *away* from the city, and it carries no Host.

the real treasure of Christ Church. There could be no clearer expression of Lanfranc's desire to restore a sense of doctrinal proportion to the worship of his community.

The manner of life at Christ Church in the later years of Lanfranc's rule is recorded in his *Constitutions*. He employed (as he said of his book against Berengar) 'scattered materials from many sources'; but as usual he had one basic text, the series of Cluniac customs recently drawn up by the monk Bernard.[1] These reflect the years of assured prestige at Cluny, a level of wealth and an elaboration of ritual to which even the restored Christ Church could hardly approximate. Not that Bernard himself preached expansion—

Hora novissima, tempora pessima, nunc vigilemus.[2]

Would that Lanfranc had left one line as self-revelatory. He simplified Bernard's text, and added practical details in the light of his own long experience. The rite of monastic profession for example differs markedly from both Bernard and the pre-Conquest usage of Christ Church.[3] But in principle Lanfranc was commending to his monks the customs of Cluny in their most up-to-date form. It was a way of life that they would understand. However attenuated and confused their observance had become, it had been established by Dunstan in the tradition of Ghent, Fleury and Cluny itself; it was not a specifically English or insular type of monasticism.[4] If the *Regularis Concordia* is at all representative of the usage of Christ Church *c.* 1070, Lanfranc's contribution was simply to make the existing observance function far more efficiently. The *Regularis Concordia*, though exalting the virtue of uniformity, is an inadequate guide to monastic practice. In the daily movement to and fro within church and claustral buildings, and in the varying liturgy throughout the year, the monk is often at the mercy of chance

---

[1] *Constitutions*, p.xiii; for the date see Appendix D.

[2] Walther 8411.

[3] *Constitutions*, pp. 108–9; cf D. H. Turner, *The Claudius Pontificals* (London, 1971: Henry Bradshaw Soc.xcvii), pp. xxxv–xxxvi.

[4] *Regularis Concordia*, ed. Symons (London, 1953: Nelson's Medieval Classics), with bibliography; cf. D. A. Bullough, 'The continental background of the reform', in *Tenth Century Studies: Essays in Comm. . . . Regularis Concordia*', ed. Parsons (London, 1975), pp. 20–36. The Easter Play (which is peculiar to the *Regularis Concordia*) was being performed at Christ Church *c.* 1070: R. W. Southern, *St. Anselm and his Biographer* (Cambridge, 1963.), p. 246.

or his own common sense. Lanfranc's customary makes it much
clearer where he is supposed to be, and why. The *Constitutions*
are a stable and unvarying framework within which communal
spirituality may flourish. The quality of the book can be seen
from its popularity throughout England for the next half-
century.[1] Though Lanfranc was not setting out to impose his
customs on other houses, they were known and used in Durham,
St. Albans and Westminster (to name only the most distinguished), and as late as *c*. 1180 they had an uncovenanted
influence on the Church in Norway.[2] A manuscript acquired by
archbishop Øystein of Nidaros during his exile in England both
contributed to the Latin liturgy of his province and was itself
rendered into Old Norse, along with Bernold's *Micrologus* and
the *Gemma Animae* of Honorius Augustodunensis. Texts which
were obsolete for thirteenth-century Europe were still useful in
establishing monastic order in the far north.

Lanfranc was a monk's monk, well versed in the finer points
of liturgical practice and daily routine. He could match the
expertise of archbishop John of Rouen on the use of the chasuble
or the vestments of a subdeacon;[3] but he was pragmatic as well
as knowledgeable. The cope, for instance, has no intrinsic
significance in the liturgy. But copes give a splendour to the
great feasts that is appropriate in a primatial see; so Lanfranc
ruled in their favour, and presented Christ Church with some
magnificent specimens that survived for three centuries.[4]
Neither ingenious nor pedantic, his willingness to spend time
and money on these outward forms is the best guide we have to
Lanfranc's conception of the monastic life. The monk's business
was the liturgical round; and it alone gave him the anonymity
in which his security lay. Though he might enjoy the friendship
and encouragement of other monks, his prior duty was to the
community. Too close a relationship with an individual could,
and occasionally did, provoke trouble. Osbern describes an

---

[1] *Constitutions*, pp. xxi–xxiv: see further A. Gransden, *The Customary of the
Benedictine Abbey of Eynsham in Oxfordshire*, p. 17 and *passim*: *Corpus Consuetudinum
Monasticarum*, ed. Hallinger (Siegburg, 1963), vol. ii.

[2] L. Gjerløw, *Adoratio Crucis* (Norwegian Universities Press, 1961), pp. 68–100,
reviewed by C. N. L. Brooke, *Journ. Theol. Stud.* N.S.xiv (1963), 210.

[3] *Lanfranci Epp.* 13.

[4] *Constitutions*, pp. 1–2 ('propter primatem sedem'); 8–9; see E. Bishop, *Liturgica
Historica* (Oxford, 1918), pp. 260–75.

alarming series of incidents that took place during the rebuilding of the cathedral.[1] The monk Aegelward was serving Lanfranc at the altar when suddenly he went out of his mind, shouting and blaspheming, and naming another monk as his companion in affliction. Several days later, when the relics of Dunstan and Elphege were being removed to the refectory, his madness broke out again, until finally Dunstan himself intervened to cure him. No doubt hysteria was to be expected when the saints were disturbed; but the crisis had originated elsewhere. In an unsettled and disorientated community Lanfranc could not present monasticism primarily in terms of inquiry or vocation: basic good order had to be established first. In these circumstances his choice of Henry as prior is easily understood.[2] The least original of the little group who came from Bec and Caen, Henry was a reliable administrator and disciplinarian, and subsequently the convinced exponent of Lanfranc's *Constitutions*. No one could have been more appropriate to the needs of the community in the 1070s.

The most notable of the Norman monks at Christ Church was in many ways Gundulf, prior of St. Étienne.[3] He came over with Lanfranc in 1070 to help him, as at Caen, in organizing the community and running the estates. No doubt he took part in the reconstruction of the cathedral; given his subsequent reputation in Rochester as a builder and as master of works for the White Tower in London, he may well have had a hand in the design. As bishop of Rochester he gave Lanfranc and Anselm steady support in local Kentish politics and in the affairs of the realm. This was worth much. Gundulf is portrayed in Rochester as a unique combination of business acumen and Anselmian piety, the second founder of the see. One of his younger contemporaries in Christ Church was Gilbert Crispin, a man with

[1] Osbern, *Miracula S. Dunstani*, cap. 19; cf. Eadmer, *Miracula S. Dunstani*, cap. 16.
[2] Henry succeeded Godric, the last Anglo-Saxon dean, in 1076 or earlier; he is already prior (and a sympathetic one) in the story of Aegelward's madness.
[3] See pre-eminently the *Textus Roffensis*, ed. P. Sawyer, *Early English MSS in Facsimile XI* (Copenhagen, 1962), fols. 171–230; cf. William of Malmesbury's characterization, 'in rebus forensibus acer et elimatus' (*Gesta Pontificum* i.72, p. 137). The *Vita Gundulfi* is heavily edifying and only moderately informative: Migne, *P.L.*clix. 813A–36C. For Gundulf's work as a builder see H. M. Colvin, *The History of the King's Works* (London, 1963), i.28–32; and for a sketch of his life as a whole R. A. L. Smith, 'The place of Gundulf in the Anglo-Norman Church', *Eng.Hist.Rev.* lviii (1943), 257–72.

a more direct grasp of Anselm's thought and the gifts to express it independently. He was appointed to Westminster *c.* 1085, without having held office in Canterbury. The other Normans are shadowy figures, who appear briefly in Anselm's letters: Albert the doctor, the young monk Maurice, who studied at Canterbury but returned to Bec, Arnost, briefly bishop of Rochester (1076), and Herluin, abbot of Glastonbury (1100).[1] In sum however these men imply that throughout Lanfranc's rule Bec and St. Étienne kept in touch with their monks overseas and that both houses were influential in the reconstruction of Christ Church. The nature of their influence is harder to define. The customs of Bec contributed little to those of Christ Church and the St. Étienne customs do not survive. But Christ Church had confraternity agreements with Bec and Caen,[2] and at a practical level the links were real. Lanfranc sent money to Bec in a year of bad harvest; and when Anselm established a priory at St. Neot's in Huntingdonshire he entrusted it to Lanfranc, Henry, Gundulf and the neighbouring abbot of Bury St. Edmunds.[3] The association lasted well into the twelfth century, under a succession of archbishops who had come from Bec. But the contact was largely at the top, archbishop to abbot rather than the Norman section of Christ Church to the parent monasteries of Bec and Caen. As the community grew, the monks of continental origin were increasingly outnumbered:[4] they transferred their loyalty to Christ Church or were promoted elsewhere; and the English began to recover some influence, though never to the point of providing a prior. If those who remembered the days before the fire of 1067 were, like Eadmer, never fully reconciled to the new regime, a convincing external harmony was achieved by the end of Lanfranc's archiepiscopate.

Coherent monastic discipline and increasing wealth made

---

[1] *Anselmi Epp.*: Schmitt, vol. iii–iv, *passim*; and see further R. W. Southern, *St. Anselm and his Biographer* (Cambridge, 1963), pp. 246–7.

[2] MS. London B. L. Cotton Claudius C.vi, fol. 171: printed by J. Dart, *The History and Antiquities of the Cathedral Church of Canterbury* (London, 1726), p. xxvii. For the customs of Bec see above, p. 27, n. 2.

[3] *Anselmi Epp.* 89: see M. Chibnall, 'The relations of St. Anselm with the English dependencies of the abbey of Bec, 1079–93', *Spicilegium Beccense* i (1959), 523–30.

[4] Eadmer remembered sixty monks in the 1070s: *Ep. ad Glastonienses* (Migne, *P.L.* clix 805D). By 1089 there were reputedly 100: D. Knowles, *The Monastic Order in England* 2nd edn. (Cambridge, 1963), p. 714.

integration easier; but perhaps the crucial factor was the education of the young monks. From *c.* 1073 the schoolmaster at Christ Church was a French monk from Beauvais, Ernulf of St. Symphorien.[1] He may have been accepted more readily in that he came from outside Normandy, the only newcomer to do so. There is no question of the quality of his learning. Beauvais, the city of Ivo of Chartres and Roscelin, is one of the dimly-perceived centres of contemporary scholarship, that should be compared with Laon and Paris rather than with Bec. Ernulf's surviving work bears this out: it is competent and modern by the standards of the late eleventh century. Lanfranc had engaged a first-class schoolmaster, who could make Eadmer and his fellows good Latinists and, at a simple level, respectable logicians. They would grow up with the basic intellectual equipment of the French schools rather than the Anglo-Saxon past. These, with the monk Maurice from Bec, were Ernulf's only pupils. There was no financial need to open the school to other students and strong disciplinary arguments against doing so: he was not in competition with the secular masters who were beginning to open schools in and around London.[2] Within Christ Church Ernulf's influence was greater than we can now discover, primarily as a schoolmaster until in 1096 he became prior, but also in the establishment of a monastic library and scriptorium over the same twenty years.

iii. the library

The pre-Conquest library of Christ Church had the virtues and defects of the old cathedral. It contained much that was of interest, and some notable rarities; but to the continental eye it was out of proportion and out of date. One of its treasures was a Carolingian Psalter from Rheims, illustrated psalm by psalm with line drawings. For example at the verse, 'Thou shalt not be afraid of any terror by night: nor for the arrow that flieth by day', the figure of Christ is beset by archers and a cloud of little

---

[1] Southern, op.cit., pp. 269–70; and see above, p. 36, nn. 1–2.

[2] R. W. Hunt, 'Studies on Priscian in the eleventh and twelfth centuries', *Med.Renaiss.Stud.* i. 2 (1943), 208. The school at Christ Church should not be seen as a link in the golden chain leading to the university of Oxford, a thesis proposed most recently by R. Foreville, 'L'école du Bec et le *studium* de Canterbury au xie et xiie siècles', *Bull.Philol.Hist.* (1955–6), 357–74.

demons in the sky. When the Psalmist continues, 'He shall give his angels charge over thee . . .', Christ is shown treading on the lion and the adder, with angels forming a mandorla round him.[1] By the ninth century the style was already archaic: the artist's model was a late Antique manuscript like the Vienna Genesis. Yet his book had an extraordinary fascination for later artists at Canterbury. A copy was undertaken *c.* 1020 and completed fifty years later, when a second was begun but never finished; and two further versions were made in the course of the twelfth century. While the artistic value of these copies is beyond question, they do show an extreme commitment to an antique model seen at one remove. Even so, manuscript illumination took on a life and invention of its own:[2] the first Canterbury copy of the Rheims Psalter is in some ways more attractive than the original. The real weakness in the Christ Church library lay in the transmission of texts. There was little knowledge of continental scholarship, and no stable tradition of book-production.

This failure in the routine skills of librarianship—choosing texts and making accurate, legible copies—had already been apparent to Dunstan and his colleagues in the late tenth century. They imported books from France and Flanders and developed a new script for Latin manuscripts which was close to that in current use on the continent.[3] In their own generation they had some success, but by *c.* 1025 the impetus was lost; and when the Lotharingian bishops of the mid-eleventh century surveyed their libraries, like Dunstan they had nothing to build on. They achieved even less than he. Leofric of Exeter endowed his cathedral with many service-books and some twenty works of literature and scholarship:[4] a Breton gospel-book further embellished at St. Bertin, several manuscripts in the reformed script of Christ Church and Glastonbury, a ninth

---

[1] E. T. Dewald, *The Illustrations of the Utrecht Psalter* (Princeton, 1953), pl.lxxxiv (Ps.91 A.V.); cf. F. Wormald, *The Utrecht Psalter* (Utrecht, 1953). Recent discussion of the Psalter and its derivatives is summarized by J. J. G. Alexander and M. Kauffmann, *English Illuminated MSS 700–1500* (Brussels, 1973: exhibition catalogue), pp. 35–43.

[2] F. Wormald, *English Drawings of the Tenth and Eleventh Centuries* (London, 1952); Alexander and Kauffmann, op.cit., nos. 8–10.

[3] T. A. M. Bishop, *English Caroline Minuscule* (Oxford, 1971), *passim.*

[4] R. W. Chambers, M. Förster and R. Flower, *The Exeter Book of Old English Poetry* (Exeter, 1933), pp. 25–30; cf. Bishop, op.cit., nos. 2, 9, 10.

century Bede. He encouraged the copying of both English and Latin texts at Exeter itself: the Rule of Chrodegang and various service books.[1] Abbot Seiwold of Bath had a similar library gathered from many sources—for example a seventh-century Augustine—but here there is no sign of a working scriptorium.[2] Though better documented than most, these two collections seem to be typical of the Anglo-Saxon library on the eve of the Conquest. It may be that the survival and growth of English as a literary language inhibited Latin learning; for although many scholars could render English into Latin and vice versa, very little original work indeed was written in either language after the early eleventh century. Nor can it be said that the monasteries and cathedrals of England had comprehensive collections in English of the books which they lacked in Latin. They contained on the one hand spectacular rarities, and on the other an utterly inadequate representation of the standard textbooks.

Lanfranc was fortunate in that some of Dunstan's books survived at Christ Church and that manuscripts were still being written in English, although the Latin script had fallen into disuse. But the collection of working scholarly texts was very thin. Exactly as Dunstan had done, he first bought manuscripts readymade, and then developed his own scriptorium at Canterbury with a distinctive, standard hand. The earliest books came either from Bec, or by the offices of Bec monks. 'You asked me for the *Moralia in Job*,' wrote Anselm. 'William [Bona Anima], abbot of St. Étienne, and Arnost [soon to be bishop of Rochester] have found a scribe, who has begun to copy our manuscript from Bec. I am doing my utmost to get you the Ambrose and the Jerome; but it is not easy.' Even the *Moralia* was still to give trouble. 'There has been a disagreement with the scribe; we have failed to engage the man whom you suggested in Brionne: and no one who is free to do the work here in Bec is sufficiently competent.'[3] The first canon-law collection in the new library came from Bec direct. Calligraphically it is of a high standard: a clear, balanced script set in a well-proportioned

---

[1] N. R. Ker, *Medieval Libraries of Great Britain*, 2nd edn. (London, 1964), p. xxi; idem, *English Manuscripts in the Century after the Norman Conquest* (Oxford, 1960), p. 19, 19, app.

[2] P. Grierson, 'Les livres de l'abbé Seiwold de Bath', *Rev.Bén.*lii (1940), 96–116.

[3] *Anselmi Epp.* 23 and 25.

page. At the end, in another and inferior hand, is the note of origin:

I Lanfranc the archbishop purchased this book from the monastery of Bec, had it brought to England and gave it to Christ Church.[1]

The same scribe was writing official documents for Lanfranc in his early years at Canterbury: the council of London in 1075 and a charter of Odo of Bayeux in favour of Christ Church.[2] His hand was scarcely good enough however for full-length manuscripts; in the 1070s these were still being imported. By the end of Lanfranc's archiepiscopate it is clear that Christ Church had its own scriptorium. One of the earliest episcopal professions to survive in the original (John of Wells: 1088) is in a script that also appears in full-length manuscripts.[3] It became the indigenous style of the house, reaching its peak in the early twelfth century. The illumination grew more ambitious: the dragons and strange creatures on Lanfranc's vestments and plate reappear in the initials of patristic manuscripts.[4] Books were even exported, notably to William of St. Carilef's new library at Durham.[5] Lanfranc himself lent a hand in the work, correcting texts and (it is said) transcribing manuscripts;[6] but the day-to-day supervision fell to others: Osbern and then Eadmer as precentors, and Ernulf as schoolmaster and prior. These men had as much effective responsibility as Lanfranc in planning the scope of the library and acquiring exemplars for the scriptorium.

If we assume that Anselm finally overcame his difficulties, the first books were purchased from Bec. With the exception of the canon-law collection mentioned above, those that survive are all patristic: Augustine, Ambrose, Jerome, Gregory the Great.[7]

---

[1] MS. Cambridge Trinity Coll.B.16.44, p. 405: Ker, op.cit., pp. 25–6, pl.5. For a discussion of the manuscript as a whole see Z. N. Brooke, *The English Church and the Papacy* (Cambridge, 1931), pp. 59–71.

[2] See Appendix A14c: Group Bc–f.

[3] Ker, op.cit., pp. 28–9, pls. 6a and 7; Appendix A14c: Group Cc.

[4] C. R. Dodwell, *The Canterbury School of Illumination* (Cambridge, 1954), pls. 13, 45–7.

[5] MSS. Durham Cathedral B.II.10 (Jerome's *Letters*) and B.IV.24 (Lanfranc's *Constitutions*).

[6] The St. Albans copy of the *Constitutions* was believed to be in Lanfranc's own hand: *Gesta Abbatum*, ed. Riley (London, 1867: Rolls Series), i.61; cf. 52, 58–9. Lanfranc certainly *corrected* texts (*obit*, lines 13–15).

[7] A list of the earliest manuscripts in the Norman library at Christ Church is

They are high quality books, folio or near-folio in size; and each individually is extremely regular in script and layout. But as a group they are so different from one another that they can scarcely reflect Bec alone: several Norman scriptoria must be represented here. Whether the books that were used as exemplars to copy in Christ Church itself normally came from Bec is harder to estimate: there are no Bec manuscripts surviving from the eleventh century and very few from the twelfth.[1] The Bec library in the 1070s must have included the texts of the *artes* and the Fathers used by Lanfranc himself and Anselm; it was no doubt a sound collection within its limits. But it could not compare with Mont-St.-Michel or Fécamp either in the range of its material or the availability of texts to be lent out as exemplars. These great houses certainly did send material to England, and it is unlikely that nothing found its way to Christ Church. Lanfranc and his assistants had to find their exemplars where they could, both in Normandy itself and, increasingly, in the Norman libraries of England. Most of the texts chosen were biblical and patristic; and it is these that remain. The pre-Conquest library with its idiosyncratic survivals and many gaps became a systematic collection of Augustine, Ambrose, Jerome, Gregory and Bede: a life-time's reading for the ordinary monk.[2] No doubt Ernulf's pupils could also find the basic texts of the *artes* and the Latin poets; Lanfranc himself donated a manuscript of Priscian, *Institutiones* i–xvi and three glossed copies of the Pauline Epistles:[3] but the collection was not primarily designed for scholars. Lanfranc's original experience as a master

---

[1] For the Bec library, see Appendix A5c. Lanfranc borrowed his own commentary on the Pauline Epistles to be copied at Christ Church (*Anselm Epp*.66): neither the Bec manuscript nor the copy now survives.

[2] N. R. Ker, *Medieval Libraries of Great Britain* 2nd edn. (London, 1964), pp. 29–40, with references p. 29; cf. R. W. Southern, *St. Anselm and his Biographer* (Cambridge, 1963), pp. 242–5; 267–8. Every monk was required to read one book per annum: *Constitutions*, p. 19.

[3] Ernulf certainly taught Virgil (*Anselmi Epp*. 64). For Lanfranc's gifts (which do not survive) see M. R. James, *The Ancient Libraries of Canterbury and Dover* (Cambridge, 1903), pp. 7, 53, and 88. The Priscian was known to the scribe of MS. Cambridge U.L.Ii.2.1 (*c*. 1100: St. Augustine's, Canterbury), who refers (fol.38v) to the 'Priscianus archiepiscopi' and again (fol.100v) to the 'liber archiepiscopi'.

---

given by C. R. Dodwell, *The Canterbury School of Illumination 1066–1200* (Cambridge, 1954), p. 17; see however N. R. Ker, 'The English Manuscripts of the *Moralia* of Gregory the Great', in *Kunsthistorische Forschungen Otto Pächt* (Vienna, 1972), pp. 78–9.

on the continent was not reflected in his library at Christ
Church.

iv. the archbishop

Lanfranc's cathedral was one of the three in England with a
monastic chapter. As in Winchester and Worcester this was a
legacy of the tenth-century reform; but in Christ Church more
than anywhere the monks symbolized the glories of the Anglo-
Saxon past, stretching back far beyond Dunstan to Theodore
and Augustine.[1] To Lanfranc it seemed appropriate enough for
an archbishop who was a monk himself. Again on similar
grounds he encouraged Gundulf to establish monks at Rochester.[2] Beyond that it is difficult to be certain that Lanfranc
endorsed the monastic chapter as such. When William of St.
Carilef made Durham monastic in 1083, Lanfranc is said to
have supported his petition for a privilege at Rome; but
Lanfranc could have had little standing in the matter beside
Thomas of York, nor was Gregory VII by then likely to listen to
him.[3] Lanfranc's monastic sympathies were easily engaged, but
not blindly; and it was obvious that the monastic chapter might
be no more than an episcopal device to annexe a rich monastery.
Bury St. Edmunds was threatened by the bishop of Thetford
and St. Peter's, Bath actually acquired by the bishop of Wells;
subsequently Coventry and Ely went the same way.[4] Only
when the bishop was himself a monk, as at Rochester, Durham
and later Norwich, was the monastic chapter at all a desirable
innovation. Even then, it had grave disadvantages, both for the
monks and their nominal head. A monk's duties were stability,

---

[1] Historically Christ Church had not been continuously monastic since the late
sixth century, but Eadmer and his contemporaries were convinced that it had been.
They found some support in Bede, *Historia Ecclesiastica* i. 23–6; iv.l, ed. Colgrave
and Mynors (Oxford, 1969), pp. 68–79; 328–33.

[2] Lanfranc's *obit*, line 38; cf. *Textus Roffensis* fol. 172, ed. Sawyer (Copenhagen,
1962: *Early Eng. MSS in Facsimile* xi), vol. II.

[3] H. S. Offler, *Durham Episcopal Charters 1071–1152* (1968: Surtees Soc. clxxix),
no. *3a, with references; W. Holtzmann, *Papsturkunden in England* ii (Berlin, 1935),
no. 2. The story reflects the wishful thinking of a later polemicist at Durham.

[4] See most conveniently John Le Neve, *Fasti Ecclesiae Anglicanae 1066–1300* ii, ed.
D. E. Greenway (London, 1971), p. ix and *passim*, with references. Before the
Conquest the bishop of Crediton had moved to St. Peter's, Exeter, and the bishop
of Ramsbury had tried to take over Malmesbury: see respectively *J.L.*4208 and
William of Malmesbury, *Gesta Pontificum* ii.83, ed. Hamilton (London, 1870: Rolls
Ser.), pp. 182–3.

anonymity and corporate, liturgical prayer. If in Normandy he often played an active part in running his diocese, not to speak of his duchy, that was a temporary expedient that really passed with the death of John of Fécamp (1078). In the later eleventh century the monk was being allotted an increasingly specialized role that was not compatible with responsibilities outside, whether administrative or pastoral. If it was argued that a cathedral chapter too should be celibate and observant, that was better achieved by the new 'regular' canons, who were already widely accepted on the continent. But they were slow to reach England; they were not the obvious alternative during Lanfranc's archiepiscopate. Walkelin had recognized the anomaly at once: his first reaction at Winchester had been to replace his monks with a large chapter of canons, and only papal intervention had stopped him.[1] A secular clerk and a much younger man, he could see how the wind was blowing. In an era when bishops on both sides of the Channel were reviewing the structure of their cathedrals, the monastic chapter could develop no new machinery of government. For Lanfranc this was no great handicap, but with the rapid expansion of diocesan administration in the early twelfth century it was a disastrous liability for his successors. By the 1130s it was absolutely clear that Walkelin had been right.

In Lanfranc's own day the burdens of administration were not great, and he shouldered them himself. His letters are in his own practised, deceptively simple Latin: they have not been delegated to some clerk with a formula-book.[2] His hand may be seen too in the organization of documents, or the collection of legal and fiscal precedents in diocesan government; but here to be honest we only assume that for any work done in his time Lanfranc was the moving spirit.[3] His chaplains included a

---

[1] *J.L.*4762–3. According to Eadmer, Lanfranc intervened to save the Winchester monks; but there is no evidence that he did more than follow Alexander II's instructions: *Historia Novorum* i, ed. Rule (London, 1884: Rolls Ser.), pp. 18–19. William of Malmesbury, abridging Eadmer, exaggerates Lanfranc's role in the Winchester dispute: *Gesta Pontificum* i.44, ed. Hamilton (London, 1870: Rolls Ser.), pp. 71–2.

[2] There is no hint here of the routine chancery practice that was established by or in the time of Theobald: A. Saltman, *Theobald, Archbishop of Canterbury* (London, 1956), pp. 190–231.

[3] D. C. Douglas, *The 'Domesday Monachorum' of Christ Church Canterbury* (London, 1944), pp. 79 and *passim*; cf. Appendix A10a and 14 below.

future abbot of Evesham;[1] they were not nonentities: but we know nothing of their activities at Canterbury. The members of the household are just as elusive. When bishop Gundulf made peace with one of his and the archbishop's major tenants in Kent, the witnesses included Lanfranc himself 'and most of his familia', undifferentiated.[2] Lanfranc had the usual officers: steward, butler, cook, dispenser, chamberlain and a constable in charge of the household knights;[3] but beyond that, as for any great household of the time, we know nothing. What can be seen is the actual topography of Lanfranc's Canterbury. Christ Church lay within the walls, east of the market and the river, north of the castle; there was no visible demarcation between the cathedral and the city. In choosing for his palace a site just within the north wall, even although it was already full of domestic housing, Lanfranc created a solid barrier against the most intrusive side of the city. Then he built a wall round the whole precinct: palace, cathedral and monastery were a self-contained complex cut off from the world.[4] Too close an involvement with Canterbury was to the detriment of the citizens as well as the monks. Throughout his archiepiscopate it was Lanfranc's sustained policy to provide for both, according to their differing and separate needs.

Whereas Caen had been a recent and predominantly ducal

[1] Walter of Evesham: *Chronicon Abbatiae de Evesham*, ed. Macray (London, 1863: Rolls Ser.), p. 96.

[2] *Textus Roffensis*, fol. 175, ed.cit. (p. 182, n. 4 above).

[3] The principal evidence is in *Domesday Monachorum* (ed.cit., p. 183, n. 3 above). The steward: Godfrey of Malling, *dapifer* (pp. 81, 83, etc., cf. p. 50). The butler: Roger *pincerna*, Osbern *pincerna*, both tenants of the archbishop *c.*1086 (p. 105). The dispenser: William *dispensator* (p. 87). The chamberlain: Ralph *camerarius* (p. 82). The constable: Richard *constabularius* (pp. 85, 93, etc.). Anselm's seneschal, William, no doubt had a predecessor under Lanfranc: A. M. Woodcock, *Cartulary of the Priory of St. Gregory, Canterbury* (London, 1956: Camden Soc. 3rd ser. lxxxviii), no. 2 (1108–9). For Anselm's household see R. W. Southern, *St. Anselm and his Biographer* (Cambridge, 1963), pp. 194–200, and for the twelfth century and later, when the evidence is plentiful, F. R. H. Du Boulay, *The Lordship of Canterbury* (London, 1966), pp. 251–64. (The monastic community had of course its own well-defined and separate officials: prior, precentor, treasurer, etc.).

[4] Lanfranc's *obit*, line 12; cf. Eadmer, *Historia Novorum*, ed.cit., p. 12: see W. Urry, *Canterbury under the Angevin Kings* (London, 1967), map 1b[4]. For a detailed plan of the precinct *c.* 1160 see M. R. James, *The Canterbury Psalter* (London, 1935), p. 53 and (better) R. Willis, *The Architectural History of the Conventual Buildings of the Monastery of Christ Church in Canterbury* (London, 1869), pp. 174–81 and pl. 2. Twenty-seven houses were demolished to make way for the palace: *Domesday Book* i.3b (fifty-two houses T.R.E.; twenty-five in 1086).

creation, Canterbury was an ancient city with immemorial vested interests; but the resources and prospects of the two were not dissimilar, and Lanfranc's experience in Caen no doubt helped him in Canterbury. Certainly it was the Norman experience that was relevant rather than the remote memory of Pavia. Canterbury depended ultimately on the commercial strength of London and its trade with the Kentish seaports: east through Canterbury to Sandwich, east and south through Canterbury to Dover. The growth of London in the tenth and eleventh centuries had greatly benefited the city; in this period the Canterbury mint was one of the most productive in England.[1] By 1086 there was a merchants' gild, an ominous development for continental prelates but not apparently for Lanfranc. The citizens of Canterbury were slow to establish legal unity: although the gild held property and may have had jurisdiction over the market, it in no sense represented the citizens as a group.[2] In any case their commercial interests were Lanfranc's too: he drew rents from city property, he had a stake in the mint,[3] and it is quite possible that he had tolls and market dues that would rise with the prosperity of the city as a whole. For his part Lanfranc established a standard liquid measure that was still in use at Canterbury in the mid-twelfth century;[4] but whether that implies his more general influence on the commercial affairs of the citizens is of course quite uncertain. Where he did intervene was in their social, educational and spiritual welfare, and that on a scale far exceeding the routine pastoral responsibilities of an archbishop.

Lanfranc's charitable foundations are the great monument of his later years in Canterbury, after the cathedral was finished (1077) and the monastic community consolidated under Henry and Ernulf. To the west of the city, on the hill of Harbledown— where the traveller suddenly has his first view of the cathedral below him—Lanfranc built a leper-hospital dedicated to St.

---

[1] G. C. Brooke, *A Catalogue of English Coins in the British Museum* (London, 1916), vol. i, p.clxxxviii; cf.clxv; ccii–cciii.

[2] Urry, op.cit., pp. 126–8, with references. For Anselm's exchange of property with the merchant gild see Urry, Charter I (in English), p. 385.

[3] Of the seven moneyers in Canterbury two belonged (notionally) to the archbishop: Brooke, op.cit., p.clxv; cf. M. Dolley, *The Norman Conquest and the English Coinage* (London, 1966), p. 13, and Urry, op.cit., p. 109.

[4] A daily pension of beer granted *c.*1177 was reckoned 'ad mensuram Lanfranci': Urry, p. 404.

Nicholas. The great fire of 1067 had been on St. Nicholas' Day;[1] it was an apt dedication once Christ Church was restored. St. Nicholas' church and alms-houses still stand, much reconstructed, but giving an impression of the site that Lanfranc chose: a hollow in the crown of the hill, well drained, generously planned, separate from the city yet not inaccessible.[2] The second hospital was to the north of Canterbury, just outside the North Gate, and now well within the present city. Dedicated to St. John the Baptist, it was for the relief of the sick and aged poor, to care for them when they were dying and give them decent burial.[3] As at Harbledown, the present buildings give an impression of the site and scale of Lanfranc's work; here a substantial fragment still survives of one of his original walls. St. John's had an establishment of clergy to serve the infirmary and chapel, and land for their maintenance: but within a few years it was merged with a more ambitious project still.

The church of St. Gregory's, Canterbury is a short distance from St. John's, on the other side of the road that runs northwards out of the city. It is Victorian from the ground up. But although there are no material remains from Lanfranc's time, exceptionally the foundation charter survives; so we can see in principle the roles that the house was designed to fill.[4] St. Gregory's had six priests and twelve *clerici*, two to assist each priest. It was financed partly from the endowments of St. John's, partly from the income of a gild of *clerici* in the city,[5] and partly from new benefactions. The priests did pastoral duty at St. John's; they were authorized to baptize and hear confession and to bury clergy and laity at St. Gregory's free of charge. In addition they ran a school 'of grammar and music'; two masters, the Norman Ebroin and the English Leofwine, are

[1] *A. S. Chron.* DE, s.a. 1067: 6 Dec.

[2] Lanfranc's *obit*, lines 22–4; cf. Eadmer, *Historia Novorum*, p. 16, and Gervase of Canterbury, *Actus Pontificum*, ed. Stubbs (London, 1880: Rolls Ser.), pp. 368–9. For the site see J. Newman, *North-east and East Kent* (London, 1969: Pevsner, *The Buildings of England*), pp. 326–7.

[3] Lanfranc's *obit*, lines 22–4; Eadmer, pp. 15–16; Newman, op.cit., pp. 249–50.

[4] Appendix A10a; cf. Lanfranc's *obit*, lines 25–9.

[5] The income derived from property in the archiepiscopal manor of Westgate, on the edge of the city. The gild of *clerici* were still drawing it in 1086 and it is not mentioned in Lanfranc's foundation charter: on the other hand St. Gregory's had certainly acquired it by *c.*1100 (*Domesday Monachorum*, p. 82); cf. F. R. H. Du Boulay, *The Lordship of Canterbury* (London, 1966), p. 43. We may speculate that St. Gregory's found room for some of the *clerici* of the gild.

among the witnesses to Lanfranc's charter. This was not a 'cathedral school' with a sophisticated curriculum and farflung students: it was essentially a town grammar school for Canter-ᵛ bury.[1] Taken as a whole then St. Gregory's did much more than reinforce the charitable work at St. John's; it was a major foundation which may well have drawn off more in funds from St. John's than it contributed in extra manpower. It was a baptismal church, like the ancient minsters directly responsible to the cathedral, in effect replacing the old baptistery which Lanfranc had pulled down. Its burial ground too would relieve the pressure on the lay cemetery at Christ Church. Finally the status of the new house was confirmed by its endowment of relics. The early archbishops (whom Lanfranc had already moved to the upper chapels in the north transept of the cathedral) were brought to St. Gregory's, together with two saints of the conversion period, Ethelburga (the first Christian queen ᵛ of Northumbria) and her sister Eadburga, co-foundresses of Lyminge, about twelve miles south of Canterbury. Although the minster itself seems to have been derelict, it was still a legal and fiscal unit of the diocese: perhaps too Lanfranc was reaffirming his title to its property.[2] Certainly he was recognizing the Anglo-Saxon past. Although there was no major cult attached to these relics, they summed up Kentish Christianity from the beginning, indebted as much to the royal house as to the professional clerics; they exactly embodied the outlook of the community that Lanfranc had originally found at Christ Church. In assigning to St. Gregory's much of the pastoral work of the cathedral Lanfranc had both freed his own community from extraneous activity and extended his influence in the city ᵛ as a whole. What is more, he had created an institution that could in principle help the archbishop with his administrative duties: the six canons were free to engage in diocesan government as the cathedral monks were not. Whether Lanfranc foresaw this development we do not know; he died before St. Gregory's was well established, and the house then took a

---

[1] The school brought Canterbury no special reputation as a centre of study: there are no links with the school of Caen nor with the twelfth-century schools at St. Albans or Oxford. For the general context to which it belongs see N. Orme, *English Schools in the Middle Ages* (London, 1973), pp. 168–9.

[2] F. Liebermann, *Die Heiligen Englands* (Hanover, 1889), i. 4–5; cf. Appendix A15b; 14b.

different course. Yet here potentially was the house of canons that the twelfth-century archbishops spent so much labour trying to institute, and which their monks so bitterly and successfully withstood.[1]

In St. Gregory's Lanfranc had taken a risk, no doubt calculated, but in the long run quite serious. The witnesses to his foundation charter include the abbot of St. Augustine's, Scotland of Mont-St.-Michel, who had come to Canterbury a month or so after Lanfranc himself. From the little we know, Scotland followed a pattern at St. Augustine's similar to Lanfranc's at Christ Church: rebuilding the church, reorganizing the estates, restocking the library, keeping the peace with his English monks. He professed obedience to Lanfranc and his successors, and in his time the great abbey outside the city walls was in at least superficial accord with the cathedral.[2] But in two respects Lanfranc's new foundation impinged on the preserve of St. Augustine's: in the pastoral rights of St. Gregory's, especially with regard to burial,[3] and in its pretensions to be a shrine of local Christianity. The latter especially was a source of friction. All the archbishops before Cuthbert (*ob.*760) were at St. Augustine's; King Ethelbert and his family were there; St. Mildred of Thanet (the King's direct descendant) had recently been moved there and a flourishing cult established.[4] To set up an alternative shrine at St. Gregory's, on however modest a scale, was to court trouble. After Scotland's death, in September 1087, the rivalry between St. Augustine's and the cathedral broke out once more.

[1] The dispute came to a head over archbishop Baldwin's attempt to establish canons at Hackington (1186–91): *Gervasii Cantuariensis Opera Historica*, ed. Stubbs (London, 1879: Rolls Ser.), i. 36–7; 499–500 and *passim; Epistolae Cantuarienses . . . 1187–99*, ed. Stubbs (London, 1865: Rolls Ser.), *passim*.

[2] Scotland built the apse and presbytery of the new abbey-church and began the nave: A. Clapham, *English Romanesque Architecture after the Conquest* (Oxford, 1934), pp. 29–30. For his survey of the estates see A. Ballard, *An Eleventh-Century Inquisition of St. Augustine's, Canterbury* (London, 1920: British Academy); for the library see N. R. Ker, *Medieval Libraries of Great Britain*, 2nd edn. (London, 1964), pp. 40–7; for his profession see Appendix A13c. A century later the Christ Church historian Gervase saw his abbacy as a time of complete harmony: 'Lamfrancus eum [sc. Scotland] ut pater filium dilexit et contra omnes iniurias protexit': *Gervasii Opera*, ed.cit. i. 70.

[3] For the burial rights of St. Augustine's see W. Levison, *England and the Continent in the Eighth Century* (Oxford, 1946), pp. 182; 198.

[4] F. Liebermann, *Die Heiligen Englands* (Hanover, 1889), i.9–17, especially the Latin version of 17: cf. Goscelin, *Vita et Translatio Mildrethae* (*B.H.L.*5960–1).

In July 1088 Lanfranc consecrated as Scotland's successor Wido, a monk of St. Augustine's (also, from his name, a Norman), and attempted to install him in the abbey.[1] But the majority of the monks, with prior Aelfwin at their head, refused to admit Wido and fled into the city to St. Mildred's church. Although Lanfranc persuaded or coerced most of the dissidents into obedience, within a few months there was a plot against the abbot's life. On Lanfranc's orders the author, a monk named Columbanus, was beaten, degraded and expelled from Canterbury. Finally after Lanfranc's death a riot broke out, during which a group of armed citizens broke into St. Augustine's and tried to kill the abbot. Gundulf and Walkelin expelled and imprisoned the monks involved and imposed on the depleted community twenty-four monks from Christ Church, one of whom was made prior of St. Augustine's. Violence of this order cannot be explained merely as the reaction of the insular Columbanus and Aelfwin to a Norman ruler: Scotland himself had had no such trouble in seventeen years. Wido was the archbishop's choice as Scotland had been the King's; both had professed obedience to Lanfranc: if the community was ever to gain freedom of election, Wido had to be resisted. But St. Augustine's had also engaged the loyalty of the citizens, as though the quarrel went deeper than the control of one ecclesiastical house by another. It can scarcely be chance that within a few years the archiepiscopal house of St. Gregory's was in fierce and open competition with St. Augustine's as one of the major shrines of Canterbury. In the 1090s the canons of St. Gregory's were advertising the relics of St. Mildred, which had, they claimed, been translated along with Ethelburga and Eadburga from Lyminge. The monks of St. Augustine replied with spirit and considerable justification that Mildred had had no connection with Lyminge in her lifetime, had never been interred there and had with the express and recorded permission of Cnut been brought to St. Augustine's from her native Thanet in 1035.[2] There she had been working miracles ever since. The

---

[1] *Acta Lanfranci*, pp. 290–2: see Appendix A14a.

[2] The claim of St. Gregory's is refuted in the *Libellus contra inanes sanctę virginis Mildrethę usurpatores* (*B.H.L.* 5962); see now *Medieval Studies* xxxix (1977), 65sqq. The *terminus a quo* is September 1091: Goscelin, *Translatio Sancti Augustini* (*B.H.L.* 781). That St. Augustine's was in the right may be argued from: i. Cnut's charter of *c.* 1035 (P. H. Sawyer, *Anglo-Saxon Charters*, London, 1968, no. 990); ii. the

canons held to their position, with no further evidence than the necessary interpolation of their foundation charter; and the controversy settled into its natural groove for the next 300 years. Of course Lanfranc himself is responsible for none of this. Yet in St. Gregory's he had founded a real source of conflict between the cathedral and St. Augustine's in the future. But in the short term St. Gregory's was the crown of Lanfranc's pastoral work as archbishop. Even the dedication matched his own career. Gregory the Great, the monk who had given up the contemplative life for the cares of government, the apostle of England,[1] the author of the primacy of Canterbury: Lanfranc could have chosen no one else.

[1] Bede, *Historia Ecclesiastica* ii.1, ed. Colgrave and Mynors (Oxford, 1969), pp. 122–35. See the foundation charter: 'beatissimi patroni nostri et tocius Anglie Gregorii pape', 'et tocius Anglorum terre patroni'. In the *Constitutions* Gregory is 'nostrae id est Anglorum gentis apostolus' (p. 61).

extraordinarily circumstantial account of the translation from Thanet; iii. miracles at Canterbury 1035–85 (*B.H.L.*5961); iv. St. Mildred's church at Canterbury castle built on St. Augustine's land, and refuge of the dissident monks in 1088.

Epilogue

The law of the Lord is perfect, converting the soul;
The testimony of the Lord is sure, making wise the simple.
The statutes of the Lord are right, rejoicing the heart:
The commandment of the Lord is pure, enlightening the eyes.
The fear of the Lord is clean, enduring for ever:
The judgements of the Lord are true and righteous altogether.

Ps.19:7–9 (A.V.)

No assessment of Lanfranc—as a master in the schools or a ruler in the Church—can or should stray far from Lanfranc the monk. Here, in the life to which he was essentially committed, Lanfranc was a traditionalist, untouched by the radical experiments of his day and scarcely sympathetic even to Anselm's exploration of prayer and monastic friendship. The legal cast of mind that had brought him success in north Italy persisted in Bec and Christ Church. The monk's duties, and his reward, were laid down beyond argument; whereas for Anselm faith and obedience were complex notions demanding hard thought, for Lanfranc this was not so: he never accepted the injunction 'Scito teipsum.'

He was still at home in the Carolingian world. The diligent and capable German bishops of the later tenth century and the eleventh, restoring the life of their clergy and the welfare of their cities, live on in Lanfranc's comprehensive work of restoration and his charitable enterprises at Canterbury. It is not surprising that the pope whom he best understood was Leo IX, who owed much of his own success to his experience as bishop of Toul. Leo improved papal administration within Rome and beyond; he exercised some sporadic authority over the episcopate in the rest of Europe and tried to control and protect the great abbeys: but he did not see his role as one of constant oversight. Papal intervention was the more effective for being infrequent; royal and comital patronage remained the major factor in church government. For Lanfranc this ancient ideal always

held good. The Gregorian vision of direct papal responsibility
for the conscience of the world, of a jurisdiction that overrode
temporal justice and the decisions of kings as a father ruling his
children: all this was being argued out, with bloodshed, during
Lanfranc's archiepiscopate; but it found no echo in England. If
Rome had moved on, William the Conqueror and Lanfranc
still held to the old ways.

In learning too Lanfranc outlived the generation to which he
contributed most. The *Liber de corpore et sanguine Domini* (*c.* 1063)
is his last piece of formal scholarship, and it is a curiously
transitional work that academically is left far behind by
Guitmund's book ten years later. Lanfranc's major work was in
the 1050s and perhaps earlier: his pioneering criticism of the
texts of classical rhetoric and (arguably) grammar, and his
commentaries on the Psalter and the Pauline Epistles. Here he
was superseded almost at once. In the 1060s Manegold of
Lautenbach, *modernorum magister magistrorum*, took the study of
grammar and rhetoric so much further that Lanfranc's criticism was rendered valueless; in the *artes* Lanfranc had done no
more than point the way. In the study of the Bible too, although
more of his work survives, it was a stage quickly passed in the
evolution of scholastic commentary. Lanfranc's enduring skill
was in language, in the exact and often felicitous expression of
given material, rather than in originality of mind. Here he was
not overtaken by the new generation. Indeed the best proof is
from the last decades of his life: in letters written in the high
style to popes and fellow-prelates, with somewhat conscious
ornament to Anselm, straightforwardly to the kings of Ireland,
but always with a force and clarity that the reader scarcely
appreciates until he tries his hand at translation. Lanfranc
would have made an excellent royal chancellor, and from the
late eleventh century onwards many men with his scholarly
training did make a career in government; the *magister* becomes
an ubiquitous figure in royal and baronial charters. But
although his letters often touch on English politics and he could
intervene decisively in affairs of state, Lanfranc's influence on
William the Conqueror and William Rufus was largely
personal: he had no regular position at court nor did he improve
or elaborate the machinery of administration. It was Rannulf
Flambard, in the decade after Lanfranc's death, who began to

show what the trained professional could do in the King's service. We have only to look at Flambard's obituary notices to be further assured that Lanfranc was *not* involved in royal administration at this level.

Lanfranc saw the contradiction inherent in the exposition of classical learning to Christian students, but he never had to face the comparable dilemma: that loyalty to Rome was ultimately incompatible with his duty to the King. In national affairs Lanfranc was a pragmatic and traditional bishop, whose immediate authority on earth was always William the Conqueror or William Rufus; at home, he was a superior resplendent in the praises of his monks, whom we ourselves see walking away through the cloister, with his hood up.

APPENDIX A: the sources for
Lanfranc's life

THE list that follows is a summary guide to the evidence for Lanfranc's life. Problems of date, authenticity and manuscript tradition are indicated mainly where they are crucial; and those authors are omitted who in substance quote their predecessors.

i. before 1070

Lanfranc's biography was written in the mid-twelfth century, when several Bec monks were very interested in history.[1] Much of the material then gathered was transcribed c. 1450 into a compendium of the early history of the house: this book passed to Christina of Sweden and thence to the papal library, where it is now MS. Vat. Reg.lat.499.[2] In 1648 Luc D'Achery published the first and major edition of Lanfranc's works. He used the resources of Bec itself and other French manuscripts deposited at the Maurist house of St. Germain-des-Prés, but not MS.Vat.Reg.lat.499, which was already inaccessible. At the Revolution the library of Bec was dispersed and the Maurist collections thrown into confusion. As a result several of the texts here listed are known in two versions: as they appear in Vat.Reg.lat.499 and according to D'Achery, who used earlier manuscripts which are now lost.

1   GILBERT CRISPIN, *Vita Herluini*   1109–17
     Gilbert Crispin came to Bec as a child oblate c. 1055. He remained there until 1080, when he joined Lanfranc at Canterbury and c. 1085 became abbot of Westminster; he died in 1117–18.[3] The *Vita Herluini* was written in his last years, after the death of Anselm (1109), and it is in part a memorial to the

---

[1] The community included an outstanding historian in Robert of Torigny and an interesting figure on the borders of history and literature in Stephen of Rouen, author of the *Draco Normannicus*. For the latter see Manitius iii. 690–4 and B. Smalley, *The Becket Conflict and the Schools* (Oxford, 1973), pp. 186–9.

[2] A. Wilmart, *Codices Reginenses Latini* ii (Vatican, 1945), 724–8.

[3] J. Armitage Robinson, *Gilbert Crispin, Abbot of Westminster* (Cambridge, 1911); cf. Fauroux, pp. 33–4 (note 77). Gilbert's account of the endowment of Bec matches a phrase in the first general charter: compare the passage 'ditioni illius . . . extiterant sibi' (Robinson, p. 91) with Fauroux, no. 98, p. 252, § 4, 'Seruitia et consuetudines . . .'

generation that Gilbert had outlived. In most respects however it is based on what he himself has seen and heard. The *Vita Herluini* was available in Bec to Robert of Torigny by 1139 and to the author of the *Vita Lanfranci* soon afterwards. The printed editions are based on this Bec manuscript, which is now lost. D'Achery's text, which is somewhat abbreviated, was reprinted by Mabillon in the *Acta Sanctorum* and again by Migne. The complete text was published in 1911 by J. Armitage Robinson, using D'Achery's edition and MS. Cambridge Corpus Christi Coll. 318 (s.xii: Rochester).[1]

1a ANON., *Altera Vita Herluini*   s.xii
This work is a rhetorical elaboration of the *Vita Herluini*, with some omissions (notably the long account of the consecration ceremony in 1077) and the addition of the letter of William of Cormeilles (no. 4a). It was printed by Mabillon from a Bec manuscript now lost.[2]

2 ANON., *Vita Lanfranci* (attrib. Milo Crispin)   *c.* 1140–56
The *Vita Lanfranci* was written after the dedication of the new choir at Christ Church (1130) and probably after the death of archbishop William (1136.)[3] Robert of Torigny does not cite it in his interpolations to William of Jumièges, which he completed at Bec *c.* 1139, but he does both use it and refer specifically to its existence in the first recension of his *Chronicle* (1156–7).[4] The ascription to Miles Crispin, precentor of Bec *c.* 1130–50, depends on a note of uncertain date in the lost Bec manuscript used by D'Achery. The note runs:

> Vitam S. Herluini edidit Gilbertus Crispinus monachus
> Beccensis, et Abbas Westmonasterii. Vitam S. Anselmi
> edidit Edmerus monachus Cantuariensis. Vitam aliorum,
> scilicet Lanfranci, Willelmi, Bosonis, Teobaldi, Letaldi,
> conscripsit Milo Crispinus cantor Becci.

It does not appear in Vat.Reg.lat.499, which is probably a direct transcript of the twelfth-century original, nor in the only

---

[1] D'Achery, *APP.*, pp. 32–40; Mabillon, *Acta Sanctorum Ord.S.Ben.Saec.VI* (Paris, 1701), ii. 342–55; Migne *P.L.*cl.697A–712D; Robinson, op.cit., pp. 87–110. D'Achery's manuscript appears in the mid-twelfth-century catalogue of Bec: see G. Becker, *Catalogi Bibliothecarum Antiqui* (Bonn, 1885), no. 127, item 100. The only other known manuscript is Vat.Reg.lat.499.

[2] *Acta Sanctorum O.S.B.* VI.ii.355–64; cf. Robinson, op.cit., p. 60. The only surviving manuscript is Rouen B.Mun. 1393, fols. 196–203 (s.xii/xiii: Jumièges).

[3] *V.L.*, pp. 1–16, reprinted by Mabillon with the full text of five letters that D'Achery had abbreviated: *Acta Sanctorum* VI.ii. 630–59 (= Migne, *P.L.*cl.29B–58C). For the date see cap. 17.

[4] Robert refers to the *Vita Lanfranci* s.a. 1042 and quotes it verbatim s.a.1089 and 1133 (ed. Delisle, i. 43, 72–7, 189).

other manuscript of the *Vita Lanfranci*, an abridged and very divergent text that may belong to Christ Church, Canterbury.[1] Miles Crispin, who wrote the fragment *De nobili genere Crispinorum* about his own family, may indeed be the author of the *Vita Lanfranci* as well: but the evidence is thin, and he had several contemporaries at Bec of a literary and historical turn of mind.[2] The text itself is based on the *Vita Herluini* and on the documents of Lanfranc's archiepiscopate: letters, councils and records of litigation. The author also knew the *Gesta Guillelmi* of William of Poitiers, in a more complete form than now survives,[3] Lanfranc's own *De corpore et sanguine domini* and Eadmer's *Vita Anselmi* and *Historia Novorum*. But his most interesting contribution is the local tradition of Bec, which had preserved the letter of William of Cormeilles (no. 4a) and ten anecdotes. Two of these had already been recounted by Eadmer:

When Lanfranc visited Rome in 1071 Alexander II rose to greet him, saying—
'Honorem exhibuimus, non quem archiepiscopatui tuo, sed quem magistro cuius studio sumus in illis quae scimus imbuti, debuimus.'

William of Malmesbury renders this as a general reference to Lanfranc's learning; but the *Vita Lanfranci* (like Eadmer) states bluntly that Alexander II studied at Bec:

Non ideo assurrexi ei (the pope explained) quia archiepiscopus Cantuariae est; sed quia Becci ad scholam eius fui, et ad pedes eius cum aliis auditor consedi.[4]

The other parallel with Eadmer is a much curtailed version of the story of the monk Aegelward who went mad while serving at Mass.[5] Judging by his treatment of other sources, the author has not modified these two stories himself; they represent

---

[1] D'Achery, p.19AB. MS. Bodleian Rawl. A.294, fols. 94–8 (s.xv[2]: English;? Christ Church Canterbury). This text was brought to my notice by Helen Clover.

[2] In addition to Robert of Torigny, Stephen of Rouen and (no. 4b) the author of the *Miracula S. Nicholai* see the compiler of the miscellany in MS. Paris B.N.lat. 13575: B. Hauréau, *Notices et extraits* (Paris, 1891), ii. 226–41.

[3] Mrs. Chibnall has shown that the coincidence of *Vita Lanfranci*, cap. 5, with a passage in Orderic Vitalis arises from a common source, which is probably the lost ending of the *Gesta Guillelmi*: see Orderic, *Hist.Eccles.* iv (Chibnall II, pp. xviii–xxi; 249–50).

[4] *V.L.*, cap. 11: cf. Eadmer, *Historia Novorum*, i (ed. Rule, p. 11), William of Malmesbury, *Gesta Pontificum* i. 42 (ed. Stubbs, p. 65) and for yet another version *Gesta Abbatum S. Albani*, ed. Riley (London, 1867: Rolls Ser.), i.46. Nothing is known of Alexander II's career before 1057, when he became bishop of Lucca: it is possible that he visited Bec *c.*1050–5.

[5] *V.L.*, cap. 14: Eadmer, *Miracula S. Dunstani*, pp. 234–7.

the tradition of Bec as distinct from Canterbury. Three of the other anecdotes in the *Vita Lanfranci* were taken up by later historians:

   a) Lanfranc falls among thieves.

   b) He accepts correction in reading aloud.

   c) Seeing William the Conqueror crowned, an onlooker exclaims, 'Ecce deum uideo!'

The remainder are not (so far as I am aware) recorded outside the *Vita Lanfranci*.[1]

3 ROBERT OF TORIGNY, *Interpolations in William of Jumièges, 'Gesta Normannorum Ducum'*   *c.* 1139
    Continuation of the 'Chronicle' of Sigebert of Gembloux   1156–86
Robert of Torigny was a monk of Bec 1128–54, when he became abbot of Mont-St.-Michel; he died in 1186. In his revision of William of Jumièges the account of Lanfranc is drawn verbatim from the *Vita Herluini*, which he expressly attributes to Gilbert Crispin.[2] In the revision of Sigebert, which is his major historical work, the Lanfranc material is again derived from the *Vita Herluini* and the *Vita Lanfranci*; but there is a residuum of two passages:

  sub anno 1032   Lanfranc and Irnerius teach Roman civil law at Bologna.

         1117   *Obit* of Ivo of Chartres, who had studied under Lanfranc at Bec.[3]

While the former is chronologically impossible, the latter must be taken seriously: it may represent an otherwise unrecorded tradition from Bec.

Further literary material from Bec

4a WILLIAM OF CORMEILLES, *Letter to abbot William of Bec* 1093–
                                           1109
William, second abbot of Cormeilles (*ob.* 1109), was a monk of Bec when Lanfranc first entered the community. His account of Lanfranc's early disillusionment with Bec is the best-attested

---

[1] *V.L.*, cap. 1, 2, 13 (anecdotes a–c); and cap. 2, 4, 8, 16 (the other five).

[2] William of Jumièges, *Gesta Normannorum Ducum* (ed. Marx, pp. 235–47; 252–6; 258–61; 267–9). For the date of Robert's additions see M. Chibnall, 'Orderic Vitalis and Robert of Torigni', in *Millénaire monastique du Mont-Saint-Michel* (Paris, 1967), ii. 133–9.

[3] *Le Chronique de Robert de Torigni*, ed. Delisle (Rouen, 1872–3: *Soc.Hist.Nor.*), i. 36, 153. Delisle distinguishes three recensions of Robert's *Chronicle*: the first written at Bec and complete by 1156–7; the second written at Mont-St-Michel and complete by 1167; and a final recension of 1182–6, also written at Mont-St-Michel, which he prints. The Lanfrancian passage s.a.1032 comes from the final recension; the other (s.a. 1117) is in the recension from Bec.

of all the anecdotes. It survives as an independent text in MS. Vat.Reg.lat.499, and it is quoted in the *Vita Lanfranci* (cap. 2) and the *Altera Vita Herluini*.[1]

4b ANON., *Miracula S. Nicholai*   *c.* 1140

One of the minor historians of twelfth-century Bec was a monk who probably lived at Conflans-St.-Honorine, the Bec priory near Paris.[2] The *Miracula S. Nicholai* has a long excursus on the foundation of Bec, drawn from the *Vita Herluini* (*Miracula* 2–4, nearly verbatim) and the *Vita Lanfranci* (*Miracula* 6–12, paraphrased).[3] The embellishments to the *Vita Lanfranci* are of some importance:

a) Lanfranc is described as 'Dorobernensis ecclesiae archipraesul et totius Britanniae Scotiae Hiberniae Archadarumque insularum primas' (cap. 6, p. 408).

b) He taught the *artes* in Italy: 'nam plures in sua patria scholas tenuerat de grammatica et rhetorica et maxime dialectica' (cap. 7, p. 409).

He studied under Berengar of Tours:

Audiens famam cuiusdam Berengerii, Turonensis ecclesiae archidiaconi, qui multos et prope omnes precellebat scientia litterarum in illis partibus, uenit ad eum, celans omnino quis esset, subdiditque se eius discipulatui. At cum nil ibi se proficere cerneret, reuera uero, ut post apparuit, intellegens eum non esse sanae doctrinae, abscessit ab eo (cap. 7, p. 409).

He visited Burgundy: 'Et iterum per se et in Burgundia et in ceteris regionibus Galliae coepit maxime scholas tenere' (cap. 7, p. 409).

c) Lanfranc's encounter with the robbers (*Vita Lanfranci* cap. 1) is modelled on a story in the *Dialogues* of Gregory the Great (cap. 8, pp. 409–10; *Dial.* i.2).

His first conversation with Herluin now includes the exchange:

---

[1] The letter was first published as an independent text in Picard's notes to the *Letters* of Anselm: reprinted Migne, *P.L.*clviii.1198D–1202D. See also du Monstier, *Neustria Pia* (Rouen, 1663), pp. 439–40, following Picard.

[2] A. Wilmart, 'Les ouvrages d'un moine du Bec: un débat sur la profession monastique au xiiᵉ siècle', *Rev.Bén.* xliv (1932), 21–46. The same monk wrote the *Miracula S. Honorinae* (*B.H.L.* 3983) and the *De libertate beccensis ecclesiae*, ed. Mabillon, *Annales Ord.S.Ben.* (Paris, 1713), v. 635–40. There is no substance in the proposed identification with Alain de Lille: P. Glorieux, 'Alain de Lille, le moine et l'abbaye du Bec', *Rech.Théol.Anc.Méd.* xxxix (1972), 51–62.

[3] *B.H.L.* 6208: printed in *Cat.Codic.Hagiog.Lat.Bibl.Nat.Paris* (Brussels, 1890), ii.405–32. The earliest dated miracle is 1103.

'Are you a clerk or a layman?'
'I am an Italian clerk and scholar, and my name is Lanfranc.' (cap. 10, pp. 410–11).

The author's main contribution is in section b): that Lanfranc taught grammar, rhetoric and above all dialectic; that he heard Berengar lecture on *scientia litterarum*; and that he visited Burgundy. The rest of his material comes from the *Vita Herluini* and the *Vita Lanfranci*, with some stylistic elaboration.

4c ANON., *Chronicon Beccense*   1150+
The first essays in general historical writing at Bec (apart from the exiguous *Annals*) were the work of Robert of Torigny himself, and the additions that were made locally to Robert's *Chronicle*, s.a. 1157–60.[1] An independent *Chronicle of Bec* was begun in the mid-twelfth century and continued into the mid-fifteenth. The part which concerns Lanfranc however is a patchwork, often inexpertly assembled, of the *Vita Lanfranci*, Robert's *Chronicle* and the *Miracula S. Nicholai*.[2]

Bec Records

5a CHARTERS
Documents relating to the continental property of Bec are (with some exceptions) divided between the originals and fragments of cartularies in the Archives Départementales at Évreux and the Maurist transcripts and some miscellaneous originals in the Bibliothèque Nationale.[3] The Parisian material was used by Porée, who quotes or refers to a number of charters, notably the general confirmation of 1077; no systematic account of the continental property has appeared since.[4] Its approximate distribution in 1077 is shown in the map at the end of this book. The English property on the other hand has been studied, and many of the documents edited, by Mrs. Chibnall.[5]

---

[1] The additions are printed by Delisle, op.cit. ii. 165–80; cf. 137–46.

[2] D'Achery, *APP.*, pp. 1–31 (Migne, *P.L.*cl.639D–90D): the manuscript is lost. Porée's edition is based on a transcript of Vat.Reg.lat.499, fols. 166–87: *La Chronique du Bec* (Rouen, 1883: *Soc.Hist.Nor.*). The *Annals of Bec*, which scarcely mention Lanfranc, have been edited twice: (i) Porée, loc.cit., pp. 1–11; (ii) L. Delisle, 'Les courtes annales du Bec', in *Notices et documents . . . Soc.Hist.France . . . cinquantième anniversaire* (Paris, 1884), pp. 93–9.

[3] G. Bourbon, *Inventaire sommaire des Archives Départementales antérieures à 1790* (Eure) Série H (Évreux, 1893), H6–101. The Maurist transcripts are now MSS. Paris B.N.lat.12884 and 13905, and the originals B.N.lat.9211.

[4] For the 1041 charter see Fauroux, no. 98 and for the 1077 charter Porée i. 645–9.

[5] M. Morgan, *The English Lands of the Abbey of Bec* (Oxford, 1946); M. Chibnall (née Morgan), *Select Documents of the English Lands of the Abbey of Bec* (London, 1951) Camden Soc. 3 ser. lxxiii.

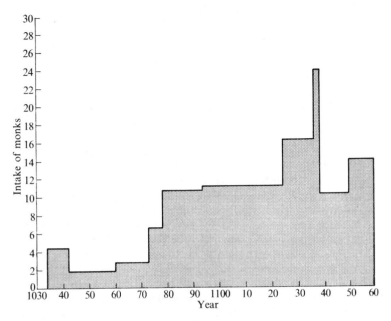

FIG. 1   Rate of Professions at Bec 1034–1159.

5b PROFESSION-ROLL; FRATERNITY-LIST; 'OBITS'

The monks of Bec, from Herluin himself to the later fifteenth century, are listed in a profession-roll that is divided according to the abbot to whom profession was made.[1] Given the dates of the abbots and a few other certainties (e.g. 1159: the deathbed profession of Robert of Neubourg), we can infer the *rate* of entry, though never the absolute number of monks. There were about two professions per annum while Lanfranc was prior: it was with Anselm that the rate began to climb. The fraternity-list on the other hand shows the relations of Bec with the world, ecclesiastical and lay. Only the great names are now recognizable: *Willelmus filius Henrici regis, Henricus iiii. Romanorum imperator, Mathildis imperatrix.*[2] The vast majority are undifferentiable and unindentifiable, as indeed they must have already have

[1] Porée ii. 629–42; some of the thirteenth-century entries are missing. The original list, now lost, was copied out in the fifteenth century (Vat.Reg.lat.499, fols. 8–15v) and printed by Porée. The graph covers 1034–1159; it includes monks professed at Bec but living in the priories.

[2] Vat.Reg.lat.499, fols. 24–9v (examples from fol. 25v); not printed.

been in the fifteenth century, when the surviving manuscript was written. Some *obits* of the eleventh and twelfth centuries are found in two later kalendars from Bec and in a fourteenth-century kalendar from the Bec priory of St. Nicaise, Meulan.[1]

5c THE LIBRARY

In 1164 Bec acquired the remarkable private library of Philip de Harcourt, bishop of Bayeux.[2] Soon afterwards a catalogue was made of the whole Bec collection, including bishop Philip's bequest.[3] As the bishop's books are also catalogued separately, any title which appears in *both* lists must be one of his: for instance the volume of Augustine, *De pastoribus* etc. (now MS. Paris B.N.lat.12211) is item 6 in the main catalogue and item 11 in bishop Philip's. The titles that remain (i.e. those appearing only in the Bec catalogue) are predominantly patristic, with the addition of Anselm, Bernard and Hugh of St. Victor. The classics and the *artes* came from bishop Philip. Very few Bec manuscripts survive now. By the seventeenth century manuscripts were being traded in for modern printed books, and at the Revolution the whole collection was dispersed. Of the pre-1164 library about a dozen manuscripts are known, of which none is pre-1100.[4] Two other manuscripts are closely associated with Bec, without strictly belonging to the library. MS. Cambridge Trinity Coll. B.16.44 is the actual book of canon law that Lanfranc purchased from Bec for Christ Church, Canterbury; and MS. Paris B.N.lat.2342 is the personal manuscript of the author of the *Miracula S. Nicholai* (no. 4b), who continued to add to his work, and have it embellished by successive artists, over the period *c.* 1090–*c.* 1140.[5]

6 CAEN RECORDS

The *acta* of William the Conqueror and Matilda for St. Étienne, Caen, and the sister-house of Holy Trinity have been edited, with a wealth of annotation, by M. Lucien Musset.[6] The total

[1] Porée ii. 579–91: MSS. Paris B.N.lat.1105 and 1208. For the St. Nicaise kalendar see A. Molinier, *Obituaires de la province de Sens* (Paris, 1906), ii. 237–42.

[2] G. Becker, *Catalogi Bibliothecarum Antiquarum* (Bonn, 1885), no. 86. As dean of Lincoln and bishop-elect of Salisbury Philip was a patron of the arts comparable with Henry of Winchester. The nucleus of his collection may well have been English.

[3] Becker, op.cit., no. 127.

[4] G. Nortier, *Les Bibliothèques médiévales des abbayes bénédictines de Normandie* (Caen, 1966), pp. 57–83, especially pp. 82–3. MSS. Paris B.N.lat.12206 and Vat.Reg.lat. 285+278 (Becker, no. 127, items 25 and 81) should be added to the list.

[5] The canon-law collection is discussed in Ch. VI. I am greatly indebted to M. François Avril of the Bibliothèque Nationale for his help with MS. lat.2342.

[6] *Les Actes de Guillaume le Conquérant et de la reine Mathilde pour les abbayes caennaises* (Caen, 1967: *Soc.Antiq.Nor.* xxxvii).

endowment of St. Étienne in 1077 is summarized in William's confirmation charter (Musset, no. 4; cf. nos. 7, 18, 19). Lanfranc witnessed transactions for both abbeys (no. 4Abis, 7, 14: St. Étienne and nos. 8, 9: Holy Trinity); but the most interesting document in which he appears is the so-called *emptiones abbatum* (no. 14; cf. 20), a record of negotiations whereby he and his two successors built up the property of St. Étienne.

Norman historians

7a WILLIAM OF POITIERS, *Gesta Guillelmi Ducis* 1074

As archdeacon of Lisieux and a court chaplain William is a rare witness from the secular clergy. For him Lanfranc is primarily the monk, one of a distinct, if not alien, group. He is the emblem of duke William's irreproachable piety:

> intima familiaritate [Lanfrancum] colebat; ut patrem uenerans, uerens ut praeceptorem, diligens ut germanum aut prolem. Illi consulta animae suae, illi speculam [a watchtower] quandam, unde ordinibus ecclesiasticis per omnem Normanniam prospiceretur commisit.

As abbot of St. Étienne Lanfranc advised duke William as the monk John had encouraged the emperor Theodosius.[1] The inflated style of the *Gesta Guillelmi* belongs to panegyric rather than history: considering how much the author saw at first hand, there is very little information to be extracted from his book.

7b ORDERIC VITALIS, *Historia Ecclesiastica* c. 1115–37

Orderic entered St. Évroult as a child c. 1085 and died a monk there in 1142. Like Robert of Torigny he began by revising Sigebert; there is no new material here on Lanfranc. For the *Historia Ecclesiastica* however his sources included the *Gesta Guillelmi Ducis*, almost certainly in a more complete form than now survives, and the *Acta Archiepiscoporum Rothomagensium*, or some cognate text; the latter may be the basis of his story that Lanfranc refused the see of Rouen. Lanfranc appears first as a neighbouring prior who intervened in the affairs of St. Évroult. Then Orderic picks out the salient points of his career at Caen and Canterbury: his exceptional learning and his refutation of Berengar, his part in English politics, particularly his support of William Rufus.[2] Orderic testifies throughout to the reputation

---

[1] *Gesta Guillelmi Ducis* i.52, ed. Foreville (Paris, 1952), pp. 126–9.

[2] For Lanfranc as prior of Bec see *Hist.Eccles.* iii (Chibnall II. 66, 90–2, 96, 148); cf. vi (Chibnall III. 232). For Lanfranc's later career see *Hist.Eccles.* iv (Chibnall II. 146, 200, 248–54, 296, 344); v (Chibnall III. 10–12, 98); vii (Chibnall IV. 90, 96); viii (Chibnall IV. 110, 120, 124–6); x (Chibnall V. 202). Lanfranc's refusal of the see of Rouen in favour of John of Avranches (*Hist.Eccles.* iv: Chibnall II. 200) is unique to Orderic. For the coincidence with *V.L.*, cap. 5, see p. 197, n. 3 above.

of Bec in the early twelfth century as a house in which even the average monk was an educated man.

Other continental witnesses

8a WILLIRAM OF EBERSBERG, *Commentary on the Song of Songs c.* 1060
Williram was a monk of Fulda, who rose to be scholasticus of Michelsberg in Bamberg (*c.* 1040) and abbot of Ebersberg (1048–85). His commentary on the Song of Songs, which is partly in German, opens with a general criticism of contemporary scholarship, in which Lanfranc alone is singled out for praise:

> Et si qui sunt qui sub scholari ferula grammaticae et dialecticae studiis imbuuntur haec sibi sufficere arbitrantes, diuinae paginae omnino obliuiscuntur, cum ob hoc solum Christianis licet gentiles libros legere, ut ex his quanta distantia sit lucis et tenebrarum, ueritatis et erroris possint discernere. Alii vero cum in divinis dogmatibus sint valentes, tamen creditum sibi talentum in terra abscondentes, ceteros qui in lectionibus et canticis peccant, derident, nec imbeccilitati eorum uel instructione, uel librorum emendatione quicquam consulti exhibent.
> Unum in Francia comperi Lantfridum nomine, antea maxime ualentem in dialectica. Nunc ad ecclesiastica se contulit studia, et in Epistolis Pauli et in Psalterio multorum sua subtilitate exacuisse ingenia; ad quem audiendum . . . multi nostrorum conflu(unt).[1]

8b SIGEBERT OF GEMBLOUX, *De scriptoribus ecclesiasticis*, cap. 155
c. 1100–12

Continuing the series of thumb-nail biographies that Jerome and Gennadius had provided for Antiquity, Sigebert sees Lanfranc as a dialectician and commentator on the Pauline Epistles, and above all as the opponent of Berengar of Tours.[2] In addition however Lanfranc is credited with a life of William the Conqueror:

> Scripsit laudes, triumphos et res gestas Guillelmi Northmannorum comitis, qui regnum Anglorum primus invasit.

Probably this is a misattribution of either the *Gesta Guillelmi Ducis* or the *Carmen de Hastingae Proelio*; but given Lanfranc's

---

[1] Martène et Durand, *Vet.Script.Ampl.Coll.* (Paris, 1724), i. 507AC. For the date see Manitius ii. 592–8.

[2] Migne, *P.L.* clx.582C–3A; new edition by R. Witte, *Catalogus Sigeberti Gemblacensis monachi de Viris Illustribus* (Frankfurt, 1974). Cf. Manitius iii.346–8. Sigebert's successors in the genre treat Lanfranc very summarily: see Honorius Augustodunensis, *De Lumin.Eccles.* iv. 14, Migne, *P.L.* clxxii. 231B–2A) and Boto of Prüfening, *De Script.Eccles.* 89 (Migne, *P.L.*ccxiii.979A).

standing with the duke it is just possible that he did write such a work.

ii. 1070–1089: archbishop of Canterbury

9a LANFRANC'S LETTERS

Lanfranc's extant letters are all found in a collection of fifty-nine letters and two provincial councils compiled *c.* 1090 and represented now by MSS. London B. L. Cotton Nero A. VII, fols. 1–39v (s.xii. in.: English) and Vatican Reg. lat.285, fols. 1–18 (s.xii. med./2: Bec).[1] D'Achery's edition is based on MS. Paris B.N.lat.13412, a late-sixteenth-century transcript of the Bec manuscript. In 1844 Giles reprinted D'Achery's text in the light of Nero A.VII, adding two authentic letters (Giles 41–2), which are missing from B.N.lat.13412, four more that relate to Lanfranc's affairs (Giles 1, 2, 9, 40) and a spurious charter (no. 10b below). Migne follows D'Achery's numbering 1–60, adding Giles 41, 42, 67 at the end. Much has been omitted from this Christ Church collection, notably the letters that Lanfranc received from successive popes and his correspondence with Anselm. The latter exists in a modern edition;[2] a conspectus of the papal letters follows below.

9b PAPAL LETTERS TO LANFRANC

Nicholas II

'Satis desideratam'	(*J.L.*4446)	1059–61[3]
Alexander II		
'Quisquis divina'	(*J.L.*4644)	14 Jan. 1068[4]
'Gratias omnipotenti'	(*J.L.*4669)	1063–70[3]
'Accepimus a	(*J.L.*4761:	
quibusdam'	*Lanfranci Epp.* 4)	1071–3

[1] See further V. H. Clover and M. T. Gibson, *The Letters of Archbishop Lanfranc* (forthcoming: Oxford Medieval Texts), introduction.

[2] Anselm's letter-collection contains sixteen addressed to Lanfranc: twelve from the period 1070–8 (nos. 1, 14, 23, 25, 27, 32, 39, 49, 57, 66, 72, 77) and four when Anselm was abbot of Bec (nos. 89–90, 103, 124), ed. F. S. Schmitt, *Anselmi Opera* (Edinburgh, 1946), vol. iii; one further letter is prefaced to the *Monologion*, ed.cit. i. 5–6. The only letters *from* Lanfranc are also found in Lanfranc's own letter-collection (*Anselmi Epp.* 30–1 = *Lanfranci Epp.* 43, 47).

[3] In MS. Cambridge Trinity Coll. B. 16. 44, the canon-law collection that Lanfranc gave to Christ Church, *J.L.*4446 and 4669 have marginal notes: 'Hanc epistolam accepit cum Becci monachus esset' (p. 211) and 'Hanc epistolam accepit dum Cadomensi coenobio praeesset' (p. 405), both by the scribe of 4669.

[4] For the date see J.-F. Lemarignier, *Étude sur les privilèges d'exemption et de juridiction ecclésiastique des abbayes normandes des origines à 1140* (Paris, 1937), pp. 144–5 app.; 160. Alexander II's letter *Charissime fili* (Migne, *P.L.*cxlvi. 1299B: no. 20) is an excerpt from *J.L.*4644.

'Pervenit ad aures'	(*J.L.*4762)	1071–3
Gregory VII		
'Qualiter nobis'	(*J.L.*4801 :*Epp.Vag.*1)	autumn 1073[1]
'Non minima ammiratione'	(*J.L.*4803 :*Reg.*i.31 ; Lanfranci *Epp.* 20)	20 Nov. 1073
'Quod ex illo tempore'	(*J.L.*5121 :*Reg.*vi.30)	25 Mar. 1079
'Saepe fraternitatem tuam'	(*J.L.*5228 :*Reg.*ix.20)	May-June 1082
Clement III (antipope)[2]		
'Fraternitati tuę'		*c.* 1085–6
'Noverit caritas tua'		1088–9
'Benedictus sit Deus'		*c.* 1086–9
Urban II		
'Non latere credimus'	(*J.L.*5351)	10 Apr. 1088[3]

9c PAPAL CORRESPONDENCE WITH WILLIAM I AND MATILDA

Alexander II		
'Omnipotenti Deo'	(*J.L.*4695)	autumn 1071
'Novit prudentia'	(*J.L.*4757)	1066–73
Gregory VII		
'Merere mentis tuę'	(*J.L.*4850 :*Reg.*i.70)	4 Apr. 1074
'Auditis nobilitatis tuę litteris'	(*J.L.*4851 :*Reg.*i.71 : Matilda)	4 Apr. 1074
'Compertum esse'	(*J.L.*5005 :*Epp.Vag.*16)	late autumn 1076
'Causam unde nos'	(*J.L.*5027 :*Reg.*iv.17)	31 Mar. 1077
'Officii nostri cura'	(*J.L.*5074 :*Reg.*v.19)	4 Apr. 1078
'Notum esse tibi credo'	(*J.L.*5166 :*Reg.*vii.23)	24 Apr. 1080
'Credimus prudentiam vestram'	(*J.L.*5168 :*Reg.*vii.25)	8 May 1080
'Ingenuitatis vestrę'	(*J.L.*5169 :*Reg.*vii.26 : Matilda)	8 May 1080
'Communis amor'	(*J.L.*5254 :*Reg.*ix.37)	winter 1083

10a LANFRANC'S CHARTERS

Lanfranc's only extant charter is:

Canterbury, St. Gregory's

'Ad universorum noticiam volumus pervenire . . .' 1086–
3 Sept. 1087

---

[1] H. E. J. Cowdrey, *The 'Epistolae Vagantes' of Pope Gregory VII* (Oxford, 1972: Oxford Medieval Texts), pp. 1–5.

[2] Printed from MS. Cambridge Trinity Coll. B.16.44, the unique manuscript, by F. Liebermann, 'Lanfranc and the Antipope', *Eng.Hist.Rev.* xvi (1901), 328–32.

[3] See A. Becker, *Papst Urban II* (Stuttgart, 1964: *Schriften Mon.Ger.Hist.*) i. 171.

MS. Cambridge Univ.Lib.Ll.ii.15, fols. 1–2 (s.xiii), ed. A. M. Woodcock, *Cartulary of the Priory of St. Gregory, Canterbury* (London, 1956: Camden Soc. 3 ser.lxxxviii), pp. 1–3.[1]

Lanfrancian grants cited by his successors include:

Anselm

to the monks of Christ Church (1093–1109)— confirmation of half the dues from the altar of Christ (presumably the high altar) in the cathedral: F. S. Schmitt, *Anselmi Opera* (Edinburgh, 1951), v, no. 474;

to the bishop and monks of Rochester (1093–1109)— confirmation of customs: P. Sawyer, *Textus Roffensis* (Copenhagen, 1962), fol. 179.

Theobald

to the monks of Rochester (1142–8)— confirmation of rights and property: A. Saltman, *Theobald, Archbishop of Canterbury* (London, 1956), no. 221;

to the same (1145)— notification of legatine judgement in their favour: ibid., no. 223.

Grants cited elsewhere include:

St. Albans

Robert, abbot of St. Albans (1151–66) cites a charter of Lanfranc as title to the wood of Northawe (Herts): H. T. Riley, *Gesta Abbatum* (London 1867: Rolls Ser.) i.164.

10b SPURIOUS CHARTERS

Durham: 'Noveritis nos hoc scriptum . . .'

MS. Durham Dean and Chapter I.i.Archiepisc.3 (s.xii) ed. W. Greenwell, *Feodarium Prioratus Dunelmensis* (Durham, 1872: Surtees Soc.lviii), pp.lxxv–lxxvi.

Glastonbury: Thirty days' indulgence granted to pilgrims. C. R. and M. G. Cheney, *The Letters of pope Innocent III concerning England and Wales* (Oxford, 1967), no. 1161.

Rochester: 'Sciatis me sursum reddidisse . . .'

MS. London B. L. Cotton Vesp.A.xxii, fol. 127v (s.xiii $\frac{2}{4}$), ed. J. Thorpe, *Registrum Roffense* (London, 1769), pp. 359, 441.

Southwark, St. Mary's Can. Reg: 'Concedimus et presentis carte pagina confirmamus . . .'

MS. London B. L. Cotton Nero C.iii, fol. 188 (original: 1139–47), ed. Giles i. 81, no. 67, reading L(anfrancus) for T(eobaldus): Saltman, op.cit. no. 252, with references.

---

[1] In its thirteenth-century form this charter has two errors: St. Mildred's body is said to have been at Lyminge 'ab antiquo' (cf. Ch. VII, § iv) and the tenant of Eynsford is wrongly given as William.

10c SEALS

The earliest archiepiscopal seal to survive for Canterbury is Anselm's.[1] The first conventual seal, which represents the pre-Conquest cathedral, presumably existed *c.* 1070; it remained in use until the mid-twelfth century. Lanfranc's cathedral, with its cherubim on the central tower, appears on the second conventual seal, which was introduced 1152–61.[2]

11 *Cognate Documents*

The following lists (11a-b) are based on H. W. C. Davis, *Regesta Regum Anglo-Normannorum*, vol. i (Oxford, 1913), corrections vol. ii (1956). They do *not* represent a critical study of the individual documents.

11a DOCUMENTS WITNESSED OR CONFIRMED BY LANFRANC—

Beneficiary	Date	Regesta, vol. i
St. Martin, Battle	1070–1	60–?61
Le Bec-Hellouin	1087	237a
St. Étienne, Caen	Sept. 1077	96 ⎫
	1081–7	105 ⎪
	1080–2	168 ⎬ [3]
	c. 1080–3	170 ⎭
Holy Trinity, Caen	1082	149–50[4]
St. Calais (Maine)	1082	147
archbishop of Canterbury	1072	64[5]
Remigius, bishop of Dorchester	1072	283[6]
Holy Trinity, Fécamp	1085	206[7]
	1086	220
St. Peter, Gloucester	1081	136a
Holy Trinity, Lessay	July 1080	125
St. Paul, London	1072–8	111 ⎫ [8]
	1080–7	274 ⎭

---

[1] See e.g. London B. L. Charters LFC.vii.5: W. de G. Birch, *Cat. Seals Dept.MSS British Museum* (London, 1887) i. 1169, pl.VI.

[2] See W. Urry, *Canterbury under the Angevin Kings* (London, 1967), p. 384; cf. Birch, op.cit., i.1368–9, pl.IX.

[3] Musset, nos. 3, 4Abis, 7, 14.

[4] Musset, nos. 9, 8.

[5] T. A. M. Bishop and P. Chaplais, *Facsimiles of English Royal Writs to A.D.1100* (Oxford, 1957), pl. xxix; cf. R. W. Southern, 'The Canterbury Forgeries', *Eng. Hist.Rev.* lxxiii (1958), 197–203.

[6] Bishop–Chaplais, op.cit., no. 14.

[7] P. Chaplais, 'Une charte originale de Guillaume le Conquérant pour l'abbaye de Fécamp . . . (1085)', in *L'Abbaye bénédictine de Fécamp: ouvrage scientifique du xiii*ᵉ *centenaire 658–1958* (Fécamp, 1959), i. 93–104.

[8] M. Gibbs, *Early Charters of the Cathedral Church of St. Paul, London* (London, 1939: Camden Soc. 3 ser.lviii), nos. 9 and 16.

SS. Mary and Aldhelm, Malmesbury	Feb. 1081	135
Rochester cathedral priory	winter 1088	301[1]
St. Albans	1087–9	314[b]
John, bishop of Wells	Sept. 1088– Mar. 1089	314
St. Peter, Westminster	1070–82	162–3

Spurious:

Battle (*Reg.* 62, 262–3, 161; London B. L. Add. Ch. 70980); Bury St. Edmunds (*Reg.* 137); Crowland (*Reg.* 222); Durham (*Reg.* 148, 195–7); St. Peter, Ghent (*Reg.* 141); Glastonbury (*Reg.* 273); Gloucester (*Reg.* 36, 167, 180, 218); Malmesbury (*Reg.* 136); Ramsey (*Reg.* 95); Rochester (Thorpe, *Registrum Roffense*, p. 441); Westminster (*Reg*, 11, 34, 90, 144);[2] Whitby (*Reg.* 228).

11b Documents addressed to or concerning Lanfranc[3]

Beneficiary	Date	Regesta, vol. i
General	*c.* 1071	50
St. Mary, Abingdon	*c.* 1071	49
	1070–84	200
St. Martin, Battle	1070–87	260
	1087–9	314a
St. Étienne, Caen	1069–70	— ⎱ 4
	1079–82	169 ⎰
Christ Church, Canterbury	1070–87	265
	1070–87	—[5]
	1071–82	————[6]

---

[1] *Textus Roffensis*, fols. 212–13; cf. C. R. Cheney, *English Bishops' Chanceries 1100–1250* (Manchester, 1950), p. 91, n. 1.

[2] For Battle see E. Searle, 'Battle Abbey and exemption: the forged charters', *Eng.Hist.Rev.* lxxxiii (1968), 449–80. For the Durham forgeries see H. S. Offler, *Durham Episcopal Charters 1071–1152* (Durham, 1968: Surtees Soc. clxxix), *no.* *3a, *4a, *4 (= *Reg.* 148, 196, 197) and *7. For Gloucester (*Reg.* 36) see Bishop and Chaplais, op.cit., p.xxi; for Ramsey see P. Chaplais, 'The original charters of Herbert and Gervase, abbots of Westminster', in *A Medieval Miscellany for D. M. Stenton* (London, 1962: Pipe Roll Soc.lxxvi), p. 97, n.3; for Rochester see P. H. Sawyer, *Anglo-Saxon Charters* (London, 1968), no. 349; and for Westminster (*Reg.* 11, 34) see Bishop and Chaplais, op.cit., p. xxi.

[3] Documents already listed in 11a (e.g. *Reg.* 60–1) are not repeated in 11b.

[4] Musset, op.cit., no. 20, 13.

[5] Lambeth Palace Lib. MS 1212, pp. 15 and 333 (s.xiii: Christ Church): protection of the archbishop's hunting; cf.*Reg.*i.265.

[6] L. C. Loyd and D. M. Stenton, *Sir Christopher Hatton's Book of Seals* (Oxford, 1950), no. 431, pl. viii (charter of Odo of Bayeux).

	1071–82	—[1]
	1071–82	—[2]
	1072–82	176
	?1077	101–2
St. Augustine, Canterbury	1070–82	175[3]
	?1072	66
	1077	98–100
	1087–8	304
St. Peter, Cluny	*c.* 1078–82	179[4]
SS. Peter and Etheldreda, Ely	1080–7	155
	1082–7	151–4 }[5]
		156–7 }
SS. Mary and Ecgwin, Evesham	1072–7	106
	1077–82	184–5
St. Paul, London	1085–7	288e
St. Benedict, Ramsey	1080–2	177
	1087	296
	1080–7	—[6]
Rochester cathedral priory	Jan. 1071	47[7]
Samson, the King's chaplain	1074–85	210
St. Albans	1072–85	218a
St. Martin, Troarn (Calvados)	1077	97
St. Peter, Westminster	1076–82	166
St. Mary, Worcester	1079–83	184

Spurious:

Battle (*Reg.* 113, 261); Christ Church, Canterbury (*Reg.* 38: see Bishop—Chaplais, no. 4); Westminster 54 (*Reg.* 54).

12 COUNCILS

Lanfranc's councils were normally held—though less frequently —in conjunction with William I's great courts: in Gloucester

---

[1] Lambeth MS. 1212, pp. 15, 187, and 332: bishop Odo notified of the return of Saltwood to Christ Church.

[2] Ibid., p. 332: confirmation of Odo's grant of four denes to Lanfranc and Christ Church. I am indebted here and on a number of similar points to the generous help of Dr. Martin Brett.

[3] See G. J. Turner and H. E. Salter, *The Register of St. Augustine's Abbey, Canterbury* (London, 1924: *Brit.Acad.Rec.Soc.Econ.Hist.* III), ii.548.

[4] C. T. Clay, *Early Yorkshire Charters viii* (*Yorks Archaeol.Soc.*, 1949), no. 3.

[5] *Liber Eliensis*, ed. Blake (London, 1962: Camden Soc. 3 ser. xcii), ii. 120 122–7; cf. pp. 426–32.

[6] *Cartularium monasterii de Rameseia*, ed. Hart and Lyons (London, 1884: Rolls Ser.), i. 233, no. cxlvi.

[7] *Textus Roffensis*, fols. 170v–1.

at Christmas, in Winchester at Easter and in London at
Whitsun.[1] An asterisk denotes surviving *acta*.

**1072	*c.* 8 April:	Winchester[2]
*1072	*c.* 27 May:	Windsor
*1075	pre-28 August:	London
*1076	1 April:	Winchester
1077–8:		London
1081	*c.* 3 January:	Gloucester
1085–6 ?midwinter:		Gloucester

13 The Primacy of Canterbury

13a THE 'SCRIPTUM LANFRANCI DE PRIMATU' *c.* 1075

MS. London B. L. Cotton Nero A.vii, the principal English
manuscript of Lanfranc's letters, contains a detailed account of
his efforts to secure a comprehensive profession of obedience
from archbishop Thomas I of York.[3] It was written after the
death of Alexander II (April 1073) and perhaps after the
transfer of the see of Lichfield to Chester (1075). The text
proper (fols. 3v–5) is followed by five relevant documents
(fols. 5–9v): Thomas's profession of 1072, the council of
Windsor (Whitsun 1072), Lanfranc's letter to Alexander II
(*Lanfranci Epp.* 3), Lanfranc's letter to Hildebrand (ibid. 5),
Hildebrand's reply (ibid. 6). This corpus is the earliest and
most reliable version of the primacy dispute; it was available to
Eadmer and extensively quoted by William of Malmesbury.[4]

13b EPISCOPAL PROFESSIONS

The South

After the consecration of Thomas of York (autumn 1070) all
the bishops of England who had already been consecrated
'diuersis in locis, ab aliis archiepiscopis uel a papa tempore
Stigandi' are said to have professed obedience to Lanfranc.
Professions survive for Wulfstan of Worcester (1062–95),
Remigius of Dorchester/Lincoln (1067–92) and Herfast of
Elmham/Thetford (1070–84).[5] There is no trace of either

---

[1] See the list in C. N. L. Brooke, 'Archbishop Lanfranc, the English bishops and
the council of London of 1075', *Studia Gratiana* xii (1967), *Collectanea Stephan
Kuttner* ii. 41–59.

[2] Further *acta* have come to light for Winchester 1072: M. Brett, 'A collection
of Anglo-Norman councils', *Journ.Eccles.Hist.* xxvi (1975), 301–8.

[3] H. Boehmer, *Die Fälschungen Erzbischof Lanfranks von Canterbury* (Leipzig, 1902),
pp. 165–7: the title is Boehmer's.

[4] Eadmer, *Historia Novorum* i. 10; William of Malmesbury, *Gesta Pontificum*
i.25–9, pp. 39–46.

[5] M. Richter, *The Canterbury Professions* (London, 1973: *Cant.York Soc.* lxvii), nos.
31–3 (Wulfstan, Remigius, Herfast); cf. *Scriptum Lanfranci*, p. 166.

renewed professions by the seven other pre-Conquest bishops or (outstandingly) the profession of Walkelin, who was consecrated after Stigand's deposition. Lanfranc himself consecrated twelve bishops to English sees. In three cases the original profession is extant; and the text survives for all the others, except Peter of Lichfield/Chester. Those marked *a* are mentioned in the *Acta Lanfranci* (no. 14a):[1]

a	Osbern, bp Exeter (1072–1103)
a	Peter, bp Lichfield/Chester (1072–85)
	Hugh, bp London (1075–84)
a	Ernost, bp Rochester (1075–6)
a	Gundulf, bp Rochester (1077–1108)
	Osmund, bp Salisbury (1078–99)
	Robert, bp Hereford (1079–95)
a	Robert, bp Chester (1086–1117)
a	William, bp Thetford (1086–91)
a	Maurice, bp London (1086–1107)
a	Godfrey, bp Chichester (1087–8)
a	John, bp Bath and Wells (1088–1122).

The North and West

Archbishop Thomas I of York (1070–1100) professed obedience to Lanfranc definitively in 1072.[2] No professions survive for Durham, his only English suffragan. York also claimed jurisdiction over Scotland, the Orkneys and the Western Isles. Archbishop Thomas probably did receive a profession from bishop Ralph of the Orkneys (1073—); whether Fothad II of St. Andrews (1059–93) also professed obedience is more doubtful.[3]

Two Irish bishops made profession to Lanfranc:

a	Patrick, bp Dublin (1074–84)
a	Donngus (Donatus), bp Dublin (*c.* 1085–95).[4]

The relations of Canterbury with the Welsh Church were initiated by Anselm.[5]

[1] The originals are for Robert of Chester, William of Thetford and John of Bath and Wells (Richter, nos. 45, 43, 47). Two others survive in a direct eleventh-century transcript (Richter, nos. 40, 46) and the rest are found in MS. London B. L. Cotton Cleopatra E.I (Richter, nos. 35, 37–41, 44). I am indebted to Dr. Richter for his generosity in allowing me to consult his book in proof.

[2] Richter, no. 34; cf. *Scriptum Lanfranci*, pp. 166–7.

[3] For Ralph see *Lanfranci Epp.* 11–12. Fothad's profession is first mentioned by Hugh the Chanter, s.a. 1109 (no. 19b below).

[4] Richter, nos. 36, 42; cf. the excellent account of the Irish professions by J. A. Watt, *The Church and the Two Nations in Medieval Ireland* (Cambridge, 1970), pp. 217–25.

[5] R. W. Southern, *St. Anselm and his Biographer* (Cambridge, 1963), pp. 132–3. For Lanfranc's alleged consecration of Herewald, bishop of Llandaff, see J. C.

13c ABBATIAL PROFESSIONS

During the twelfth and thirteenth centuries the archbishops of Canterbury received professions of obedience from a number of abbots both in their own diocese (e.g. Faversham) and elsewhere in their province (e.g. Glastonbury). The only known professions to Lanfranc are from St. Augustine's, Canterbury, which was a special case:

    a   Scotland, abbot of St. Augustine's (1070–87)

    a   Wido, abbot of St. Augustine's (1087–93)[1]

14 *Christ Church Records*

14a ACTA LANFRANCI   1070–93

The A-text of the *Anglo-Saxon Chronicle*, which ends in 1070, is followed by a series of Latin annals of Lanfranc's archiepiscopate, based on the records at Christ Church.[2] The author uses the episcopal professions, documents of the litigation at Penenden Heath, Lanfranc's *obit* and a few of his letters. He contributes valuable details of Lanfranc's councils and a long account of the resistance to abbot Wido at St. Augustine's. The *Acta* were probably entered in several stages: the dispute with Thomas of York (based on the *Scriptum Lanfranci*); councils and consecrations 1071–89; the revolt at St. Augustine's, Canterbury, and the accession of Anselm. Eadmer's statement that Lanfranc 'ipsemet de rebus ecclesiasticis quae suo tempore gestae sunt ueracissimo et compendioso [sc. summary] calamo scripserit' could refer to these *Acta*.[3]

14b DOMESDAY MONACHORUM   *c.* 1100

The so-called *Domesday Monachorum* is a more comprehensive document than the name implies.[4] It records the estates of Christ Church (both archiepiscopal and monastic) and some related property, the archbishop's tenants and the ecclesiastical dues (such as chrism-money) that implied jurisdiction. The description of the estates and their tenants is approximately

---

[1] C. Eveleigh Woodruff, 'Some early professions of canonical obedience to the see of Canterbury by heads of religious houses', *Archaeol.Cantiana* xxxvii (1925), 60–1.

[2] Cambridge Corpus Christi Coll. 173, fol.32r-v, ed. Plummer, *Two Saxon Chronicles Parallel* (Oxford, 1892), i. 287–92; facsimile by R. Flower and H. Smith, *The Parker Chronicle and Laws* (London, 1941); and cf. p. 218, n.1 below.

[3] *Historia Novorum* i. 13.

[4] D. C. Douglas, *The 'Domesday Monachorum' of Christ Church Canterbury* (London, 1944). See further R. S. Hoyt, 'A pre-Domesday Kentish assessment list', in *A Medieval Miscellany for D. M. Stenton* (London, 1962: Pipe Roll Soc. lxxvi), pp. 189–202 and F. R. H. du Boulay, *The Lordship of Canterbury* (London, 1966), pp. 37–50; 113.

Davies, *Episcopal Acts . . . relating to Welsh Dioceses 1066–1272* (Cardiff, 1946), i. 57-9.

comparable with the account in *Domesday Book*. There are many discrepancies of detail and the order is different; but essentially both *Domesday Book* and *Domesday Monachorum* show the Christ Church estates in the last years of Lanfranc's archiepiscopate. *Domesday Monachorum* in its present form however is about a decade later than *Domesday Book;* it summarizes several earlier documents and is the key to others in the twelfth century.

Earlier documents

1   *the plea at Penenden Heath*   1072
See J. Le Patourel, 'The reports of the trial on Penenden Heath', in *Studies in Medieval History presented to F.M. Powicke*, ed. R. W. Hunt *et al.* (Oxford, 1948), pp. 15–26; add MS. London B. L. Cotton Tiberius C.ix, fols. 45–6.[1]

2   *further estates and revenues recovered subsequently*   1078–9
See D. C. Douglas, 'Odo, Lanfranc and the Domesday Survey', in *Historical Essays in honour of James Tait*, ed. J. G. Edwards *et al.*, (Manchester, 1933), pp. 47–57; F. R. H. Du Boulay, *The Lordship of Canterbury* (London, 1966), pp. 38–41.

3   *Domesday Book* i. 3–5   1086
The exact relation of Domesday Book to *Domesday Monachorum* is still in dispute. While *Domesday Monachorum* is not a straight derivative of Domesday Book, it is likely that they both reflect fairly sophisticated estate records kept at Christ Church during Lanfranc's archiepiscopate.
See *Victoria County History: Kent* (London, 1932), iii. 203–52; S. Harvey, 'Domesday Book and its predecessors', *Eng.Hist.Rev.* lxxxvi (1971), 753–73; V. H. Galbraith, *Domesday Book: its place in administrative history* (Oxford, 1974), pp. 78–84.

4   *obit* of William the Conqueror   1087
William's *obit* at Christ Church records twenty-seven estates which, directly or indirectly, he had restored to the archbishop and community. The list includes the estates recovered at Penenden Heath and those named in the fragment of 1078–9. Most of the others appear as Christ Church property in Domesday Book.
See Le Patourel, op.cit., pp. 24–6; Du Boulay, op.cit., pp. 41–6.

Later documents

5   *Textus Roffensis*   *c.* 1122
This earliest cartulary of Rochester contains the main evidence

---

[1] MS. Tiberius C.ix is a fifteenth-century recension that emphasizes the archiepiscopal *consuetudines* and abridges the description of the estates: P. Sawyer, *Textus Roffensis* ii (Copenhagen, 1962), 16 app.

for the restoration of Rochester cathedral and the recovery of its lands. Lanfranc is actively involved throughout his archiepiscopate, from Penenden Heath to the anxious bargaining with William Rufus in 1088 over the building of Rochester castle (fols. 173–4v).

See P. Sawyer, *Textus Roffensis* ii (Copenhagen, 1962: Early English MSS. in Facsimile xi), with bibliography.

6 list of the archbishop's tenants   1171

As Becket was in exile in 1166, the *cartae baronum* include no return for Canterbury. In the list of 1171, which makes good this deficiency, several of the families established in Lanfranc's time are still in possession: hence further details of their position in the eleventh century may be inferred from the more exhaustive account of the later twelfth.

See H. M. Colvin, 'A list of the archbishop of Canterbury's tenants by knight-service in the reign of Henry II', *Kent Records* xviii (1964), 1–40; F. R. H. Du Boulay, *The Lordship of Canterbury* (London, 1966), pp. 61–2.

14c LANFRANC'S SCRIBES

The handful of official documents surviving from Lanfranc's years in Canterbury is too small and disparate to allow the identification of individual scribes. Nor can we assert that any one scribe was formally retained as an (or the) archiepiscopal scribe. At the same time it is clear that these early documents fall into distinct groups:[1]

A *Scribes already active in St. Étienne, Caen*

These hands are similar (particularly *a* and *b*), but not identical.

a Caen, Arch. Orne H.421, no. 2 1063–6

                                     Musset, no. 1, pl. I (there entitled H. 421, no. 1)

b Canterbury Dean and   1072
    Chapter Cart.Ant.A.2   *Pal.Soc.*, pl. 170; cf. Bishop and Chaplais, pl. xxix

---

[1] The list below is based on the following: T. A. M. Bishop and P. Chaplais, *Facsimiles of English Royal Writs to A.D.1100* (Oxford, 1957); H. Boehmer, *Die Fälschungen Erzbischof Lanfranks von Canterbury* (Leipzig, 1902); E. A. Bond and E. M. Thompson, *Palaeographical Society Facsimiles* 1 ser. (London, 1873–83), iii; C. N. L. Brooke, 'Archbishop Lanfranc, the English bishops and the council of London of 1075', *Studia Gratiana* xii (1967), App. I (communication from T. A. M. Bishop); C. R. Dodwell, *The Canterbury School of Illumination* (Cambridge, 1954); D. C. Douglas, 'Odo, Lanfranc and the Domesday Survey', in *Historical Essays in honour of James Tait*, ed. J. G. Edwards *et al.*; N. R. Ker, *English Manuscripts in the Century after the Norman Conquest* (Oxford, 1960); Musset; *Regesta*, Richter; E. M. Thompson *et al.*, *New Palaeographical Society facsimiles* 2nd ser. (London, 1913–30), ii. I am greatly indebted to Dr. Pierre Chaplais for his assistance with this section.

c Caen, Arch. Orne H.421,   1077
   no. 1   Musset, no. 3, pl. II
                        (there entitled H.421, no. 2)

B *Scribes actives at Christ Church in the 1070s*
Nos. c–f below are the same scribe.

  a London B. L. Cotton Faust. 1070–2
    B.vi, fol. 94   Boehmer I

  b London B. L. Cotton Calig. 1073+
    A.xv, fol. 120–38   Dodwell, p. 21

  c Cambridge St. John's Coll. 1075
    236   Brooke/Bishop, p. 57

  d Cambridge Trinity Coll.   1070–85
    B.16.44., p. 405: colophon Ker, pp. 25–6; Brooke,
    'Hunc librum . . .'   loc.cit.

  e Canterbury Dean and   ?1077
    Chapter S.246   Ker, loc.cit.; Brooke,
                        loc.cit.; *Regesta* i. 101

  f London B. L. Cotton   1079–80
    Aug.ii.36   Douglas, at p. 48; Ker,
                        loc.cit.; Brooke, loc.cit.

C *Scribes active at Christ Church in the 1080s*
The main evidence here is the episcopal and abbatial professions, both originals (Cart.Ant.C.115) and early transcripts (Cart.Ant.C.117). The hands of a-b are very similar, as are d-g.

  a Canterbury Cath.Cart.Ant. 1086
    C.115, no. 1   *New Pal. Soc.* ii, pl. 64
    (William, bp of Elmham)

  b C.115, no. 2   1086
    (Robert, bp of Chester)   ibid., loc.cit.

  c C.115, no. 7   1088
    (John, bp of Wells)   ibid., loc.cit.

  d C.117, no. 1   1088+
    (Godfrey, bp of Chichester)

  e C.117, no. 2   1088+
    (Wido, abbot of St. Augustine's)

  f C.117, no. 3   1088+
    (Osbern bp of Exeter)

  g C.117, no. 4   1088+
    (Osmund, bp of Salisbury) Ker, *English Manuscripts,* pl. 6

  h C.117, no. 5   1088+
    (John, bp of Wells)

Lanfranc's autograph 'signum' and subscription
Canterbury Dean and Chapter 1072
Cart.Ant.A.2 (*signum* and   (scribe Ab above)
   subscription)
Cambridge St. John's Coll. 236 1075
(*signum* and arguably   (scribe Bc above)
   subscription)
Archives Dépt. Seine-Maritime 1085[1]
7.H.2151 (*signum* only)

14d 'OBITS' AND EPITAPHS
The principal text here is the long *obit* printed in Appendix B.
This Christ Church text is exceptionally detailed: the normal
entry in both English and continental houses was 'Lanfrancus
archiepiscopus', or something equally brief. The epitaphs are
strictly conventional:

   i. Anselm's contribution to Lanfranc's mortuary roll—*inc.*
     Archiepiscopii non diuitias nec honores . . . *expl.* Pro semet
     supplex et sedulus ipse laborat.[2]

   ii. Anonymous verses, attributed to a monk of Crowland—*inc.*
     Eheu ploret Anglia simul et Italia . . . *expl.* Ut te ducem
     laureatus habeat perpetuum.[3]

   iii. A Canterbury text, probably the inscription on Lanfranc's
     tomb—*inc.* Hic tumulus claudit quem nulla sub orbe latino
     . . . *expl.* Vtque sibi detur requies orando iuuate.[4]

   iv. Verses attributed to Philip de Harvengt O. Prémonst. (*ob.*
     1183)—*inc.* Vixisti venerande pater sapienter et aeque . . .
     expl. Prompsit luna dies, nocte solutus abis.[5]

iii. after 1089

15   *Canterbury Sources*
15a THE ANGLO-SAXON CHRONICLE   s.xi[2]
Lanfranc appears remarkably seldom in the *Chronicle*, considering the Canterbury provenance of several recensions (A, F, and

---

[1] See p. 208 n. 7 above.

[2] *V.L.*, pp. 17–18 (Migne *P.L.*clviii.1049A–50B: Walther 1428; add Vat. Reg.
lat.499, fol.71r-v. See L. Delisle, *Rouleaux des morts du ixe au xve siècle* (Paris, 1866),
no. xxiv; cf. Orderic Vitalis, *Hist.Eccles.* viii (Chibnall IV. 170) and Robert of
Torigny, *Chronicle* i. 75–6.

[3] E. du Méril, *Poésies populaires latines du moyen âge* (Paris, 1847), pp. 251–5: MS.
Douai B.Mun.852 (*olim* 801), fol.152; Walther 5297. The opening lines are printed
by Mabillon, *Acta Sanctorum O.S.B.* saec. VI (Paris 1701), ii. 660. For the association
with Croyland see *Historia Ingulfi: Rerum Anglicarum Scriptorum Veterum* (Oxford,
1684), i.96.

[4] MS. Cotton Nero A.VII, fol. 40, printed only in Giles i.313.

[5] Migne, *P.L.*cciii.1393: abridged D'Achery (*V.L.* pagination), p. 42 (Migne,
*P.L.*cl.98B); Walther 20769.

the archetype of E) in the later eleventh century and the detailed account of events in which Lanfranc was personally involved, for example the revolts of 1075 and 1088. The author of the archetype of E, who had known the Conqueror's court at first hand, sees Lanfranc's duties as strictly ecclesiastical: the consecration of Thomas as archbishop and William Rufus as king. The councils of the king are noted and described, but never (except in one brief phrase) the archbishop's. The D-text does however give the exact date of the fire at Christ Church: 6 December 1067.[1]

15b ANNALES ANGLO-SAXONICI   s.xi[ex].
A series of marginal notes added to a Christ Church kalendar, MS. London B. L. Cotton Caligula A.xv, has two useful items (fol. 135): s.a.1073 (*rectius* 1077) consecration of the new cathedral on 9 April; s.a. 1085 translation of St. Eadburga (only) from Lyminge to St. Gregory's, Canterbury.[2]

15c CANTERBURY WORLD-CHRONICLE   s.xiii[ex].
MS. Canterbury Dean and Chapter Add. 17 contains two fragments of a world-chronicle in Old French, the second of which (pp. 7–18) covers the late tenth to the late eleventh centuries.[3] The author gives a detailed account of Lanfranc's archiepiscopate, based on Canterbury material; but he preserves nothing that is not found in the surviving Latin sources.

16   *The cult of Dunstan*
16a OSBERN, *Miracula S. Dunstani*   *c.* 1090
In the Anglo-Saxon community *c.* 1070 Osbern is the only adult monk of whom anything is known personally. He came to accept and admire Lanfranc; but he kept (or more probably developed) a vision of the heroic age of Dunstan. There are six relevant chapters in his *Miracula*:[4]

   17   Lanfranc's reverent translation of Dunstan during the rebuilding of the cathedral.
   18   Dunstan supports Lanfranc in a secular lawsuit.
   19   Dunstan cures the monk Ægelward.

[1] D. Whitelock *et al.*, *The Anglo-Saxon Chronicle* (London, 1961), pp. 146; 153–68; cf.pp.xi–xviii. In the A-text the annal for 1070 begins as an Anglo-Saxon rendering of the *Scriptum Lanfranci*; but from 'he refused and said that he ought not to do it' to the end it diverges: T. A. M. Bishop and P. Chaplais, *Facsimiles of English Royal Writs to A.D.1100* (Oxford, 1957), no. 3. This in turn is followed by the *Acta Lanfranci* (no. 14a).

[2] F. Liebermann, *Ungedruckte Anglo-Normannische Geschichtsquellen* (Strasbourg, 1879), p. 4. The consecration of the cathedral has been reckoned erroneously as seven years from the fire of 1067 rather than from Lanfranc's arrival in 1070.

[3] N. R. Ker, *Medieval Manuscripts in British Libraries* (Oxford, 1976), ii. 305–6. I am indebted to the Dean and Chapter of Canterbury and the cathedral librarian for their help.

[4] W. Stubbs, *Memorials of St. Dunstan* (London, 1874: Rolls Ser.), pp. 142–55.

20 Lanfranc is cured by a vision of Dunstan on horseback.
21 Lanfranc's chaplain is cured at the same moment.
22 Two miracles concerning prisoners.

In sum these miracles assert that it was by Dunstan's help that Lanfranc was so successful an archbishop.

16b EADMER, *Miracula S. Dunstani*   *c.* 1105–9

Osbern's book was revised by Eadmer, his younger contemporary at Christ Church.[1] Eadmer had no new material, but like Osbern he had lived through the events. He was a much better stylist: he could present, for example, the story of Ægelward (Osbern, cap. 19) more vividly and at half the length. But he is still writing from a literary text rather than his own memory.

17a EADMER, *De reliquiis S. Audoeni*   1123+

Eadmer gives a valuable description here of the structure and internal organization of the pre-Conquest cathedral and of Lanfranc's cathedral that replaced it.[2]

17b EADMER, *Vita Anselmi* (1116); *Historia Novorum i-iv* (*c.* 1115)

For the biographer of Lanfranc the *Vita Anselmi* is a lost opportunity.[3] Eadmer says nothing of Lanfranc's intellectual or spiritual influence on Anselm, beyond the bare statements that it was on his account that Anselm came to Bec and on his advice that he became a monk there. Eadmer does however give a detailed account of the only meeting of the two men that he himself witnessed: Anselm's visit to Christ Church in 1079, when he convinced Lanfranc that St. Elphege was a martyr. Finally Eadmer refers briefly to Lanfranc's construction of a church at Harrow.

The *Historia Novorum* on the other hand has a systematic account of Lanfranc's archiepiscopate.[4] Eadmer had abundant material: his own *Miracula S. Dunstani*, Lanfranc's letters, the *Scriptum Lanfranci*, the litigation over the estates and the Christ Church *obit*. He seems to have known the *Acta Lanfranci*, though he makes little use of it.[5] His version of the primacy dispute is

---

[1] Stubbs, op.cit., pp. 232–41; for the date see R. W. Southern, *St. Anselm and his Biographer* (Cambridge, 1963), p. 281, n.2.

[2] *De reliquiis S. Audoeni*, ed. Wilmart, 'Edmeri Cantuariensis cantoris noua opuscula de sanctorum ueneratione et obsecratione', *Rev.Sciences Rélig.* xv (1934), 362–7.

[3] *Vita Anselmi* I. v-vi; xxix–xxx; II.vi, ed. Southern, 2nd edn. (Oxford, 1972: Oxford Medieval Texts), pp. 8–11; 48–54; 67–8. For the church at Harrow cf. *Regesta* i. 265.

[4] *Historia Novorum* i, ed. Rule (London, 1884: Rolls Ser.), 10–25. Eadmer also gives a short account of Lanfranc's dealings with William Rufus (pp. 25–6) and with abbot Baldwin of Bury St. Edmunds (lib.iii, pp. 132–3).

[5] *Acta Lanfranci*, p. 288, 'ut ei contra morem assurgeret': cf. *Historia Novorum* i. 10–11, 'Cui quod Romanam . . . intranti assurgens'.

tinged with romance: Alexander II stands by while Lanfranc reinstates both Thomas of York and Remigius of Dorchester in the sees of which they have just been deprived. But in the main Eadmer's panegyric is a serious assessment, based on both documents and his own personal acquaintance over nearly twenty years.

 18   GERVASE OF CANTERBURY   s.xii[2]

The last major witness to the Canterbury tradition is Gervase, monk of Christ Church 1163–*c*.1200 and towards the end of his life sacristan. His *Actus Pontificum* has a full-length portrait of Lanfranc, based almost entirely on the *Vita Lanfranci* and William of Malmesbury but naming Lanfranc's parents: Aribald and Roza.[1] In his *Gesta Regum* (again modelled on William of Malmesbury) Gervase refers to the belief, very relevant to the contemporary disputes with archbishop Baldwin, that it was Lanfranc who had first divided the monastic property from the archiepiscopal; he himself held that the division went back to Theodore in the seventh century.[2]

Gervase's real contribution however is the *Tractatus de combustione et reparatione Cantuariensis ecclesiae*, in which he describes the cathedral as it was before the fire of 1174.[3] The western half of the church that Gervase knew was still substantially Lanfranc's; he specifies some of the ornaments that Lanfranc had provided and the position of his grave in the Trinity chapel. In conjunction with the plan of the monastic complex as a whole that was drawn up for prior Wibert *c*.1160[4] the *Tractatus* enables at least part of Lanfranc's church to be seen with some clarity.

19   *Northern writers*

19a   ANON., *De iniusta uexatione Willelmi episcopi primi*   1089–91

The *De iniusta vexatione* is a record of the negotiations between William of St. Carilef, bishop of Durham, and William Rufus in 1088, when the bishop was involved in, or compromised by, the baronial revolt against the king.[5] It consists of three letters from bishop William to the king (spring–summer 1088) and a purportedly eye-witness account of the bishop's trial at Salisbury

---

[1] *Gervasii Opera*, ed. Stubbs (London, 1879–80: Rolls Ser.), ii. 364.

[2] Ibid. ii. 64 and 341; cf. Gervase's earlier pamphlet, *Persecutio causae contra Baldewinum archiepiscopum* (ibid. i.43): see further Ch. VI.

[3] Ibid. i. 9–16; cf. Osbern, *Miracula S. Dunstani* 22, p. 154.

[4] M. R. James, *The Canterbury Psalter* (London, 1935), pp. 53–6; cf. A. Saltman, *Theobald, Archbishop of Canterbury* (London, 1956), no. 46.

[5] *Symeonis Monachi Opera*, ed. Arnold (London, 1882: Rolls Ser.), i. 170–95. The tractate proper begins 'Rex Willelmus iunior dissaisivit Dunelmensem episcopum . . .' (p. 171) and ends '. . . rex permisit episcopo transitum' (p. 194).

(2–3 Nov. 1088). Whereas Lanfranc is the royal counsellor who materially assists in convicting a fellow-ecclesiastic, bishop William appears as the upholder of legal principle: his lands must be restored to him before he stands trial; and he is entitled to trial in an ecclesiastical court. The sophistication of these arguments, together with certain difficulties in the transmission of the text, have led Professor Offler to propose that the *De iniusta vexatione* is a retrospective polemic written in the second quarter of the twelfth century. It is 'a *Tendenzschrift* composed at leisure with the reference books available at a date when the new canon law was more freely current in England than was probable in 1088',[1] rather than a piece of contemporary journalism. Certainly there is no case for dating the tractate between the bishop's return from exile in 1091 and his death in 1096. But the exceptionally skilful historical drama composed a generation later by an unknown hand for an unknown purpose is a fairly desperate last resort. Urban II's letter of April–June 1089 confirms that bishop William had appealed immediately to Rome.[2] Urban must have received some account of the affair, with supporting documents: not perhaps the *De iniusta vexatione* complete, but something similar, on the lines for example of the *Scriptum Lanfranci* (no. 13a above). If the *De iniusta vexatione* was written at once, in the winter of 1088, it was written in Normandy, where more canon law and lawyers were available than in Durham, and where, too, William had a sympathetic audience. It is a *Tendenzschrift*, without question, but one I think that was written in the heat of the affair itself. The arguments may have been brushed up: but we need not doubt that St. Carilef was tried at Salisbury in such a mixed assembly as the tractate describes; nor need we resist the impression that the personalities in that council ring true.

⸱ 19b HUGH THE CHANTER, *History*   1127

Given that Hugh's main concern is the primatial dispute between York and Canterbury, his account of Lanfranc is remarkably generous.[3] Lanfranc was a scholar, who had taught archbishop Thomas of York. He was a royal counsellor, warning

---

[1] H. S. Offler, 'The tractate *De iniusta vexacione Willelmi episcopi primi*', *Eng.Hist. Rev.*lxvi (1951), 321–41: passage quoted pp. 334–5. But see R. W. Southern, *St. Anselm and his Biographer* (Cambridge, 1963), pp. 147–50, and M. Chibnall, *The 'Ecclesiastical History' of Orderic Vitalis* (Oxford, 1973: Oxford Med. Texts), IV. xxvii–xxx.

[2] *J.L.* 5397; cf. A. Becker, *Papst Urban II* (Stuttgart, 1964: *Mon.Ger.Hist. Schrift.*), i. 173–6.

[3] Hugh the Chanter, *The History of the Church of York 1066–1127*, ed. Johnson (London, 1961: Nelson's Medieval Texts), pp. 2–7, 11.

William the Conqueror of the danger that an independent archbishop of York might support a rival king, and advising him to
enforce the restitution of estates by York to Worcester. For the
primatial dispute itself Hugh had the text of the 1072 council,
an obscure report (not otherwise known) that the issue was
again discussed in 1086 by the king and both archbishops, and a
letter (1093) from Urban II to Thomas of York deploring his
submission to Canterbury.[1]

20 WILLIAM OF MALMESBURY, *Gesta Pontificum* (*c.* 1120–5); *Gesta
Regum* (1118–25); *Vita Wulfstani* (1124+).
William's formal account of Lanfranc is in the *Gesta Pontificum*.[2]
He knew the *Vita Herluini* and Eadmer's *Miracula S. Dunstani*,
Vita Anselmi and *Historia Novorum* and he had independent access
to some of the Christ Church records used by Eadmer:
Lanfranc's letters, the *Scriptum Lanfranci*, the litigation at
Penenden Heath and subsequently, and the forged primatial
privileges. The *Vita Lanfranci* did not yet exist: most of the
material that William has in common with the *Vita Lanfranci*
comes from the *Vita Herluini*. But the type of anecdote characteristic of the *Vita Lanfranci* was already in circulation: William
contributes the story of Herfast (bishop of Elmham), the ducal
chaplain whom Lanfranc snubbed for his illiteracy and an
instance of Lanfranc's prophetic gift, when Gundulf and two
friends consulted the *sortes vergilianae* at Bec.[3] There is a reference
to his contempt for bishop Wulfstan as an ignorant man and an
extraordinary tale of his establishment of the cult of St.
Aldhelm.[4]

In the *Gesta Regum* Lanfranc is a less prominent figure; and
much of what William does say is repeated in more detail in the
Gesta Pontificum. Lanfranc does appear however as the confidant
of Waltheof, earl of Northumbria (a story also found in
'Florence of Worcester'). It was on Lanfranc's advice (or
possibly Wulfstan's) that William the Conqueror abolished the
slave trade to Ireland and again on Lanfranc's advice that Odo
of Bayeux was imprisoned in 1082 'not as bishop of Bayeux but
as earl of Kent'.[5]

[1] W. Holtzmann, *Papsturkunden in England* (Berlin, 1935–6), ii. 103; cf. Becker,
op.cit., pp. 177–9.
[2] *Gesta Pontificum*, i. 24–44, ed. Hamilton (London, 1870: Rolls Ser.), pp. 37–73.
A new edition is in preparation for Oxford Medieval Texts.
[3] *Gesta Pontificum* ii. 74, ed.cit., p. 150 (Herfast); i. 72, p. 137 (Gundulf).
[4] *Gesta Pontificum* iv. 143, p. 284 (Wulfstan); v. 269, p. 428 (Aldhelm).
[5] *Gesta Regum* iii. 255, ed. Stubbs (London, 1889: Rolls Ser.), ii. 314; cf. *Florentii
Wigorniensis Chronicon*, ed. Thorpe (London, 1848), ii. 10–12. For the slave trade and

In the *Vita Wulfstani* Lanfranc is presented as a consistent supporter of bishop Wulfstan: he consigns the see of Lichfield to Wulfstan during the vacancy of 1070–2 and helps him to resist the domination of York. It is by Lanfranc's advice that even ecclesiastical magnates are required to hold household knights in readiness against a Danish invasion (1086). Finally Nicholas, later prior of Worcester, is sent as a young man to learn the monastic life from Lanfranc at Christ Church.[1] William of Malmesbury saw Lanfranc in terms of the scholars and bishops of the 1120s. He belonged to a simpler and more honest age:

> Non tunc episcoporum ambitus, non tunc abbatum uenalitas proficiebat: ille majoris gloriae, amplioris gratiae, apud regem et archiepiscopum erat, qui tenacioris sanctitudinis opinionem habebat.[2]

If Lanfranc was a better prelate than William's ambitious contemporaries, it could not be supposed that his scholarship was more primitive. It is William who draws the definitive picture of Lanfranc the dialectician, supreme in one art rather than competent in several.[3]

iv. the thirteenth century onwards

After 1200 there is little hope of finding fresh evidence of the historical Lanfranc. But there is still a lively trade in anecdote. The Wyclifite controversy of the late fourteenth century revived interest in Berengar and so incidentally in Lanfranc as his successful opponent. Most of this late material derives either from William of Malmesbury or from Lanfranc's *De corpore et sanguine domini* itself; but occasionally a late chronicler records a story that has apparently been circulating as oral tradition. These anecdotes are comparable with the stories in the *Vita Lanfranci*; but they are less appropriate to Lanfranc and of course much less well authenticated.

21a WILLIAM DE MONTIBUS, *Lectures on the Psalter*   *c.* 1170
William's discussion of Ps. 67: 31, as reported by his pupil Samuel, monk of Bury St. Edmund's, includes the earliest known version of Lanfranc's appearance incognito to refute

---

[1] *Vita Wulfstani* ii. 1; iii. 16–17, ed. Darlington (London, 1928: Camden Soc. 3 ser.xl), pp. 25–6; 56–7.

[2] *Gesta Regum* iii. 267, ed.cit. ii. 326.

[3] See particularly *Gesta Pontificum* i. 41, ed.cit., pp. 63–5; cf. R. W. Southern, 'The Canterbury Forgeries', *Eng.Hist.Rev.*lxxiii (1958), 213 app. Notice also *Gesta Pontificum* i. 43, p. 69.

Odo's imprisonment see respectively *Gesta Regum* iii. 269 and iv. 306, ed.cit. ii. 329 and 360–1.

Berengar at the council of 1059. Until that moment he had concealed his learning even from his abbot.[1]

21b THOMAS OF ECCLESTON, *De adventu fratrum minorum in Angliam*
s.xiii med.

Another version of William de Montibus' story is attributed to Eustace of Merk, one of the early Franciscan wardens at Oxford and later (*c.* 1257) *custos* of York.[2] Searching for a monastery that is truly observant Lanfranc, disguised as a fool, enters Bec. At the 1059 council, still incognito, he refutes Berengar, who is here allowed the last word: 'Aut tu es Lanfrancus, aut tu es diabolus!'[3]

22 ANON., *Liber Exemplorum* no. 86   1270–9

Like Thomas of Eccleston the author is a Franciscan. Lanfranc was walking by the Seine, wrapt in theological speculation, when he noticed a child scooping up water from the river into a little hole in the sand. 'You will never finish that task!' Lanfranc exclaimed. 'And you will never reach the end of your argument,' said the child; and vanished.[4] Half a century earlier Caesarius of Heisterbach, the Cistercian, had told the same story of 'quidam scholasticus'; in the *Liber Exemplorum* and a related collection of about the same date Lanfranc is the central figure, as he is later for Knighton (no. 24 below). Finally the scene is moved from the Seine to the Mediterranean and the story applied to St. Augustine.[5] But originally it referred to one of the *moderni*, possibly even Lanfranc himself.

23 RANULF HIGDEN, *Polychronicon* vi–vii   s.xiv[1]

Higden's account of Lanfranc is based mainly on William of Malmesbury, *Gesta Pontificum* and *Gesta Regum*. He gives the *Liber de corpore et sanguine domini* the misleading title of *Liber*

---

[1] MS. Oxford Bodleian 860, fol. 70rb-va (s.xiii[1]: Bury). I owe this reference to the late Franco Giusberti.

[2] *De adventu fratrum minorum in Angliam*, ed. Little (Manchester, 1951), p. 64. For Eustace of Merk see A. B. Emden, *Biog.Reg.Oxford* (Oxford, 1958), ii. 1262.

[3] The theme of the scholar who conceals his learning is implicit in Gilbert Crispin's account of Lanfranc's early years at Bec (*V.H.*, pp. 96–7). The search for the observant monastery was originally Herluin's (ibid., pp. 91–2): for the meeting incognito with Berengar cf. *Miracula S. Nicholai* cap. 7.

[4] *Liber Exemplorum ad usum praedicatorum*, ed. Little (Aberdeen, 1908: *Brit.Soc. Franc.Stud.* i), pp. 48–9, cf. p. 140.

[5] The main references are given in Caesarius of Heisterbach, *Libri Miraculorum*, ed. Hilka (Bonn, 1937), pp. 75–6: see in particular the *Speculum Laicorum* (also Franciscan: dated 1279–92), ed. Welter (Paris, 1914), no. 549, p. 106. The whole question is admirably surveyed by H.-I. Marrou, 'Saint Augustin et l'ange', in *L'Homme devant Dieu: mélanges . . . H. de Lubac* (Lyons, 1964), ii. 137–49.

Scintillarum and refers obscurely to Lanfranc's attitude to the financial exactions of William the Conqueror.[1]

24 HENRY KNIGHTON, *Chronicle* ii. 5 s.xiv[2]

Though Knighton adds nothing to our knowledge of Lanfranc, he is often cited as a source, even where he is quoting Higden (no. 23) verbatim.[2] Lanfranc came incognito to the 1059 council and refuted Berengar in person (no. 21b); he was rebuked by the child for his theological speculation (no. 22).

25 'ST LANFRANC'

There was no medieval cult of Lanfranc, official or popular, nor was he beatified or canonized later on. From time to time however he is given an honorary title. For William de Montibus in the later twelfth century he is 'beatus'; for Thomas of Eccleston in the thirteenth 'sanctus'; and for Capgrave in the early sixteenth 'sanctus Lanfrancus archiepiscopus et confessor'.[3] The Maurists regarded him as *de facto* 'beatus', principally for his defence of the doctrine of the Eucharist; and the matter was still the subject of learned comment in 1939.[4]

---

[1] *Polychronicon Ranulphi Higden*, vi, caps. 23–7, vii, caps. 1–6, ed. Lumby, vol. vii (London, 1879: Rolls Ser.); see principally pp. 208; 334–6. The *Vita Dunstani* (p. 338) has not been identified.

[2] *Chronicon Henrici Knighton*, ed. Lumby (London, 1889: Rolls Ser.), i. 87–95. The phrase 'quando in scholis militavimus' (p. 90) has led many scholars to assume that Lanfranc studied with Berengar at Chartres: for a trenchant criticism of this view see F. Novati, 'La leggenda di Lanfranco da Pavia', in *Studi letterari e linguistici . . . P. Rajna* (Milan, 1911), pp. 705–16; and for a perceptive study of the 'legend' itself E. Gorra, 'La *leggenda* di Lanfranco da Pavia e di Alano da Lilla', *Boll.Soc.Pav. Stor.Patr.* xii (1912), 265–97.

[3] Appendix A21ab; John Capgrave, *Nova Legenda Angliae* (London, 1516), fols. 213v–18v.

[4] *Bull.Soc.Ant.Norm.* xlvii (1939), 303–5: meeting of 2 June, contributions by Hersent and Lesage, with bibliography. See also E. Hora, 'Zur Ehrenrettung Lanfranks, des Erzbischofs von Canterbury (ca.1005–1089)', *Theol.Quartalschr.* cxi (1930), 317–19.

APPENDIX B: Lanfranc's *obit*

LANFRANC died on 28 May (5 kal. Jun.) 1089. His *obit* and anniversary as celebrated at Christ Church were printed by Wharton from MS. L below: *Anglia Sacra* (London, 1691), i. 55–6. The text that follows is based on C.

C   London B. L. Cotton Claudius C.VI s.xii[in].

A few pages of the twelfth-century *obit*-book of Christ Church are fortuitously bound up with Burchard's *Decretum* (fols. 1–169) and Lanfranc's *Constitutions* (fols. 174v–202). Lanfranc's *obit* is on a half sheet of parchment (fol. 173) 238 × 194 mm. It is carefully punctuated to bring out the repetitive, rhymed clauses, which were chanted rather than spoken. Noted by Wharton (p. xxi), whose reference to Cotton Nero C. IX is misleading.

A   London B. L. Arundel 68 s.xv[2]

The fifteenth-century *obit*-book survives here complete (fols. 12–52). At 5 kal. Jun. there are several short obits, then the rubric (fol. 28v) 'Semper legatur in ordine suo licet in ebdomado pentecostis' and Lanfranc's obit following (fols. 28v–9). The only material change is lines 51–2; but the minor variants, which spoil the rhythm, show that the recitation of the obit had become less formal.

L   London Lambeth Palace Lib. 20 s.xvi,[in].

This is a fair copy of A with some fine illumination, made after 1500 (archbishop Morton is included: fol. 218v), but not long after. The title of Lanfranc's *obit* is expanded from A: 'Semper legatur obitus Lanfranci in ordine suo licet in/fol. 189v ebdomado pentecosten contigerit'; there are no significant variants from A in the text itself (fol. 189v).

[a]Obiit felicis memoriȩ LANFRANCVS archiepiscopus
catholice fidei fidelissimus obseruator. et firmissimus roborator.
qui cooperante gratia Dei ȩcclesiam istam[b] à fundamentis
    fundauit.[bb] consummauit.
multis et honestis ornamentis. aliis ex auro mundissimo factis.
5   aliis auro gemmisque paratis. aliis etsi sine auro ac gemmis.
magnifice tamen laudandis ornauit.
multis[c] ac religiosis monachorum personis ditauit.

multa multumque reuerenda religione decorauit.
Hic etiam claustra. celaria. refectoria. dormitoria
10 cęterasque omnes necessarias officinas.[d]
et omnia edificia infra ambitum curię consistentia.
cum ipso ambitu mirabiliter miranda ędificauit.
Pretioso insuper ornamento librorum.
ęcclesiam istam apprime honestauit.
15 quorum[e] quamplurimos per semetipsum emendauit.
Archiepiscopum quoque eboracensem.
cęterosque huius regni episcopos a subiectione huius ęcclesię resilientes.
ad ueram et debitam subiectionem reuocauit.
Per hunc[f] etiam et ipso faciente. omnes illas terras
20 quę in anniuersaria die regis WILLELMI commemorantur. longo
tempore amissas.
ęcclesia ista recuperauit.
Extra ciuitatem larga habitacula fecit.
quę pauperibus et infirmis repleuit.
quibus de propriis rebus uictum et uestitum sufficienter largiri pręcepit.
25 Similiter foris ciuitatem beati GREGORII ęcclesiam composuit.
in qua clericos posuit.
a quibus morientes et unde sibi sepulturam[g] possent pręparare non habentes
[gg]absque pretio susciperentur.
suscepti illuc deferrentur.[h] delati honeste sepelirentur.
30 In maneriis ad archiepiscopum pertinentibus multas et honestas ecclesias
edificauit. multas et honestissimas domos pręparauit.
quę[i] et archiepiscopis essent delectationi et honori.
et pauperibus hominibus qui archiepiscopis domos sepissime pręparabant.
essent tanti laboris sulleuationi.
35 Ecclesiam[j] rofensem a fundamentis incepit. inceptam honeste perfecit.
quam multis et honestis decorauit ornamentis.
insuper et reuerendam inibi monachorum religionem instituit.
Terras de ęcclesia longo tempore ablatas ipse adquisiuit.
quas monachis ad uictum et uestitum habere permisit.
40 Necnon ęcclesiam sancti ALBANI fundauit. et fere consummauit.
Quam etiam multis et pretiosis ornamentis ampliauit.

PRONVNTIATO anniuersario domni LANFRANCI archiepiscopi in
capitulo. omnes simul fratres procedant in ęcclesiam canentes *Verba mea*.

[a]. iterum obiit *A* item obiit *L* [b]. istam ecclesiam *AL*[bb] et consummauit *L*
[c]. et multis ac *L* [d]. officinas necessarisa *AL* [e]. quorum: quibus *AL*
[f]. hunc: hoc *AL* [g]. sepulturam sibi *AL* [gg] et absque *AL* [h]. differentur *AL*
[i]. quę: quod *AL* [j]. ecclesiam etiam *AL*

10–13 Cf. Eadmer, *Historia Novorum* i, p. 12, lines 17–19.
20 See Appendix A 14b4.
25–6 *Historia Novorum* i, p. 16, line 3.
30–1 Ibid. i, p. 16, lines 17–19.
42–54 *Constitutions*, pp. 64–6: feasts of the third rank.

interim sonantibus omnibus signis. Post cęnam pulsato signo ad uigilias.
omnes solito more conueniant. ipsas uigilias festiue peragant. duo tertium.
45 tres sextum. quattuor nonum responsorium canant. In crastino quisque
sacerdos missam^k pro eo celebrare debet. et qui missam non cantat.
quinquaginta psalmos cantet. Missa in conuentu in albis festiue celebretur.
Ad quam cantor et cum eo duo alii fratres sint cappis induti. tres ad
responsorium. quattuor ad tractum similiter in cappis. Ad pauperes
50 pascendos ipso die secretarius debet^l dare solidos quindecim celararius uero
uiginti quinque.^m Seruitium refectorii festiue fieri.ⁿ sicut in festiuitate
unius apostoli. Ęcclesia parata permaneat sicut in festiuitate SANCTI
AVGVSTINI. donec peragatur seruitium.

^k. missam unam *AL* ^l. secretarius debet: thesaurarii debent *AL*
^m. solidos quindecim celararius uero uiginti quinque: solidos xl *AL*
ⁿ. fieri debet *AL*

---

43   Ps. 5: one of the Psalms for the dead.
51–2   The names of the officials change, but the payment remains
at 40 (15+25) *solidi*. A similar payment was made on
Gundulf's anniversary at Rochester: 4+24 *solidi*+120
denarii (*Textus Roffensis*, fol. 197r-v).

APPENDIX C: a note on the primatial forgeries

A DEFINITIVE account of the primatial forgeries would require a full-scale article, turning as much on the palaeographical and diplomatic problems raised as on the comparison of texts. I am concerned only to say why I believe that the forgeries (II–VIII) were available to Lanfranc and why, if they were indeed extant, they were not cited in the disputes with York before 1123. I am indebted at every turn to Wilhelm Levison, whose study of 'the charters of king Ethelbert' goes far beyond the seventh century.

As in all ancient foundations that lacked a full and recent confirmation of their property and rights, forgery was endemic in Christ Church throughout the eleventh century and the first half of the twelfth. The monk Eadwi Basan (c. 1010–20) copied genuine royal charters and constructed false ones; one of his successors contrived the profession of archbishop Ealdwulf of York (992–5) to Aethelheard of Canterbury; and c. 1070 yet another forger produced a seventh-century papal letter that established the community at Christ Church as perpetually monastic.[1] Finally (for our purposes) a fourth forger was at work c. 1120–30, who specialized in the conversion of genuine eleventh-century writs and the interpolation of the Anglo-Saxon Chronicle.[2] These set the scene for the forgeries that are the subject of this note: nine papal privileges, variously interpolated, which emphasize the primacy of Canterbury over Britain or over all the English.[3] Whereas the other Christ Church forgeries are patently the work of the community, stopping the gaps in their imperfect title-deeds, these primatial privileges are at first sight the archbishop's affair: they reflect his ambitions in the kingdom rather

---

[1] For Eadwi Basan see T. A. M. Bishop, *English Caroline Minuscule* (Oxford, 1971), nos, 24–5, with references. Ealdwulf's profession is based on that of Eadwulf of Lindsey (796): Richter, no. 1. For the monastic privilege of c. 1070 (*J.L.* 1998; cf. 4761) see above, p. 169 n. 1.

[2] T. A. M. Bishop and P. Chaplais, *Facsimiles of English Royal Writs to A.D. 1100* (Oxford, 1957), nos. 3–4.

[3] H. Boehmer, *Die Fälschungen Erzbischof Lanfranks von Canterbury* (Leipzig, 1902), pp. 147–61: I have followed Boehmer's numbering II–X (*J.L.* 2007; 2021; 2095; 2132; 2133; 2243; 2510; 3506; 3687).

than the convictions and anxieties of his monks. But this first impression is I think misleading: the primatial forgeries, like the rest, were conceived by the community itself in its own ✓interest.

The primatial privileges are based on genuine papal letters of the seventh to tenth centuries, addressed to English recipients, normally bishops but in one instance (no. V) king Ethelred of Mercia and his Northumbrian sub-kings Alfred and Aldulf. The interpolations assert the primacy of Canterbury 'in all parts of the British Isles' ('totius Britanniae regionis': no V) and 'over all the churches of Britain' ('omnium ecclesiarum Britanniae': no. VI). Eight of these privileges (nos. II–IX) were inserted by various hands, hence possibly at various dates, in Athelstan's Gospel-book, one of the treasures of Christ Church.[1] The ninth (no. X) was extant by July 1123; for all nine are included in the collection of canon law, episcopal professions and papal letters which is now MS. London B. L. Cotton Cleopatra E.i.[2] Eadmer and William of Malmesbury quote the nine in extenso in the same order as the Cotton manuscript.[3] It is then beyond dispute that all nine primatial forgeries were known by the summer of 1123, and that they remained in circulation thereafter; what is much less certain is when they came into existence. Palaeographically the eight in the Athelstan Gospel-book are all later than the monastic privilege of *c.* 1070 (Boehmer I): they could be as late as *c.* 1120; they might well be somewhat earlier.

There is solid reason to believe that the texts of II–VIII were already in existence, or were being devised, at the beginning of Lanfranc's archiepiscopate, whatever the date at which they were copied into the Gospel-book. Writing to Alexander II in May 1072 Lanfranc lists the popes who have given support to the primacy of ✓Canterbury:[4]

[1] MS. London B. L. Cotton Tiberius A.ii: see N. R. Ker, *Catalogue of Manuscripts containing Anglo-Saxon* (Oxford, 1957), no. 185; cf. idem, 'Membra Disiecta', *British Museum Quarterly* xii (1938), 130–1. The privileges are written by three different scribes: A (nos. V–VI); B (no. II); C (nos. III–IV, VII–IX). They are not in chronological order.

[2] MS. Cotton Cleopatra E.i. fols. 41ra–7vb: the privileges are in chronological order. For the date July 1123 see R. W. Southern, 'The Canterbury Forgeries', *Eng.Hist.Rev.*lxxiii (1958), 219.

[3] Eadmer, *Historia Novorum* v, pp. 262–76; William of Malmesbury, *Gesta Pontificum* i. 31–9, pp. 47–62.

[4] *Lanfranci Epp.* 3. 'Vltimum quasi robur totiusque causae firmamentum prolata sunt antecessorum uestrorum Gregorii, Bonefacii, Honorii, Vitaliani, Sergii, item Gregorii, Leonis, item ultimi Leonis privilegia atque scripta quae Dorobernensis ecclesiae praesulibus Anglorumque regibus aliis atque aliis temporibus variis de causis sunt data aut transmissa.'

LANFRANC'S LETTER		PRIVILEGES, NUMBERED ACCORDING TO BOEHMER
Gregory I		Nil[1]
Boniface	II	Boniface V (619–25) to Justus
Honorius	III	Honorius I (625–38) to Honorius
Vitalian	IV	Vitalian (657–72) to Theodore
Sergius	V	Sergius I (687–701) to the kings of Mercia and Northumbria
	VI	Sergius I to the bishops of Britain
item Gregory	VII	Gregory III (731–41) to the bishops of England
Leo	VIII	Leo III (795–816) to Æthelheard
Leo IX		Nil

Lanfranc's popes correspond to nos. II–VIII; the authors of IX–X are not cited, and there is nothing in the privileges to match Gregory I and Leo IX. Lanfranc never quotes the *text* of his papal letters. Even so, the coincidence is too marked to be accidental: either Lanfranc is referring to the privileges or the privileges are based on Lanfranc's list. The obvious explanation is the former: Lanfranc knew the forgeries and cited them; he was not so rash as to send to the papal chancery direct quotations from their own altered privileges. Some years ago Sir Richard Southern argued the alternative case: that the privileges are based on Lanfranc's letter.[2] In Bede's *Historia Ecclesiastica*[1] and in the routine papal documents that Christ Church had accumulated over the centuries, Lanfranc had sufficient material to suggest a plausible list of popes, though certainly not enough to provide direct quotations. When Alexander II died (April 1073), the issue lapsed at Rome: what Gregory VII had refused as archdeacon he was unlikely to concede as pope. In England the archbishop of Canterbury still claimed primacy; but over the next fifty years (1072–1122) neither the primatial forgeries (supposing them to have existed), nor Lanfranc's list of popes, nor even Lanfranc's letter are cited in his support. The primatial dispute blew up again briefly in 1086;[3] it was renewed in 1093 at Anselm's consecration, in 1101 at the accession of Gerard of York, in 1109 at the consecration of Thomas II, in 1114 at the accession of both Ralph d'Escures and Thurstan: above all in 1119–21 the claims of Canterbury were asserted most urgently against the papal directive that Thurstan be

---

[1] Lanfranc is referring to Gregory the Great's letter to Augustine: Bede, *Historia Ecclesiastica* i.29, ed. Colgrave and Mynors (Oxford, 1969: Oxford Med. Texts), pp. 104–7.

[2] Southern, op.cit., pp. 193–226.

[3] Hugh the Chanter, *History*, s.a. 1086. ed. Johnson (London, 1961: Nelson's Med.Texts), pp. 5–6.

received in England and allowed to assume his office. Throughout this entire half-century, when the primatial forgeries *would have* strengthened the hand of the archbishop of Canterbury, they are mentioned only twice, in neither case unmistakably. In 1093 Osbern the precentor refers to the privileges of Boniface, Honorius, Vitalian and Agatho (arguably nos. II–IV and an addition to the series); and in 1109 Henry I, having scrutinized the papal privileges (unspecified) of Christ Church and the royal writ of 1072, was convinced of the primacy of Canterbury over York.[1] These dubious instances apart, it is as though the forged privileges did not exist; and Sir Richard proposes just that solution: they did not. It is only in the spring of √ 1123, in an ill-advised move by the community after the death of Ralph d'Escures, that the complete set of primatial forgeries (II–X) is suddenly submitted to Rome, and at once discredited. Surely then these forgeries were invented during Ralph's last illness, on the basis of Lanfranc's list of popes? The historical context proposed is comprehensive and exact; if there are palaeographical or textual difficulties,[2] these can be met: the whole problem is removed from Lanfranc's biography lock, stock and barrel.

Sed contra. Whereas the historical argument for 1121–3 is rigorous and convincing, the actual substance of the privileges is curiously vague. We might expect that texts forged in and for the specific crisis of 1121–3 would assert clearly the primacy of Canterbury over York. No. VII comes near to doing so. Gregory III consigns to archbishop Tatwin jurisdiction over 'omnes ecclesias Britanniae earumque rectores ... ut omnis homo totius Angliae regionis tuis canonicis iussionibus oboediat et te sciat esse speculatorem atque primatem totius insulae'; the church of Canterbury is 'prima et mater ... aliarum omnium'. Although York is not mentioned by

---

[1] 'Ecce etenim sponsa mea, sancta Cantuariensis ecclesia, apost oli mei Petr benedictione a principio sanctificata, piissimo piissimi Gregorii studio nobiliter fundata, sanctorum Bonifacii, Honorii, Vitaliani, Agathonis et ceterorum orthodoxorum patrum singulari semper privilegio donata' (*Anselmi Epp.* 149); Eadmer, op.cit. iv, p. 209. For Agatho see the Roman council of 679, interpolated in England s.xi[2]: W. Levison, *England and the Continent in the Eighth Century* (Oxford, 1946), p. 190, n. 2, with references.

[2] Some unresolved difficulties in Sir Richard's argument are: (i) *palaeographical*. Whereas nos. II–X were certainly added to Cotton Cleopatra E.i *c.* 1121–3, it is much less clear that nos. II–IX were added in several rather archaic hands to the Athelstan Gospel-book only a few months earlier. (ii) *textual*. The texts in the Athelstan gospel-book are repeatedly at variance with II–IX as found in Cleopatra E.i and in Cotton Claudius E.v (1127+). (iii) *textual*. The material common to Claudius E.v and MS. Cambridge Trinity Coll.B.16.44 on the one hand, and to Claudius E.v and Cleopatra E.i on the other *may* imply another Canterbury manuscript, now lost, of the complete Ps.-Isidore with local additions at the end.

name, the implication is inescapable. But the language elsewhere is more reserved. For instance in no. VIII Leo III confirms jurisdiction over 'omnes Anglorum ecclesias', with a side glance at monasteries and nunneries as well as the episcopate proper; Christ Church is a 'sedes metropolitana'. Formosus (no. IX) speaks of 'omnes Anglorum episcopos' and of Canterbury as 'metropolim primamque sedem episcopalem . . . regni Anglorum'; John XII writing to Dunstan (no. X) refers to 'primatum . . . tuum'. The others (nos. II–VI) belong to the seventh and early eighth centuries, when York was not yet in practice the principal see in the north. Boniface V (no. II) sees Christ Church as the 'metropolitanam et primitivam sedem' and Canterbury as the *political* capital of the English people: the arch-bishop shall be the 'metropolitanus totius Britanniae', with jurisdic-tion over 'omnes provinciae . . . regni Anglorum'. Honorius I (no. III) uses similar terms: ('primatum omnium ecclesiarum Britanniae' and 'caput omnium ecclesiarum Anglorum populorum'. Archbishop Theodore (no. IV), who did exercise a de facto primacy (however he himself understood it), is simply given the oversight of 'omnes ecclesias in insula Britanniae positas'. Finally pope Sergius I calls archbishop Beorhtweald 'totius Britainnae regionis primum pontifi-cem' (no. V), having the 'primatum omnium ecclesiarum Brit-anniae' (no. VI). In none of the privileges is there specific mention of York. That is perhaps a minor point, though it argues greater sophistication than was shown in other respects by the putative monastic forgers of 1121–3. What is more serious is that of the four privileges (nos. VII–X) which are late enough to be relevant only one (no. VII) asserts the primacy of Canterbury with real vigour. John XII's letter to Dunstan (no. X) is especially puzzling, given Dunstan's historic importance in the English Church and the devo-tion to his memory at Canterbury. All that was required in 1121–3 to confound archbishop Thurstan was one privilege, clear, compre-hensive and acceptable to Rome: Dunstan seems the obvious choice. Instead nine were concocted, of which eight are virtually useless. All this, presumably, on the basis of Lanfranc's letter, which was not itself quoted at Rome.[1]

In such an impasse it is worth looking for a moment beyond Christ Church. The monks of St. Augustine's also produced forgeries in this period, equally bold and far-reaching, though the 'primacy' of the house is touched on only in passing. There is a foundation privilege from St Augustine himself, sealed with a leaden bull, seven royal and papal privileges of the seventh century, two privileges of

---

[1] Hugh the Chanter, *History*, s.a.1123, ed.cit., pp. 114–15; cf. Southern, op.cit., pp. 223–4.

John XII (955–63) and Edward the Confessor's grant of Thanet.[1]
All these eleven privileges assert and reinforce the exempt status of
the first monastery in England: in the words of no. 10 the *mater
primaria* of the English houses. No. 5 is certainly prior to *JL*. 1998
(Boehmer I), and the group as a whole belongs to the late eleventh
and early twelfth centuries. The St. Augustine's forgeries are then
comparable in date (though the date is imprecise) with the primatial
forgeries in Christ Church. Are they also comparable in purpose?
There are coincidences of language, but not such as to suggest a
common author.[2] The more grandiose claim of St. Augustine's to
monastic 'primacy' may very well be a counter-claim to Christ
Church; but it is not central to the St. Augustine's privileges as a
whole. The two groups have no more in common than the defence of
their respective houses and their liberty from external interference;
had one been produced in Canterbury and the other (say) in
Malmesbury or Evesham, that would conclude the matter. But they
are the work of immediate rivals in the same city; the communities
of Christ Church and St. Augustine's were each mutually the public
for the other's propaganda—propaganda which inevitably involved
the local families of Canterbury in a way that we cannot now
recover.[3] The claims of the monks of St. Augustine's were matched
by the monks of Christ Church, the status of whose community was
most convincingly demonstrated by the supreme status of the archbishop, their head. 'We are exempt' was countered by 'We are
primatial'. As the St. Augustine's forgeries seem to have been constructed over at least a generation, so the Christ Church forgeries
have no internal features that require a twelfth-century date; their
fabrication can equally be seen as a process initiated before 1070 and
continuing into the twelfth century. The forgeries of each house were
written with an eye to the other, neither having absolute priority.
On this view nos. II–VIII were known to Lanfranc (1072); II–IX
had been entered in the Athelstan Gospel-book by (on palaeographical grounds) *c*. 1120; and finally II–X were entered in Cleopatra
E.i (1121–3) and produced in Rome (1123).

We return to the question of why, if they were extant, the prima-

---

[1] Levison, op.cit., pp. 181–2, and see the entire discussion pp. 174–233. The
complete list (following Levison's numbering) is: nos. 1–3 Ethelbert of Kent, no. 4
St. Augustine, no. 5 Boniface IV (*J.L.*1997), no. 6, Eadbald of Kent, no. 7
Adeodatus (*J.L.* 2104), no. 8 Agatho, nos. 9–10 John XII (*J.L.* 3678–9), no. 11
Edward the Confessor.

[2] Some of the St. Augustine's forgeries were (in all reasonable likelihood) the
work of Guerno, a monk of S. Médard, Soissons: Levison, *op.cit.*, pp. 207–8.

[3] See Ch. VII, §iv. The St. Augustine's forgeries were used in 1108 (scrutiny by
Henry I) and 1120 (privilege of Calixtus II) in ways comparable with the Christ
Church privileges: Levison, op.cit., p. 179.

tial forgeries were ignored. In the first place they were not designed to support the primacy of Canterbury over York; they were for consumption nearer home. For Lanfranc they were momentarily useful in implying *papal* approval of his petition to Alexander II: that the primacy of Canterbury over York be expressed definitively in a new privilege. But within England the only effective support was a royal diploma, such as Lanfranc secured, with the maximum formality and publicity, in the spring of 1072:

In presentia ipsius (regis) et episcoporum atque abbatum ventilata est causa de primatu quem Lanfrancus Dorobernensis archiepiscopus super Eboracensem ęcclesiam iure suę ęcclesię proclamabat . . .
Et tandem aliquando diversis diversarum scripturarum auctoritatibus probatum atque ostensum est quod Eboracensis aecclesia Cantuariensi debeat subiacere eiusque archiepiscopi ut primatis totius Britannię dispositionibus in iis que ad christianam religionem pertinent in omnibus oboedire.[1]

There is the reality of Lanfranc's victory over York; and, as Professor Brooke has pointed out, to the end of his life archbishop Ralph regarded this royal diploma as his basic title to primacy.[2] Nor was it ineffective. Until the disarray of Ralph's last years, the archbishop of Canterbury did exercise a de facto, if contested, primacy over York. Then, *c.* 1120, the absence if a clearcut *papal* privilege (such as Lanfranc had tried to secure) was a fatal weakness to the cause of Canterbury; fifty years earlier it had not been worth the journey to Rome.

If an author must be sought for the primatial forgeries, the obvious candidate is Osbern the precentor, who arguably refers to them in 1093;[3] but essentially they reflect the hopes and convictions of the community as a whole *c.* 1070 and in the generation following. They cannot reasonably be attributed to any of the archbishops, Lanfranc or his successors.

[1] Bishop–Chaplais, no. xxix.
[2] C. N. L. Brooke, 'The Canterbury Forgeries and their author II', *Downside Review* lxix (1951), 219.
[3] See n. 1, above.

APPENDIX D: handlist of Lanfranc's writings

EXTANT

1 THE 'ARTES'

note on Priscian, *Institutiones* i. 12

note on the verb *sum*

    R. W. Hunt, 'Studies on Priscian in the eleventh and twelfth centuries', *Med.Renaiss.Stud.*I.ii (1943), 194–231, especially 206 app. and 224.

note on Cicero, *De Inventione* i. 48.89

    MS. Hereford Cathedral P.i.4, fol. 17v (s.xii[1]: English).

note on *Rhetorica ad Herennium* ii. 26.42

    R. W. Hunt, op.cit., pp. 207–8.

2 PATRISTICA

notes on Augustine, *De Civitate Dei*

notes on Gregory the Great, *Moralia in Iob*

    M. T. Gibson, 'Lanfranc's notes on patristic texts', *Journ. Theol.Stud.* n.s. xxii (1971), 435–50.

notes on Cassian, *Collationes*

    D'Achery, p. 252 (Migne, *P.L.* cl. 443A–4B)

note on ?Jerome, *Ep.* xviiiA.

    R. W. Hunt, op.cit., p. 208.

3 THE BIBLE

notes on Psalms 13:3 and 17:30 (Vulgate).

    See Appendix A8a; B. Smalley, 'La *Glossa Ordinaria:* quelques prédécesseurs d'Anselme de Laon', *Rech.Théol.Anc. Méd.* ix (1937), 365–400, especially 375.

Commentary on the Pauline Epistles

    D'Achery, pp. 1–229 (Migne, *P.L.* cl. 105D–406A) B. Smalley, op.cit.; M. T. Gibson, 'Lanfranc's commentary on the Pauline Epistles', *Journ.Theol.Stud.*, n.s. xxii (1971), 86–112.

Pauline commentaries which draw on Lanfranc's work include the following (all unpublished):

a)   Metz/Tegernsee commentary, s.xi[2]

MSS.: Berlin (E.) Deutsche StaatsB. Phill. 1650; Munich StaatsB. Clm. 18530a.

Smalley, op.cit., pp. 386–8; C. Eder, 'Die Schule des Klosters Tegernsee im frühen Mittelalter', *Stud.Mitt.Gesch. Benediktinerordens* lxxxiii (1972), 113–14.

b) Anselm of Laon, commentary on the Pauline Epp., inc. 'Pro altercatione scribit Romanis' s.xi[ex]
MSS: Cornell University Lib. M.27; Milan B.Ambros. C.122 inf.; Cologne DomB. 25–6; London B.L. Add. 16942; Manchester John Rylands Lib. lat.23; Oxford Bodleian Lib. Auct.D.i.13; Padua B. Antoniana xv. 339–40; Paris B.N. lat. 480; Stockholm Kungl.B. A.141; and many others, generally s.xii.

c) Anonymous master (?French) s.xii[in].
MS: Paris B.N. lat. 12267
Smalley, op.cit., pp. 379–80.; W. Affeldt, *Die weltliche Gewalt in der Paulus-Exegese* (Göttingen 1969: *Forsch. Kirchen- und Dogmengesch.* xxii), pp. 146–9, 289–90.

4 DE CORPORE ET SANGUINE DOMINI   1063–1070
D'Achery, pp. 230–51 (Migne, *P.L.* cl.407A–42D); critical list of manuscripts by R. B. C. Huygens, 'Bérengar de Tours, Lanfranc et Bernold de Constance', *Sacris Erudiri* xvi (1965), 358–77.
J. de Montclos, *Lanfranc et Bérenger: la controverse eucharistique du xie siècle* (Louvain, 1971: *Spic.Sacr.Lovan.* 37). For the date see *Lanfranci Epp.* 3.

5 LETTERS   1070–1089
See Appendix A9a. D'Achery, pp. 299–329 (Migne, *P.L.* cl.515C–50B). Edition forthcoming by V. H. Clover and M. T. Gibson (Oxford Medieval Texts).
Criticism of individual letters—*3* R. W. Southern, 'The Canterbury Forgeries', *Eng.Hist.Rev.* lxxiii (1958), 193–226.
4 V. H. Clover, 'Alexander II's letter *Accepimus a quibusdam* and its relationship with the Canterbury Forgeries', in *La Normandie bénédictine*, ed. Langé (Lille, 1967), pp. 417–42.
54 F. Barlow, 'Domesday Book: a letter of Lanfranc', *Eng. Hist.Rev.* lxxviii (1963), 284–9; V. H. Galbraith, 'Notes on the career of Samson, bishop of Worcester (1096–1112)', ibid. lxxxii (1967), 86–101.

6 MONASTIC CONSTITUTIONS   1079–1089
Decreta Lanfranci, ed. D. Knowles (London, 1951: Nelson's Medieval Texts); reprinted in *Corpus Consuetudinum Monasticarum*, ed. Hallinger (Siegburg, 1967), vol. iii; add MSS. Oxford Bodl.lat.theol. d.29, fols. 1–44v (s.xii[2], English: complete) and Wood empt.4, fol. 22v (*c.* 1100, English: Knowles, ed.cit., pp. 1–3).

˄ As Elphege appears in the kalendar, the *Decreta Lanfranci* cannot be earlier than 1079: see *Vita Anselmi* I.xxx. The so-called commentary on the *Decreta* attributed to prior Hamelin of St. Albans has no connection with Lanfranc's work nor (it would appear) with Hamelin: E. Martène and U. Durand, *Thesaurus Novus Anecdotorum* (Paris, 1717), v. 1453–6; cf. J. Leclercq, 'La vêture *ad succurendum* d'après le moine Raoul', *Analecta Monastica* iii: *Studia Anselmiana* xxxvii (1955), 166.

7 VERSES ON THE 'QUATTUOR TEMPORA' (Ember days)   ?1072

Ebdomada primā Martis ieiunia prima;
Iunius ebdomadā iubet hec celebrare secundā;
Tercia Septembris iubet hec, eademque Decembris:
Tollit enim Christi mensi natale Decembri
Quartam. quam ratio. quam par sibi cesserat ordo.

Walther, no. 5057; add MS. Bristol Baptist Coll.Z.c.23 (sold Sotheby's, 13 Dec. 1976, lot 56), from which the above text is taken. I am much indebted to the librarian of the Baptist College for his help.

Lost

Lantfrancus de dialectica: entry in an eleventh-century catalogue of St. Aper, Toul.

G. Becker, *Catalogi Bibliothecarum Antiqui* (Bonn, 1885), no. 68, item 250.

Questiones Lantfranci: entry in an eleventh-century catalogue of an unidentified library in Saxony.

Becker, op.cit., no. 54 item 6. The monastic church to which the library belonged was consecrated in 1064 by the bishops of Minden and Osnabrück: A. Wilmanns, 'Der Katalog der Lorscher Klosterbibliothek aus dem zehnten Jahrhundert', *Rheinisches Museum* xxiii (1868), 408–10.

Dubia et spuria

Texts marked with an asterisk are certainly spurious.

I   THE BIBLE

*revision of the text of the Vulgate
H. Glunz, *The Vulgate in England* (Cambridge, 1933), pp. xvii–xviii, 158–95. None of the manuscripts cited here has any demonstrable connection with Lanfranc.

*commentary on the Song of Songs
*commentary on the Apocalypse
Histoire littéraire viii (Paris, 1747), 297–8. The Maurists were presumably misled here by the description of MS. London B. L. Royal 4.B.IV: 'Lanfrancus et D.Augustinus super

quasdam Pauli Epistolas, Apocalypsin et Cantic. Cantic-
orum': E. Bernard, *Catalogus Librorum MSS Angliae et Hiberniae*
(Oxford, 1697), II.i.no. 8159 (and 7861).

2 THEOLOGY, HOMILETICS, LITURGY

*poem 'Ad se nos dominus cupiens remeare benignus'
attributed to Lanfranc in MS. S. Omer B.Mun. 115 (s.xii:
Clairmarais, O. Cist.); rectius Fulbert of Chartres.
A Boutemy, 'Notes additionelles à la notice de Ch.Fierville
sur le MS 115 de S. Omer', *Rev. Belge Phil.Hist.* xxii (1943), 8.
Walther, *Initia Carminum* 439.

*concordance to the Bible
attributed to Lanfranc by Samuel Gale (*ob.* 1754); no reason
given: MS. Oxford Bodleian Rawl. G. 26 (S.C. 14759),
s.xiii.

**De diversis casibus missae*
attributed to Lanfranc in MS. Oxford Corpus Christi Coll.
155, fols. 269v–74 (s.xv: Rievaulx, O.Cist.)
A. G. Watson, *The Manuscripts of Henry Savile of Banke* (London,
1969), p. 20.

**Elucidarium* (rectius Honorius Augustodunensis)
Attributed to Lanfranc in two manuscripts: London B. L.
Royal 5.E.VI, fol. 1 (s.xii[1]: English); Paris B. S. Geneviève
1443 (s.xiii: French). In MS. Cambridge Corpus Christi
Coll. 308, p. 86 '(L)andfrancus' is named in the margin as the
source of *Elucidarium* iii. 33.
See further Y. Lefèvre, *L'Elucidarium et les Lucidaires* (Paris,
1954: *Bibl.Éc.Franc.Athènes Rome* 180) and V.I.J. Flint, 'The
original text of the *Elucidarium* of Honorius Augustodunensis
from the s.xii English MSS', *Scriptorium* xviii (1964), 91–4.
It is possible that Honorius made use of a Lanfrancian
sentence-collection, now lost.

**Liber de corpore et sanguine domini metrice compositus*
attributed to Lanfranc in MS. Oxford Bodleian Add.A.103,
fol. 50v–63 (S.C. 28964) s.xv: rectius Petrus Pictor
(Manitius iii. 877–83).
Migne, *P.L.* clxxi. 1199A–1212D; 1198D–9A; Walther
13623; 16200

**De octo quae observari debent a monachis*
attributed to Lanfranc in MS. Oxford Brasenose Coll. 12,
fol. 192v, s.xv: rectius 'Radulphus monachus', probably the
abbot of Battle (1107–24).
Migne, *P.L.*cl.637D–9B; new edition with bibliography by
D. H. Farmer, 'Ralph's *Octo Puncta* of monastic life', *Studia
Monastica* xi (1969), 19–29. See also R. W. Southern, *St.*

Anselm and his Biographer (Cambridge, 1963), pp. 206–9. Only the Brasenose manuscript corresponds with Migne (639B–40C: 'Regnum Dei . . . inuenitur habere').

*'ordo' for the coronation of William Rufus (Claudius III)
suggested attribution by D. H. Turner, *The Claudius Pontificals* (London, 1971: Henry Bradshaw Soc.xcvii), pp. xxxix–xlii; 115–22.
The major difficulty in the view that Claudius III was *composed* with William Rufus in mind is the provision for crowning the Queen. Again Rufus had more need to demonstrate continuity with his father's rule than to bring an Anglo-Saxon coronation liturgy into line with modern practice on the continent.

*exposition of saints' lives
attributed to Lanfranc by A. J. MacDonald, *Lanfranc: A Study of his Life, Work and Writing* 2nd edn. (London, 1944), p. 29.
an uncharacteristic misreading of J. de Crozals, *Lanfranc* (Paris, 1877), p. 55: 'des livres saints'.

3 LETTERS
'Indicatum est mihi'
Lanfranci Epp. 60; *terminus ad quem* 1117: G. Morin, 'Rainaud l'ermite et Ives de Chartres: un épisode de la crise du cénobitisme au xie–xiie siècle', *Rev.Bén.*xl (1928), 109–10.
attributed to Lanfranc in the *Liber Pancrisis*: MS. London B. L. Harley 3098, fols. 66v–7; cf. O. Lottin, *Psychologie et morale aux xiie et xiiie siècles* (Gembloux, 1959), v. 9–14.
'Quotienscunque necessariis'
attributed to Lanfranc by J. A. Giles, *Anecdota Bedae Lanfranci et aliorum* (London, 1851: Caxton Soc.) pp. 79–83, on the strength of the title:
'Domini I . . . L. summae fidei sinceritate deuotus'.

4 CANON LAW
abridgement of Pseudo-Isidore
See Ch. VI, § ii.
Z. N. Brooke, *The English Church and the Papacy (Cambridge,* 1931); S. Williams, *Codices Pseudo-Isidoriani,* (New York, 1971): further description of manuscripts, with bibliography; H. Fuhrmann, *Einfluss und Verbreitung der pseudoisidorischen Fälschungen* (Stuttgart, 1973: *Schriften Mon.Ger.Hist.* XXIV), ii. 419–22, with references.

De celanda confessione
attributed to Lanfranc in MSS. Paris B. N. nouv. acq. lat. 2243, fol.50 (s.xii) and Paris B. Arsenal 391, fol. 10v (s.xiii). Migne, *P.L.*cl.625B–38C; P.Anciaux, *La Théologie du*

*sacrament de pénitence au xii*ᵉ *siècle* (Louvain, 1949), pp. 31–46;
F. Behrends, 'Two spurious letters in the Fulbert collection',
*Rev.Bén.*lxxx (1970), 254.

In its assumption that sacramental confession is a generally
accepted practice for laity and clergy alike this text is probably not earlier than *c.* 1100. It may well belong to the same
Parisian context as the *De Sacramentis* of Hugh of St. Victor.
The author's involved Latin style, as D'Achery noted, and his
arguments from allegory are quite unlike Lanfranc's work as
a whole.

5 HISTORY

Gesta Guillelmi (lost)
> attributed to Lanfranc by Sigebert of Gembloux: see
> Appendix A8.
> F. Barlow, 'A view of archbishop Lanfranc', *Journ.Eccles.Hist.*
> xvi (1965), 163, n.3.

De rebus ecclesiasticis tractatus (lost)
> attributed to Lanfranc by Eadmer: see Appendix A14a.

Works dedicated to Lanfranc

1067 Guy of Amiens, *Carmen de Hastingae Proelio*
> ed. C. Morton and H. Muntz (Oxford, 1972: Oxford
> Medieval Texts). See however R. H. C. Davis, 'The *Carmen
> de Hastingae Proelio*', *Eng.Hist.Rev.* xciii (1978): I am grateful
> to Professor Davis for allowing me to read this article in
> typescript.

c. 1080 Goscelin, *Vita Sancte Edithe Virginis*
> ed. A. Wilmart, *Analecta Bollandiana* lvi (1938), 5–101; 265–
> 307

Editions and select critical
literature since 1500

1516   London   Wynkyn de Worde, *Nova Legenda Anglie*, fols. 213v–18v: *De sancto Lanfranco archiepiscopo et confessore* (based on *V.L.* and English chronicles).
See C. Horstman, *Nova Legenda Anglie* (Oxford, 1901), ii. 133–43.

1528   Basel   J. Sichard, *Philastrii episcopi Brixiensis haereseon catalogus*, fols. 99vff: *Lanfranci Cantuariensis de eucharistiae sacramento libellus aduersus Berengarium Turonensem.*
See P. Lehmann, *Johannes Sichardus und die von ihm benutzten Bibliotheken* (Munich, 1912), p. 60, no. xvi.

1540   Rouen   F. Carré and G. le Rat, *Lanfrancus cantuariensis archiepiscopi in Berengarium Turonensem hereticum de corpore et sanguine Domini dialogus . . .*, pp. 17–76.
See J. de Montclos, *Lanfranc et Bérenger: la controverse eucharistique du xie siècle* (Louvain, 1971), pp. 257–8.

1550   Basel   Anonymus, *Mikropresbytikon*, pp. 525–46: Lanfranc, *De Eucharistiae Sacramento adversus Berengarium Liber.*

1551   Louvain   J. Costerus, *De ueritate corporis et sanguinis domini nostri Iesu Christi in eucharistiae sacramento*, pp. 1–25: Lanfranc, *De Eucharistiae Sacramento aduersus Berengarium Liber.*

1555   Basel   J. Heroldt, *Orthodoxographa*, pp. 1279–1301: Lanfranc, *De Eucharistiae Sacramento aduersus Berengarium Liber.*

1561   Louvain   J. Vlimmer, *De veritate corporis et sanguinis Domini nostri Iesu Christi in sacrosancto Eucharistiae sacramento*, fols. 1–28v.
See N. R. Ker, 'English manuscripts owned by Johannes Vlimmerius and Cornelius Duyn', *The Library* xxii (1941–2), 205–7.

1575   Paris   M. de la Bigne, *Sacra Bibliotheca Sanctorum Patrum* IV. 213E–44A: reprint of the text in *Mikropresbytikon* (1550).

1589   Paris   idem, 2nd edn., vol.VI.355A–86A.

1610   Paris   idem, 3rd edn., vol.VI.299A–324C.

1618   Cologne   idem, revised and expanded at Cologne, vol. XI.336G-48D; reprinted several times.

1626   Douai   C. Reyner, *Apostolatus Benedictinorum in Anglia*, Appendix, pp. 211–53: Lanfranc, *Decreta*.

1632   Dublin   J. Ussher, *Veterum Epistolarum Hibernicarum Sylloge* (prints four of Lanfranc's letters and two episcopal professions)

1648   Paris   L.D'Achery, *Beati Lanfranci Cantuariensis archiepiscopi . . . opera omnia.*

1688   Antwerp   *Acta Sanctorum* VI, 28 May, pp. 832–54: *Vita Lanfranci.* The Bollandists have conflated the twelfth-century *Vita Lanfranci* with excerpts from Eadmer, *Historia Novorum* (ed. Selden, 1623).

1691   London   H. Wharton, *Anglia Sacra* i.6 (s.xiv life), 55–6 (*obit*), 78–82 (episcopal professions).

1701   Paris   J. Mabillon and Th. Ruinart, *Acta Sanctorum Ordinis S. Benedicti saec. VI.* ii. 630–60: *Vita Lanfranci* (D'Achery's text with slight alterations).

1737   London   D. Wilkins, *Concilia Magnae Britanniae et Hiberniae* i.322–8; 361–9 (letters and conciliar legislation); 328–61 (*Constitutions*).

1745   Venice   L. D'Achery, *Lanfranci Opera*: reprint of 1648 edition, with slight changes in the order of texts.

1747   Paris   *Histoire littéraire de la France* viii. 260–305. The Maurist account of Lanfranc's life.

1775   Venice   J. D. Mansi, *Sacrorum Conciliorum Nova et Amplissima Collectio* xx. 19–34; 449–56. Letters and conciliar legislation.

1834   Berlin   *Berengarii 'De Sacra Coena'*, ed. A. F. and F. Th. Vischer.

1844   Oxford/ Paris   J. A. Giles, *Beati Lanfranci Archiepiscopi Cantuariensis opera quae supersunt omnia* 2 vols.

1849   Paris   A. Charma, *Lanfranc, notice biographique, littéraire et philosophique.*

1854   Paris   J.-P. Migne, *Patrologia Latina*, cl.9A–764B: *B. Lanfranci . . . Opera Omnia.*

1858   London/   W. and M. Wilks, *The Three Archbishops:*
       Edinburgh *Lanfranc, Anselm, à Becket.*
1877   Paris   J. de Crozals, *Lanfranc archevêque de Canterbéry:*
                 sa vie, son enseignement, sa politique.
1901   Évreux   A. A. Porée, *Histoire de l'abbaye du Bec* 2 vol.
1902   Caen/Paris E. Longuemare, *Lanfranc moine bénédictin con-*
                 seiller politique de Guillaume le Conquérant.
1902   Leipzig   H. Boehmer, *Die Fälschungen Erzbischof Lan-*
                 franks von Canterbury.
1908   Montpellier N. Tamassia, 'Lanfranco arcivescovo di Canter-
                 bury e la scuola pavese', *Mélanges Hermann*
                 Fitting ii. 189–201.
1909   Oxford   J. Armitage Robinson, 'Lanfranc's monastic
                 constitutions', *Journ.Theol.Stud.* x. 375–88.
1911   Milan   F. Novati, 'La leggenda di Lanfranco da Pavia',
                 in *Studi Letterari e Linguistici . . . P. Rajna,* pp.
                 705–16.
1912   Pavia   E. Gorra, 'La *Leggenda* di Lanfranco da Pavia e
                 di Alano da Lilla', *Boll.Soc.Pav.Stor.Patr.* xii
                 (1912), 265–97.
1926   Oxford   A. J. MacDonald, *Lanfranc: a study of his life,*
                 work and writing.
1930   Augsburg E. Hora, 'Zur Ehrenrettung Lanfranks des
                 Erzbischofs von Canterbury (ca.1005–1089)',
                 Theol.Quartalschr. cxi.288–319.
1931   Cambridge Z. N. Brooke, *The English Church and the Papacy.*
1937   Louvain   B. Smalley, 'La *Glossa Ordinaria*: quelques
                 prédécesseurs d'Anselme de Laon', *Rech.Théol.*
                 Anc.Méd. ix. 365–400.
1944   Oxford   A. J. MacDonald, *Lanfranc,* 2nd edn.
1948   Oxford   R. W. Southern, 'Lanfranc of Bec and Berengar
                 of Tours', in *Studies in Medieval History presented*
                 to F. M. Powicke, ed. R. W. Hunt *et al.,* pp. 27–
                 48.
1950–1 Downside C. N. L. Brooke, 'The Canterbury Forgeries
       Abbey   and their author', *The Downside Review* lxviii.
                 462–76; lxix. 210–31.
1951   London   D. Knowles, *The Monastic Constitutions of*
                 Lanfranc: Nelson's Medieval Classics.
1956   Milan/   T. Gregory, 'Lanfranco da Pavia', in A.
       Naples   Viscardi *et al., Le origini: la letteratura italiana:*
                 storia e testi i. 420–33.
1958   London   R. W. Southern, 'The Canterbury Forgeries',
                 Eng.Hist.Rev. lxxiii. 193–226.

1965 London   F. Barlow, 'A view of archbishop Lanfranc', *Journ.Eccles.Hist.* xvi. 163–77.

1967 Siegburg   D. Knowles, *Decreta Lanfranci Monachis Canturiensibus Transmissa*: vol. III *Corpus Consuetudinum Monasticarum*, ed. Hallinger (=*Monastic Constitutions* 1951, revised edn).

1971 Louvain   J. de Montclos, *Lanfranc et Bérenger: la controverse eucharistique du xie siécle*.

1971 Oxford   M. T. Gibson, 'Lanfranc's *Commentary on the Pauline Epistles*', *Journ.Theol.Stud.* n.s. xxii. 86–112; idem, 'Lanfranc's notes on patristic texts', ibid. xxii. 435–50.

Index of Manuscripts

ARCHIVES

General Index

Abbo, abb.Fleury, 16–17, 88 n.
Abelard, 14, 49, 57, 62, 88 n., 96
Abingdon, 114 n., 157
Acta Archiepiscoporum Rothomagensium, 203
Acta Lanfranci, 115 n., 118 n., 141 n., 142, 189 n., 212–13, 219
Adalbert, archbp. Bremen, 125 n.
Adalbert, bp. Laon, 12, 16–17
Adalbert, bp. Orkneys, 125 n.
Adalbert, bp. Prague, 2
Adam of Bremen, 125 n.
Adelaide, dau. William the Conqueror, 127 n.
Adelmann of Liège, 16 n., 68, 88 n.
Ægelward, m. Christ Church, 175, 197, 218–19
Ælfric, archbp. Canterbury, 171
Ælfwin, pr. St. Augustine's, Canterbury, 189
Ælfwine, abb. Ramsey, 167 n.
Ælsi, abb. Ramsey, 159
Æthelbald, kg. Mercia, 112 n.
Æthelheard, archbp. Canterbury, 117, 169, 231, 233
Æthelmaer, bp. Elmham, 114–15, 118 n., 148
Æthelric, bp. Selsey, 114–15, 133, 145
Æthelsige, abb. St. Augustine's, Canterbury, 114, 167–8
Æthelwig, abb. Evesham, 156, 158
Æthelwine, bp. Durham, 114
Agatho, pope, 234
Agnes, empress, 127
Alberic, m. of Monte Cassino, 95
Albert, abb. Marmoutiers, 19
Albert, m. of Bec, 176
Alcuin, 12
Aldhelm, 222
Aldulf, kg. Northumbria, 169, 232–3
Alexander II, pope, 70
relations with Lanfranc, 25, 103, 151, 183 n., 197, 205–6, 220
— with Normandy, 109–11

— with England, 116, 131–4, 137–8, 148, 169, 206
— with St. Augustine's, Canterbury, 167, 169
and primacy of Canterbury, 118–21, 232–3, 237
Alexander de Villa Dei, 46 n.
Alfred, kg. Northumbria, 169, 232–3
Alphanus, archbp. Salerno, 15 n.
Ambrose, bp. Milan, 61–2, 66, 179–81
on Eucharist, 40, 71–6, 80, 83, 89, 92
on Pauline Epistles, 54, 57–9
see also 'Ambrosiaster'
'Ambrosiaster', 59
Anastasius, 21, 88 n.
Angelomus of Luxeuil, 86 n.
Angers, 65, 69 n., 82, 94 n.
Anglo-Saxon Chronicle, 126 n., 160 n., 162 n., 168 n., 186 n., 217–18, 231
anima mundi, 48
Anjou, 38, 70, 101
bishops, *see* Eusebius Bruno
counts, *see* Fulk Nerra, Geoffrey Martel
Annales Anglo-Saxonici, 218
Anselm, archbp. Canterbury, 20 n., 25, 155
pr. Bec, 27, 44 n., 54 n., 170 n., 179–81, 201
abb. Bec, 32 n., 36, 37
archbp. Canterbury, 125, 128 n., 135 n., 139, 152 n., 175–6, 185 n., 207–8, 212, 233
relations with Lanfranc, 34–5, 37, 171, 192
spirituality, 28–9, 127 n., 191
writings, 3, 26, 35, 43, 56, 82, 89, 202
Anselm, abb. Bury St. Edmunds, 158 n.
Anselm of Besate, 13–14, 17, 85
Anselm of Laon, 47–8, 50 n., 62
Ansfrid, abb. Préaux, 68
anthropomorphites, 41
Antiochene exegesis, 59
Aristotle, 78, 80, 90–1, 95–6

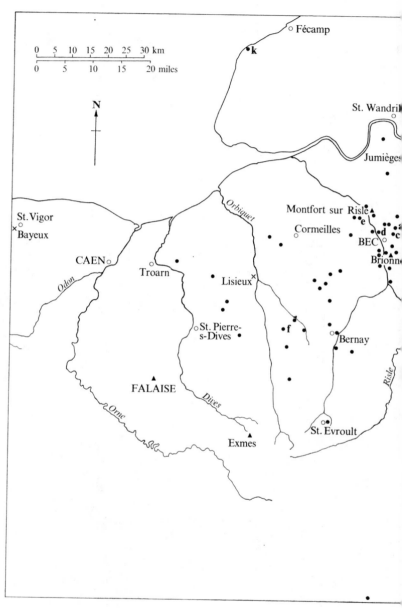

MAP 1 Property held by the Monastery of Bec in 1041

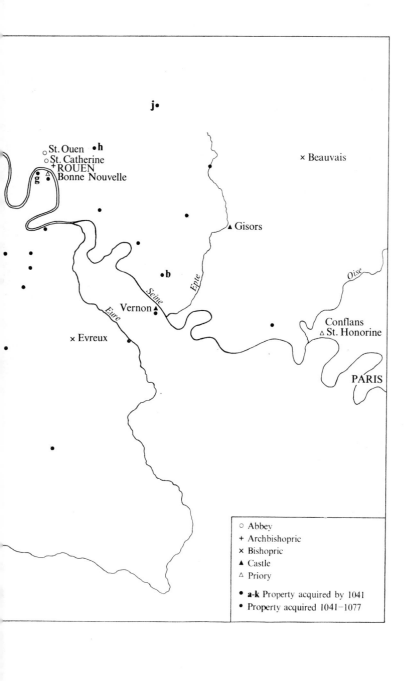

j•

St. Ouen ○ •h
St. Catherine ○
+ ROUEN
g ○ △ Bonne Nouvelle
•

× Beauvais

▲ Gisors

•b

Vernon ▲

Evreux ×

Conflans
△ St. Honorine

PARIS

○	Abbey
+	Archbishopric
×	Bishopric
▲	Castle
△	Priory
• a-k	Property acquired by 1041
•	Property acquired 1041–1077